Adobe®
Dreamweaver® CS5
①②③④⑤⑥⑦ on Demand

Steve Johnson

Perspection, Inc.

Que® Que Publishing, 800 East 96th Street, Indianapolis, IN 46240 USA

Adobe® Dreamweaver® CS5 On Demand

Library of Congress Cataloging-in-Publication Data is on file

ISBN-13: 978-0-7897-4444-9

ISBN-10: 0-7897-4444-9

Printed and bound in the United States of America

First Printing: April 2010

13 12 11 10   4 3 2 1

Que Publishing offers excellent discounts on this book when ordered in quantity for bulk purchases or special sales.

For information, please contact: U.S. Corporate and Government Sales

  1-800-382-3419 or corpsales@pearsontechgroup.com

For sales outside the U.S., please contact: International Sales

  1-317-428-3341 or International@pearsontechgroup.com

Trademarks

All terms mentioned in this book that are known to be trademarks or service marks have been appropriately capitalized. Que cannot attest to the accuracy of this information. Use of a term in this book should not be regarded as affecting the validity of any trademark or service mark.

Adobe, the Adobe logo, Acrobat, Bridge, Device Central, Dreamweaver, Extension Manager, Flash, InDesign, Illustrator, PageMaker, Photoshop, Photoshop Elements, and Version Cue are registered trademarks of Adobe System Incorporated. Apple, Mac OS, and Macintosh are trademarks of Apple Computer, Inc. Microsoft and the Microsoft Office logo are registered trademarks of Microsoft Corporation in the United States and/or other countries.

Warning and Disclaimer

Every effort has been made to make this book as complete and as accurate as possible, but no warranty or fitness is implied. The authors and the publishers shall have neither liability nor responsibility to any person or entity with respect to any loss or damage arising from the information contained in this book.

Publisher
Paul Boger

Associate Publisher
Greg Wiegand

Acquisitions Editor
Laura Norman

Managing Editor
Steve Johnson

Author
Steve Johnson

Editor
Adrian Hyde

Page Layout
James Teyler

Interior Designers
Steve Johnson
Marian Hartsough

Photographs
Tracy Teyler

Indexer
Katherine Stimson

Proofreader
Adrian Hyde

Team Coordinator
Cindy Teeters

Acknowledgements

Perspection, Inc.

Adobe Dreamweaver CS5 On Demand has been created by the professional trainers and writers at Perspection, Inc. to the standards you've come to expect from Que publishing. Together, we are pleased to present this training book.

Perspection, Inc. is a software training company committed to providing information and training to help people use software more effectively in order to communicate, make decisions, and solve problems. Perspection writes and produces software training books, and develops multimedia and Web-based training. Since 1991, we have written more than 100 computer books, with several bestsellers to our credit, and sold over 5 million books.

This book incorporates Perspection's training expertise to ensure that you'll receive the maximum return on your time. You'll focus on the tasks and skills that increase productivity while working at your own pace and convenience.

We invite you to visit the Perspection web site at:

www.perspection.com

Acknowledgements

The task of creating any book requires the talents of many hard-working people pulling together to meet impossible deadlines and untold stresses. We'd like to thank the outstanding team responsible for making this book possible: the writer, Steve Johnson; the editor, Adrian Hyde; the production editors, James Teyler and Beth Teyler; proofreader, Adrian Hyde; and the indexer, Katherine Stimson.

At Que publishing, we'd like to thank Greg Wiegand and Laura Norman for the opportunity to undertake this project, Cindy Teeters for administrative support, and Sandra Schroeder for your production expertise and support.

Perspection

About The Author

Steve Johnson has written more than 50 books on a variety of computer software, including Adobe Photoshop CS4, Adobe Flash CS4, Adobe Dreamweaver CS4, Adobe InDesign CS4, Adobe Illustrator CS4, Microsoft Windows 7, Microsoft Office 2007, Microsoft Office 2008 for the Macintosh, and Apple Mac OS X Snow Leopard. In 1991, after working for Apple Computer and Microsoft, Steve founded Perspection, Inc., which writes and produces software training. When he is not staying up late writing, he enjoys playing golf, gardening, and spending time with his wife, Holly, and three children, JP, Brett, and Hannah. Steve and his family live in Pleasanton, California, but can also be found visiting family all over the western United States.

We Want To Hear From You!

As the reader of this book, *you* are our most important critic and commentator. We value your opinion and want to know what we're doing right, what we could do better, what areas you'd like to see us publish in, and any other words of wisdom you're willing to pass our way.

As an associate publisher for Que, I welcome your comments. You can email or write me directly to let me know what you did or didn't like about this book—as well as what we can do to make our books better.

Please note that I cannot help you with technical problems related to the topic of this book. We do have a User Services group, however, where I will forward specific technical questions related to the book.

When you write, please be sure to include this book's title and author as well as your name, email address, and phone number. I will carefully review your comments and share them with the author and editors who worked on the book.

Email: feedback@quepublishing.com

Mail: Greg Wiegand
         Que Publishing
         800 East 96th Street
         Indianapolis, IN 46240 USA

For more information about this book or another Que title, visit our Web site at *quepublishing.com/register*. Type the ISBN (excluding hyphens) or the title of a book in the Search field to find the page you're looking for.

Contents

Introduction

Welcome to *Adobe Dreamweaver CS5 On Demand*, a visual quick reference book that shows you how to work efficiently with Dreamweaver CS5. This book provides complete coverage of basic to advanced Dreamweaver skills.

How This Book Works

You don't have to read this book in any particular order. We've designed the book so that you can jump in, get the information you need, and jump out. However, the book does follow a logical progression from simple tasks to more complex ones. Each task is presented on no more than two facing pages, which lets you focus on a single task without having to turn the page. To find the information that you need, just look up the task in the table of contents or index, and turn to the page listed. Read the task introduction, follow the step-by-step instructions in the left column along with screen illustrations in the right column, and you're done.

What's New

If you're searching for what's new in Dreamweaver CS5, just look for the icon: **New!**. The new icon appears in the table of contents and throughout this book so you can quickly and easily identify a new or improved feature in Dreamweaver CS5. A complete description of each new feature appears in the New Features guide in the back of this book.

Keyboard Shortcuts

Most menu commands have a keyboard equivalent, such as Ctrl+P (Win) or ⌘+P (Mac), as a quicker alternative to using the mouse. A complete list of keyboard shortcuts is available on the Web at *www.perspection.com*.

How You'll Learn

How This Book Works

What's New

Keyboard Shortcuts

Step-by-Step Instructions

Real World Examples

Workshops

Adobe Certified Expert

Get More on the Web

Step-by-Step Instructions

This book provides concise step-by-step instructions that show you "how" to accomplish a task. Each set of instructions includes illustrations that directly correspond to the easy-to-read steps. Also included in the text are time-savers, tables, and sidebars to help you work more efficiently or to teach you more in-depth information. A "Did You Know?" provides tips and techniques to help you work smarter, while a "See Also" leads you to other parts of the book containing related information about the task.

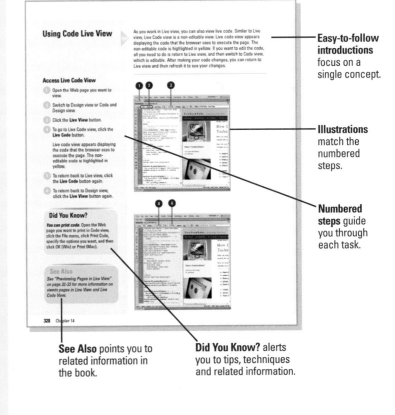

Easy-to-follow **introductions** focus on a single concept.

Illustrations match the numbered steps.

Numbered steps guide you through each task.

See Also points you to related information in the book.

Did You Know? alerts you to tips, techniques and related information.

Real World Examples

This book uses real world example files to give you a context in which to use the task. By using the example files, you won't waste time looking for or creating sample files. You get a start file and a result file, so you can compare your work. Not every topic needs an example file, such as changing options, so we provide a complete list of the example files used throughout the book. The example files that you need for project tasks along with a complete file list are available on the Web at *www.perspection.com*.

Real world examples help you apply what you've learned to other tasks.

Workshops

This book shows you how to put together the individual step-by-step tasks into in-depth projects with the Workshop. You start each project with a sample file, work through the steps, and then compare your results with a project results file at the end. The Workshop projects and associated files are available on the Web at *www.perspection.com.*

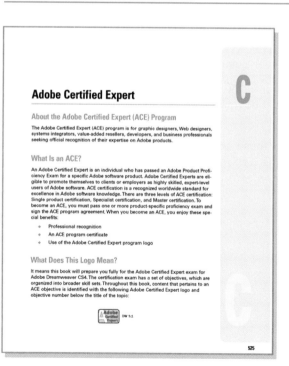

The **Workshops** walk you through in-depth projects to help you put Dreamweaver to work.

Adobe Certified Expert

This book prepares you fully for the Adobe Certified Expert (ACE) exam for Adobe Dreamweaver CS5. Each Adobe Certified Expert certification level has a set of objectives, which are organized into broader skill sets. To prepare for the certification exam, you should review and perform each task identified with an ACE objective to confirm that you can meet the requirements for the exam. Information about the ACE program is available in the back of this book. The Adobe Certified Expert objectives and the specific pages that cover them are available on the Web at *www.perspection.com.*

Get More on the Web

In addition to the information in this book, you can also get more information on the Web to help you get up to speed faster with Dreamweaver CS5. Some of the information includes:

Transition Helpers

◆ **Only New Features.** Download and print the new feature tasks as a quick and easy guide.

Productivity Tools

◆ **Keyboard Shortcuts.** Download a list of keyboard shortcuts to learn faster ways to get the job done.

More Content

◆ **Photographs.** Download photographs and other graphics to use in your Dreamweaver documents.

◆ **More Content.** Download new content developed after publication.

You can access these additional resources on the Web at *www.perspection.com*.

Keyboard Shortcuts

Adobe Dreamweaver CS5

If a command on a menu includes a keyboard reference, known as a keyboard shortcut, to the right of the command name, you can perform the action by pressing and holding the first key, and then pressing the second key to perform the command quickly. In some cases, a keyboard shortcut uses three keys. Simply press and hold the first two keys, and then press the third key. Keyboard shortcuts provide an alternative to using the mouse and make it easy to perform repetitive commands.

If you're searching for new keyboard shortcuts in Dreamweaver CS5, just look for the letter **N**. The **N** appears in the Keyboard Shortcuts table so you can quickly and easily identify new or changed shortcuts.

Additional content is available on the Web.

Keyboard Shortcuts		
Command	Windows	Macintosh
Menu Commands		
File		
New	Ctrl+N	⌘+N
Open	Ctrl+O	⌘+O
Browse in Bridge	Ctrl+Alt+O	⌘+Option+O
Open in Frame	Ctrl+Shift+O	⌘+Shift+O
Close	Ctrl+W	⌘+W
Close All	Ctrl+Shift+W	⌘+Shift+W
Save	Ctrl+S	⌘+S
Save As	Ctrl+Shift+S	⌘+Shift+S
Print Code	Ctrl+P	⌘+P
Preview in Browser		
Primary Browser (IExplore)	F12	F12
Device Central	Ctrl+Alt+F12	⌘+Option+F12

1

Working Together with Adobe Programs

Introduction

Adobe programs are designed to work together so you can focus on what you need to do, rather than on how to do it. In fact, the Adobe programs share tools and features for your most common tasks so you can work uninterrupted and move seamlessly from one program to another. Adobe Creative Suite is an integrated collection of programs that work together to help you create designs in print, on the Web, or on mobile devices. When you install Adobe Creative Suite or a stand-alone Adobe program, you also get additional Adobe programs—Bridge, CS Live, ConnectNow, Device Central, Extension Manager, and ExtendScript Toolkit—to help you perform specific jobs, such as locating, downloading, and modifying images for projects, managing files and program extensions and testing files for different mobile devices.

Adobe Bridge is a program that lets you view, open, modify, and manage images located on your computer from any Adobe Creative Suite program. Adobe Bridge is literally the glue that binds Adobe Creative Suite programs together into one cohesive unit with shared tools. Bridge allows you to search, sort, filter, manage, and process image files one at a time or in batches. You can also use Bridge or Mini Bridge to do the following: create new folders; rename, move, delete and group files; edit metadata; rotate images; create web galleries and contact sheets; and run batch commands. You can also import files from your digital camera and view file information and metadata.

What You'll Do

Explore Adobe Programs

Explore Adobe Bridge

Get Started with Adobe Bridge

Get Photos from a Digital Camera

Work with Raw Images from a Digital Camera

Work with Images Using Adobe Bridge

Set Preferences in Adobe Bridge

Automate Tasks in Adobe Bridge

Use Mini Bridge

Explore CS Live Services

Share My Screen

Review CS Documents

Explore Adobe Device Central

Check Content Using Adobe Device Central

Use Adobe Extension Manager

Additional content is available on the Web.

1

Preparing and Planning a Web Site

1

Introduction

You might have heard the expression: A journey of a thousand miles begins with the first step. While that makes perfect sense, there is one other thing that must be accomplished before taking that fateful step... proper planning.

Attempting to design a complex Web site without proper planning would be akin to taking a trip from New York to California without the benefit of any roadmaps. You might understand that you need to travel in a westerly direction; however, without proper planning, you would probably make a lot of wrong turns before arriving at your final destination. Planning therefore is a fundamental part of any journey, and it's a fundamental part of any Web design project.

Planning for a new Web site involves understanding in two key areas: knowledge of the applications you will be using (the logical side), and knowledge of what direction you want to take this new Web project (the creative side).

Dreamweaver will help any Web design project run more smoothly; whether you are building a Web site from scratch, collaborating with a Web-design team, or anywhere in between. So, before starting the planning process, you need knowledge of Dreamweaver and what's it's capable of doing.

Regardless of the scope of your project, take some time in advance to think through the architecture of your site (the layout structure of the pages as a whole, and the options for navigating the site), develop a look-and-feel (graphic design and interface), and gather the content (the information you want to include on the site pages). When this preliminary work is done, you can plunge into the development, staging, launching, and the very important maintenance of the site.

Creating a comprehensive plan of the project will simplify the process of creating a complex Web site, and like a road map, will help to keep you on track as you make that journey of a thousand miles.

Beginning with a Plan

Before you fire up the software and start cranking out Web pages, take a step back from the process, and ask yourself what you're aiming at by designing this Web site. You can get help in answering that question by asking yourself five more questions. Just turn to journalism 101, and ask yourself the 5 basic W questions: Who, What, When, Where, and the all-important, Why.

◆ **Who** is designing this site?

◆ **What** are the goals of the site?

◆ **When** will the site be completed?

◆ **Where** is my target audience?

◆ **Why** am I doing this?

Who is designing this site?

In this case the answer would be you. You're responsible for everything from the creation of the graphics to the typing of the text, even to the compression of the video. Since you know Dreamweaver, the construction of the site... from the ground up, is all up to you. At least you think it is...

For example, you might know Dreamweaver from top to bottom, but do you also know some of the other applications you might need to use, such as: Photoshop, Illustrator, Flash, and Fireworks; just to name a few. If your knowledge of other essential applications is lacking, you might need to bring other experts into the mix. In addition, many Web designers can assemble Web pages with their eyes closed, but lack a fundamental understanding of how to load and manage the site out to the server. And what about marketing your site? Did you ever hear the expression, build it and they will come? Well, a lot of people built Web sites and nobody comes. Why? No one knew they

existed. The question: *Who is designing this site?* helps you focus not only on the end game, but who is going to help you get there.

What are the goals of the site?

You would be surprised (or maybe you wouldn't) how many people want to build a Web site, but have no clear goals as to what they want the site to accomplish (just talk to some of my clients). A Web site is about communication, plain and simple. For example my goal for this book is to teach you how to use Dreamweaver in a logical and creative way, plain and simple. We could say that the goal of our fictional Web site is to obtain more business, that's what most business sites are designed to do. However, we also want an element of the site devoted to pure and free information; maybe an area devoted to tips and tricks on taking good photographs. A Web site can have more than one goal, but it's important to define them at the get go. If you don't have any clearly defined goals for your site, how are you going to be able to tell if you're successful? When my dad would take us on one of his famous across-the-country vacations, my sister and I would be in the back seat singing the mantra of all children everywhere: *Are we there yet?* Without a good, well-defined set of goals, how are you ever going to know if you've arrived? Later we'll talk about how you monitor those goals; for now just set them. If you don't know, or understand, the ultimate goals of your site, then stop right now, and don't move forward until you can define them.

When will the site be completed?

While this may seem trivial, I've known many a good Web designer who have gone out of business because they promised and never delivered. Since you'll be designing this site on your own, this question becomes even more important because it gives you a date to strive for. Believe me, it's very easy to let other considerations interfere with the completion of the site. And here's another good reason… in the business world, a make-or-break time for many is the holiday shopping season. From the end of November to the end of December, many retailers make most of their money.

You believe that you can sell a lot of your photographs during this time of the year, so you plan for the site to be up and running for the holidays. But what does that really mean? In truth it means having the site up and running by August, at the latest. This gives the site time to be indexed by all the search engines, and it gives you time to iron out any possible kinks in the operation of the site. The worst thing you want to happen is to get the site up by mid November, and then discover that your shopping cart module is full of problems. Set a reasonable, reachable date, and then work toward that goal. Reasonable and reachable is obtained based on your knowledge of the site, its complexity, how long it will take you to do things, and how much time in the day you have to devote to the project.

Where is my target audience?

How are you going to know what to put into your site unless you understand where your audience is coming from? By coming from, I don't mean their geographical location (although that can be important). When I design a Web site for a client, I want to get to know the people that will be visiting the site. In reality, that's not very practical. After all, you're not going to knock on the front door of each and every possible visitor, sit down with

a cup of tea, and discuss his or her likes and dislikes.

What I'm looking for in the discovery phase is a general idea of who my visitors might be: What kind of people would buy my photos and videos? Once I've got a handle on the demographics of my audience, I can design the site around those parameters. For example, I would design a Web site for six-year olds much differently than a site for a major corporation such as: General Electric, or Williams-Sonoma. We'll talk more about how you'll accomplish this later in this chapter; however, it's important to understand your target audience.

Why am I doing this?

While this may seem close to the goals for the site, it's simply a motivating tool. For example, the goal of the site is to increase my business, but in the end my goal is to share my photographic work with the world. It might also be security. For example, you work for someone else as a photographer in his or her studio, and because business is not that great, you feel that you could be in the unemployment queue before long. Your objective for designing this Web site is a personal goal you've had for years: To start your own business and become a photographer in your own rights.

Designing a Web site is not just about making money. You would be surprised how simply asking yourself the question: *Why am I doing this?*, will motivate you to not only to get the job completed on time, but to do the absolute best job possible. Hey, this could just be your dream come true.

Creating a Visual Mind Map

There are many ways to expand a simple idea into a complex design. My personal favorite way is through the creation of a mind map.

Mind maps have many applications in personal, family, education, and business. Ideas are inserted into the map around a center thought (the seed), without the organization that comes from hierarchy or sequential arrangements (grouping and organizing is reserved for later stages).

A Mind Map consists of four essential elements:

◆ The **idea** (seed) is placed in the center of a blank page.

◆ The main **themes** of the central idea radiate from the central image on connecting lines or branches.

◆ Each branch holds a **key word**, and secondary ideas radiate out from each branch.

◆ The branches form a **connected structure** back to the central idea.

I find the best time to create a mind map of a project is when I'm fully rested and calm with the world. Remember, a mind map is all about free association.

Getting back to the mind map of our fictional Web site... The name of your business is YouTechTube, a place to store and display home videos on technology. Start the process by getting away from any possible distractions; turn off the television, get away from cell phones. Music is totally optional, and might help to focus your mind by eliminating any distracting background noise. The supplies you need are some plain white paper, and few colored pencils, the answers to the 5 W questions, and an uncluttered mind.

Start by drawing a circle in the middle of the page, and write the title of your site in the circle. You draw a line out from the center circle, like the branch of a tree, and on the branch you write the word, Applications. Then, using smaller branches, you begin listing the applications you believe will be needed to accomplish your goal: Dreamweaver, Flash, Photoshop, Final Cut Pro, etc. As you write down Final Cut Pro, you realize that you don't have much experience with that application; however, it will be very important in the design and compression of your video files. A good friend of yours, Harold Driver, is an expert and so you make a smaller branch next to Final Cut Pro and write, Contact Harold.

The process of free association is that one thought will inevitably lead to another related thought. If at any time you seem at a standstill, simply reread the answers you gave to the 5 basic W questions, and it should give you the mental inspiration to continue.

Once the mind map is complete, you might want to clean it up by entering the information from the hand-drawn sketch into a word processor. Sometimes by retyping the details of the mind map, it helps to spot things you might have forgotten. If you prefer doing your mind maps on a computer, check out the following Web sites:

◆ **Mindmap.** http://www.mindmap.com/EN/mindmaps/definition.html

◆ **Inspiration.** http://www.inspiration.com/

◆ **MindGenius.** http://www.mindgenius.com/

◆ **Mind manager.** http://www.mindjet.com/uk/

◆ **Mind tools.** http://www.mindtools.com/

◆ **Open source Freemind.**
http://freemind.sourceforge.net/wiki/
index.php/Main_Page

Remember that a mind map does not lock you in stone; it simply presents ideas on how you are going to proceed with the construction of your Web site.

The process of mind mapping a simple project can go very quickly. The more complex the project, the more involved the mind map. However, it's time well spent. Most studies show that planning complex projects will wind up saving you time... up to twenty percent.

Mind map

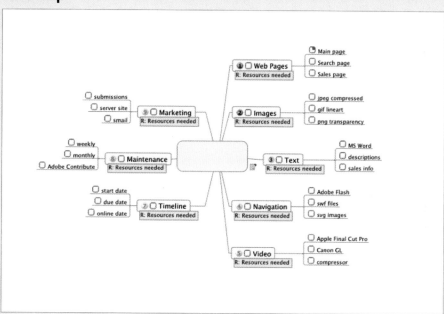

Once the mind map is complete, take some time to hand-draw some sketches of what the pages of your Web site will look like. You can start out (like I do) by drawing rectangles on a piece of paper, and crudely outlining where you want to place elements on the page; like arranging the furniture in a room, place page elements where they will be most comfortable and accessible to your visitors.

You don't have to be pretty; just get a general idea of how the site will be visually laid

out. You might even add notations as to colors and text. Eventually, you'll clean up these crude sketches by creating them on graph paper that matches the width to height ratio for each page, but more on that later.

The final step after the creation of the sketches is to give them the names you will use when you create them in Dreamweaver. Since these are file names, they should conform to standard file-naming conventions.

Generating a Timeline

You've generated a comprehensive mind map, and you've got some page sketches... you're doing great. You now have the information you need to proceed to the next step, and that's the creation of a flow chart. While the mind map gives you all the details of how your Web site is to be constructed, it does not give you that information in chronological order.

The flow chart takes the information obtained from the mind map and places it into an ordered timeline. For example, what do you work on first, second, third? Do you call Harold and ask for his help today on Final Cut Pro, or can it wait a bit? The flow chart is like the construction of a house; you start with the foundation, and move on. What do you think would happen if the drywall workers sealed up the walls to a new home before the electricians had a chance to install the internal wiring?

In our case, you might design a really cool navigation system in Flash (took days of time); however, as you build the site, you realize that you left several pages out. Now, you've got to consume more time by going back and changing the Flash Navigation. The flow chart will help to reduce or eliminate such problems. It will also let you know where you stand in the construction of the site, and will help you complete your site successfully and on time.

Sample Timeline

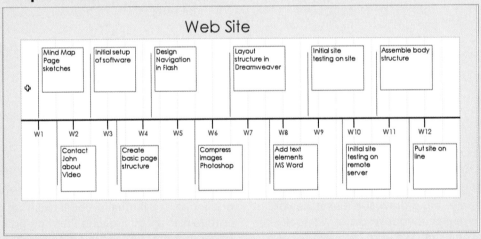

Assembling the Site

The majority of what you've accomplished so far is without the use of your computer (unless you're using your computer to generate the mind maps or flow charts). While the process may seem tedious, in reality it's quite straightforward. As a matter of fact, once you have experienced the benefits of proper site planning, you'll never design another project without having a plan.

The next part of this process involves the gathering together of the "stuff" you will need to complete the project. That will include applications, images, animations, text; all the things that make up a proper site. Believe it or not, in a typical Web project, Dreamweaver might be one of the last places you go; not the first. Think of it this way, Dreamweaver is a Web design layout application. In order to use it, you need things to "lay out."

Gathering Information About Your Visitors

I mentioned earlier that the statement: "Build it and they will come," is not necessarily true, especially when it comes to Web design. You need information. If you haven't already done a demographic study (also called the discovery phase) based on your target audience, do so now. If this seems a bit overwhelming, there are a lot of sites that specialize in giving you exactly this sort of information.

The following list is just a few of the existing discovery sites:

◆ http://www.omniture.com/

◆ http://www.pewinternet.org/

◆ http://internet-statistics-guide.netfirms.com/

◆ http://www.w3.org/

A demographic study will give you an idea of what kind of people will visit your site, who they are, and what kind of Web knowledge they have. This information is invaluable in creating the design of your site. For example, the portion of your site that deals with video, could be made much more efficient if you used the latest compression codec from Adobe Flash; however, your study shows that most of your potential visitors do not have the current version of the Flash player, so you decide to downsize the videos to match what your visitors have. A demographic study is all about giving your visitors an enjoyable experience. If they like it, they'll be back.

Creating a Marketing Plan

While you haven't started the actual creation of the site, it's not too early to start your marketing plans. There are thousands of new Web sites going up on the Internet every week. How do you get known? Well, first off, Web search engines will find you; they employ programs called Web robots that go to all the Web servers on the planet, and patiently index each site. That way they can offer their visitors the ability to access information from any site, anywhere on or off the planet. The more sites like yours they index, the more money they can charge their advertisers. That means they are aggressive and they will find you. That doesn't mean that you sit by and wait, submission of your site to search engines is one of the first steps in getting your name out there to the world.

If you have the bucks, there are companies out there that will help you with the submission process. For example, the following sites will get you going, but for a price:

- http://www.wpromote.com/
- http://www.addpro.com/
- http://www.prioritysubmit.com/

If you would rather take a crack at the process yourself, there are a lot of ways to shout "Here I Am" without spending any of your hard-earned cash.

Search engine submission, or registration refers to the act of getting your Web site listed with search engines. Unfortunately, getting listed does not mean that you will necessarily rank well for particular terms. It simply means that the search engine knows your pages exist, and if your visitors type in the right search words, they will find you.

For example, Yahoo has two submission options: "Standard," which is free, and "Yahoo Express," which involves a submission fee. Anyone can use Standard submission to submit for free to a non-commercial category.

How do you submit? Type the following URL into your browser:

http://search.yahoo.com/info/submit.html

That will bring up a list of submission options. Select you option, fill out the form, and you're finished.

Most search engines give you the ability to submit your site for free, or for a price. In many cases the only difference is how long it takes for your site to appear.

You should always prepare before submitting. This preparation means that you have written a 25 word or less description of your entire Web site. That description should make use of the two or three key terms that you hope to be found for. In our fictitious site, you would use words like Photography and Video.

You should consider researching what are the best terms for your site, rather than guessing at these. The site:

http://searchenginewatch.com/

has a list of resources that will allow you to do such research. Avoid the use of marketing language in your description. You should use distinct keyworks instead. So, your description might go something like: *video, technology, training, and social network, etc.*

Creating a Storyboard

Many Web professionals use a technique called **storyboarding**. Storyboarding gives you a visual look at the layout of the site, and what type of organization you need to use. This will also give you a first look at how you want to build your navigational system.

A Linear Storyboard

The linear method connects pages one to another in an almost book-like fashion. The visitor has two choices: to move forward, or to move back... one page at a time.

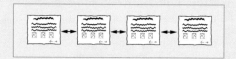

A Hierarchical Storyboard

Hierarchical navigation models have a distinct top-down design. The idea is that there is an index or home page, and that page branches to other main pages, and so on. It resembles a business organizational chart, with the most important person at the top. This gives the visitor to your site a sense of direction, and is a popular Web organizational model.

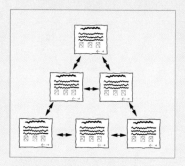

A Wheel Storyboard

The wheel method is like spokes connected to a main hub. The main hub would have links to all the other pages within the site; however, it does require the visitor to return to the hub before moving to another page.

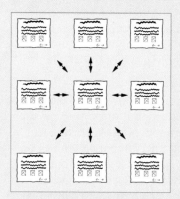

The Complete Storyboard

The Complete method takes into account the dynamic nature of the Web and its ability to navigate anywhere at any time. Typically, it involves a main or index page, connected with a sophisticated menu system that allows the visitor to access any portion of the Web with 2 to 3 clicks, and a single click will always take them back to the main page. This is the most widely used navigational method.

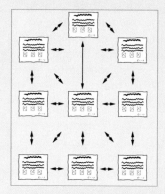

Once you've chosen and created a storyboard, you should have a thumbnail of each of the proposed pages within your Web site, and the file name for each page.

Creating a Site Local Root Folder

The final act to perform is the creation of work folders. The work folders should contain all the elements of the Web site. You first start with a local root folder for the site. The **local root folder** contains all the elements of the Web site; every single piece of the site is included within this folder.

For example, your site local root folder is named, *youtechtube*, and there would be subfolders for the elements of the Web site, like: *Web Pages*, and all the Web pages you designed in Dreamweaver would be placed within this subfolder. You use Photoshop and Fireworks to manage all of the site's images, and they are placed in the folder named, *Images*. Flash Objects, CSS, PDF documents; each kind of document is placed within its own personal folder. Later in this book, you'll learn how to link this *site root folder* to Dreamweaver and create a working site.

Imagine the control you'll exert over the construction of a site when you create this type of organization. Even a modest Web site can have hundreds of parts. Let's say that you need to modify one of your PDF documents; however, you didn't create separate folders, you put everything into one folder. Now, you have to scroll through over one hundred file names, looking for that one PDF file. Fortunately, you work smart, you simply open the PDF folder and, BANG, there it is, ready to be double-clicked. Work smart...

Creating a site root folder is not just a requirement of using Dreamweaver; in addition, it will help you in the creation, and of the moving of the site. If everything involving the construction of your Web site is contained within a single folder, it helps to keep you organized and in control... and being in control is an important part of being creative.

Although planning may seem like a lot of work, it really isn't. Especially when you add in the amount of time and frustration you'll save when the site is complete.

Have fun, and don't forget to enjoy the journey.

Create a Local Root Folder

1. Right click your mouse on the desktop, and then select **New Folder** from the popup menu (Macintosh) or right-click the desktop, point to **New**, and then click the **Folder** button from the popup menu.

2. Name the folder according to the site you're working (in this example, *youtechtube*).

3. Double click to open the folder, and then add additional subfolders to the local root folder.

All elements dealing with the construction of this Web site should be contained within this local root folder, and its corresponding subfolders.

Getting Started with Dreamweaver CS5

2

Introduction

Adobe Dreamweaver CS5 is the industry leading Web development tool for building Web sites and applications. It provides a combination of visual layout tools, application development features, and code editing support, enabling developers and designers at every skill level to create visually appealing, standards-based sites and applications quickly and easily. From leading support for Cascading Style Sheet (CSS) design to hand-coding features, Dreamweaver provides the tools professionals need to get the job done. In addition, developers can use Dreamweaver with the server technology of their choice to build powerful Internet applications that connect users to databases, live data feeds, and legacy systems.

Dreamweaver is an application that's rooted in the real world. In the real world, new or updated browsers come into the marketplace every year, and this creates problems in compatibility. Dreamweaver solves this problem by giving you powerful error-checking tools, and even gives you the ability to use Live Data View, and see exactly how your pages will perform on virtually any browser.

In the real world, server technologies change quickly. Dreamweaver's extensible architecture makes server compatibility a snap by giving you the tools to customize for third-party server models. In the real world, computer operating systems change. Dreamweaver's CS5 not only supports use on Windows and Macintosh systems; in addition, there is now support for the new Intel-based Macintosh computers.

Web designers come at all levels of experience. Dreamweaver's user-friendly interface helps you out. If you're relatively new to the application, you can jump right in and begin designing simple Web pages. If you are an experienced designer, you will be able to access the power and control that this application offers, and take your Web designs where no one has gone before.

What You'll Do

Understand System Requirements

Install Dreamweaver

Get Started

View the Dreamweaver Window

Create a Web Site

Open a Web Site

Create a Blank Web Page

Create Web Pages from Templates

Create a Web Page from a Sample

Save a Web Page

Open an Existing Web Page or File

Work with Views

Switch Between Pages and Views

Preview a Web Page

Get Help While You Work

Get Dreamweaver Updates on the Web

Close a Web Site or File

Finish Up

Understanding System Requirements

System Requirements

Before you can install Dreamweaver, you will need to make sure that your computer meets the minimum system requirements. Dreamweaver CS5 is supported on both Windows and Macintosh computers.

While many designers bemoan the fact that their older computer systems will not support the newer applications, in the long run it's all for the best. The original versions of Dreamweaver (many years ago) were simply non-visual HTML editing applications. Dreamweaver CS5 is not only doing things that were not even dreamed of in years past; it's also faster. As a Web designer, time is an important part of getting the job done, and getting it done quickly.

If I can accomplish more work in less time, it gives me more time to be creative, and able to meet my deadlines. And that's a good thing. So think of system requirements as the power behind the applications, that's going to help you do more, better work, and all in less time.

For Windows Computers

You need to have a computer with the following minimum configuration:

- Intel Pentium 4, Intel Centrino, Intel Xeon, Intel Core Duo, or AMD Athlon 64 (or compatible) processor.
- Microsoft Windows 7, Windows Vista with Service Pack 1, or Windows XP with Service Pack 3 or higher.

- 1 GB of RAM, 2 GB or above recommended.
- 1 GB of available hard-disk space (additional free space required during installation).
- 1,024 x 768 monitor resolution with 16-bit video card.
- DVD-ROM drive.
- Internet connection required for activation, registration, and some CS online services.

For Macintosh Computers

You need to have a computer with the following minimum configuration:

- Multicore Intel processor; Intel-based Macintosh.
- Mac OS X 10.5.7, or higher.
- 1 GB of RAM, 2 GB or above recommended.
- 1 GB of available hard-disk space (additional free space required during installation).
- 1,024 x 768 monitor resolution with 16-bit video card.
- DVD-ROM drive.
- Internet connection required for activation, registration, and some CS online services.

Installing Dreamweaver

The process of installing the Dreamweaver application is fairly straight-forward; you insert the Dreamweaver CS5 install disc into your DVD drive or download the software online to your computer, double-click the setup program and simply follow the on-screen instructions. The first thing that will happen is that the installer will check to see if you have the minimum system requirements. If you meet the minimums, the installer will guide you through the steps to complete the installation. The whole process takes about ten minutes, and at the end of the process you can launch Dreamweaver for the first time. Remember to have your serial number handy, because you will have to type it in during the installation process. It's a good idea to have that serial number in a safe place, just in case you would need to reinstall Dreamweaver.

Install Dreamweaver CS5

1 Insert the Dreamweaver CS5 DVD into your DVD ROM drive, or download the software online to your hard disk.

2 If necessary, double-click the DVD icon or open the folder with the downloaded software, and then double-click the setup icon.

3 Follow the on-screen instructions to install the product; the installer asks you to read and accept a licensing agreement, enter a serial number, indicate the language you want, enter or create an Adobe ID or skip the step, and specify where you want to install the software.

Did You Know?

Most Adobe applications can be downloaded. It's all very simple, you go to *www.adobe.com*, click the Products menu item, and then select the application you want to purchase. You will need a credit card (of course), and a lot of bandwidth.

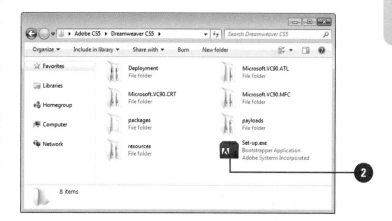

Getting Started

The launching of Dreamweaver can be accomplished in one of several ways. You could access the application by opening the Dreamweaver folder and double-clicking on the application icon (Macintosh or Windows). You could create an alias of the application, by right clicking on the Dreamweaver program icon and selecting Make Alias (Macintosh) or Create Shortcut (Windows).

Start Dreamweaver in Windows

1. Click the **Start** button on the taskbar.

2. Point to **All Programs**, and then click **Adobe**.

3. Point to an Adobe Collection CS5 menu, if needed.

4. Click **Adobe Dreamweaver CS5**.

5. If you're starting Dreamweaver CS5 for the first time, you might be prompted to specify the following initial settings:

   ◆ Enter or create an Adobe ID to register the product, click **Submit**, and then click **Done**.

   ◆ Select the check boxes with page types you want to set Dreamweaver as the default editor, and then click **OK**.

   The Dreamweaver window opens, displaying the Welcome screen.

Did You Know?

You can create and use a shortcut icon on your desktop to start Dreamweaver (Win). Click Start on the taskbar, point to All Programs, right-click Adobe Dreamweaver CS5, point to Send To, and then click Desktop (Create Shortcut). Double-click the shortcut icon on your desktop to start Dreamweaver.

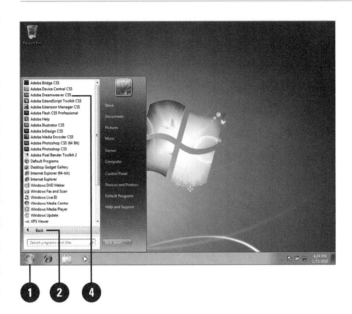

Welcome screen

Start Dreamweaver in Macintosh

1 Open the Applications folder (located on the main hard drive).

2 Open the Adobe Dreamweaver CS5 folder.

3 Double-click the **Dreamweaver CS5** application icon.

4 If you're starting Dreamweaver CS5 for the first time, you might be prompted to specify the following initial settings:

◆ Enter or create an Adobe ID to register the product, click **Submit**, and then click **Done**.

◆ Select the check boxes with page types you want to set Dreamweaver as the default editor, and then click **OK**.

The Dreamweaver window opens, displaying the Welcome screen.

Did You Know?

You can create a shortcut on the Macintosh. Drag and drop the Dreamweaver application icon to the bottom of the screen, and then add it to the shortcuts panel.

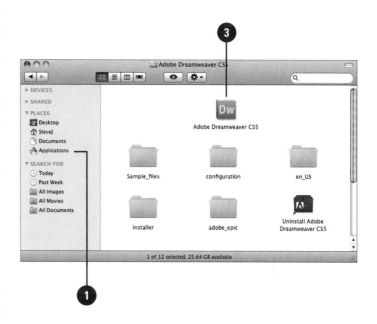

Shortcut for Adobe Dreamweaver CS5

For Your Information

Activating Dreamweaver

In order to curb theft of their products, Adobe requires you to activate the Dreamweaver application. The first time you open it, you will be prompted to enter your serial number, and then activate Dreamweaver. You will be able to delay the activation process for up to 30 days; however, on day 31 the application will cease to run until activated. Activation can be accomplished by the Internet, or by phone.

You can launch Dreamweaver and open a document at the same time. Simply double-click on the document icon (i.e. index.html). If the document was originally created within Dreamweaver, the file automatically opens in the Dreamweaver application.

Viewing the Dreamweaver Window

The Dreamweaver Graphical User Interface or GUI (pronounced "GOOEY") is the Web designer's workplace. Inside its document window and 19 main work panels you will find all the tools you need to design everything from a simple Web page, to a complex site.

Applications Bar
Displays options for working with and switching between documents and applications.

Workspace menu
Switches between workspaces.

Panel Windows
Gives you access to authoring tools and attribute settings for elements.

Welcome screen
Provides easy access links to create and open Dreamweaver documents.

Document Window
Displays open Dreamweaver documents along with the Document bar and Related Files bar.

Document Bar
Displays buttons for viewing and working with documents in Dreamweaver.

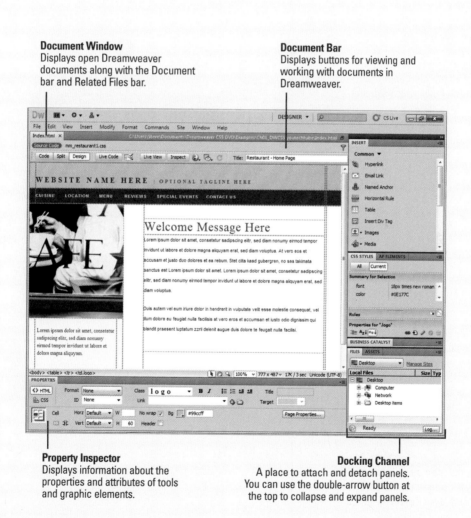

Property Inspector
Displays information about the properties and attributes of tools and graphic elements.

Docking Channel
A place to attach and detach panels. You can use the double-arrow button at the top to collapse and expand panels.

Creating a Web Site

Before you create a Web site, you need to create a local root folder where you'll store all the elements that make up the site. Web sites are more than just a bunch of Web pages. All the images, videos, navigational buttons, documents, scripts, etc., are separate files that must be uploaded into those pages. Defining a Web site instructs Dreamweaver that the local root folder is the folder location that contains all the elements of your site. In turn, Dreamweaver will keep track of the files within the folder, automatically update them as needed, and give you access to them, while you're working. The Site Setup dialog box (**New!**) doesn't force you to complete the site setup unless it's required. As you work on your site and a task needs information from the Site Setup dialog box, Dreamweaver opens it and highlights the required setting.

Create a New Web Site

1. Define a local root folder where you'll store all the elements that you will use to build your Web site.

2. Start Dreamweaver.

3. Click the **Site** menu, and then click **New Site**.

   Dreamweaver gives you several categories on the creation of a Web site: Site, Servers, Version Control, and Advanced Settings.

4. Click the **Site** category.

5. Name your site (Site names are not file names, so feel free to use any naming convention you wish).

6. Enter the location of your local root folder, or click the **Browse For Folder** icon, located to the right of the input box, navigate to the folder you want to use as the root folder, and then click **Select**.

7. Click the **Servers** category.

8. To specify the server (*optional at this point; you can do it later*) that will host your pages on the web, click the **Add New Server** button, specify the server name, FTP address, username and password, and root directory on the Basic tab, and then click **Save**.

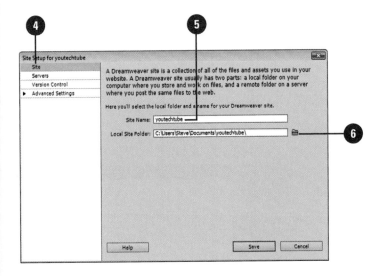

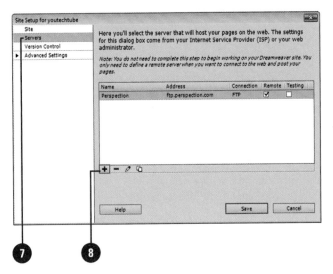

9 Click the **Version Control** category.

10 To use version control software (*optional at this point; you can do it later*), click the **Access** list arrow, click **Subversion**, and then specify the protocol type, server address and settings, and username and password.

11 Click the **Advanced Settings** category.

A list of subcategories appears, where you can set advanced settings. We'll deal with Advanced Settings in Chapter 20.

12 Click **Save** to complete the process.

Dreamweaver creates a site definition based on your options and your choice of the local root folder (In our example, youtechtube).

When you define a site in Dreamweaver, the Assets and Files panels will now display a list of all your folders and files.

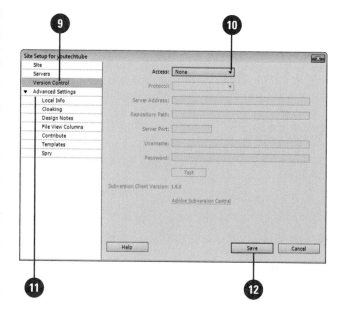

See Also

See "Setting Advanced Site Definitions" on page 474 for information on using the Advanced tab in the Site Definition dialog box.

For Your Information

Creating a Local Root Folder

The first step to a successful Web site is careful planning, and the creation of a local root folder. Since this is covered in Chapter 1, we'll assume that you've already taken care of this very important part of the design process. Remember, the local root folder contains all the elements that you use to build your Web site and all the individual pages and parts that it contains. It's very possible that you've already put in a lot of computer time before coming to this very important first step in Dreamweaver. For example, you may have created many of the images and graphics that you're going to use by working in Adobe Photoshop and Illustrator. You may have designed some Adobe Flash animations, and you might have even used Microsoft Word and Excel to generate some text documents and spreadsheets. All of these elements would be in the local root folder. In keeping with Chapter 1, we call this local root folder, *youtechtube*. Now that you have your local root folder, the next step is to inform Dreamweaver that this is the folder you'll be using for the creation of this particular Web site.

Opening a Web Site

Adobe Dreamweaver allows you to manage multiple sites. When you open Dreamweaver it will load the Web site last used. If, however, you need to work on another Web site it's a simple matter to redirect Dreamweaver to the needed site using the Manage Sites dialog box, which you can also use to create, edit, duplicate, remove, export, and import sites.

Open Predefined Sites

1 Click the **Site** menu, and then click **Manage Sites**.

2 Select the site from the listed options.

3 Click **Done**.

Dreamweaver closes the first site and loads all the assets for the selected site.

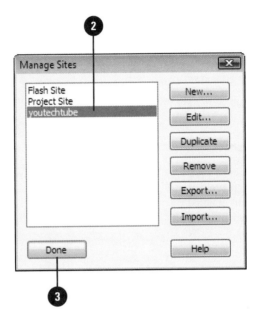

Creating a Blank Web Page

The whole point of using Dreamweaver is the creation of Web pages. In turn, these pages will load static and dynamic content, and be bundled together with a good navigational system; finally winding up as a complete Web site. The process of creating a site can become involved; however, it all begins with the creation of the first page. A new page is a blank slate for you to draw. A new Web page can be literally anything from a text page to a high-end page dealing with animation, video, audio, CSS, incontext editing (**New!**) or any combination of the above.

Create a Blank Web Page

1. Click the **File** menu, and then click **New**.

   TIMESAVER *Press Ctrl+N (Win) or ⌘+N (Mac).*

   The New Document dialog box opens.

   TIMESAVER *To create a Web page without the dialog box, click the file type you want at the Welcome Screen.*

2. Click the **Blank Page** category.

3. Select the Page Type you want (in this example, HTML).

4. Select the Layout you want (in this example, 1 column, elastic, centered).

5. Click the **DocType** list arrow and select the option you want.

6. Click the **Layout CSS** list arrow, if available, and select the option you want.

7. Click the **Link** button to attach a CSS file to the current document.

8. To add an editable region for a blank HTML page, select the **Enable InContext Editing** check box (**New!**).

9. Click **Create**.

   Dreamweaver creates the new page and opens it.

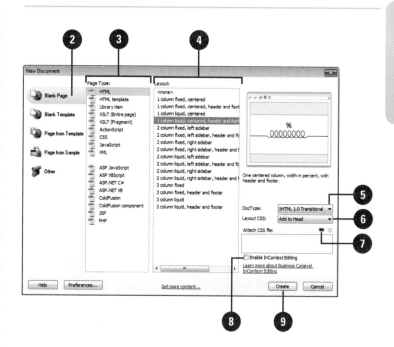

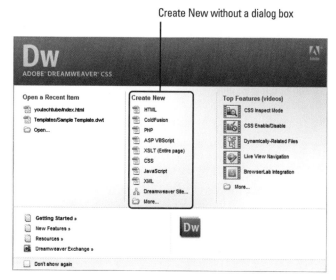

Create New without a dialog box

Creating a Web Page from a Blank Template

A Dreamweaver template is a common structure created and used for all or some pages of a Web site. Each section of a Web site can have its own template with variations in structure or color from the others. Templates are fantastic timesaving tools because they allow you to create pages that share the same design but different content, and if you modify a template document, you immediately update the design of all pages that were created from that template. Dreamweaver templates are special master files that contain editable and locked regions. Pages based on a template enable Dreamweaver users to edit parts of a Web page within the editable regions without the risk of accidentally changing the locked regions. This is a major advantage, because if you are creating a site that will be maintained by other users you can specify which parts of pages editors can and cannot change.

Create a Blank Template

1. Click the **File** menu, and then click **New**.

2. Click the **Blank Template** category.

3. Select the Template Type you want (in this example, HTML Template).

4. Select the Layout you want (in this example, 2 column, elastic, left sidebar).

   In this example leave the Doc Type and Layout CSS at their default values of XHTML 1.0 Transitional, and Add to Head, respectively.

5. Click **Create**.

   Dreamweaver opens the template.

6. Click the **File** menu, click **Save**, click **OK** if necessary to dismiss the no editable region alert, specify a name, and then click **Save**.

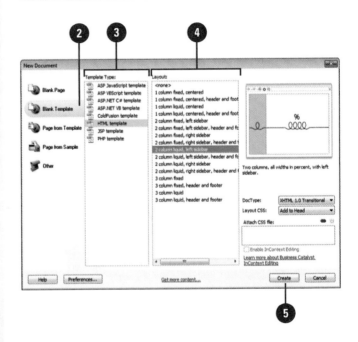

For Your Information

Storing Templates

When you work with templates, Dreamweaver automatically creates a folder called Templates, and all template files are stored in this folder. If you move a template file outside that folder, Dreamweaver will not be able to create new files based on that template. In addition, it creates problems when you insert paths for hyperlinks. Keep your templates within the Templates folder.

Create Editable Regions

① Use your cursor to select an area of the image that you want to have the ability to edit. An editable area can be defined as an AP element, or table, or table cell, etc.

② Click the **Insert** menu, point to **Template Objects**, and then select from the following Region options:

◆ **Editable Region.** Use this option to allow contributors to the Web page the ability to change or modify that selected area.

◆ **Optional Region.** Use this option to define a section of the page that will or will not be shown, depending on what the content contributor decides.

◆ **Repeating Region.** Use this option to allow contributors to the Web page the ability to duplicate the region. For example, creating a table that holds customer comments, and the contributor needs the ability to generate new pages, and add more rows to the table, as needed.

③ Enter an appropriate name for the Region.

④ Click **OK**.

The selected area now takes on the appropriate characteristics.

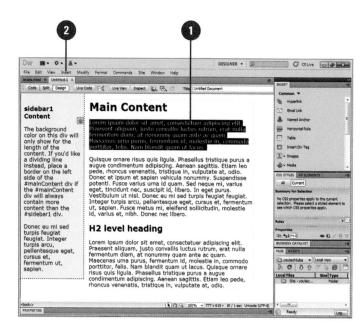

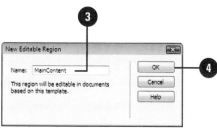

Editable Region

Creating a Web Page from a Template

Instead of creating a Web page from scratch, you can create a new Web page based on the existing template, which can save you a lot of time and effort. In the New Document dialog box, you can select your own custom template designs available in the Page From Template category or click Get More Content to open the Dreamweaver Exchange on the Web to download more template page designs.

Create a Web Page from an Existing Template

1. Click the **File** menu, and then click **New**.

   TIMESAVER *Press Ctrl+N (Win) or ⌘+N (Mac).*

   The New Document dialog box opens.

2. Click the **Page From Template** category.

3. Select the site that contains the template you want.

4. Select the template you want to use.

5. Select or clear the **Update Page When Template Changes** check box.

6. Click **Create**.

7. Click the **File** menu, click **Save**, specify a name, and then click **Save**.

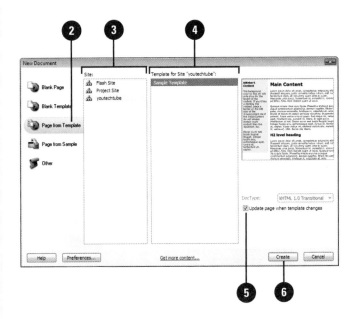

Did You Know?

You can create a document from a template in the Assets panel. Open the Assets panel using the Windows menu, click the Templates icon to view the list of templates, right-click (Win) or Control-click (Mac) the template you want, click New From Template, and then save the document.

Creating a Web Page from a Sample

If you're not sure where you start, you can use one of Dreamweaver's sample designs as a starting point for a new page and then make any changes you want to customize it to suit your specific needs. In the New Document dialog box, you can preview sample file designs and then create a new document based on the one you want to use. You can select from sample pages with CSS (Cascading Style Sheets), frames, themes (starter pages for Entertainment, Lodging, etc.), and basic types (starter pages for Commerce, Data, Images, etc.). When you create a new document, Dreamweaver makes a untitled copy of the sample file, which you can save with a new name.

Create a Web Page from a Sample

1. Click the **File** menu, and then click **New**.

    TIMESAVER Press Ctrl+N (Win) or ⌘+N (Mac).

    The New Document dialog box opens.

2. Click the **Page From Sample** category.

3. Select the type of sample folder you want to use: CSS Style Sheet, Frameset, Starter Page (Theme), or Starter Page (Basic).

    TIMESAVER At the Welcome Screen, click the type of sample file you want.

4. Select the sample page you want.

5. If available, click the **DocType** list arrow, and then select from the available options.

6. Click **Create**.

    Dreamweaver creates the new page and opens it.

7. Click the **File** menu, click **Save**, specify a name, and then click **Save**.

8. If the Copy Dependent Files dialog box appears, set the options you want, and then click **Copy**.

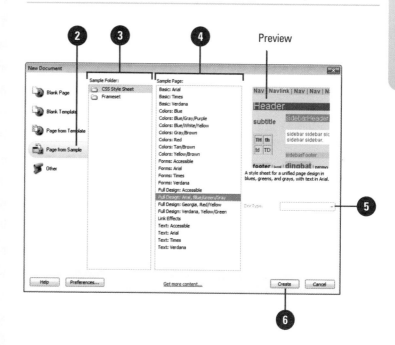

Saving a Web Page

Web pages should be saved as soon as they're opened. Naming conventions should be according to a predefined list of names that you created during the planning stage of the project. It's important to save pages early, that way if there's any problem such as: the application locking up, you will be able to start again from the last-saved version. Another important reason is error checking and validating. Web pages must be in a saved state before performing any validation.

Save a Web Page

① Click the **File** menu, and then select from the following options:

- ◆ **Save.** If the file is new, you will be prompted to enter a proper file name and location for the new page. If the file has been previously saved, Dreamweaver saves the file, using the original file name and location (without prompting).

  TIMESAVER *Press Ctrl+S (Win) or ⌘+S (Mac).*

- ◆ **Save As.** Use this option to make a copy of a file; you will be prompted to give the file a new name and location.

  TIMESAVER *Press Ctrl+Shift+S (Win) or ⌘+Shift+S (Mac).*

- ◆ **Save All.** Use this option if you have more than one file open, and you want to save all of them at the same time. If any of the files are new, you will be prompted to enter a file name and location.

- ◆ **Save All Related Files. (New!)** Use this option to save web site related files, which includes external CSS rules, server-side includes, external JavaScript files, parent templates files, library files, and iframe source files.

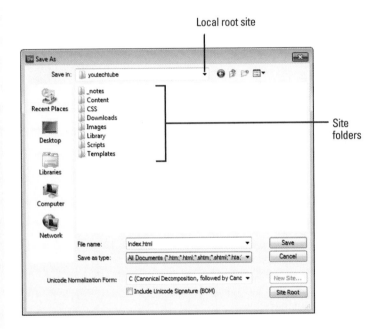

Local root site

Site folders

For Your Information

Naming Conventions for Files and Elements

When you name your files and elements in Dreamweaver, it's important to use standard guidelines for naming to make sure your Web site works properly on different server platforms, such as Windows or UNIX. Keep the following in mind: (1) Use underscores in place of spaces and avoid special characters (colons, slashes, periods, and apostrophes), and (2) use shorter names; filenames on the Mac cannot be more than 31 characters.

- **Save As Template.** Use this option to save the open document as a template. A template is a reusable document that contains editable regions.

2 Navigate to the drive and folder location where you want to save the file.

3 Type a name for the file, or use the suggested name.

When naming files, avoid using spaces and special characters, or punctuation.

For this example, leave the other options at their default levels.

4 Click **Save** to finalize the process.

5 Click **Copy**.

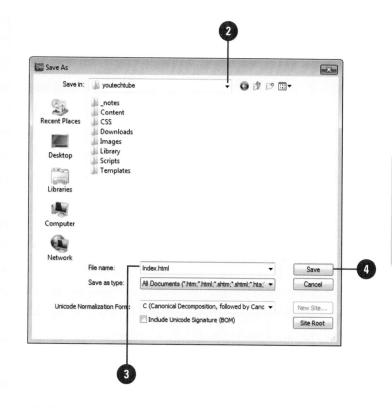

Did You Know?

You can revert to the last saved version of a document. Click the File menu, click Revert, and then click Yes to revert to the previous version, or click No to keep your changes. If you save a document and then exit Dreamweaver, you cannot revert to the previous version when you restart Dreamweaver.

Macintosh and Windows computers systems are not case sensitive. Therefore when you create a file name for a Web page (or the files loaded on the page), you won't have a problem validating that page on your computer; however, when you move the site to the server, many servers are case-sensitive, and the same pages may not load correctly. For example, if a Web page is named Index.html and you call it using index.html. It validates on your computer, but it might not work on the server… pay attention to case.

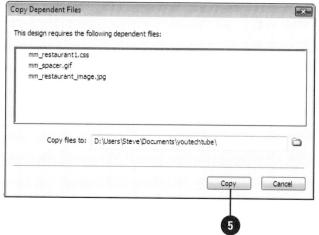

Opening an Existing Web Page or File

Opening a Web page is a simple procedure. You can use the Open section on the Welcome screen, Open commands on the File menu, or Adobe Bridge CS5 (a stand-alone file management program that comes with Dreamweaver CS5) to open Web related files in several formats. You can open a Web page from your local hard drive, a network drive, or a Web server using an Uniform Resource Locator (URL). By default, Dreamweaver opens the last Web site you worked on every time you open the program. If you open a new page while another site is still open, the new page opens in a new Dreamweaver window. Web pages using the HTML—Hypertext Markup Language—are the primary file types you open in Dreamweaver, however, you can open other types too. As an editor, you can use Dreamweaver to open many types of Web related files, including style sheets, scripts, text, xml, and libraries. For Web pages you recently opened, you can quickly reopen them again by pointing to Open Recent on the File menu, and then selecting the Web page you want to open.

Open an Existing Web Page or File

1. Click the **File** menu, and then click **Open**.

   TIMESAVER *Press Ctrl+O (Win) or* ⌘+O *(Mac).*

2. Navigate to the drive and folder location where you want to open the Web page.

3. Click the **Files Of Type** list arrow (Win) or **popup** (Mac), and then select the type of file you want to open.

4. Select the page you want to open in the working folder, or type the URL of the page you want.

5. Click **Open**.

6. If the file is read-only, click **View**, **Make Writable**, or **Cancel**.

   If you click View, a lock icon (**New!**) appears in the Document tab to the left of the name.

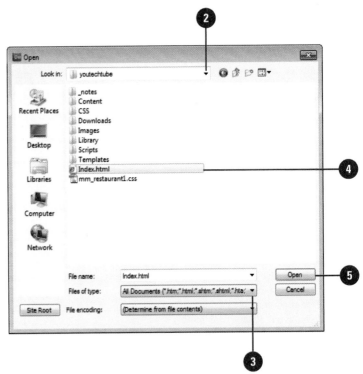

Open a Recently Opened Document

◆ **File Menu**. Click the **File** menu, point to **Open Recent**, and then click the file you want to open.

◆ **Welcome Screen**. At the Welcome Screen, click the file you want to open under Open A Recent Item.

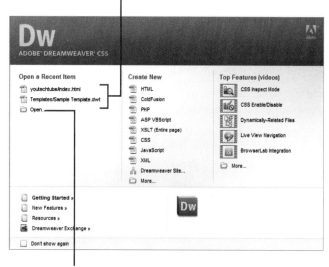

Click to open recently opened files

Click to access the Open dialog box

Did You Know?

You can open a recent file quickly from the Start menu (Win). Click the Start button, point to Recent Items (Vista) or My Recent Documents (XP), and then click the file name you want to open.

You can browse and open files in Adobe Bridge. Click the File menu, click Browse In Bridge, select a work-space display to view your files the way you want, navigate to the drive or folder where the file is located. To open the file, double-click the file icon. To return back to Dreamweaver, click the File menu, and then click Return To Adobe Dreamweaver.

Common Dreamweaver File Types

File Type	Description
HTML	Hypertext Markup Language (.html or .htm) files display Web pages in a browser.
CSS	Cascading Style Sheet (.css) files are used to format and position HTML content in a consistent manner.
GIF	Graphics Interchange Format (.gif) files are used for graphics, such as logos, containing a max of 256 colors.
JPEG	Joint Photographic Expert Group (.jpeg) files are used for graphics, such as photographs, requiring more than 256 colors.
XML	Extensible Markup Language (.xml) files contain data in raw form that can be formatted using XSL.
XSL	Extensible Stylesheet Language (.xsl or .xslt) files are used to style XML data.
CFML	ColdFusion Markup Language (.cfm) files are used to process dynamic Web pages.
ASPX	ASP.NET files (.aspx) files are used to process dynamic Web pages.
PHP	Hypertext Preprocessor (.php) files are used to process dynamic Web pages.

Working with Views

When you open a Web page, Dreamweaver displays three view buttons on the Document toolbar and uses View menu commands to help you work more efficiently.

Code view displays the HTML and any embedded code for a page.

Split Code view displays the screen in half vertically (**New!**). Both halves display page code. Only available on View or Layout menu.

Code and Design view displays the screen in

half vertically (**New!**). One half displays the current page in Code view and the other half displays the current page in Design view.

Design view displays Web pages in WYSIWYG (What You See Is What You Get) for editing.

In a split screen display, you can change the placement of the content. Click the View menu, and then click Split Vertically (horizontal when unchecked), or Design View on Left or Design View on Top.

Code view

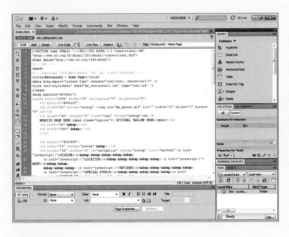

Split Code view

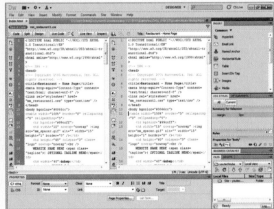

Design view

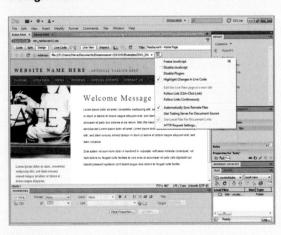

Code and Design view

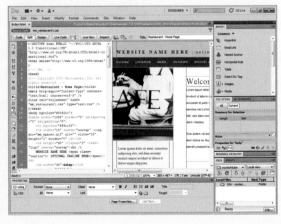

Switching Between Pages and Views

The tabs across the top of the Document window indicate the currently open Web pages. You can click the tab to display the page or site you want. Below the tab in the Document window, the view buttons—Code, Split, and Design—appear for the current page. Design view displays the page or site as it appears on screen, while Code view displays the HTML code that makes up the page or site. Split (Code and Design) view shows you Code view at the top and Design view at the bottom, while Split Code view shows code at the top and bottom.

Switch Between Web Pages

◆ **Web Pages.** Click the tab with the name you want to display.

TIMESAVER *Press Ctrl+Tab or Ctrl+Shift+Tab to cycle thru tabs.*

Click tabs to switch between open files

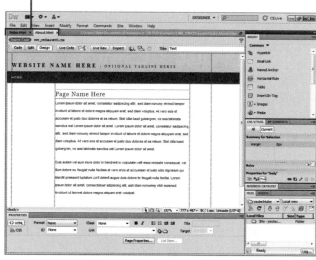

Switch Between Page Views

◆ **Switch Views.** Click the **Code**, **Split**, or **Design** button below the tab on the Document toolbar in the Document window, or click the **View** or **Layout** menu, and then click the view you want: **Code**, **Split Code**, **Design**, and **Code and Design**.

   ◆ The Split Code command (no button available) displays code in a split screen.

   TIMESAVER *Press Ctrl+`* (accent above Tab key) to cycle to the view you want.*

Click to display the Layout menu   Click to switch views

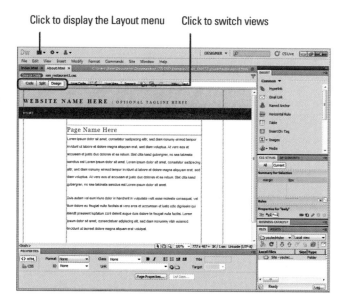

Previewing Pages in Live View

As you work on your site, you will probably want to see what individual pages look like. Instead of previewing pages in an external browser, you can view pages as they will appear in a browser in Dreamweaver using Live view, a non-editable view. You switch to Live view from Design view, which becomes frozen. However, you can still use Code view to make changes and then refresh it back in Live view. In Live view, you can set options (**New!**) to follow links in pages, type URLs using the Browser Navigation bar (**New!**), and edit browsed pages from your site in a new tab. In addition, you can also freeze JavaScript and the page in its current state. This allows you to make and refresh changes to step through different states of an interactive element, such as menus, which you can't do in Design view. While in Live view, you can also view Live Code, which is a non-editable view of the executed code on the page. When code states change, Live Code highlights the code in different colors (**New!**) for easy viewing.

Preview a Web Page in Live View and Live Code View

1. Open the Web page you want to view.

2. Switch to Design view or Code and Design view.

3. Click the **Live View** button.

4. If you want, make changes in Code view, in the CSS Styles panel, in an external CSS style sheet, or in another related file.

    ◆ You can open related files by using the Related Files toolbar.

5. Click the **Refresh** button in the Document toolbar or press F5 to view any changes.

6. To go to Live Code view, click the **Live Code** button.

    Live code view appears displaying browser code. The non-editable code is highlighted in different colors for code state changes.

7. To return back to Live view, click the **Live Code** button again.

8. To return back to Design view, click the **Live View** button again.

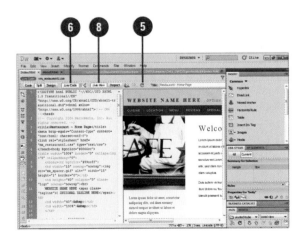

Select Live View Options

1 Open the Web page you want to view.

2 Switch to Design view or Code and Design view.

3 Click the **Live View Options** button on the Browser Navigation toolbar (**New!**), or click the **View** menu, point to **Live View Options**, and then select any of the following:

◆ **Freeze JavaScript.** Freezes elements that use JavaScript.

◆ **Disable JavaScript.** Displays the page as if the browser doesn't have JavaScript enabled.

◆ **Disable Plug-ins.** Displays the page as if the browser doesn't have plug-in enabled.

◆ **Highlight Changes in Live Code.** Highlights code state changes in different colors (**New!**).

◆ **Show Browser Navigation Bar.** Use to navigate pages (**New!**).

◆ **Edit the Live View Page in a New Tab.** Opens Live view page in a new tab for editing (**New!**).

◆ **Follow Link** or **Follow Links Continuously.** Allows you to follow links in Live view (**New!**).

◆ **Automatically Sync Remote Files.** Automatically updates remote files (**New!**).

◆ **Use Testing Server For Document Source.** Used for dynamic pages. Uses the file version on the site's testing server as the Live view source.

◆ **Use Local Files For Document Links.** Used for non-dynamic sites. Uses the local file version as the Live view source.

◆ **HTTP Request Settings.** Allows you to set advanced settings for displaying live data.

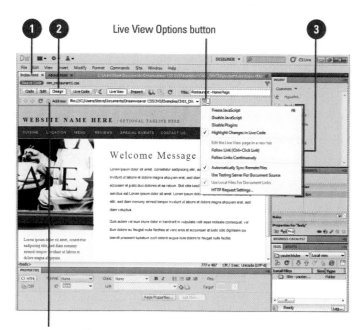
Live View Options button

Browser Navigation Bar

For Your Information

Using the Browser Navigation Bar in Live View

The Browser Navigation bar (**New!**) allows you to navigate to pages in Live view. The Browser Navigation bar includes similar options to those in a Web browser. You can enter a URL in the Address bar, and use the Back, Forward, Refresh, and Home buttons to navigate to pages in Live view. The Home button displays your original document. On the right side of the bar is the Live View Options button, which you can use the display content in Live view or Live Code view. To show or hide the Browser Navigation bar, click the View menu, point to Live View Options, and then click Show Browser Navigation Bar, or click the View menu, point to Toolbars, and then click Browser Navigation.

Previewing Pages in Browser

As you work on the development of your site, you will probably want to occasionally stop and see what the individual pages look like when previewed within a specific browser. One of the most used features for testing your site is the Preview In Browser feature. This is one of the most used when working in Dreamweaver. It lets you see what your site will look like in a particular Internet browser. When testing a particular Web page, it's a good idea to check it out in more than one browser, and in more than one version of the browser on different operating systems. For example, it may look great in Safari on the Macintosh, and not even work in Internet Explorer on Windows. If you don't have access to other browsers and operating systems, you can use Adobe Browser-Labs, an online service that you can use from within Dreamweaver, to view your Web pages.

Preview a Web Page

1. Open the Web page you want to view.

2. Click the **File** menu, point to **Preview In Browser**, and then select a browser from the available options.

   ◆ **Adobe BrowserLab.** An online service that allows you to view using different browsers and operating systems.

3. If the Web page needs to be saved, you will be prompted to save the page before continuing.

   The Web page opens and displays in the selected browser. Check the page display and links.

4. When you're done, close the browser.

Did You Know?

What it means when you get an error previewing a Web page. The preview in browser function may return a "page cannot be found" error if any of the characters in the path of the local folder have a different letter case than the path of the testing server folder.

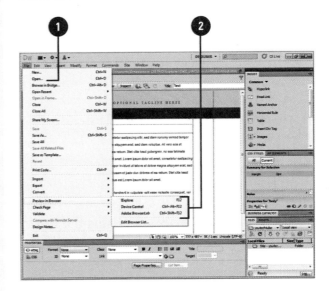

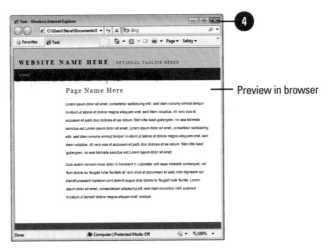

Preview in browser

Edit the Browser List in Preferences

① Click the **File** menu, point to **Preview In Browser**, and then click **Edit Browser List**.

② Click the **Plus** (+) button to add another browser to the list.

③ Give the new browser a name.

④ Click **Browse**, and then locate the browser you want to add to your list.

⑤ Select the browser, and then click **Open**.

⑥ Select the **Primary Browser** or **Secondary Browser** check box to decide whether this new browser is the primary or secondary browser.

⑦ Click **OK** to return to the Preferences dialog box.

⑧ Click **OK** to close the dialog box and save your changes.

⑨ Click the **File** menu, and then point to **Preview In Browser**.

Your new browser option is added to the list.

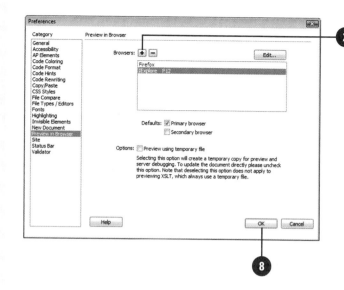

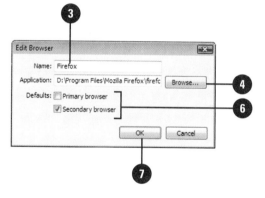

Did You Know?

You can use keyboard shortcuts to preview pages. The Primary Browser launches when you press the F12 key. The Secondary Browser launches when you press Ctrl+F12 (Win) or ⌃⌘+F12 (Mac).

For Your Information

Using Adobe BrowserLab

Adobe BrowserLab is an online service that allows you to test pages of your Web site using different browsers and operating systems. You can use it as a standalone service or within Dreamweaver. In Dreamweaver, you can preview local web content from your local site, or from a remote or testing server. To set file location preferences, click the CS Live menu, click BrowserLab to open the panel, click the Location list arrow, and then click Local or Server. You can preview a page from Design or Live view. To preview a page, click the File menu, point to Preview In Browser, and then click Adobe BrowserLab, or click the Preview button in the Adobe BrowserLab panel.

Getting Help While You Work

When you start Dreamweaver Help, the Adobe Community Help window opens (**New!**), displaying help categories and topics. You can search product help from Local Help, Community Help, or Adobe.com by using keywords or phrases or browsing through a list of categories and topics to locate specific information. Local Help accesses product help on your local computer, Community Help accesses product help online, and Adobe.com accesses related help information on Adobe.com. When you perform a search using keywords or phrases, a list of possible answers is shown from the search location. In addition, comments and ratings from users are available to help guide you to an answer. You can add feedback and suggestions by signing in to Adobe.com.

Get Dreamweaver Help

1. Click the **Help** menu, and then click **Dreamweaver Help**, or type a keyword in the Search box.

    TIMESAVER *Press F1 (Win) or* ⌘+/ *(Mac).*

2. To search another CS product, click the **Select Product** list arrow, and then select a CS product.

3. To set search options, click **Search Options** to expand it, and then select any of the following:

    ◆ **Search This Help System Only.** Select to constrain the search to the selected product.

    ◆ **Search Location.** Select Local Help, Community Help, or Adobe.com.

    ◆ **Filter Results.** For Adobe.com, select a filter option.

4. Click Help categories (plus sign icons) until you display the topic you want or type in keywords to search in the **Search** box.

5. Click the topic you want.

6. Read the topic, and if you want, click any links to get information on related topics or definitions.

7. When you're done, click the **Close** button (Win) or click the **Adobe Help** menu (Mac), and then click **Quit Adobe Help**.

Search box

Search results

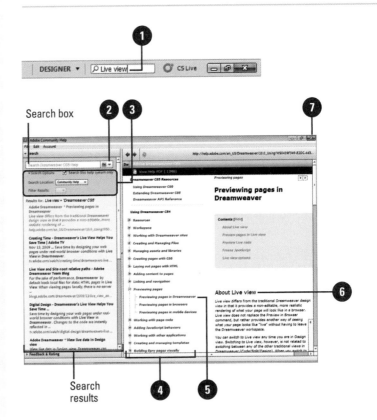

Get Additional Help

Click the **Help** menu, and choose from the following options:

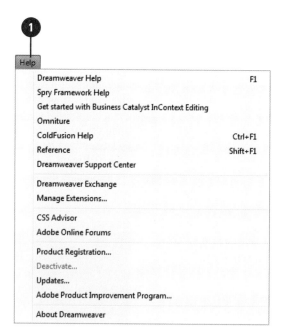

- **Dreamweaver Help.** Standard help systems for all areas of Dreamweaver.

- **Spry Framework Help.** Online help for Spry, an open source Ajax framework developed by Adobe which is used in the construction of Rich Internet Applications.

- **Get Started with Business Catalyst InContext Editing.** Online information about Adobe InContext Editing.

- **Omniture.** Online information about the Omniture company.

- **ColdFusion Help.** Online help for CFML (ColdFusion Markup Language). CFML is a tag-based Web scripting language supporting dynamic Web page creation and database access.

- **Reference.** Gives you access to fourteen books and manuals with product information.

- **Dreamweaver Support Center.** Gives you access to Adobe online support, and allows you to search through an extensive LiveDocs data base.

- **Dreamweaver Exchange.** Gives you access to the Adobe Marketplace & Exchange with tools and resources.

- **Manage Extensions.** Opens Adobe Extension Manager CS5.

- **CSS Advisor.** Gives you access to information about using Cascading Style Sheets (CSS).

- **Adobe Online Forums.** Gives you access to the Adobe online forums, where you can get information from contributors.

For Your Information

Participating in Adobe Product Improvement

You can participate in the Adobe Product Improvement Program. Click the Help menu, click Adobe Product Improvement Program, and then follow the on-screen instructions. This is an opt-in program that allows you to test Adobe products and make suggestions for future products. This program enables Adobe to collect product usage data from customers while maintaining their privacy.

Getting Dreamweaver Updates on the Web

As time passes, Dreamweaver—like any other program—will change. There are two types of changes to a program: updates and patches. Updates are improvements to a program such as a new feature, option, or command. Patches are software fixes for problems discovered after the public release of the program. The good news is that both updates and patches are free, and once downloaded, are self-installing. Adobe gives you two ways to check for changes. You can check manually by going to the Adobe web site, or automatically through the Adobe Updater. The Adobe Updater Preferences dialog box allows you to set update options for Dreamweaver and other installed Adobe products, such as Bridge. You can also set an option to have Adobe notify you of updates in the menu bar (**New!**).

Get Dreamweaver Updates on the Web

1. Click the **Help** menu, and then click **Updates**.

   Adobe checks your software with the latest available version and automatically updates it.

2. To manually check, click the **Check For New Updates** button.

3. To change preferences, click **Preferences**, select the update options you want, and then click **Done**.

4. Click **Quit**.

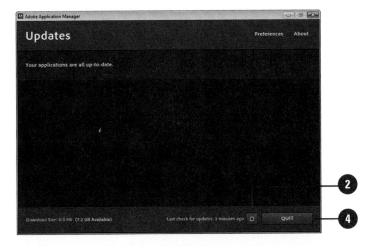

Did You Know?

You can deactivate or activate Dreamweaver to use on another computer. You can use your serial number on only one computer at a time. If you're moving from one computer to another, you can deactivate your serial number on one computer and then activate it another one. Click the Help menu, click Deactivate, click Suspend Activation (saves serial number) or Deactivate Permanently (removes serial number), and then click Done. To activate it, click the Help menu, and then click Activate.

Closing a Web Page or File

After you finish working on a Web page, you can close it and open another one, or close it and exit Dreamweaver. Closing a Web page makes more computer memory available for other processes. Closing a Web page is different from exiting Dreamweaver: after you close a Web page, Dreamweaver is still running until you exit it. You can use the Exit command on the File menu (Win) or Quit Dreamweaver command on the Dreamweaver menu (Mac) to close a document and exit Dreamweaver, or you can use the Close button on the Document tab. If you try to close a document without saving your final changes, a dialog box opens, asking if you want to do so.

Close a Web Page or File

1. Click the **Close** button on the Document tab, or click the **File** menu, and then click **Close**.

   TIMESAVER *Click the Close button in the Document window or press Ctrl+W (Win) or ⌘+W (Mac).*

2. Click **Yes** to save any Web page changes; click **No** to close the Web page or file without saving any changes; or click **Cancel** to return to the Web page or file without closing it.

Did You Know?

You can close all Web pages at one time. Click the File menu, and then click Close All Pages or press Ctrl+Shift+W (Win) or ⌘+Shift+W (Mac).

You can cascade or tile Document windows. To cascade document windows, click the Windows menu, and then click Cascade. To tile documents, click the Windows menu, and then click Tile Horizontally or Tile Vertically (Windows), or Tile (Mac).

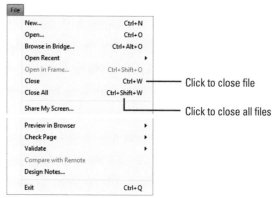

Click to close file

Click to close all files

Finishing Up

As much as we enjoy working in Dreamweaver, the time will finally come when you want to shut down for the day. The process of closing out a Dreamweaver Web site, is not difficult; as a matter of fact, it's no more complicated than closing down any application. Dreamweaver is smart, if you attempt to exit or quit before saving that last file you were working on, Dreamweaver prompts you to save or ignore any changes.

Exit or Quit Dreamweaver

1. Use any of the following methods:

    TIMESAVER *Press Ctrl+Q (Win) or ⌘+Q (Mac).*

    - Click the **Close** button on the Dreamweaver program window title bar.

    - In Macintosh, click the **Dreamweaver** menu, and then click **Quit Dreamweaver**.

    - In Windows, click the **File** menu, and then click **Exit**.

2. Click **Yes** to save any Web changes, or click **No** to ignore any changes.

    Dreamweaver performs an orderly shutdown of the program.

Click to exit Dreamweaver

Working Within the Dreamweaver Environment

3

Introduction

Getting to know the Dreamweaver authoring environment makes you more effective and efficient as you create Web pages and manage Web sites. You'll get to know the parts of the Dreamweaver window, which include toolbars and panels.

The Toolbars contain buttons that you can use to perform common tasks. Dreamweaver comes with four toolbars. The main one is the Document toolbar, which appear by default. The Document toolbar appears under an open document tab and allows you to change views, specify a title, manage files, preview pages, enable or disable page view options, and perform document validation. The Dreamweaver window also included panels. Panels are windows that allow you to view, organize, and change elements and related options in a document. The Insert panel provides the commands for inserting various types of objects. The Properties panel is a specialized panel that allows you to change object specific attributes and options. To work efficiently in Dreamweaver you need information about the active document. Dreamweaver displays current information about the active document and common display tools on the Status bar, located at the bottom of the document window. For example, working with the Zoom tool on the Status bar gives you one more way to control the view size to exactly what you see in Dreamweaver. In addition, you can use rulers, guides, and the grid to help you lay out artwork and objects with precision.

Dreamweaver uses built-in keyboard shortcuts designed specifically for Dreamweaver. The built-in keyboard shortcuts are organized into sets, which you can duplicate and customize to create your own personalized set. Dreamweaver allows you to set preferences to customize the way you work in the program.

What You'll Do

Examine the Dreamweaver Window

Work with Toolbars

Resize Panels

Work with Panels

Dock and Undock Panels

Group and Ungroup Panels

Create a Workspace

Use the Status Bar

Change the View with the Zoom Tool

Work with Rulers

Work with the Grid and Guides

Create Keyboard Shortcuts

Set General Preferences

Set New Document Preferences

Work with Colors

Set Highlighting Color Preferences

Examining the Dreamweaver Window

When you start Dreamweaver, the program window displays several windows of varying sizes you can use to create Web pages. These windows include the Program window, Document window, various panels, and the Properties panel. Depending on your installation and previous program usage, not all of these windows may appear, or additional ones may be visible. You'll do the bulk of your work in Dreamweaver with these windows.

In Dreamweaver, windows appear in the Program window. The **Program window** displays an Application bar at the top of the

Document Window
Displays open Dreamweaver documents, panels, and the Properties panel.

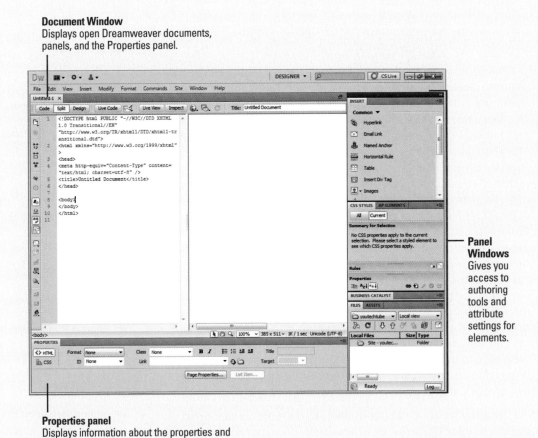

Panel Windows
Gives you access to authoring tools and attribute settings for elements.

Properties panel
Displays information about the properties and attributes of tools and graphic elements.

screen with a program icon, menu bar (depending on screen size), menus (Layout, Extend Dreamweaver, Site, and Workspace), Search bar, CS Live menu (**New!**), resizing buttons, and a Close button.

A menu bar appears on or below the Applications bar with menu names. A **menu** is a list of commands that you use to accomplish specific tasks. A **command** is a directive that accesses a feature of a program. Dreamweaver has its own set of menus, which are located on the menu bar along the top of the Dreamweaver window. On a menu, a check mark identifies a feature that is currently selected (that is, the feature is enabled or on). To disable (turn off) the feature, you click the command again to remove the check mark. A menu can contain several check marked features. A bullet (Win) or diamond (Mac) also indicates that an option is enabled, but a menu can contain only one bullet-or diamond-marked feature per menu section. To disable a command with a bullet or diamond next to it, you must select a different option in the section on the menu.

When you perform a command frequently, it's faster, and sometimes more convenient, to use a shortcut key, which is a keyboard alternative to using the mouse. When a shortcut key is available, it is listed beside the command on the menu, such as ⌘+F3 (Mac) or Ctrl+F3 (Win) for the Properties command on the Window menu.

Below the menu bar is the Insert toolbar, which appears by default and provides tabs with a variety of different buttons. A **Toolbar** contains a set of commonly used buttons you can quickly access to help you to create Web pages. Dreamweaver comes with five different toolbars, which you can show or hide to customize the Program window.

The **Document window** displays open Dreamweaver documents. Dreamweaver uses tabs to make it easier to switch back and forth between documents. Below a Document tab is the Related Files and Document toolbar. Each document tab includes a Minimize, Maximize, and Close button at the top, and a **Status bar** at the bottom, which displays current information about the active document and common display tools.

A **panel** is a window you can collapse, expand, and group with other panels, known as a panel group, to improve accessibility and workflow. A panel appears with a shaded header bar, which includes the window title and additional options. A panel group consists of either individual panels stacked one on top of the other or related panels organized together with tabs, such as the Files panel, to navigate from one panel to another. Dreamweaver provides a wide variety of panels you can use to work with different aspects of a Web page, including CSS Styles, Databases, Tags, and Frames, which you can open and close from the Window menu. As you open, close, and move around windows and panels to meet your individual needs, you can save the location of windows and panels as a custom panel layout set, which you can display again later.

The **Properties panel**, known more commonly as the **Property Inspector**, at the bottom of the Program window provides a convenient way to view and change attributes of any selected object or multiple objects, such as graphics and shapes, on a Web page. After you select an object, relevant commands and associated fields for it appear in the Property Inspector.

Working with Toolbars

Toolbars contain buttons you can click to carry out commands you use frequently. Dreamweaver provides 4 different toolbars—Style Rendering, Document, Standard, Browser Navigation (**New!**), and Coding—and the Insert panel for you to use to execute commands. The Insert panel provides the commonly used commands for inserting various types of objects. The Insert panel, displays subpanels, such as Common, Layout, Forms, Data, Spry, Text, and Favorites, you can use to access buttons. The Style Rendering toolbar allows you to work with different media types. The Document toolbar appears by default under an open document tab and allows you to change views, specify a title, manage files, preview pages, enable or disable page view options, and perform document validation. The Standard toolbar provides common file and editing commands, such as Open, Save, Print, Cut, Copy, Paste, Undo, and Redo. The Browser Navigation toolbar is available in Live view and allows you to follow links and browse pages (**New!**). The Coding toolbar is available in Code and Split views and makes it easier to work with code. You can quickly show or hide the toolbars you need or are no longer using to customize the way you use Dreamweaver.

Show and Hide Toolbars

◆ To display a toolbar, click the **View** menu, point to **Toolbars**, and then click a toolbar to select the check mark.

   TIMESAVER *You can also right-click (Win) or Control+click (Mac) any of the toolbars and then click a toolbar.*

◆ To hide a toolbar, click the **View** menu, point to **Toolbars**, and then click a toolbar to deselect the check mark.

   TIMESAVER *To display or hide the Insert toolbar, press Ctrl+F2, or click the Window menu, and then click Insert.*

Did You Know?

You can show and hide the Application bar. Click the Window menu, and then click Application Bar (**New!**).

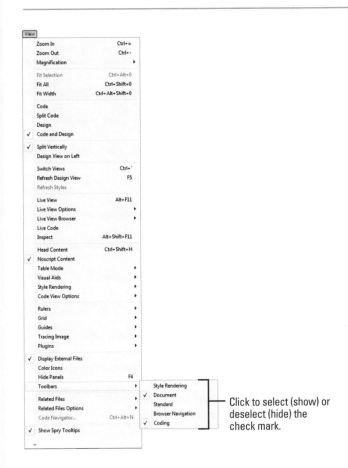

Click to select (show) or deselect (hide) the check mark.

Resizing Panels

If you need more workspace, you can use the double-arrow button (at the top of a panel group) to quickly minimize a panel group, such as the one on the right side of the Dreamweaver window. When you click the double-arrow button, the panel group collapses to icons, which increases the size of the workspace. You can click the icons to display the panel. When you click the double-arrow button again, the panel group reopens. If you need to increase or decrease the size of a docking panel, you can drag the resize bar at the top-left side of the panel group to resize it as you would any window.

Minimize and Maximize Panels

◆ To minimize or maximize a docking channel, click the **Double-arrow** button at the top of panel group.

The double-arrow direction indicates whether the panel minimizes or maximizes.

For example, if the double-arrow points to the left of the Tools panel that means when you click it the Tools panel minimizes. If the double-arrow points to the right that means when you click it the Tools panel maximizes.

◆ To have an expanded panel icon automatically collapse or hide when you click away, right-click (Win) or control+click (Mac) a panel, and then click **Auto-Collapse Icon Panels** or **Auto-Show Hidden Panels**.

Double-arrow button; maximized panel

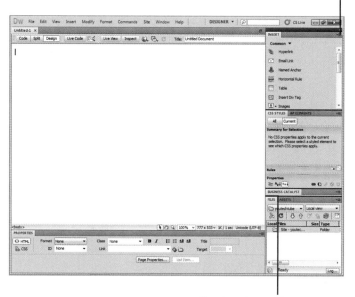

Drag to resize panel

Double-arrow button; minimized panel

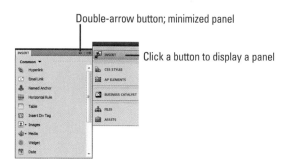

Click a button to display a panel

Working with Panels

Panels are windows that allow you to view, organize, and change elements and related options in a document. In Dreamweaver, you work with several panel windows at one time. Instead of continually moving, resizing, or opening and closing windows, you can collapse or expand individual panels within a window with a single click to save space. A panel appears with a header, which includes the tab titles and three accessibility options: the Minimize/Maximize button, the Close button, and an Options menu. The entire set of panels includes a double arrow you can use the collapse and expand the entire panel between icons with text and full panels. You use the Minimize/Maximize button to collapse or expand panels. The Options menu provides you with panel specific commands, including group, rename, maximize, close a panel, and use the Help system.

Open and Close a Panel

1 Click the **Window** menu.

2 Click a panel name, such as Properties, Files, History, or CSS Styles.

> **TIMESAVER** *To close panels or panel group, right-click (Win) or option-click (Mac), and then click Close or Close Group.*

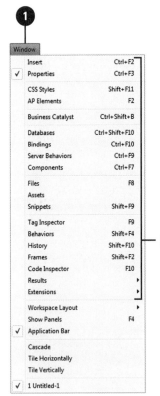

Panels on Window menu

Collapse and Expand a Panel

1 To collapse or expand an open panel, click the header bar or double-click the title tab on the header bar of the panel.

> **TIMESAVER** *To hide and show all panels, click the Window menu, and then click Hide Panels.*

> **TIMESAVER** *To Auto-Collapse Icon Panels or Auto-Show Hidden Panels, right-click (Win) or option-click (Mac), and then select a command.*

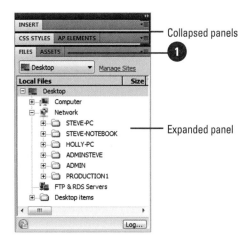

Collapsed panels

Expanded panel

Use the Panel Options Menu

1 Open or expand a panel.

2 Click the **Options** menu on the right side of the panel header bar.

3 Click a command from the list (commands vary). Common commands include:

- ◆ **Help.** Accesses Help.

- ◆ **Close.** Closes the currently displayed tab in the panel.

- ◆ **Close Group.** Closes all the tabs in the panel.

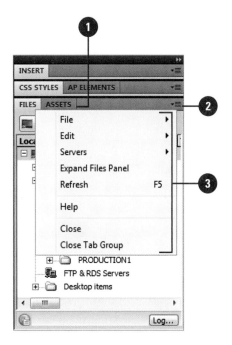

Docking and Undocking Panels

You can dock and undock, or temporarily attach and detach, panels or panel groups. You can display panels using the Window menu, and then drag them around the program window to dock or undock them to other panels. You can even dock or undock the Properties panel. However, document panels cannot be docked. When you drag a panel over a dockable area, an outline around the target dock appears. When you release the mouse button, the panel snaps to the dockable area and stays there until you move it. You can even drag a panel tab to a new position. If you attempt to dock a panel over an undockable area, no outline appears.

Dock a Panel

1. Position the pointer on the panel tab or panel set header bar.

2. Drag the window away from the panel to a panel.

   ◆ **Add to Panel.** Drag to a panel until a blue rectangle appears around the panel.

   ◆ **Append to Panel.** Drag to a panel until a blue line appears along the side of the panel.

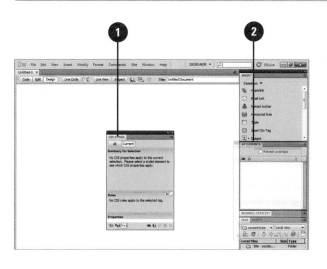

Undock a Panel

1. Position the pointer on the panel tab or panel set header bar.

2. Drag the window away from the panel to an empty area of the Dreamweaver window.

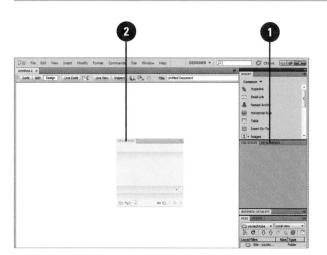

Grouping and Ungrouping Panels

You can group panels together to improve organization and workflow. When you group panels together, you can stack one on top of the other, or group related panels together as a tabbed panel group, such as the Component Inspector panel. You can add a panel to an existing panel group or you can create a new panel group. If you no longer need panels grouped together, you can ungroup them. You can use the panel gripper to group or ungroup as well as dock or undock panel windows.

Group Panels Together

1. Position the pointer on the panel tab or panel set header bar.

2. Drag the window away from the panel to another panel window.

   ◆ **Add to Panel.** Drag to a panel until a blue rectangle appears around the panel.

   ◆ **Append to Panel.** Drag to a panel until a blue line appears along the side of the panel.

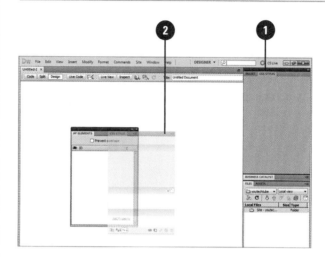

Ungroup Panels

1. Position the pointer on the panel tab or panel set header bar.

2. Drag the window away from the panel to an empty area of the Dreamweaver window.

See Also

See "Working with Panels" on page 46 for information on using panels, or "Docking and Undocking Panels" on page 48 for information on moving panels around the screen.

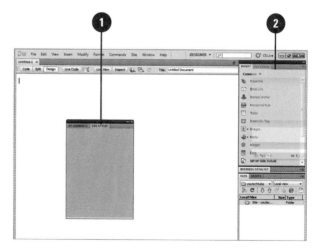

Creating a Workspace

As you work with Dreamweaver, you'll open, close, and move around windows and panels to meet your individual needs. After you customize the Dreamweaver workspace, you can save the location of windows and panels as a custom workspace. You can create custom workspaces, or use the default ones provided by Dreamweaver, such as Designer, Code, Dual Screen, and App Developer. If you no longer use a custom workspace, you can remove it at any time. You can also rename a custom workspace to better recognition and use.

Create a Workspace

1. Open and position the panels you want to include in a panel set.

2. Click the **Window** menu, point to **Workspace Layout**, and then click **New Workspace**.

   TIMESAVER *Click the Workspace menu on the menu bar (Win) or title bar (Mac) to access workspace commands.*

   The New Workspace dialog box opens.

3. Type a name in the Name box.

4. Click **OK**.

   The panel set is now saved.

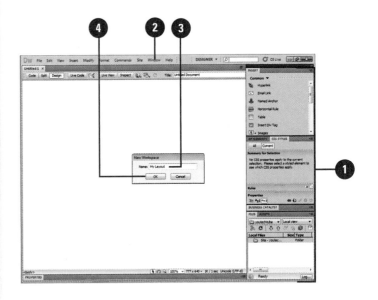

Display a Workspace

1. Click the **Window** menu, point to **Workspace Layout** or click the **Workspace** menu, and then select a panel option:

   ◆ **Custom Panel Name.** Displays a custom panel layout in which you created.

   ◆ **Predefined Layouts.** Displays the default panel layout: App Developer, App Developer Plus, Classic, Coder, Coder Plus, Designer, Designer Compact, or Dual Screen.

Workspace menu with panel name

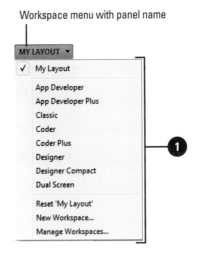

Delete a Workspace

1. Click the **Workspaces** menu, and then click **Manage Workspaces**.

   The Manage Workspaces dialog box opens.

2. Select the panel set you want to delete.

3. Click **Delete**.

4. Click **Yes** to confirm the deletion.

5. Click **OK**.

   The panel set is now deleted.

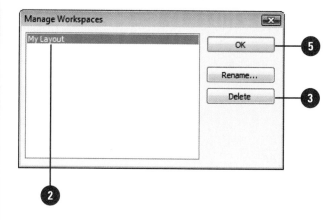

Did You Know?

You can hide all panels. Click the Window menu, and then click Hide Panels to select the check mark.

Rename a Workspace

1. Click the **Workspaces** menu, and then click **Manage Workspaces**.

   The Manage Workspaces dialog box opens.

2. Select the panel set you want to rename.

3. Click **Rename**.

4. Type a new name, and then click **OK**.

   The panel set is now renamed.

5. Click **OK**.

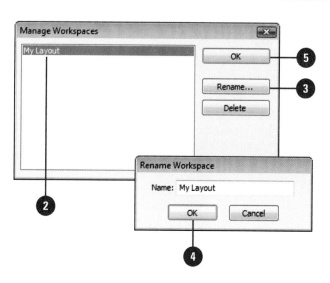

Using the Status Bar

To work efficiently in Dreamweaver you need information about the active document. Details about the document's size and estimated download time all help in the design and preparation of the page. Dreamweaver displays current information about the active document and common display tools on the Status bar, located at the bottom of the document window. The Status bar displays the Tag selector for the current selection and the estimated document size and download time, and allows you to use the Select, Hand, or Zoom tools, set document magnification, or resize the Document window.

Use the Status Bar

1 View the display information or click a tool on the Status bar:

◆ **Tag Selector.** Shows the hierarchy of tags surrounding the current selection.

◆ **Select Tool.** Use to enable or disable the Select tool.

◆ **Hand Tool.** Use to drag a document into the Document window.

◆ **Zoom Tool.** Use to increase or decrease the magnification level for a document.

◆ **Set Magnification.** Use to select a predefined magnification level.

◆ **Window Size.** Use to resize the Document window to a predefined value in Design view.

◆ **Document Size And Estimated Download Time.** Shows the estimated document size and download time for the page.

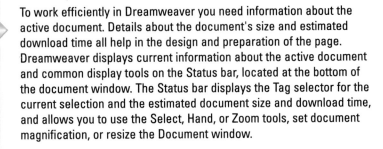

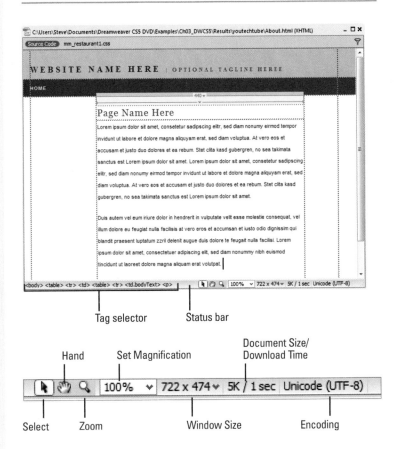

Tag selector   Status bar

Hand   Set Magnification   Document Size/ Download Time

Select   Zoom   Window Size   Encoding

Set Windows Size and Connection Speed from the Status Bar

① Click the **Dreamweaver** (Mac) or **Edit** (Win) menu, and then click **Preferences**.

② Click the **Status Bar** category.

③ Set the options you want:

◆ **Window Sizes.** Specify the window sizes you want to appear in the Status bar.

◆ **Connection Speed.** Select the connection speed (in kilobits per second) you want to use to calculate the download size that appears in the Status bar.

④ Click **OK**.

Did You Know?

You can display the download size for an image. When you select an image, the image's download size appears in the Properties panel.

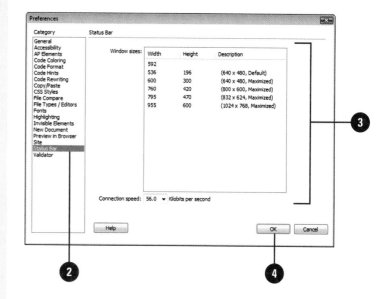

Changing the View with the Zoom Tool

Working with the Zoom tool gives you one more way to control exactly what you see in Dreamweaver. The Zoom tool does not change the active image, it only lets you view the image at different magnifications. The Zoom tool is located on the Status bar, and resembles a magnifying glass. Increasing the magnification of an image gives you control over what you see and gives you control over how you work. Large documents are difficult to work with and difficult to view. Many documents, when viewed at 100 percent, are larger than the maximized size of the document window. When this happens, viewing the entire image requires reducing the zoom.

Zoom In or Out the View

1. Select the **Zoom** tool on the Status bar.

2. Use one of the following methods to zoom in:

   ◆ **Click On The Document.** The image increases in magnification centered on where you clicked.

   ◆ **Drag To Define An Area With The Zoom Tool.** The image increases in magnification based on the boundaries of the area you dragged.

   TIMESAVER *Press Ctrl+= (Win) or ⌘+= (Mac) to zoom in.*

3. To zoom out, hold down the Alt (Win) or Option (Mac) key, and then click on the screen to reduce the zoom of the active document.

   The zoom reduction centers on where you click on the active document.

   TIMESAVER *Press Ctrl+- (Win) or ⌘+- (Mac) to zoom out.*

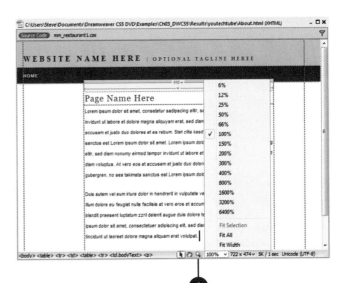

Working with Rulers

Carpenters know that precise measurements are essential to making things fit, so they have a rule: Measure Twice, Cut Once. In keeping with the idea that precise measurements are essential, Dreamweaver gives you ruler bars. Ruler bars are located on the top and left sides of the active document window. Rulers serve a very important role. Ruler guides help you correctly align design elements. As a matter of fact, if you're not working on a flat glass or LCD monitor, the curvature of the monitor can give you a false impression of the vertical and horizontal. By using guides you have access to precise alignment systems.

Work with Rulers

1. Click the **View** menu, and then point to **Rulers**.

2. Select the options you want:

   ◆ **Show.** Click to show or hide the ruler.

   TIMESAVER *Press Ctrl+Alt+R (Win) or* ⌘*+Option+R (Mac) to show or hide the ruler.*

   ◆ **Reset Origin.** Click to set the ruler back to the default.

     ◆ **Change the Origin.** Drag the ruler-origin icon (at the upper-left corner) anywhere on the page.

   ◆ **Pixels**, **Inches**, or **Centimeters.** Click to select the type of measurement you want to appear on the ruler.

   TIMESAVER *Right-click in the ruler bar to open a menu you can use to change the measurement system.*

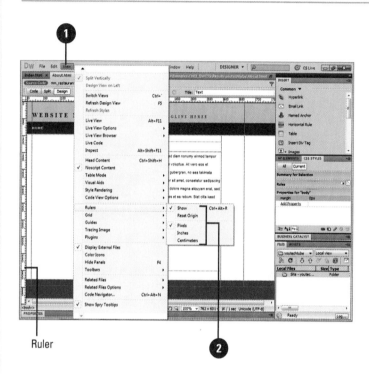

Ruler

Did You Know?

You can choose what type of Point/Pica size to use. Click Postscript (72 points/inch) or click Traditional (72.27 points/inch). Postscript is more widely used, and Dreamweaver defaults to this option.

Working with the Grid and Guides

Dreamweaver comes with guides, grids, and rulers to help you lay out artwork and objects with precision. A grid is a series of crisscrossed lines that aid in aligning objects to each other on the Stage. A guide is a horizontal or vertical line you can position to align objects. Grids and guides are modifiable. You can change their visibility, position, color, and frequency. To align several elements to a grid or guide line, you first turn Snap to Grid or Snap to Guides on. Then you can drag the elements to align them to the grid or a guide. These items are invisible by default, but they can be easily turned on and adjusted. Though you see them in the Dreamweaver development environment, they are invisible on the viewable page. Use guides to align art and objects to each other on vertical or horizontal paths, or turn on the grid for use in designing a layout that is proportional and balanced.

Use the Grid

① Click the **View** menu, and then point to **Grid**.

② Select the option you want:

◆ **Show.** Click to show or hide the grid.

TIMESAVER *Press Ctrl+Alt+G (Win) or ⌘+Option+G (Mac) to show or hide the grid.*

◆ **Snap To Grid.** Click to enable or disable objects aligning to a grid line.

TIMESAVER *Press Ctrl+Alt+Shift+G (Win) or ⌘+Option+Shift+G (Mac) to enable or disable Snap To Grid.*

◆ **Grid Settings.** Click to open the Grid Settings dialog box, where you can set the grid color, settings, spacing, and display, either lines or dots.

Grid

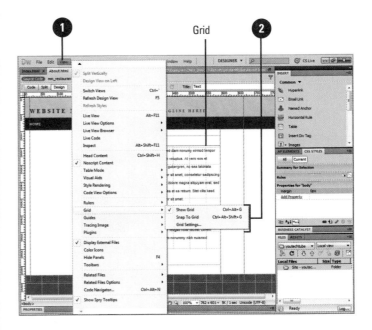

Grid Settings

Use Guides

1 Click the **View** menu, point to **Guides**, and then select the options you want:

◆ **Show Guides.** Click to show or hide the guides.

◆ **Snap To Guides** or **Guides Snap To Elements.** Click to enable or disable objects aligning to guides or guides to objects.

◆ **Edit Guides.** Click to set the guide color, distance color, and other settings.

◆ **Lock Guides.** Click to lock the existing guides in place.

◆ **Clear Guides.** Click to remove all guides.

2 Move to the vertical or horizontal Ruler bar, and then click and drag into the document.

3 Click the **Select** tool on the Status bar to drag existing guides to a new position (make sure Lock Guides is not selected).

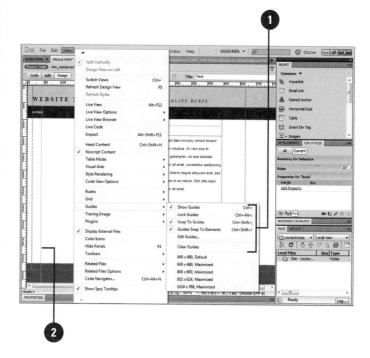

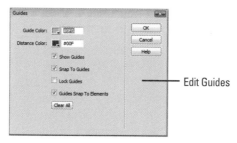

Edit Guides

Did You Know?

You can remove one guide at a time. Make sure Lock Guides is clear, and then click the Select tool. Drag the existing guide you want removed back to the corresponding Ruler bar.

You can use keyboard shortcuts to work with guides. ⌘+; (Mac) or Ctrl+; (Win) shows and hides guides, Option+⌘+; (Mac) or Ctrl+Alt+; (Win) locks and unlocks guides, Shift+⌘+; (Mac) or Ctrl+ Shift+; (Win) to turn Snapping to guides on and off, and Shift+⌘+/ (Mac) or Ctrl+Shift+/ (Win) to turn Snapping guides to elements on and off.

For Your Information

Setting Precise Measurements Using Guides

If you want to use exact measurements while you work with guides to create a Web page design, you can set guides to a precise location or view the exact distance between guides. To view and move a guide to a specific location, double-click the guide, enter the exact location you want, and then click OK. To view the distance between guides, press Ctrl (Win) or (Mac), and hold down the mouse pointer anywhere between the two guides. The unit of measure that appears is the same as the unit of measure for the rulers.

Creating Keyboard Shortcuts

Dreamweaver uses built-in keyboard shortcuts designed specifically for Dreamweaver. A complete list of the keyboard shortcuts is available in the back of this book. The built-in keyboard shortcuts are organized into sets, which you can duplicate and customize to create your own personalized set. If you use other programs, such as Adobe Illustrator or Adobe Photoshop, and you are more comfortable using their keyboard shortcuts for common commands, you can select a built-in keyboard shortcut set from any of the graphics programs to use in Dreamweaver.

Create a Keyboard Shortcut Set

1. Click the **Dreamweaver** (Mac) or **Edit** (Win) menu, and then click **Keyboard Shortcuts**.

2. Click the **Current Set** list arrow, and then select a set.

3. Click the **Duplicate Set** button.

4. Type a name for the new shortcut set.

5. Click **OK**.

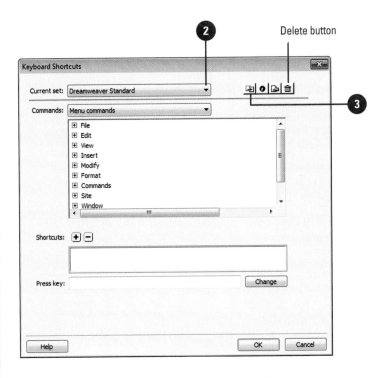

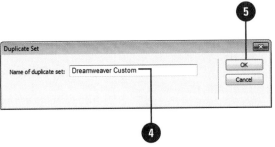

Did You Know?

You can delete a custom keyboard shortcut set. Click the Dreamweaver (Mac) or Edit (Win) menu, click Keyboard Shortcuts, select a shortcut set from the Current Set list arrow, and then click the Delete button. You cannot delete a built-in keyboard shortcut set that comes with Dreamweaver.

You can rename a custom keyboard shortcut set. Click the Dreamweaver (Mac) or Edit (Win) menu, click Keyboard Shortcuts, select a shortcut set from the Current Set list arrow, click the Rename Set button, enter a new name, and then click OK. You cannot rename a built-in keyboard shortcut set that comes with Dreamweaver.

Add or Remove a Keyboard Shortcut

1. Click the **Dreamweaver** (Mac) or **Edit** (Win) menu, and then click **Keyboard Shortcuts**.

2. Click the **Current Set** list arrow, and then select the set in which you want to change.

3. Click the **Commands** list arrow, and then select a shortcut category, such as Menu Commands, Drawing Tools, Test Movie Menu Commands, and Workplace Accessibility Commands.

4. Select the command for which you want to add or remove a shortcut in the Commands list.

5. Do the following:
   - ◆ To add a shortcut, click the **Add Shortcut** (+) button, and then press the key combination to enter the new shortcut key in the Press Key box.
   - ◆ To remove a shortcut, click the **Remove Shortcut** (-) button.

6. Click **Change**.

7. To add or remove additional shortcuts, repeat Steps 2-6.

8. Click **OK**.

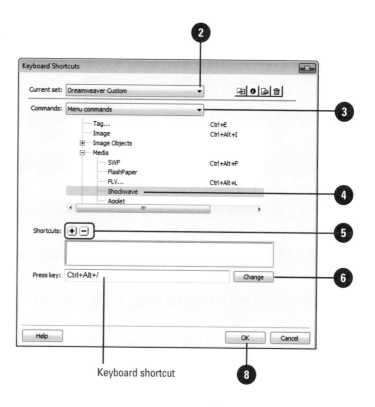

Keyboard shortcut

Setting General Preferences

Dreamweaver allows you to set general preferences to customize the way you work in the program. You can specify what you want to display or open when you launch Dreamweaver and how you want to edit content. Some of the preferences allow you to show or hide the Welcome Screen, allow multiple consecutive spaces when editing, enable or disable the Related Files toolbar along with file discovery and display for static and dynamic (such as includes and server scripts) files (**New!**), specify to the number of history steps (undo levels), and select a spelling dictionary.

Set General Preferences

1. Click the **Dreamweaver** (Mac) or **Edit** (Win) menu, and then click **Preferences**.

2. Click the **General** category.

3. Select from the following options:

   - **Open Documents In Tabs (Mac).** Select to open all documents in a single window with tabs.

   - **Show Welcome Screen.** Select to show welcome screen (Default on).

   - **Reopen Documents On Startup.** Select to open any documents that were opened the last time you closed Dreamweaver (Default off).

   - **Warn When Open Read-Only Files.** Select to get an alert when you open a locked file (Default on).

   - **Enable Related Files.** Select to enable the Related Files toolbar along with file display. To discover and show dynamic includes and server scripts, click the **Discover Dynamic-Related Files** list arrow, and then click **Manually, Automatically,** or **Disabled** (**New!**).

   - **Update Links When Moving Files.** Specify the action you want: Prompt (Default), Never, Always.

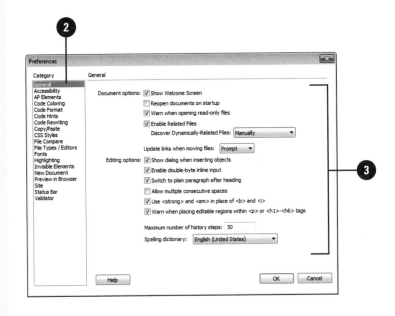

- **Show Dialog When Inserting Objects.** Select to prompt you when inserting objects using the Insert bar or Insert menu.

TIMESAVER *To temporarily override this setting, Ctrl-click (Win) or ⌘-click (Mac) when creating and inserting objects.*

- **Enable Double-Byte Inline Input.** Select to enter double-byte text, such as Japanese characters (Default on).

- **Switch To Plain Paragraph After Heading.** Select to press Enter (Win) or Return (Mac) after a heading paragraph to switch to a plain paragraph in Design view (Default on).

- **Allow Multiple Consecutive Spaces.** Select to allow typing two or more spaces in Design view to create nonbreaking spaces that appear as multiple spaces in a browser (Default off).

- **Use <strong> And <em> In Place Of <b> And <i>.** Select to apply <strong> instead of <b> and <em> instead of <i> (Default on).

- **Warn When Placing Editable Regions Within <p> Or <h1><h6> Tags.** Select to display a warning when you save a template when true (Default on).

- **Maximum Number Of History Steps.** Specify the number of steps the History panel keeps.

- **Spelling Dictionary.** Click to select a dictionary language. The dialect is in parenthesis.

4 Click **OK**.

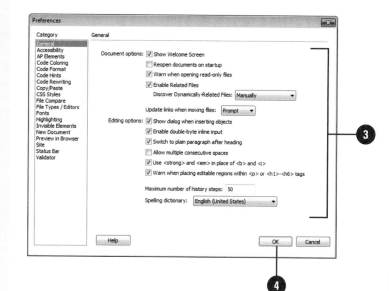

Setting New Document Preferences

When you create a new document, Dreamweaver allows you to set the default document type you want. The New Document preference options allow you to specify the default document, extension, document type definition (DTD), and file encoding. DTD allows you to select XHTML 1.0 Transitional or XHTML 1.0 Strict to make new Web pages XHTML-compliant. File encoding makes sure your Web browser and Dreamweaver use the right character set for the selected language.

Set New Document Preferences

1. Click the **Dreamweaver** (Mac) or **Edit** (Win) menu, and then click **Preferences**.

2. Click the **New Document** category.

3. Select from the following options:

   - **Default Document.** Select the type of document you want to use as default (Default HTML).

   - **Default Extension.** Enter the file extension you want to use for the HTML extension, either .html or .htm. (Default .html).

   - **Default Document Type (DTD).** Select to the XHTML document type definition (DTD) you want.

   - **Default Encoding.** Specify the encoding you want to use for new documents and opened documents without any specified encoding. This makes sure your Web browser and Dreamweaver use the right character set for the selected language. The default for HTML encoding is Unicode (UTF-8), which safely represents all characters.

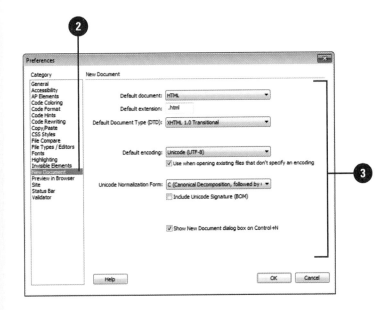

- ◆ **Use When Opening Existing Files That Don't Specify An Encoding.** Select to apply encoding to when you open a file without encoding.

- ◆ **Unicode Normalization Form.** If you select Unicode (UTF-8) for encoding, select the form option you want: C, D, KC, or KD. Form C is the most common one used for the Web in the Character Model. The others are provided by Adobe.

- ◆ **Include Unicode Signature (BOM).** If you select Unicode (UTF-8) for encoding, you can select this option to include a Byte Order Mark (BOM), which is a 2-4 bytes at the beginning of a text file that identifies a file as Unicode, and order the bytes. This is optional.

- ◆ **Show New Document Dialog Box On Control+N.** Select to show the New Document dialog box or clear to automatically create a document with default settings when you use the shortcut key Ctrl+N (Win) or ⌘+N (Mac).

4 Click **OK**.

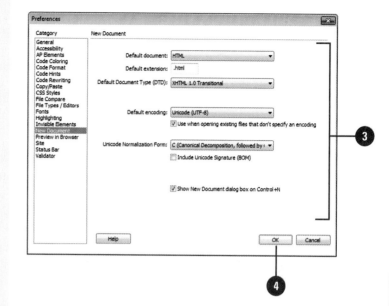

Working with Colors

Since Web pages appear in Web browsers, you want to use colors on your pages that are Web-safe, so they appear consistently on every browser. A **Web-safe** color appears the same in Microsoft Internet Explorer and Netscape Navigator on both Windows and Macintosh system when running in 256-color mode.

RGB (red, green, blue) is a set of color values that describe colors. RGB identifies a color by a set of hexadecimal numbers, an internal computer numbering scheme, that specify the amounts of red, green, and blue needed to create the color. RGB colors appear best over the Web (true color representation without dithers or substitutes) when you use only **browser safe colors**, which is a standard set of 216 color combinations. These RGB values are 0, 51, 102, 153, 204, or 255 in decimal or 00, 33, 66, 99, CC, or FF in hexadecimal. When you use the system color dialog boxes, you use decimal values. You use hexadecimal values in Code view, the Properties panel, and some dialog boxes, such as the Preferences dialog box.

Using the Color Picker

When you want to change a color, you can click any color box available in many dialog boxes, such as the Preferences dialog box, and the Property Inspector to open the color picker. The color picker allows you to select a color for different page elements.

When you click a color box, the color picker appears, displaying the eyedropper cursor and a palette with a bar at the top and a swatch of colors at the bottom. The bar displays the currently selected color and its hexadecimal number. To the right is the **Default Color button**, which clears the current

color without choosing a different color. Next to the Default Color button is the **Color Wheel button**, which opens the system color picker. The system color picker is the standard color selector provided by the operating system, either Windows or Macintosh. The menu in the upper-right corner of the color picker allows you to expand your color selection. You can select different color palettes, including Color Cubes, Continuous Tone, Windows OS, Mac OS, and Grayscale. The Color Cube (default color palette) and Continuous Tone palettes are Web-safe while the Windows OS, Mac OS, and Grayscale are not. If you are using a non Web-safe palette, you can use the Snap To Web Safe command to have Dreamweaver replace the selected color with the closest Web-safe color. You can use the eyedropper to select a color swatch from the palette or pick a color from anywhere on your screen inside or outside Dreamweaver.

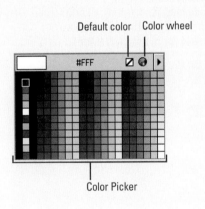

Default color   Color wheel

Color Picker

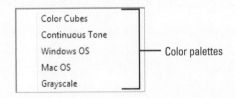

Color palettes

Using the System Color Picker

When you click the Color Wheel button in the color picker, a system color picker dialog box opens. In Windows, you can use the Color dialog box, which displays basic and custom color squares and a color matrix with the full range of colors in the color spectrum, to help you select a color. You can enter RGB (Red, Green, Blue) values or hue, saturation, and luminosity (also known as brightness) values to specify a color. **Hue** is the color created by mixing primary colors (Red, Blue, and Yellow). **Saturation** is a measure of how much white is mixed in with the color. A fully saturated color is vivid; a less saturated color is washed-out pastel. **Luminosity** is a meas-ure of how much black is mixed with the color. A very bright color contains little or no black. You can also change the hue by moving the pointer in the color matrix box horizon-tally, the saturation by moving the pointer vertically, and the luminosity by adjusting the slider to the right of the color matrix box. On the Macintosh, you click one of the color modes and select a color, using its controls. You can select RGB values by selecting the color sliders at the top of the dialog box; or by entering values (color numbers) to select a color. You can select hue, saturation, and brightness (or luminosity) values by selecting the color sliders at the top of the dialog box or entering values (color numbers). The color you select appears in the ColorSolid box.

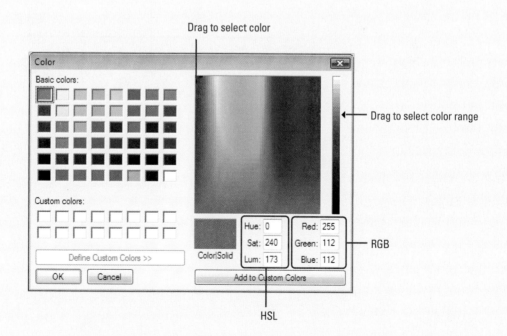

Drag to select color

Drag to select color range

RGB

HSL

Setting Highlighting Color Preferences

You use the Highlighting section of the Preferences dialog box to specify the colors you want to use for the following items in Dreamweaver: Mouse-Over, Editable regions, Nested editable, Locked regions, Library items, Third-party tags, or untranslated or translated live data. You can select the color you want by using a color swatch or entering a color id number in Hexadecimal (Hex). In addition, you can also determine whether you can show or hide your color selection.

Set Highlighting Color Preferences

1. Click the **Dreamweaver** (Mac) or **Edit** (Win) menu, and then click **Preferences**.

2. Click the **Highlighting** category.

3. Click the color box and select a color or enter a color Hex number for the options you want.

4. Select or clear the **Show** check box next to an option to show or hide the color selection.

5. Click **OK**.

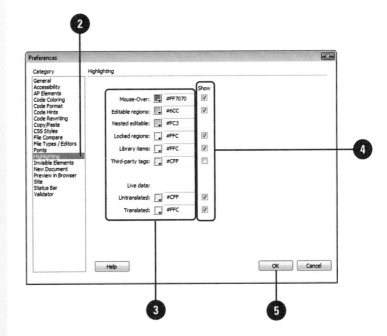

Managing Web Site Files

4

Introduction

A Web site is made up of numerous files. As you continue to create more and more Web pages and other files for a Web site, keeping track of them becomes an important job. Managing Web site files is an important part of creating an organized site that one or more developers can work on.

In Dreamweaver, there are three main site folders: local root, remote, and testing server. The local root and testing server folders are the working development folders for your Web site, while the remote folder is the Web server folder that visitors access on the Web. Instead of using Windows Explorer (Win) or Finder (Mac) to manage and work with Web site files, you can use the Files panel. When you create or open a Web site, the Files tab in the Files panel displays all the site's files, which you can use to quickly and easily manage individual Web pages, files, and folders. If you can find a file on your site, you can also use the Files panel to help you locate it.

If you're creating a custom template or sharing files with someone who needs them for use in another program, you can use the Save As dialog box to change the file type for a Web page or other related file.

When you create a Web page, one of the first things to do is to apply some general settings to your page. The Page Properties dialog box lets you specify the default font family and font size, background color, margins, link styles, and many other aspects of page design. You can assign new page properties for each new page you create, and modify those for existing pages. Dreamweaver allows you to embed these changes to the page using HTML or CSS (Cascading Style Sheets), depending on your preference.

What You'll Do

Explore Web Site Files and Folders

Set Up Site Folders

View the Files Panel

Open and Create Files in the Files Panel

Manage Files and Folders in the Files Panel

Find Files in the Files Panel

Save a File with Different Formats

Identify Dreamweaver File Formats

Set the Home Page

Prepare to Set Page Properties

Set Appearance Page Properties

Set Link Page Properties

Set Heading Page Properties

Change Title and Encoding Page Properties

Insert a Tracing Image

Use Visual Aids

Work with Invisible Elements

Select Elements

Exploring Web Site Files and Folders

A Web site consists of linked documents and related files organized into folders. You can use Dreamweaver to organize and manage your site files and folders, and maintain your links. With Dreamweaver, you can create, develop, and work with site files and folders on your local hard disk and upload them to a Web server where visitors on the Web can access it.

Working with Site Folders

The development environment for a Dreamweaver site consists of three main folders: Local root, Remote, and Testing server. The **local root** folder, known as the "local site," stores your site files and folders you work on during development. You can store the local root folder on your local computer or a network server. The **remote** folder, known as the "remote site," stores your site files and folders for production on the Web. The remote folder is typically the Web server, known as a production server, where visitors access your site on the Web. If you plan to use dynamic pages—Web pages that change based on circumstances—in your Web site, the Web server also needs to run an application server. An **application server** is a network server with software, such as ColdFusion, ASP, ASP.NET, JSP, or PHP, that processes dynamic pages. If you want to test dynamic pages during development, you also need a **testing server** folder, which provides a place to generate and display dynamic content while you work. You can store the testing server folder on your local computer or application server. In order to set up a testing server folder, you need to define the local and remote folder first.

Web site development takes place in the local folder, while Web site final production takes place in the remote folder. After you finishing developing files and folder in your local folder, you can upload them to your remote folder. The folder structure in the local and remote folders should always be the same. If the folder structure is not the same, files upload to the wrong location and links to files don't work. So, making sure the folder structure of the local and remote are the same is very important.

You can name and specify the location of the local folder. However, the remote folder name and location is typically provided by your Web server administrator. After you find out the name and location of your remote folder, you can establish a connection to it from Dreamweaver. If the remote folder name and location is not available at the moment, you can still set up a local folder now and start creating Web site files, and then specify the remote and testing folders later.

Typically, you work on files in your local folder and then upload them to your remote folder. However, you can also work on files directly on your remote site in Dreamweaver. When you make a change to a remote site file make sure you also update the local site file too so they are both the same.

Setting Up Site Folders

In Dreamweaver, there are three main site folders: local root, remote, and testing server. The local root folder is the working development folder for your Web site. The remote folder is the Web server folder for your Web site. This is the location on the Web where visitors access your Web site. The testing server folder is a development folder for generating and displaying dynamic page content while you work. A **dynamic page** is a Web page that changes based on circumstances. The other type of Web page is a **static page**, which only changes when you edit it. You can set up site folders when you create a new site or edit an existing one. If you don't know the settings for the remote and testing server folders, you can set up a local folder now, start creating Web site files, and then specify the remote and testing folders later.

Set Up Site Folders

1. Use one of the following methods:

   ◆ New Site. Click the **Site** menu, and then click **New Site**.

   ◆ Exist Site. Click the **Site** menu, click **Manage Sites**, select the site you want, and then click **Edit**.

2. Click the **Site** category.

3. Click the **Browse For Folder** icon, locate the local folder you want to use, and then click **Select**.

4. Click the **Servers** category.

5. Click the **Add New Server** button, specify the server name, connection type, address, username and password, and root directory on the Basic tab (**New!**).

6. Click the **Advanced** tab, and then select testing server model and access method you want to use to display dynamic page content (**New!**).

7. Click **Save**, and then click **OK** to cache files, if necessary.

8. Select the check box for the **Remote** and **Testing** server you want to use (**New!**).

9. Click **Save**.

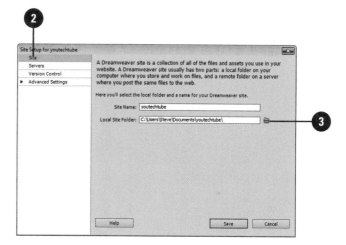

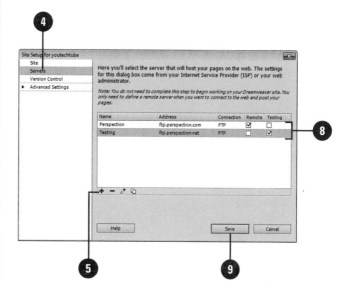

Viewing the Files Panel

The Files panel is a useful place for managing files and folders. When you create or open a Web site, the Files tab in the Files panel displays all the site's files. If you want to change locations, you can use the Site list arrow in the Files panel to select a remote server, local drive, or desktop. The Files tab displays the file hierarchy of all the folders and files in your Web site in different views, either local, remote, testing, or repository version control from Subversion. Using the plus sign (+) and the minus sign (-) to the left of an icon in the Files tab allows you to display different levels of folders in your Web site without opening and displaying the contents of each folder. If you want to display two different views, you can expand the Files panel.

View Files in the Files Panel

1 Select the Web site in which you want to view.

2 Click the **Window** menu, and then click **Files** to display the Files panel.

3 Click the **Site** list arrow, and then select the location where you want to view files.

4 Click the **Site Files View** list arrow, and then select the view you want.

- ◆ **Local View.** Displays the folder structure of the site on your computer (Default view).

- ◆ **Remote Server.** Displays the folder structure of the site on a Web server.

- ◆ **Testing Server.** Displays the folder structure of the testing and local site.

- ◆ **Repository View.** Displays the Version Control site files using Subversion.

5 Perform the commands you want to display folder structure and contents:

- ◆ To show the file and folder structure, click the **Plus** sign (+).

- ◆ To hide the file and folder structure, click the **Minus** sign (-).

- ◆ To display the contents of a folder, click the folder icon.

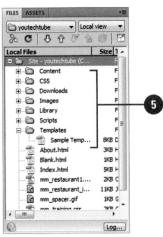

Work with the Files Panel in Expanded View

1 Select the Web site in which you want to view.

2 Click the **Window** menu, and then click **Files** to display the Files panel.

The Files panel appears, displaying the Files tab.

3 Click the **Expand** button to expand the Files panel.

The Files panel expands to display the remote site, testing site, or site map on the left and the local site on the right.

4 Click a button on the toolbar to display the view you want:

- ◆ **Remote Server.** Displays the remote site.

- ◆ **Testing Server.** Displays the testing site.

- ◆ **Repository Files.** Displays the Version Control site files using Subversion.

5 Click the **Collapse** button again to collapse the Files panel.

See Also

See "Managing Files and Folders in the Files Panel" on page 74 for information on working with site files in different views.

Click to expand/collapse

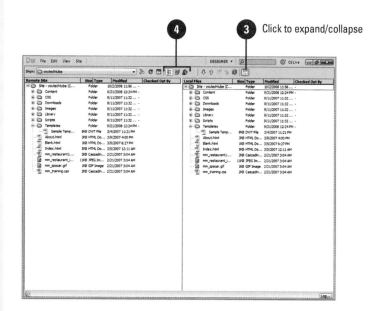

Opening and Creating Files in the Files Panel

Instead of using Windows Explorer (Win) or Finder (Mac) to manage and work with Web site files, you can use the Files panel. After you open a Web site, you can quickly open files using the Files panel instead of using the Open command on the File menu. The Files panel displays all the files for the working site. If you want to open a file for another site, you need to use the Open command on the File menu, or switch the working site and use the Files panel. In addition, you can create a new file. When you do, Dreamweaver creates the new file in the same folder as the selected file.

Open a File in Files Panel

1. Select the Web site in which you want to view.

2. Click the **Window** menu, and then click **Files** to display the Files panel.

3. Click the **Site** list arrow, and then select the location where you want to view files.

4. Click the **Site Files View** list arrow, and then select **Local View**.

5. Use any of the following methods:

   ◆ Double-click the file icon.

   ◆ Right-click (Win) or Control-click (Mac) the file icon, and then click **Open**.

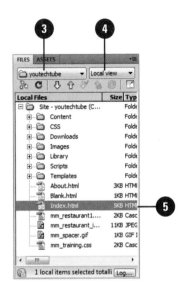

Did You Know?

You can refresh the Files panel. If you don't see a file or folder you know is in the Files panel, click the Refresh button (Dreamweaver sites only) or right-click (Win) or Control-click (Mac), and then click Refresh.

Create a File in Files Panel

1. Select the Web site in which you want to view.

2. Click the **Window** menu, and then click **Files** to display the Files panel.

3. Click the **Site** list arrow, and then select the location where you want to view files.

4. Click the **Site Files View** list arrow, and then select **Local View**.

5. Select a file where you want to place the new one.

6. Right-click (Win) or Control-click (Mac), and then click **New File**.

7. Enter a name for the file or folder, and then press Enter (Win) or Return (Mac).

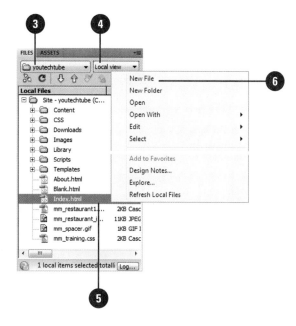

Did You Know?

You can control what applications open specific files. For example, you might want to open your .gif files using Fireworks, or you might want to use Photoshop. Click the Dreamweaver (Mac) or Edit (Win) menu, and then click Preferences. Click the File Types/Editors category, make your changes, and then click OK.

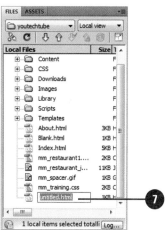

Managing Files and Folders in the Files Panel

After you create a Web site, you can use the Files panel to quickly and easily manage individual Web pages, files and folders. If a file or folder name is not exactly what you want, you can quickly rename it. You can create and name a new folder and move pages to a different location. If you no longer need or want a file or folder, you can remove it. In addition, you can move files and folders around in the same way you can in Windows Explorer (Win) or Finder (Mac). If you no longer need a file, you can quickly delete it.

Rename a Site File or Folder in Files Panel

1 Select the Web site with the file or folder you want to rename.

2 Click the **Window** menu, and then click **Files** to display the Files panel.

3 Right-click (Win) or Control-click the file or folder icon you want to rename, point to **Edit**, and then click **Rename**.

   TIMESAVER *Click the file name in the Files panel, and then click the file again to highlight it.*

4 Type a new name, and then press Enter (Win) or Return (Mac).

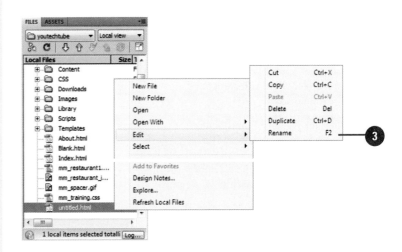

Did You Know?

You can delete a site file or folder. In the Files panel, right-click (Win) or Control-click (Mac) the file or folder you want to delete, click Delete, and then click Yes.

Create a New Site Folder in Files Panel

1. Select the Web site where you want to create a new folder.

2. Click the **Window** menu, and then click **Files** to display the Files panel.

3. Locate and select the file or folder where you want to place the new folder.

4. Right-click (Win) or Control-click (Mac), and then click **New Folder**.

5. Enter a name for the file or folder, and then press Enter (Win) or Return (Mac).

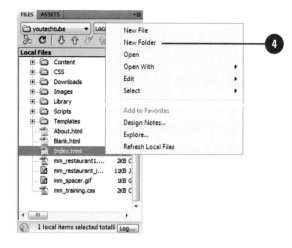

Move a Site File or Folder in Files Panel

1. Select the Web site with the file or folder you want to move.

2. Click the **Window** menu, and then click **Files** to display the Files panel.

3. In the Files panel, display the file or folder you want to use.

4. Drag the page icon to the position where you want it to occupy on your site.

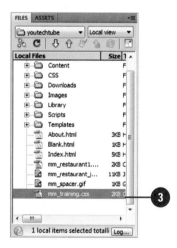

Finding Files in the Files Panel

If you can find a file on your site, you can use the Files panel to help you locate it. The Files panel allows you to quickly find files in your site. If you have a file open and your not sure which site it belongs to, you can find it using the Locate in Site command. If you want to find the newest files in your local or remote site, you can select them using commands on the Options menu in the Files panel. As you work on files, you can also use find commands to locate currently checked out or recently modified files.

Find Files in a Site

1. Select the Web site with the files you want to find.

2. Click the **Window** menu, and then click **Files** to display the Files panel.

3. Use any of the following methods to find a file:

   ◆ **Open File In Site.** Open the file in the Document window, click the **Site** menu, and then click **Locate In Site**, or click the **Options** menu, point to **Edit**, and then click **Locate In Local Site**.

   The file appears selected in the Files panel.

   ◆ **Newer Local Files.** Click the **Options** menu, point to **Edit**, and then click **Select Newer Local**.

   ◆ **Newer Remote Files.** Click the **Options** menu, point to **Edit**, and then click **Select Newer on Remote Server**.

   ◆ **Checked Out Files.** Click the **Options** menu, point to **Edit**, and then click **Select Checked Out Files**.

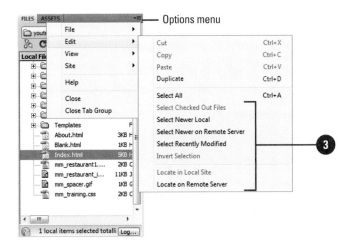

Options menu

See Also

See "Checking Site Files In and Out" on page 498 for information on checking out files.

Find Recently Modified Files in a Site

① Select the Web site with the files you want to find.

② Click the **Window** menu, and then click **Files** to display the Files panel.

③ Click the **Options** menu in the Files panel, point to **Edit**, and then click **Select Recently Modified**.

④ Do either of the following to indicate search dates you want:

◆ To report on all files modified in the last several dates, click the **Files Created Or Modified In The Last** option, and then enter the number of days you want.

◆ To report on all files modified within a specific time, click the **Files Created Or Modified Between** option, and then specify a data range.

⑤ If you are working on an Adobe Contribute site, enter a user name to limit your search to files modified by a specific user.

⑥ Click the option you want to specify where to view the files listed.

◆ **Local Machine.** Select if the site uses static pages.

◆ **Testing Server.** Select if the site uses dynamic pages.

◆ **Other Location.** Use to enter a specific location path.

⑦ Click **OK**.

Dreamweaver saves your settings and highlights the files based on the search criteria.

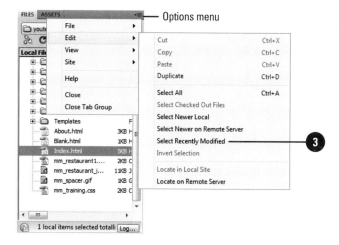

Options menu

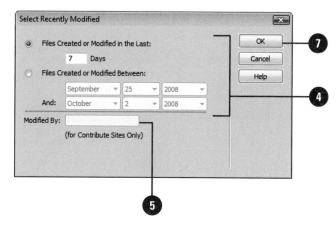

Saving a File with Different Formats

A file type specifies the file format (for example, a Web page .htm or .html) as well as the program and version in which the file was created (for example, Dreamweaver). You might want to change the type if you're creating a custom template or sharing files with someone who needs them for use in another program. You can use the Save As dialog box to change the file type for a page. The Save As Type list arrow displays a list of the available formats for the program or current selection.

Save a File as a Different Type

1. Open and display the file you want to save in a different format.

2. Click the **File** menu, and then click **Save As**.

3. Locate the drive and folder location where you want to save the file.

4. Type a name for the file, or use the suggested name.

5. Click the **Save As Type** list arrow, and then click the file type you want.

6. Click **Save**.

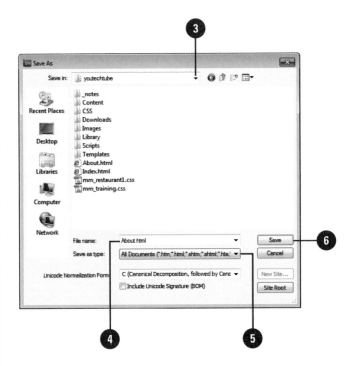

See Also

See "Identifying Dreamweaver File Formats" on page 79 for information on selecting the right file format.

Identifying Dreamweaver File Formats

Dreamweaver Open and Save File Formats

File type	Extension	Used to open or save
All Documents	*.*	Complete Web site
HTML Files	.htm, .html	Web pages as an HTML file
Server-Side Includes	.shtm, .shtml, .stm, .ssi, .inc	Web pages with incorporated files from a Web server
JavaScript Files	.js	Scripts in the JavaScript language
XML	.xml, .xsd,.xsl, .xslt, .dtd, .rss	Web pages as an XML file
Library Files	.lbi	Web page elements as a reusable file
Template Files	.dwt	Web pages as a changeable Dreamweaver template
Style Sheets	.css	Web pages as a cascading style sheet
Active Server Pages	.asp, .asa	Web pages as a Microsoft Active Server Page
Active Server Plus Pages	.aspx, .aspcx, .asmx, .cs, .vb, .config, .master	Web pages as a changeable Microsoft Active Server Page that utilizes ActiveX scripting usually VB Script or Jscript code
ColdFusion Templates	.ctm, .ctml, .cfc	Web pages as a changeable ColdFusion template that integrates databases and Web pages
ActionScript	.as, .asc, .asr	Scripts in the Flash scripting language, including Communication and Remote (Open only) files
Text	.txt	Web pages as a text file
PHP	.php	Web pages as a PHP script file
Lasso Files	.lasso	Scripts for internet applications development which use browsers to connect to HTTP and database servers
Java Server Pages	.jsp, .jst	Web pages as a JavaScript script file
Fireworks Script	.jsf	Scripts in the Fireworks scripting language (Open only)
Tag Library Descriptor Files	.tld	Tag library files (Open only)
Java Files	.java	Scripts in the Java language
WML	.wml	Web pages as an XML language used to specify content and user interface for WAP devices; WML (Wireless Markup Language)
EDML	.edml	Scripts for server behavior code
VB Script Files	.vbs	Scripts in the Visual Basic for Applications language
VTML	.vtm, .vtml	Tag library files that list every installed tag; VTML (Visual Tool Markup Language)

Setting the Home Page

A home page is the first page visitors see when they visit your site. The home page for a Web site is typically named *index.htm* or *index.html*. When you type a URL, such as *www.perspection.com*, most Web servers look for a Web page name *index.htm* or *index.html*. Check with your Web hosting service to determine how you should name your home page. If you need to change the name of your home page, you can do it directly within Dreamweaver using the Files panel.

Rename a Web Page as the Home Page

1. Select the Web site with the Web page you want to change.

2. Click the **Window** menu, and then click **Files** to display the Files panel.

3. Right-click (Win) or Control-click the file icon you want to rename, point to **Edit**, and then click **Rename**.

   TIMESAVER *Press F2 or click the file name in the Files panel, and then click the file again to highlight it.*

4. Type a new name, such as index.htm or index.html, and then press Enter (Win) or Return (Mac).

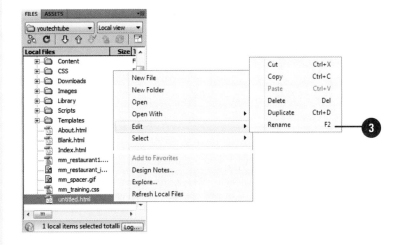

Preparing to Set Page Properties

When you create a Web page, one of the first things to do is to apply some general settings to your page. The Page Properties dialog box lets you specify the default font family and font size, background color, margins, link styles, and many other aspects of page design. You can assign new page properties for each new page you create, and modify those for existing pages. Dreamweaver provides the ability to embed these changes to the page in one of two ways: HTML or CSS.

Dreamweaver formats text using CSS (Cascading Style Sheets), by default, and it would prefer to set page preferences in this manner. If you use the default CSS setting, Dreamweaver uses CSS tags for all properties defined in the Appearance (CSS), Links (CSS), and Headings (CSS) categories of the Page Properties dialog box. The CSS tags defining these attributes are embedded in the head section of the page. To view the tags, simply click the Code button, located in the upper left corner of the document window, and Dreamweaver changes the view from Design to Code. Scroll up to the Head section of the document and view the property codes.

If, however, you want to use HTML tags, you can set page preferences in the Appearance (HTML) category of the Page Properties dialog box. The options are similar to those in the Appearance (CSS) category.

The page properties you choose apply only to the active document. If a page uses an external CSS style sheet, Dreamweaver doesn't overwrite the tags set in the style sheet, as this affects all other pages using that style sheet.

Appearance (CSS) options

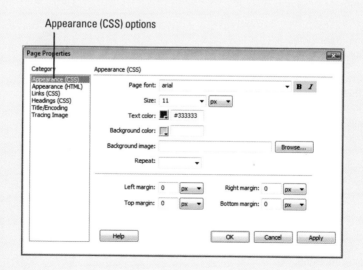

Setting Appearance Page Properties

The Appearance category in the Page Properties dialog box allows you to set the default options for CSS and HTML you want for page font type and size, text and background color. You can also use a picture as the background for a page and specify how it appears. If you'd like to add some interest to your pages, you can add a background color. If the background image contains any transparent areas, the background color appears. When selecting background colors, some creative judgment is required. For example, if you choose a dark color for your background, make sure you use a light color for your text (the most commonly used is white) to generate the appropriate contrast required for easy reading.

Set Appearance Page Properties

1. Open the Web page you want to change.

2. Click the **Modify** menu, and then click **Page Properties**.

3. Click the **Appearance (CSS)** or **Appearance (HTML)** category.

4. Select from the following options:

    ◆ Page Font and Size. Specify the font type and size you want.

    ◆ Text and Background Color. Specify the text and background color you want.

    ◆ Background Image. Specify the font type, size, and text color you want.

    ◆ Repeat. Specify how you want the background image to appear on the page. **No-repeat** appears once; **Repeat** appears tiled horizontally and vertically; **Repeat-x** appears horizontally; and **Repeat-y** appears vertically.

    ◆ Margins. Specify the page margins you want. Most designers place zeros in all four boxes (top, bottom, left, right), so when a visitor opens the page, all elements align to the upper left corner of the page.

5. Click **OK**.

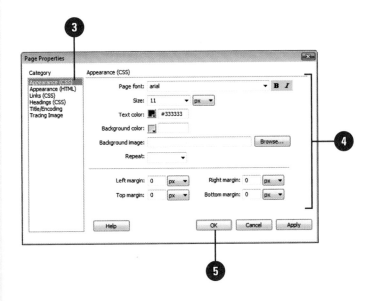

Appearance (HTML) category

Setting Link Page Properties

The Links category in the Page Properties dialog box allows you to change the default nature of the links on a page. For example, a word defined as a link has a blue underline, by default. You could change the color to red. You can specify link colors for text, visited, rollover, and active links. In addition, you can even choose not to use an underline, or only have it appear when the visitor rolls over the text.

Set Link Page Properties

1. Open the Web page you want to change.

2. Click the **Modify** menu, and then click **Page Properties**.

3. Click the **Links (CSS)** category.

4. Select any of the following font options:

   ◆ **Link Font.** Specifies the default font family to use for links. (Default uses entire page font set in the Appearance category).

   ◆ **Bold or Italic.** Specifies whether to use bold or italic for links.

   ◆ **Font Size.** Specifies the default size to use for links.

5. Select a color for the following options:

   ◆ **Link Color.** Displays color for linked text.

   ◆ **Visited Links.** Displays color for links you visit.

   ◆ **Rollover Links.** Displays color for links you point at.

   ◆ **Active Links.** Displays color for links you click.

6. Click the **Underline Style** list arrow, and then select the underline option you want.

7. Click **OK**.

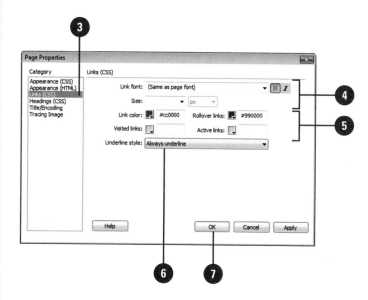

Setting Heading Page Properties

The Headings category in the Page Properties dialog box allows you to specify the default settings for up to six heading styles. You can specify the font type, size, color, and formatting. For example, you can specify that every H2 heading style that is applied to text is 14 points and red. In addition, you have the option of choosing whether the heading styles are Bold or Italic style.

Set Heading Page Properties

1. Open the Web page you want to change.

2. Click the **Modify** menu, and then click **Page Properties**.

3. Click the **Headings (CSS)** category.

4. Specify the Heading font you want.

5. Click the **Bold** and/or **Italic** buttons if you want.

6. Specify the specific font size and color of the H1 through H6 heading styles you want.

7. Click **OK**.

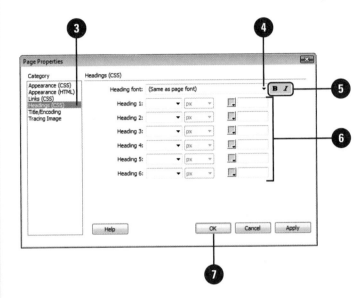

Changing Title and Encoding Page Properties

The Title/Encoding category in the Page Properties allows you to change the Web page title and specify the document encoding type you want. A Web page title is the text that visitors see on the title bar of their Web browser when they display the Web page. The document type and encoding options in the Page Properties dialog box allow you to specify the language you want to use for a Web page. File encoding makes sure your Web browser and Dreamweaver use the right character set for the selected language. The standard settings for a simple HTML page are: Document Type (DTD) XHTML 1.0 Transitional, Encoding Unicode 4.0 UTF-8, and Unicode Normalization None.

Change Title and Encoding Page Properties

1 Open the Web page you want to change.

2 Click the **Modify** menu, and then click **Page Properties**.

3 Click the **Title/Encoding** category.

4 Enter the title you want for the Web page title bar.

> **TIMESAVER** *Enter a title in the Title box on the Document toolbar.*

5 Select from the following options:

♦ **Document Type (DTD).** Select XHTML 1.0 Transitional or XHTML 1.0 Strict to make new Web pages XHTML-compliant.

♦ **Encoding.** Select the language you want. The default for HTML encoding is Unicode (UTF-8), which safely represents all characters.

♦ **Unicode Normalization Form.** If you select Unicode (UTF-8) for encoding, select the form option you want: C, D, KC, or KD. Form C is the most common one used for the Web in the Character Model. The others are provided by Adobe.

6 Click **OK**.

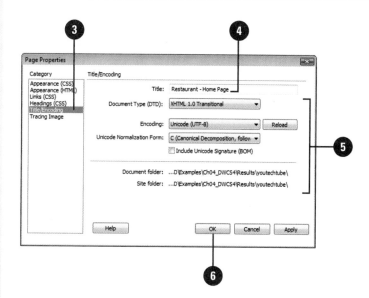

Changing Page Properties for a Tracing Image

A **tracing image** is a JPEG, GIF, or PNG formatted image that lays in the background to help you layout the page. For example, you could comp your site in Fireworks and then bring it into Dreamweaver to use as a guide to align tables and layers. Tracing images are not saved with the final document and don't appear in a Web browser. It doesn't matter how big or complex the tracing images are because they are only used by Dreamweaver during the design phase. Once the file is saved and moved to the server, the tracing image goes away, and the file retains its original small size.

Change Page Properties for a Tracing Image

1 Open the Web page you want to change.

2 Click the **Modify** menu, and then click **Page Properties**.

3 Click the **Tracing Image** category.

4 Click **Browse**, locate the image you want to use, select it, and then click **OK**.

TIMESAVER *Click the View menu, point to Tracing Image, and then click Load to insert a tracing image.*

5 Drag the **Transparency** slider to the percentage level you want for the image.

6 Click **OK**.

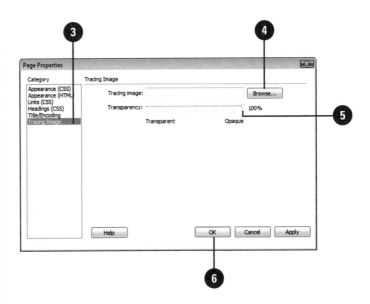

See Also

See "Using a Tracing Image" on page 204 for information on using a tracing image to create a Web page.

Using Visual Aids

When you're working in Design or Split view, you can use visual aids in Dreamweaver to make it easier to work with page elements, such as borders, backgrounds, and outlines that are normally invisible. Sometimes it's hard to adjust elements without being able to see the edge. For example, the Table Borders and Frame Borders commands on the Visual Aids submenu on the View menu make it easier to view and change the borders in tables and frames on a page. You can show or hide all the visual aids at once or select each item individually. The Visual Aids submenu highlights the menu icon or displays a checkmark when a visual aid is turned on.

Show or Hide Visual Aids

◆ **All.** Click the **View** menu, point to **Visual Aids,** and then click **Hide All**.

   TIMESAVER *Press Ctrl+Shift+I to show or hide all visual aids.*

◆ **Individual.** Click the **View** menu, point to **Visual Aids,** and then click each item you want to show or hide.

   ◆ CSS Layout Backgrounds.

   ◆ CSS Layout Box Model.

   ◆ CSS Layout Outlines.

   ◆ AP Element Outlines.

   ◆ Table Widths.

   ◆ Table Borders.

   ◆ Frame Borders.

   ◆ Image Maps.

   ◆ Invisible Elements.

Click to hide all visual aids

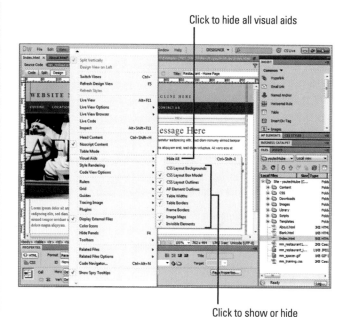

Click to show or hide individual visual aids

Working with Invisible Elements

Dreamweaver uses many styles of elements to create a Web page. Some of the elements are invisible, such as text and images, and some are not, such as anchors and line breaks. The invisible elements in a Web page are important to the structure and functionality of a page. However, they are not always necessary to view and make changes to a Web page unless you specifically want to work with an invisible element. You can use the Preferences dialog box to select the invisible elements you want to show or hide. After you set your invisible element preferences, you can use the Visual Aids submenu on the View menu to show (enable) or hide (disable) the Invisible Elements command. Showing invisible elements might slightly change the layout of a page, however, it's only temporary until you hide them.

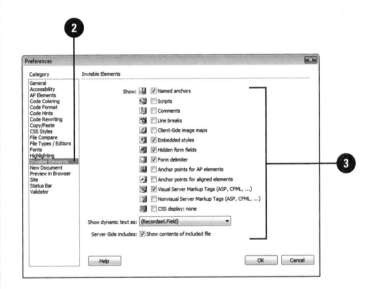

Set Invisible Element Preferences

1. Click the **Dreamweaver** (Mac) or **Edit** (Win) menu, and then click **Preferences**.

2. Click the **Invisible Elements** category.

3. Select or clear the check box options you want to show or hide:

   ◆ **Named Anchors.** Displays an icon to mark anchor locations.

   ◆ **Scripts.** Displays an icon to mark JavaScript or VBScript.

   ◆ **Comments.** Displays an icon to mark the location of comments.

   ◆ **Line Breaks.** Displays an icon to mark the location of line breaks <br>.

   ◆ **Client-Side Image Maps.** Displays an icon to mark the location of client-side image maps.

   ◆ **Embedded Styles.** Displays an icon to mark the location of CSS styles embedded in the body section of a document.

   ◆ **Hidden Form Fields.** Displays an icon to mark the location of form fields that are set to "hidden."

- **Form Delimiter.** Displays the border of a form to make it easier to insert form fields.

- **Anchor Points For AP Elements.** Displays an icon to mark the location of code defining an AP Element, which is an element with an absolute position assigned to it. AP elements are not invisible, just the code defining it.

- **Anchor Points For Aligned Elements.** Displays an icon to mark the location of HTML code for elements that work with the align option, such as images, tables, ActiveX objects, plug-ins, and applets.

- **Visual Server Markup Tags.** Displays the location of visual server markup tags, such as Active Server Pages tags and ColdFusion tags, whose content cannot be displayed.

- **Nonvisual Server Markup Tags.** Displays the location of nonvisual server markup tags, such as Active Server Pages tags and ColdFusion tags, whose content cannot be displayed.

- **CSS Display: None.** Displays an icon to mark the location of hidden content using the display:none property.

- **Show Dynamic Text As.** Displays any dynamic text on your page in the format of {Recordset:Field} by default.

- **Server-Side Includes.** Displays the content of each server-side include file from the Web server.

4 Click **OK**.

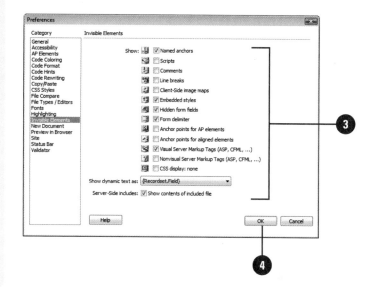

Selecting Elements

Before you can work with an element, such as text or an image, you need to select the element first. If an element is invisible, you need to make it visible before you can select it. You can select an element in Design view by simply clicking the element. If you want to select the complete tag associated with an element, you can use the tag selector. The tag selector appears at the bottom of the Document window on the Status bar. The tag selector shows the tags within the current selection or insertion point. The leftmost tag in the tag selector is the outermost tag in the selection. Simply select the code or place the insertion point where you want to select a tag, and click the tag you want to select in the tag selector.

Select Elements

◆ **Visible Element**. In Design view, click the element or drag across it.

◆ **Invisible Element**. Click the **View** menu, point to **Visual Aids**, and then click **Invisible Elements**. You can select the invisible elements as visible ones.

◆ **Tags**. Select the code or place the insertion point where you want to select a tag, and then click the tag you want in the tag selector.

Tags selected

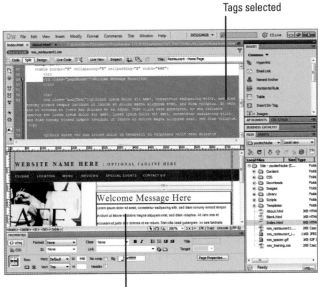

Table cell selected

Working with Web Page Text

Introduction

Now that you've created a Web page, it's time to throw in some text to get the message across. Text comes in many forms: from headings and paragraphs, bulleted points, and body text written especially for the Web. Your job as a Web designer is to make it all flow together in a logical, attractive, understandable fashion.

Many designers who come from the professional printing industry are surprised at the lack of typographic control on a normal Web page. Specific fonts are suggested, not specified, sizes are relative, and line spacing seems to be imaginary. Designers of print-to-paper are used to exacting standards and control. For example, tell a print designer that although he specified the *Benguiat* font to be used in his brochure design, the readers might wind up with *Times New Roman*, or *Garamond*. That designer would be out the door and looking for a new print shop. Yet, that's what sometimes happens on the Internet.

Some Web designers, to achieve the desired look, respond by converting their text into graphics, but don't. For one reason, text converted into graphics bloats the size of the page and increases download times; another reason is that text converted to graphics is not searchable.

Cascading Style Sheets (CSS) are more and more becoming a real option and give the Web designer almost as much control as the print designer.

In this chapter we're going to talk about text as it relates to standard Web page construction: adding text to a page, modifying text, using text to attract attention, formatting text, checking text... text, text, text.

What You'll Do

Add Text to Web Pages

Import Tabular Data

Import Content from Microsoft Documents

Insert Special Characters and the Date

Select Text

Copy and Paste Text

Set Copy/Paste Preferences

Modify Font Combinations

Format Characters and Paragraph Text

Control Line Spacing

Insert Horizontal Rules

Create Ordered and Unordered Lists

Create Definition Lists

Modify Lists

Apply and Create Text Styles

Find and Replace Text or Code

Check Spelling

Use Undo and Redo

Set Font Preferences

Adding Text to Web Pages

Working with text is not just about placing letters on a page; it's about using text as a page design element and it's also about readability. What's the use of adding text to a Web page if it's too small to read, or the font is not one that renders well on a pixel-based monitor? Remember, there are fonts that look good on paper, and fonts that look good on a computer monitor. Dreamweaver is going to help us out with the formatting part of the equation; it's up to you to make the words sound good. The cool thing about working with text in Dreamweaver is the choices you have; for example, you can choose to type text directly into a page, or copy and paste the text from a word processing document. Text is added to the Web page in several ways: you can open up a blank Web page and just start typing; however, you have very little control over text formatting. Another way is to create a table, and insert the text into the individual table cells. This gives you the ability to control your margins and paragraph formatting. The newest way is through the use of individual layers. Layers not only give you the ability to control your paragraph formatting; in addition, they give you the ability to move the layers, even stacking one layer on another.

Add Text to a Web Page

1. Open the Web page you want to add text.

   In this example we use a Web page with an inserted table.

2. Click with your mouse in the table cell that you want to add text.

3. Begin typing the text that you want to add.

4. Press the Enter (Win) or Return (Mac) key to start a new paragraph.

   Dreamweaver adds text based on its default formatting parameters, and automatically wraps the text when it comes to the end of the table cell.

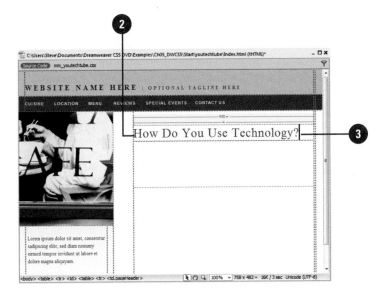

Importing Tabular Data

If you have data in tabular form, such as a database or spreadsheet, you can import the data as delimited text files. Before you can import the data, you need to export or save the data in the database or spreadsheet as a delimited text file, which is a file format with the data separated by tabs, commas, colons, or semicolons. From here, you can import the data file to your page in Dreamweaver and format it as a data table. When you import the data, you can specify the table layout and formatting options you want.

Import Tabular Data

1. Open the Web page you want to import content.

2. Click in the location where you want to insert content.

3. Click the **File** menu, point to **Import**, and then click **Tabular Data**.

4. Click **Browse**, navigate to the location with the file you want to import, select the delimited file, and then click **Open**.

5. Click the **Delimiter** list arrow, and then select the delimiter type you used when you exported or saved the file.

6. Click the **Fit To Data** or **Set To** option. If you selected the Set to option, enter a specific width or a percentage of the browsers window width you want (in pixels).

7. Enter the cell padding and cell spacing you want (in pixels).

8. Click the **Format Top Row** list arrow, select the formatting option you want, and then enter the table border width you want (in pixels).

9. Click **OK**.

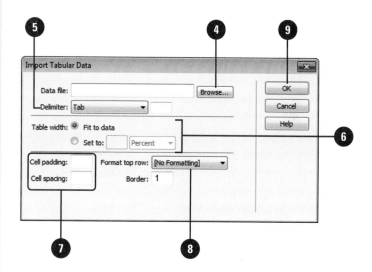

Importing Content from Microsoft Documents

If you're a Windows user you can import Microsoft documents directly onto your Web pages. You can use the Import submenu on the File menu to import content from Microsoft Word or Microsoft Excel documents into your Web pages. If you want to create a link to a Microsoft Word or Excel document, you can simply drag the document file to where you want the link in your page. If the document file is not located inside the local root folder, Dreamweaver prompts you to copy the file to the root to maintain proper site organization. In addition, when you upload your page to your Web server, you need to make sure you also upload the Microsoft Word or Excel document, so the link works properly.

Import Content from Microsoft Word or Excel

① Open the Web page you want to import Microsoft content.

② Click in the location where you want to insert content.

③ Click the **File** menu, point to **Import**, and then click **Word Document** or **Excel Document**.

④ Navigate to the location with the Microsoft document you want to import.

⑤ Select the document.

⑥ Click **Open**.

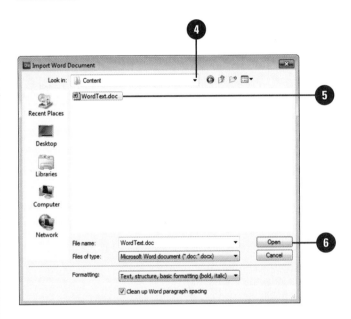

See Also

See "Cleaning Up Word HTML" on page 464 for information on cleaning HTML in a Word document.

Create a Link to a Microsoft Word or Excel Document

1 Open the Web page where you want to create a link to Microsoft content.

2 Drag the Word or Excel file from its current location to your page and position the link where you want it.

◆ You can use the Files panel to drag a file to the Document window. Click the **Window** menu, and then click **Files**.

3 Click the **Create A Link** option.

4 Click **OK**.

5 If the document file is not located inside your root folder, click **Yes** to copy the document to the site root.

The Copy File As dialog box opens.

6 Click **Save**.

The name of the linked file appears as the link text, which you can change.

Drag here

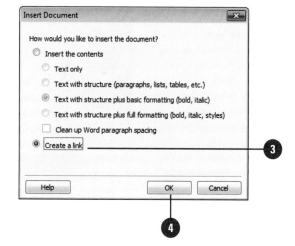

Inserting Special Characters and the Date

In word processing you have all the letters of the alphabet, and you have special characters. Special characters help to further define what you're saying. For example, you could say that your Web site has a copyright date of 2007, or you could use a special character, and say it this way: ©2007. HTML only allows one space between characters. If you want to add more, you can use the Non-Breaking Space command on the Special Characters submenu. The Special Characters submenu also allows you to insert other characters, such as character with accents and other international characters. However, the visitor's browser must support the "other" character inserted for it to be visible to the user; therefore testing is essential. In addition to special characters, you have the ability to add things like the current date and even the time, and have the date/time items automatically update with the passage of time. When you use the Insert Date option your pages will always reflect the correct date.

Insert a Special Character

1. Open the Web page you want to insert special characters.

2. Click to place the insertion point where you want to insert text.

3. Choose one of the following options:

   ◆ Click the **Insert** menu, point to **HTML**, point to **Special Characters**, and then select a special character from the available options.

   ◆ Select the **Text** tab on the Insert bar, click the **Characters** button, and then select from the available special character options.

   Dreamweaver places the special character at the insertion point.

For Your Information

Special Characters vs Decorative Fonts

Special characters are not to be confused with decorative fonts. Some fonts, like Zapf Dingbats, and Symbols, are designed to give you small graphics (like a pointing finger, or smile face) in place of the letters of the alphabet. Special characters are actually coded into the HTML document, so that they produce exactly the symbol requested.

Insert Other Characters

① Open the Web page you want to insert other characters.

② Click to place the insertion point where you want to insert text.

③ Click the **Insert** menu, point to **HTML**, point to **Special Characters**, and then click **Other**.

④ Select a character from the available list. A copy of the HTML code used to display the character appears in the insert box in the upper left.

⑤ Click **OK**.

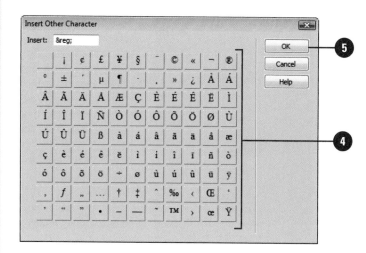

Add the Date and Time

① Open Dreamweaver, and then open a Web document.

② Click to place the insertion point where you want to insert text.

③ Choose from the following options:

◆ Click the **Insert** menu, and then click **Date**.

◆ Select the **Common** tab on the Insert bar, and then click the **Date** button.

The Insert Date dialog box opens.

④ Select the format you want the day and date to display.

⑤ Select a format for the time (optional).

⑥ Select the **Update Automatically On Save** check box to update the date/time every time the page is saved.

⑦ Click **OK**.

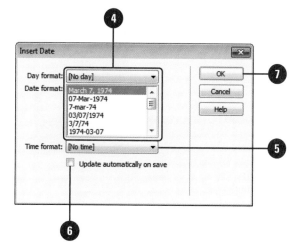

Selecting Text

Like any other application that process text, Dreamweaver needs a que from you as to what you want to do. If you plan to make a change to the current text, you need to inform Dreamweaver of that fact by making a selection. There are several ways that you can select text in Dreamweaver. The first thing to notice is that Dreamweaver does not have a specific text tool. That's because the cursor is sensitive to the area it's hovering over. For example, if you hover over an image, and click your mouse, Dreamweaver selects the image; however, if you're hovering over a section of text and click your mouse, Dreamweaver turns into a text tool, and create an insertion point into the text. That's why Dreamweaver doesn't have that old familiar Toolbox, like you see in applications such as: Photoshop, Illustrator, and Flash because it's the position of the cursor in the document that automatically determines what happens. Of course, once the text is selected, it can be modified, deleted, even copied.

Standard Selection Techniques

♦ **Single Click.** Creates an insertion point within the body of text.

♦ **Double Click.** Selects a single word (separated by spaces or a paragraph return).

NOTE *If the word ends with punctuation (period, comma, etc), they will not be selected.*

♦ **Triple Click.** Selects one paragraph (all text between two paragraph returns; including any punctuation).

♦ **Click and Drag.** Click within a body of text and drag the mouse to select a group of text. Release the mouse and the dragged text remains selected.

♦ **Click release Shift Click.** Click once within the body of text and release. Then move to another area, hold the shift key and click once. All the text between the two mouse clicks is selected.

Selected text

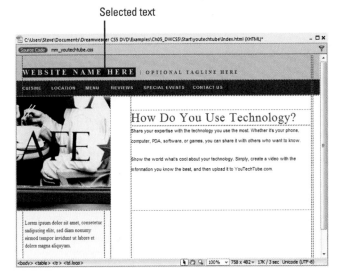

Select Using the Status Bar

1 Click to place the insertion point where you want to select text, and then look at the Status bar.

The tags for the area you've selected appear on the left side of the Status bar.

2 Click the specific tag you want in the Status bar to select the tag within the code.

For example, when you click the <p> (paragraph) tag, all the text associated with that tag appears selected.

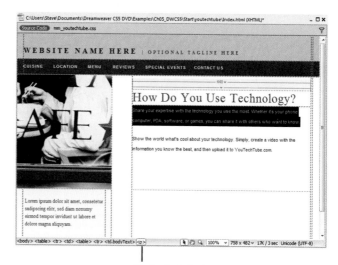

Text selected using
tags on the Status bar

Did You Know?

The tag selector is not just for text. For example, if you choose an image <alt> tag, the corresponding image within the document will be selected. This is a quick and easy way to make selections within complex Web documents.

You can use the Select All command to select all of the text within the selected body. Click once within the text body, click the Edit menu, and then click Select All, or press Ctrl+A (Win) or ⌘+A (Mac).

Copying and Pasting Text

If you cut or copy text from a file in any other application (word processor, spreadsheet, or database), Dreamweaver inserts the copied text at the insertion point of the cursor. Understand that the default Paste command has limited control over the formatting of text: It can only paste plain, unformatted text; bold, italic, or other formatting options are not carried over with the text... unless you're using Microsoft Word. By default, performing a copy/paste command from MS Word retains most font formatting. Unfortunately, unless you change the Preferences of the Paste option, the Copy/Paste commands have limited control over text. For example, you have a heavily formatted section of text in Microsoft Word and you want to bring the text into Dreamweaver without any formatting because you plan to use a Style Sheet to do all the document formatting. That's where the Paste Special command comes into play. With Paste Special, you can control what formatting options are used when pasting the text.

Copy and Paste

1. Open a text document within your word processor (i.e. Microsoft Word).

2. Select the text that you want to paste into Dreamweaver.

3. Click the **Edit** menu, and then click **Copy**, or click the **Copy** button on the Standard toolbar or Home tab (Vista).

4. Open Dreamweaver, and the Web page you want to add the text.

5. Click to place the insertion point where you want to insert text.

6. Click the **Edit** menu, and then click **Paste**.

   Dreamweaver pastes the copied text at the insertion point.

Did You Know?

You can access the copy/paste preferences directly from the Paste Special dialog box. When you select the Paste Special command, simply click the Paste Preferences button, and you can make your changes permanent.

Copy and Paste Special

① Open a text document within Microsoft Word.

② Select the text that you want to paste into Dreamweaver.

③ Click the **Edit** menu, and then click **Copy**, or click the **Copy** button on the Standard toolbar or Home tab (Vista).

④ Open Dreamweaver, and the Web page you want to add the text.

⑤ Click to place the insertion point where you want to insert text.

⑥ Click the **Edit** menu, and then click **Paste Special**.

⑦ Select from the following options:

- ◆ **Text Only.** Pastes text without formatting.

- ◆ **Text With Structure (paragraphs, lists, tables, etc.).** Pastes structured text without formatting.

- ◆ **Text With Structure Plus Basic Formatting (bold, italic).** Pastes structured text and simple HTML formatting.

- ◆ **Text With Structure Plus Full Formatting (bold, italic, styles).** Pastes structured text, HTML formatting, and CSS styles.

- ◆ **Retain Line Breaks.** Select this option to keep line breaks.

- ◆ **Clean Up Word Paragraph Spacing.** Select this option if you've chosen Text With Structure, or Text With Structure Plus Basic Formatting, and want to eliminate extra spacing between paragraphs.

⑧ Click **OK**.

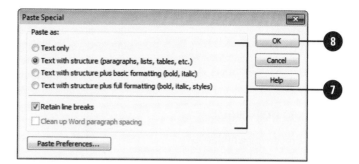

For Your Information

Working with Word Processing Programs

To assist in generating text on my Web pages, I work with Microsoft Word and Adobe Dreamweaver open at the same time. This way I'm able to type text in an application I'm comfortable with (MS Word), and quickly drag from my word processor directly into my Dreamweaver Web page. If you're copying text that contains multiple paragraphs, make sure your paragraphs are separated by two returns. When pasted into Dreamweaver, the paragraph breaks are preserved. If you just have a single return between paragraphs, Dreamweaver converts the paragraphs to line breaks.

Setting Copy/Paste Preferences

You can use the Copy/Paste section of the Preferences dialog box to customize how the Paste command inserts text into a Web page. You can set special paste preferences as default options to paste text from other programs. You can set options to paste text only, text with structure, such as paragraphs, list and tables, and text with structure and formatting, including HTML and CSS styles.

Set Copy/Paste Preferences

1. Click the **Dreamweaver** (Mac) or **Edit** (Win) menu, and then click **Preferences**.

2. Click the **Copy/Paste** category.

3. Select from the following check boxes:

   ◆ **Text Only.** Pastes unformatted text.

   ◆ **Text With Structure (paragraphs, lists, tables, etc.).** Pastes structured text without formatting.

   ◆ **Text With Structure Plus Basic Formatting (bold, italic).** Pastes structured text and simple HTML formatting.

   ◆ **Text With Structure Plus Full Formatting (bold, italic, styles).** Pastes structured text, HTML formatting, and CSS styles.

4. Select the **Retain Line Breaks** check box to keep line breaks in pasted text.

5. Select the **Clean Up Word Paragraph Spacing** check box if you selected the Text with Structure or Text with Structure Plus Basic Formatting option, and want to eliminate extra space between paragraphs when you paste your text.

6. Click **OK**.

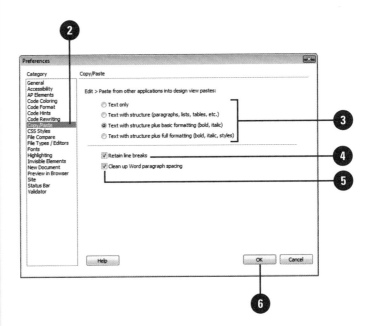

Modifying Font Combinations

When you select one of Dreamweaver's default fonts, you'll notice that they come in groups of three: A primary font, secondary font, and general font. This is known as a **font combination**. Font combinations determine how a browser displays text in your Web page. A browser uses the first font in the combination that is installed on the user's system. For example, if you choose the Arial and the visitor does not have Arial, the browser attempts to find Helvetica, if it can't find Helvetica, it substitutes a sans-serif font. If none of the fonts in the combination are installed, the browser displays the text as specified by the user's browser preferences. You can use the Edit Font List command to set the font combinations that appear in the Properties panel and the Font submenu on the Format menu.

Modify Font Combinations

1. Click the **Format** menu, point to **Font**, and then click **Edit Font List**.

2. Select the font combination you want to edit.

3. Use any of the following to add, modify, or remove the selected font combination.

   ◆ **New Combination.** Click the Add button (Plus), select a font from the Available Fonts list, and then click Left Arrow button to add it to the font list.

   ◆ **Delete Combination.** Select the font combination you want to remove, and then click the Subtract button (Minus).

   ◆ **Add Fonts.** Select a font from the Available Fonts list, and then click Left Arrow button to add it to the font list.

   ◆ **Remove fonts.** Select a font from the Chosen Fonts list, and then click Right Arrow button to remove it from the font list.

   ◆ **Change Combination Order.** Select the font combination you want to arrange, and then click the Up or Down arrows.

4. Click **OK**.

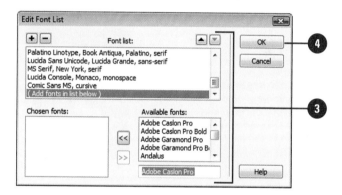

Formatting Characters

Selecting text is one thing; knowing what to do with it once it's been selected is another. Dreamweaver has a set of character formatting tags that allows you to change the size, color and style of the text, and then generate the specific HTML tags. Remember, formatting text is not just about changing the text; you also have you ask yourself the question of why you're changing it. Does that heading text really need to be THAT big… Is it OK to change the color of text to red? Many a good Web site has gone down the tubes because of bad design. Remember, do not change the text just because you can; change it because it reflects the overall design of the site.

Format Text Characters

1 Open the Web page you want to format.

2 Select a word inside the text that you want to modify.

   TIMESAVER *Press Ctrl+A (Win) or ⌘+A (Mac) to select all of the text within the selected body.*

3 Click the **Window** menu, and then click **Properties** to open the Properties panel.

4 Click **HTML** to format HTML tags or click **CSS** to modify CSS.

5 Choose from the following type of formatting options:

   ◆ Format. Click the button and choose from the predefined styles. Leave this option at its default value.

   ◆ Class. Displays the class style currently applied to the text. If no styles have been applied the option displays No CSS. Leave this option at its default value.

   ◆ Bold. Click to **bold** the selected text.

   ◆ Italic. Click to *italicize* the selected text.

   ◆ Font. Click to change the font type of the selected text.

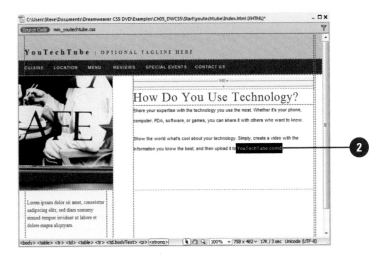

◆ **Size.** Click the **Size** button, and then first choose how you want to measure font sizes (percent, pixels, points, etc), and then change the size in the input field. For example, if you're fonts by percentage (default), and you change the size to 50 percent, the selected text will be half the size of the standard font; 200 percent, twice the size, etc.

◆ **Text Color.** Click the **Text Color** button, and then choose a new color for the selected text, or click in the coding box and type in the hexadecimal code value for the desired color.

NOTE *Hexadecimal codes are preceded by a pound sign (#), and are three sets of double-digit number values representing the percentages of red, green, and blue, respectively.*

Formatted text characters

Did You Know?

You can make multiple formatting changes at once. After you select the text you want to change, if you click the Page Properties button on the Properties panel, you can perform all of your formatting changes to the text, and change options to the Page Properties at the same time.

Formatting Paragraph Text

Paragraph text formatting differs from standard text formatting in one way: The changes made impact the entire paragraph, not just the individual words. For this reason, paragraph formatting does not require you to select the paragraph; you just have to click inside the paragraph you want to change. Once the paragraph is selected you can work with Dreamweaver's paragraph style options.

Format Paragraph Text

1. Open the Web page you want to format.

2. Select a word inside the text that you want to modify.

3. Click the **Window** menu, and then click **Properties** to open the Properties panel.

4. Click **HTML** to format HTML tags or click **CSS** to modify CSS.

5. Choose from the following type formatting options:

   ◆ **Format.** Click the **Format** button and select one of the available options.

   NOTE *The paragraph style applies the default style for an <p> HTML tag, as do the H1 thru H6 Heading styles.*

   ◆ **Align.** Select one of the justification buttons: **Align Left**, **Align Right**, **Align Center**, or **Justify** to change the justification of the active paragraph.

   ◆ **Indent.** Click the **Text Indent** or **Text Outdent** button to indent (in or out) the left margin of the text paragraph.

   ◆ **Ordered/Unordered.** Click the **Ordered List** or **Unordered List** button to convert the select paragraph into a list.

   The formatting options are applied to the selected text.

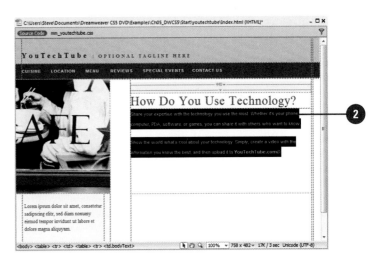

CSS properties

Controlling Line Spacing

One of the problems with formatting text on a Web page is the problem of controlling line spacing. For example, when you press the Enter key to create a new paragraph, HTML create a <p> or paragraph tag, jumps you down to the next line, and leaves a bit of extra space between the lines; however, what if you don't want the extra space? HTML takes care of this pesky problem by giving us another obscure HTML code called a line break, or the <br> tag.

Control Line Spacing

1. Open the Web page you want to change.

2. Click your mouse inside the document and begin typing.

3. Use either of the following to control line spacing:

   ◆ **Paragraph.** Press the Enter key.

   Dreamweaver inserts the paragraph tag <p> into the text and adds extra line spacing between the two lines.

   ◆ **Line Break.** Press the Shift + Enter keys.

   Dreamweaver inserts the line break tag <br> into the text and does not add any extra space between the lines.

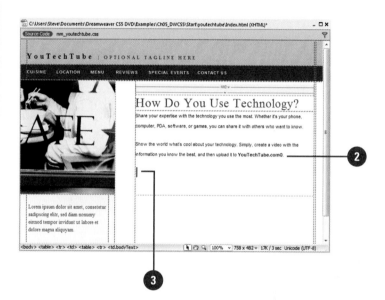

Inserting Horizontal Rules

Horizontal lines have a variety of uses in the construction of a Web page. Whether they're used to separate sections of a page or to underline an important piece of text, you have several decisions to make. Inserting a horizontal line provides a simple, yet effective way to highlight the information you want visitors to see. Lines have a variety of properties that you can modify, including width, height, alignment, and color.

Insert a Horizontal Line

1. Open and display the Web page you want to use.

2. Click where you want to insert a horizontal line.

3. Click the **Insert** menu, point to **HTML**, and then click **Horizontal Rule**.

Inserted horizontal line

Modify a Horizontal Line

1 Open and display the Web page with the horizontal line you want to change.

2 Select the horizontal line you want to modify.

3 Select the formatting options you want in the Properties panel:

◆ **W.** Width of the line. Specified in pixels or as a percentage of the window width.

◆ **H.** Height of the line in pixels.

◆ **Align.** Alignment of the line on the page.

◆ **Shading.** Select the check box to create a shaded line.

Creating Ordered and Unordered Lists

Most word processors have the ability to create bulleted or numbered lists of information. A bulleted list can itemize a topic's points or catalog the properties of an object. A numbered list is helpful for giving step-by- step instructions. A list can break up the page and simultaneously draw the viewer's eye to key details. Lists are an important alternative to the basic textual tools of paragraphs and headings. In this chapter, you can study Dreamweaver's tools for designing and working with each of the three basic types of lists available in HTML: ordered lists, unordered lists, and definition lists. An ordered list is used when it's important that the listed items appear in a sequential order. As a professional chef, I use ordered lists all the time for the steps to a specific recipe. An unordered list is used when the sequence of the listed items is of no great concern. Again, as a chef, I use unordered lists to display my list of ingredients to a recipe.

Create an Ordered List

1. Open the Web page you want to format.

2. Click within the document where you want to insert the ordered list, or select a group of text that you want to convert into a list.

3. Click the **Window** menu, and then click **Properties** to display the Properties panel.

4. Click **HTML** to format HTML tags.

5. Click the **Ordered List** button in the Properties panel.

   Dreamweaver inserts the Roman numeral 1 into the document.

6. To add items to the list, type an item, and then press Enter (Win) or Return (Mac).

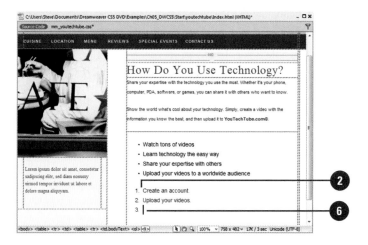

Did You Know?

You can create a nested or indented list. A nested list is a list that contains another list. Select the items you want to nest, click the Indent button in the Properties panel, or click the Format menu, and then click Indent.

Create an Unordered List

1. Open the Web page you want to format.

2. Click within the document where you want to insert the unordered list, or select a group of text that you want to convert into a list.

3. Click the **Window** menu, and then click **Properties** to display the Properties panel.

4. Click the **Unordered List** button in the Properties panel.

   Dreamweaver inserts a default round bullet into the document.

5. To add items to the list, type an item, and then press Enter (Win) or Return (Mac).

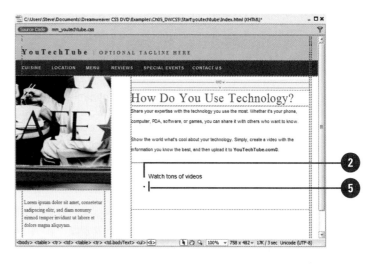

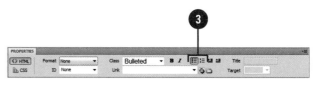

Create a List Using Existing Text

1. Open the Web page you want to format.

2. Select the paragraphs you want to make into a list.

3. Click the **Unordered List** or **Ordered List** button in the Properties panel, or click the **Format** menu, point to **List**, and then select the type of list you want: **Unorder List**, **Ordered List**, or **Definition List**.

2 List changed to bullets

Creating Definition Lists

A definition list doesn't use leading characters (bullets or numbers) to map the items; instead, definition lists are used in areas like glossaries. I might create a definition list explaining cooking terminology. A definition list does not use bullets to identify the items, and it's composed of two lines: the first line is for the name of the item, and the second line is indented and describes the item; hence the name, definition list. If you happen to have a very long definition, and you want to separate it into two or more paragraphs, don't press the Enter key; that will take you to a new definition term. Simply press the Shift plus Enter key to create a soft return, and then type the second paragraph.

Create an Definition List

1. Open the Web page you want to format.

2. Click within the document where you want to insert the definition list.

3. Click the **Format** menu, point to **List**, and then click **Definition List**.

4. Type a definition term and press the Enter (Win) or Return (Mac) key. The new line is automatically indented.

5. Type in a definition description.

6. Press the Enter (Win) or Return (Mac) key to add another definition term, and press Enter (Win) or Return (Mac) again to add the corresponding definition description.

   The Definition list can be continued for as long as you want.

7. Press the Enter (Win) or Return (Mac) key twice to end the list and return to the normal paragraph style type.

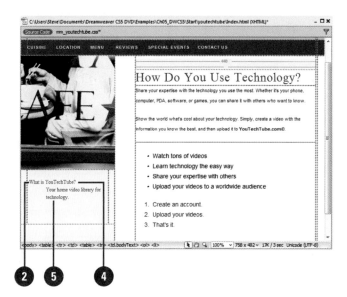

Modifying Lists

After you create a list, you can use the List Properties dialog box to make changes to it. Some of the list options you can change include number style, number reset, or bullet style. You can make changes to the entire list or to a specific item in the list.

Modify a List

1. Click anywhere within the ordered list you want to modify, or click a specific item that you want to change.

2. Click the **Format** menu, point to **List**, and then click **Properties**.

3. To modify the list use the following options:

   ◆ Click the **List Type** list arrow, and then click **Bulleted List**, **Numbered List**, **Directory List**, or **Menu List**.

   ◆ Click the **Style** list arrow, and then select the style you want.

   NOTE *You'll see different options based on the list type chosen.*

   ◆ Enter the starting number you want to use by the list (available only when creating a numbered list).

4. To modify an individual item:

   ◆ Click the **New Style** list arrow to change the style of the active list item.

   ◆ Enter the reset count number you want to use by the active list item (available only when creating a numbered list).

5. Click **OK**.

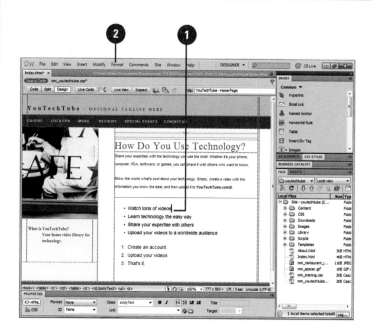

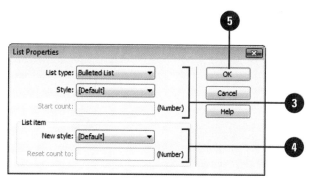

Applying Text Styles

Dreamweaver gives us the ability to change the style of text. A **style** is a collection of formatting settings saved with a Web site or template that you can apply to text, graphics, and tables at any time. Changing the style of text is useful when you want to draw the reader's eyes to a particular phrase or word. For example, using a bold font might indicate that the word is very important. Dreamweaver accomplishes this by using two types of tags: physical tags and logical styles. **Physical tags** change how the text looks (bold, italic, underline, etc). **Logical styles** define a certain look or style. For example, a paragraph style, or a heading style changes the text, based on pre-defined values. In addition, when you use logical styles for HTML text, it becomes easier to find what you're looking for. For example, you could conduct a search to find all paragraphs defined as citation text. Dreamweaver provides you with built-in styles, or you can create your own user-defined styles.

Apply a Built-In Text Style

1. Open the Web page you want to apply a text style.

2. Select the character, word, or words that you want to apply the text style.

   If you select a word or words and apply a style, the style will only affect the selected text. If you click inside a paragraph and apply a style, the style will change the entire paragraph.

3. Click the **Format** menu, point to **Style**, and then select from the following options:

   - Bold, Italic, Underline

   TIMESAVER *You can also change the font style in the Properties panel. Click the Bold, Italic, or Underline buttons you want to apply.*

   - Strikethrough, Teletype, Emphasis, Strong

   - Code, Variable, Sample, Keyboard

   - Citation, Definition, Deleted, Inserted

Apply a Built-In Font and Size Style

1. Open the Web page you want to apply a text style.

2. Select the character, word, or words that you want to apply the text style.

   If you select a word or words and apply a style, the style will only affect the selected text. If you click inside a paragraph and apply a style, the style will change the entire paragraph.

3. Click **CSS** in the Properties panel to apply or create a CSS rule.

4. Choose from any of the following style options:

   ◆ Font. Click the **Font** list arrow, and then select the font style you want.

   ◆ Size. Click the **Size** list arrow, and then select the point size you want.

   NOTE *You can also change the font using the Format menu. Click the Format menu, point to Font, and then select a style.*

5. If the New CSS Rule dialog box appears, select the following options:

   ◆ Selector Type. Specify a selector type: Class, ID, Tag, or Compound.

   ◆ Selector Name. Select or enter a name for your selector.

   ◆ Rule Definition. Select where to define the rule, either a current document or external CSS file.

6. Click **OK**.

For Your Information

Using the <strong> and <em> Tags

The two style tags <b> bold and <i> italic are common use tags in Dreamweaver; however, it is better to use the, <strong> for bold and <em> for italic. Dreamweaver allows you to specify which tags to use. Click the Edit (Win) or Dreamweaver (Mac) menu, click Preferences, click the General category, select the Use <strong> and <em> in place of <b> check box, and then click OK.

Creating Text Styles

While embedding physical tags or logical styles into a document is a very common way to change the look of text, the Web design community is moving to Cascading Style Sheets. Cascading Style Sheets can be used in conjunction with logical styles to define how that style works when viewed by the visitor, and give you more control over what your visitors will see. It's also important to understand that the visual look of standard HTML styles and tags are defined by the browser application, and may appear different when viewed on different browsers. If you modify a style, you make the change once, but all text tagged with that style changes to reflect the new format.

Create a CSS Text Style

① Open the Web page you want to create a customized style.

② Click the **Format** menu, point to **CSS Styles**, and then click **New**.

◆ You can also click the **New Style** button on the CSS Styles panel.

③ Choose from the following options:

◆ Selector Type. Select the **Class (can apply to any tag)** option.

◆ Selector. Enter a name for the style.

NOTE *Class names should begin with a period (if you don't add it, Dreamweaver will), and have no spaces or additional punctuation.*

◆ Define In. Select the **This Document Only** option or select an existing external style sheet.

④ Click **OK**.

⑤ Click the **Type** category.

⑥ Format the font based on the available options.

⑦ Click **OK**.

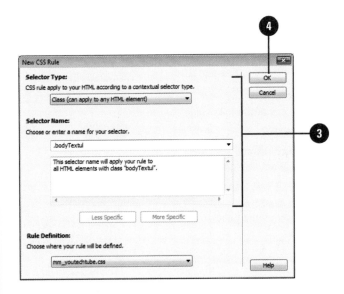

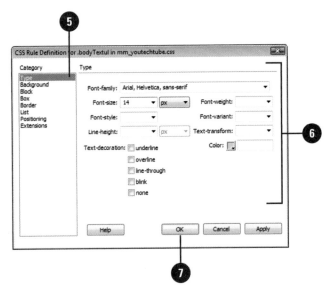

Apply a CSS Text Style

1. Open the Web page you want to apply a CSS text style.

2. Select in the paragraph that you want to apply the custom style.

   Remember the style you created can only be used within the original document. If you open another document, you will not be able to use this new style.

3. Click the **Format** menu, point to **CSS Styles**, and then click the name of the new style, or click the **Targeted Rule** list arrow in the Property Inspector for CSS, and then click the name of the new style.

   TIMESAVER *You can also change the Style in the Properties panel. Click the Style list arrow, and then select the style you want to apply.*

   The new style is applied to the selected text.

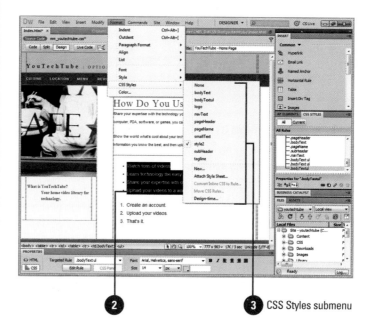

③ CSS Styles submenu

③ Targeted Rule list arrow

Renaming Styles

If you no longer like the name you specified for a style or the name doesn't adequately describe the formatting style, you can rename it using the Style list arrow in the Properties panel. The Style list arrow provides access to the Rename command where you can change the name of a style.

Rename a Style

1. Open the Web page you want to rename a style.

2. Click the **Window** menu, and then click **Properties** to open the Properties panel.

3. Click **HTML** in the Properties panel.

4. Click the **Style** list arrow, and then click **Rename**.

5. Click the **Rename Style** list arrow, and then select the style you want to rename.

6. Type a new name for the style.

7. Click **OK** to close the dialog box and save your changes.

   The Results panel appears, displaying the selected style.

Style list arrow

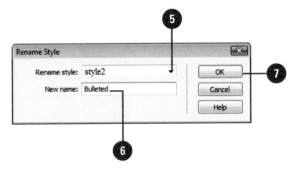

Finding Text

If you need to quickly find another instance of a word or phrase in a Web page, you can use the Find Selection command instead of the Find and Replace command. All you need to do is select an instance of the text or phrase you want to find, and then select the Find Selection command on the Edit menu, or press Shift+F3. After you find the selection, you can use the Find Next command to locate the next occurrence of the selection.

Find Text by Selection

1. Open the Web page you want to find text.

2. Select a word or phrase.

3. Click the **Edit** menu, and then click **Find Selection**.

   TIMESAVER *Press Shift+F3 to find the current selection.*

   Dreamweaver goes through the document, finds and highlights the next occurrence of the selected word.

4. To locate the next occurrence of the word, click the **Edit** menu, and then click **Find Next**.

   TIMESAVER *Press F3 to find the next occurrence of the current selection.*

Locates the next instance of "Upload"

Finding and Replacing Text or Code

Suppose that you discover you need to change a word throughout a Web page or entire site. You do not need to read through the document to find every instance of the word and manually change it. The Find and Replace command can do that for you. Dreamweaver can find every instance for you, and walk you through the Web site from page to page until all the corrections have been made. In addition to text, you can also find and replace code. You can search one or more Web page or an entire Web site. The results of performing a Find All and Replace All appear within the Results window under the Search tab, and results remain there until the next time you perform a Find All or Replace All. If you select a word or group of words before opening the Find and Replace dialog box, the words automatically are added to the Find box.

Find and Replace Text or Code

1. Open the Web page you want to find and replace text.

2. Click the **Edit** menu, and then click **Find and Replace**.

3. Choose from the following Find and Replace options:

   ◆ **Find In**. Click to determine what documents you want to search; everything from the current document to the entire site.

   ◆ **Search**. Click to determine what logical parts (Text or Source Code) of the document you want searched.

   ◆ **Find**. Enter the text that you want to find.

   ◆ **Replace**. Enter the text (optional) that you want to use to replace the text entered in the Find input box.

   ◆ **Load Query**. Click Load Query button to load a previously saved Find and Replace query.

   ◆ **Save Query**. Click Save Query button to save the current Find and Replace query.

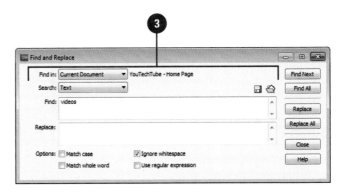

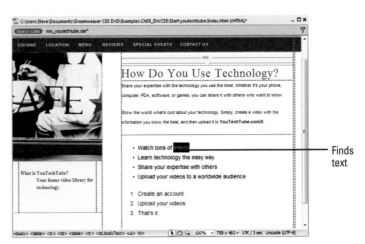

Finds text

4 Choose from the following Find and Replace options:

- ◆ **Match Case.** Select to make the Find text case sensitive (charlie, as opposed to Charlie).

- ◆ **Match Whole Word.** Select to match whole words.

- ◆ **Ignore Whitespace.** Select to treat all whitespace as a single space for the purpose of matching.

- ◆ **Use Regular Expression.** Select to use string expressions to help locate information.

5 Choose from the following controls to find what you want:

- ◆ **Find Next.** Find the next occurrence of the Find input field, based on the current position of the cursor.

- ◆ **Find All.** Find all occurrences of the Find input field.

- ◆ **Replace.** Find the next occurrence of the Find input field and replace it with the text in the Replace field.

- ◆ **Replace All.** Find all occurrences of the Find input field and replace with the text in the Replace field.

6 Click **Close** to exit the Find and Replace dialog box.

The Results panel appears for the Find All and Replace All.

TIMESAVER *Press F3 (Win) or* ⌘+G *(Mac) to perform a search again without displaying the Find and Replace dialog box.*

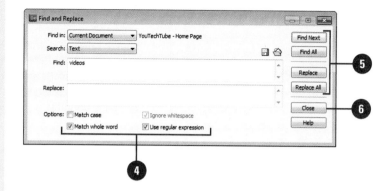

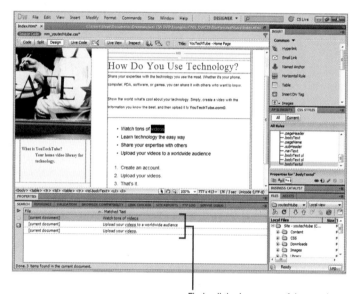

Finds all the instances of the word "video" in the Results Panel.

Using the Results Panel

The results of performing a Find All and Replace All search in the Find and Replace dialog box appear within the Results window under the Search tab. The search results remain there until the next time you perform a Find All or Replace All. You can access the search results by opening the Results panel. Within the Results panel, you can quickly highlight a specific result, open the Find and Replace dialog box, stop a search in progress, and save the search results in the XML.

Use the Results Panel

1. Open the Web page you want to find and replace text.

2. Click the **Window** menu, and then click **Results** to open the Results panel.

   The list of pages containing the previous search results opens in the Results panel at the bottom of the Dreamweaver window.

3. Click the **Search** tab if necessary.

4. Choose from the following Find and Replace options:

   ◆ **Highlight Selection.** Double-click a selection from the Results panel to open the file if necessary and highlight the selection in the document.

   ◆ **Find and Replace.** Click to open the Find and Replace dialog box.

   ◆ **Stop.** Click to stop a search in progress.

   ◆ **Save Report.** Click to save the search results as a report in the XML file format.

5. Click the **Window** menu, and then click **Results** to close the Results panel.

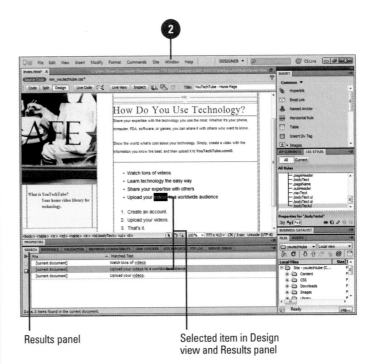

Results panel

Selected item in Design view and Results panel

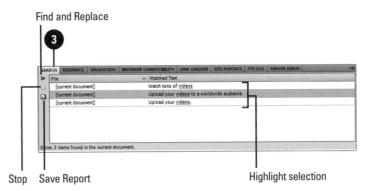

Find and Replace

Stop   Save Report

Highlight selection

Defining Acronyms and Abbreviations

If your Web page contains acronyms, such as MADD for Mothers Against Drunk Driving, and abbreviations, such as CE for Copy Editor, you can define them using HTML tags for use with search engines, spell checkers, language translation programs, or speech synthesizers.

Define Acronyms and Abbreviations

1 Open the Web page you want to define an acronym or abbreviation.

2 Select the acronym or abbreviation in the text.

3 Click the **Insert** menu, point to **HTML**, point to **Text Objects**, and then click **Acronym** or **Abbreviation**.

4 Enter the full text of the acronym or abbreviation.

5 Enter the language you want, such as en for English, it for Italian, or de for German.

6 Click **OK**.

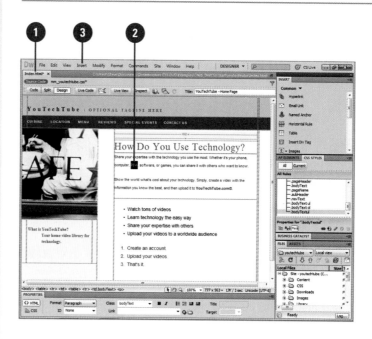

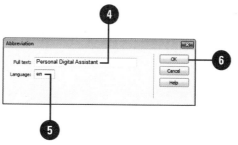

Checking Spelling

One of the worst things that you can do (well, almost one of the worst) is to have misspelled words on your Web page. Not only do they distract the reader, they distract from the overall impression of professionalism that you're trying to imply. Besides, since everyone on the planet knows there's something called a spellchecker there's simply no excuse for misspelled words. Fortunately, Dreamweaver includes a simple spellchecker to help avoid such awkward moments. You should always spell check a Web page before it's moved online. One other fine point: Using a spellchecker does not mean that the words are used correctly. For example, to, too, and two, are all spelled correctly; however, they have very different meanings. So, the order of events follows: Spell Check first; then read the text (called type editing), and be sure that it makes sense.

Check Spelling

1. Open the Web page you want to spell check.

2. Click the **Commands** menu, and then click **Check Spelling**.

   TIMESAVER *Press Shift+F7 to check spelling.*

   Dreamweaver begins the spell check process and stops on the first problem word.

3. Use the following options to work with the problem word:

   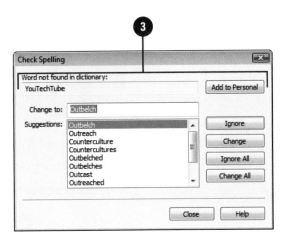

   - ◆ **Word Not Found In Dictionary.** Displays the offending word, and highlights the word in the Web page document.

   - ◆ **Change To.** Type in the word you want to use to substitute for the offending word.

   - ◆ **Suggestions.** Choose an option from the listed suggestions.

   - ◆ **Add To Personal.** Click to add the offending word to Dreamweaver's personal dictionary. Excellent for names or technical terms that are spelled correctly, but keep coming up as misspelled.

4 Choose from the following controls to change the selection:

- ◆ **Ignore.** Ignore the word, proceed to the next offending word, and don't add the word to the personal dictionary.

- ◆ **Change.** Change the word; based on the text in the Change To dialog box, or the appropriate selected suggestion.

- ◆ **Ignore All.** Ignore all occurrences of the offending word, but don't add to the personal dictionary.

- ◆ **Change All.** Change all occurrences of the offending word.

5 Click **Close** to close the Check Spelling dialog box, or click **OK** when the spell check is completed.

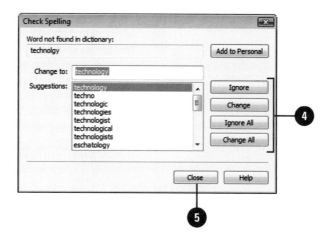

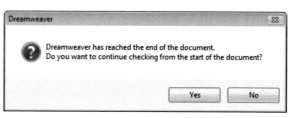

Did You Know?

You can spell check in more than English. Adobe uses the LILO (Linguistic Library Optimized) speller engine, which supports 37 different dictionaries (**New**!). The default dictionary matches the installed version of Dreamweaver. Click the Edit (Win) or Dreamweaver (Mac) menu, click Preferences, click the General category, click the Spelling dictionary list arrow, select the dictionary language you want, and then click OK. You can download dictionaries for additional languages from the Dreamweaver Support Center. Click the Help menu, and then click Dreamweaver Support Center.

Using Undo and Redo

Probably one of the greatest inventions of the computer industry is the ability to Undo, and Redo. Now, if we could just figure out how to give real life an undo feature... that would be something. Dreamweaver gives us the ability to undo our past mistakes, and redo something we wished we had not removed. The History panel shows the actions you've just taken in Dreamweaver, and enables you to undo or repeat any number of steps. History gives us the ability to control our working environment, and allows us to try creative ideas; knowing full well, that if we make a mistake, it's a simple matter to go back in time. The History panel is Dreamweaver's time machine.

Undo or Redo One Action at a Time

◆ Click the **Edit** menu, and then click **Undo,** or click the **Undo** button on the Standard toolbar to reverse your most recent action, such as typing a word or formatting a paragraph.

   TIMESAVER *Press Ctrl+Z (Win) or ⌘+Z (Mac) to undo.*

◆ Click the **Edit** menu, and then click **Redo,** or click the **Redo** button on the Standard toolbar to restore the last action you reversed.

   TIMESAVER *Press Ctrl+Y to redo your undo.*

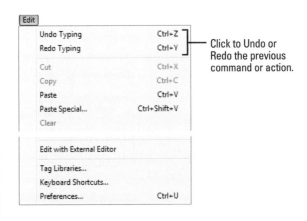

Click to Undo or Redo the previous command or action.

Undo and Redo buttons on the Standard toolbar

Undo or Redo Actions Using the History Panel

1. Open a Web document, and perform several actions (i.e. create text, insert an image, etc).

2. Click the **Window** menu, and then click **History** to open the History panel.

   TIMESAVER *Press Shift+F10 to open the History panel.*

   You'll see a line-by-line listing of all the steps performed to the current Web document.

3. To perform a multiple undo, click the arrow located to the left History panel, and then drag it up the list.

   Every item listed under the arrow will be undone.

   NOTE *To perform a multiple redo, click the arrow, and drag it down the list. All items above the arrow (including the item the arrow is pointing) will be restored.*

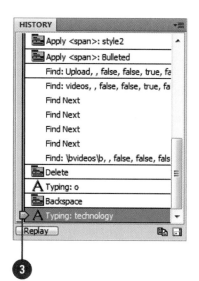

Did You Know?

You can change the number of History Steps. The default number of History steps is 50; while that may seem enough for most folks, you can change the number of steps in Preferences. Click the Edit (Win) or Dreamweaver (Mac) menu, click Preferences, click the General category, and then change the number of steps. The maximum value for history steps is 9,999... that's a lot of steps. When you're done, click OK.

Setting Font Preferences

You can use the Fonts section of the Preferences dialog box to view encoding for the selected font and size you want. File encoding makes sure your Web browser and Dreamweaver use the right character set for the selected language. The fonts you select in the Preferences dialog box don't affect the page display in a Web browser, however, it does affect the page display in Dreamweaver. You can specify the font and size you want to use in Code view, or as a proportional or fixed font.

Set Font Preferences

1 Click the **Dreamweaver** (Mac) or **Edit** (Win) menu, and then click **Preferences**.

2 Click the **Fonts** category.

3 Select the encoding type you want to view.

4 Select from the following check boxes:

◆ **Proportional Font.** Select the font and size you want to use to display normal text, such as paragraphs, headings, and tables.

◆ **Fixed Font.** Select the font and size you want to use to display text within pre, code, and tt tags.

◆ **Code View.** Select the font and size you want to use for all text in Code view.

5 Select the **Use Dynamic Font Mapping** check box.

6 Click **OK**.

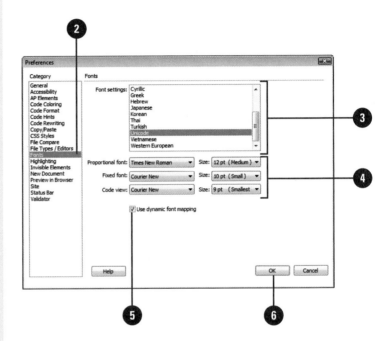

Working with Web Page Images

Introduction

Is it true that a picture is worth a thousand words? Is it also true that every time a writer begins talking about images they use that same timeworn phrase? Am I ever going to get to the point? To be honest, a picture can be worth much more than a thousand words; in fact, a well-placed image can articulate more than words can ever convey. For example, ever try to verbally describe a sunset? Go ahead, I'll wait; give it a try.

Communication comes in three forms: Visual, Vocal, and Verbal, and on a Web page the right visual image can be very powerful. On the other hand, placing images on a Web page can produce the opposite effect. I call it the why-did-they-use-that-image syndrome.

Good designers don't use images just because they can, but because they are needed to convey a specific message. Images should be used to drive your message home; they should blend seamlessly with the Web page, and the text on the pages. Don't use images because you can, use them because you need them to convey your message.

Dreamweaver makes the insertion of images a snap; in fact, it's as simple as a drag and a drop. In turn, Dreamweaver creates the compliant HTML tags within the document to make the image display correctly on a variety of browsers. Once the images have been inserted, Dreamweaver's graphical user interface allows you to modify the images in terms of size and position. You can even set up external editing applications, such as Adobe Photoshop and Fireworks, to revise the images on the fly.

In addition to adding simple images to a Web page, you can use graphics for navigational aids, rollover buttons, and even image maps.

What You'll Do

Use Web Friendly Graphics

Define an Image Folder

Insert Images

Insert Images from Photoshop

Update Images from Photoshop

Insert Images from Fireworks

Optimize Images Using Fireworks

Use Low Source Images

Modify Images

Align Images

Edit Images

Change Image Brightness and Contrast

Change Image Sharpness

Crop an Image

Use an External Editor

Set File Types/Editors Preferences

Create Rollover Images

Insert an Image Placeholder

Using Web Friendly Graphics

The Internet did not always support the use of graphics. As a matter of fact, its original use was for sharing of textual data among scientists and the U.S. Military. That was yesterday... Today, the Internet supports static graphics, animations, video, and audio, along with all that textual data.

Preparing images for the Internet involves knowing what file formats are best to use for the Internet. Web friendly formats are designed to help the image appear good, load as quickly as possible, be compatible with all the major browsers on the market, and work seamlessly on any operating system (Macintosh, Windows, etc).

The formats that meet those requirements are then submitted to the World Wide Web Consortium, the international organization that controls and organizes the Internet. If they put their blessing on the format, it becomes a Web standard, and then all the browser manufacturers scramble to make their browsers compatible with that format. Eventually, the new browsers find their way into the marketplace, and designers begin using the formats in their Web pages.

The three major file formats that are considered the standard for static images are: GIF, JPEG, and PNG.

Depending on the type of image, and how you're using it, each one of these formats has their advantages and disadvantages.

The GIF Format

Short for Graphics Interchange Format, the GIF format (pronounced, jiff) is a unique Web compression technique that supports 8-bit images with a maximum of 256 colors. GIF is for images with distinct colors, such as line drawings, black and white images and small text groups that are only a few pixels high. With an animation editor, such as Adobe Fireworks, GIF images can be put together for animated images. GIF also supports transparency, where a color or colors can be set to transparent in order to let the color on the underlying Web page to show through. The compression algorithm used in the GIF format is called RLE (Run Length Encoding). This compression algorithm works best with solid colors, like you would encounter in clipart, or text; and since most clipart does not include many colors, the 256 maximum color restriction works just fine.

The GIF format is also considered lossless. In other words, images saved in the GIF format will be compressed without the removal of any color information. Therefore, when they're displayed on the visitor's browser, the image will be exactly what you saved, in terms of quality.

The JPEG Format

Short for Joint Photographic Experts Group, the JPEG (pronounced j-peg) is a Web format designed primarily for the compression and display of photographs. JPEGs allow for 24-bit images using millions of colors. To make JPEGs usable, the large amount of color information must be compressed, which is accomplished by removing what the compression algorithm considers unneeded information. JPEG compression is "lossy," meaning that the compression scheme sacrifices some image quality, in exchange for a reduction in the file's size. JPEG files can range from small amounts of lossless compression to large amounts of lossy compression. This is a common standard on the Web, but the data loss generated in its compression makes it undesirable for printing purposes. JPEG images do not support any level of transparency, and will fill transparent areas of the image with a user-defined matte color.

Once an image has been compressed using the JPEG format and saved, the color information that was removed can never be recovered. Therefore, it's best when editing an image to save a copy as the JPEG, so as to retain the original image information.

The PNG Format

Short for Portable Network Graphic, (pronounced ping) the PNG format was designed to be a patent-free successor to the GIF format. Though not designed specifically for the Web, PNG offers particular benefits in this environment such as improved image compression (10 to 30 percent smaller than the GIF format), two dimensional interlacing, storage of text with the image making it possible for search engines to gather information and offer subject searching for images in a standard way. In addition, the PNG format is used for lossless compression and displaying images on the web.

The PNG format comes in two sizes, the PNG-8 (used in place of the GIF format), and the PNG-24 (used in place of the JPEG format).

The advantages of PNG are that it supports images with millions of colors and produces background transparency without jagged edges. The disadvantages are that PNG images will not show up on older browsers (pre 4.0), and when using the full PNG-24 format with transparency, they can be comparatively larger in file size than JPEG images.

One other interesting feature of the PNG format is its ability to adjust the gamma of an image across operating systems. Typically, an image will display differently on a Mac or Windows monitor. The PNG format adjusts the image so that it appears the same... regardless of operating system.

Adobe Fireworks and Adobe Flash use the PNG as their native format, so that means all the power of the format, including transparency, and opacity settings are fully supported.

Defining an Image Folder

It's important to set up a folder within your site folder that holds all of the images for a specific Web project. Creating this folder can be accomplished when you set up the site, or it can be made later. There are several advantages to setting up an image folder: it helps Dreamweaver in the organization of your site, and helps you locate images when you need to work on them. Since we're about to start adding images to our site, it's a good idea to stop and define this folder. Once the folder is created, you should copy all of your Web images into this folder. In addition, when you attempt to add an image to a Web page that is outside the site folder, Dreamweaver prompts you to copy the file to your site, and when you do, it adds the new images into the defined folder. All things considered, creating an image folder is a smart, efficient thing to do.

Define an Image Folder

① Open your site folder, and create a new folder.

In this example, we'll use the obvious and call the new folder, Images.

② Click the **Site** menu, and then click **Manage Sites**.

③ Select your site from the available options.

④ Click **Edit**.

⑤ Click the **Advanced Settings** category.

⑥ Click the **Local Info** category.

⑦ Click the **Browse For Folder** icon located to the right of the Default Images Folder Input box.

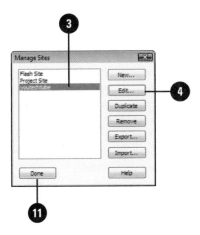

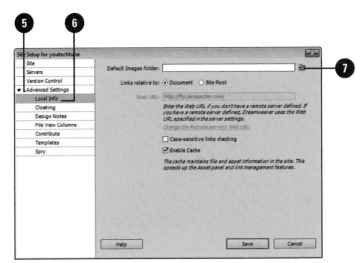

8 Navigate to the Local root folder, and then select the Images folder you want to use.

9 Click **Select** (Win) or **Choose** (Mac) to record the folder's location, and exit the Search dialog box.

10 Click **Save** to close the Site Setup dialog box, and then click **OK**, if necessary to recreate the cache.

11 Click **Done** to save your changes.

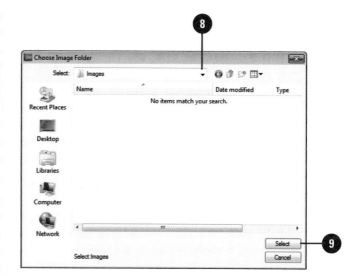

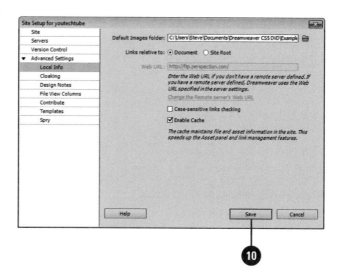

Inserting Images

The three basic elements of any static Web page are text, images, and links. Adding a static image to a Web page can be as simple as a drag and a drop. By the way, the term "static" simply refers to any non-moving Web image. A static image is not video; it does not dance, move, or sing… it just sits there. You can also add dynamic images, which are images that change. For example, an advertising banner cycles through different images. Images can be added directly to a Web page or they can be added within a section of text: called an inline image. Dreamweaver gives you several ways to add images to your Web pages. The method you choose to add images depends on how you like to work with Dreamweaver. Any time you add an image to a Web page, Dreamweaver (by default) asks you to type in a description, and alternate text. This information is used by screen reader applications (i.e. JAWS) for visually impaired users; therefore it's important that this information is added to the image.

Insert an Image

1. Open the Web page you want to insert an image.

2. Click to place the insertion point where you want to place the image.

3. Using one of the following methods to insert an image:

   ◆ **Assets Panel.** Open the Assets panel, select the image you want to add to the page, and then drag the thumbnail, or filename of the image into the Web page.

   ◆ **Folder.** Open a folder on your desktop that contains Web friendly images, and then click and drag from the folder directly into the Web page.

   ◆ **Insert Panel.** Click the **Common** tab on the Insert panel, click the **Image** button arrow, click **Image**, select the image from the available options, and then click **OK**.

   ◆ **Insert Menu.** Click the **Insert** menu, click **Image**, select the image from the available options, and then click **OK**.

Select Image Source dialog box

Insert Menu option

Select the image you want to insert.

④ If the image you selected is not contained within the site folder, click **Yes** to the alert asking for permission to make a copy of the image, and place it within the site folder, and then click **Save** in the Copy File As dialog box.

The Image Tag Accessibility Attributes dialog box opens.

⑤ Click in the Alternate Text Input field and type a very short description for the image.

For example, if the image is of a cell phone, you might enter the words, Image of a cell phone, or just, cell phone.

NOTE *If you prefer to leave this field blank, click the arrow to the right of the input box, and select the empty option.*

⑥ Click the file folder icon, located to the right of the Long Description input box, and then select the file that contains a longer description of the image.

NOTE *The Long Description option is a plain text document, which contains a longer description of the image. For example, if the image is of a sunset, you could describe the place and time the image was captured. Remember, the alternate text and long description are primarily used by the visually impaired. This file should be created in a text processor, saved as plain text, and placed inside the site folder.*

⑦ Click **OK** to add the image to the Web page.

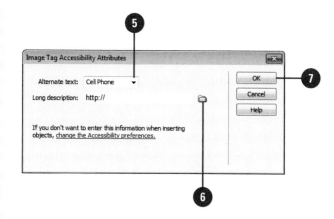

Inserted image

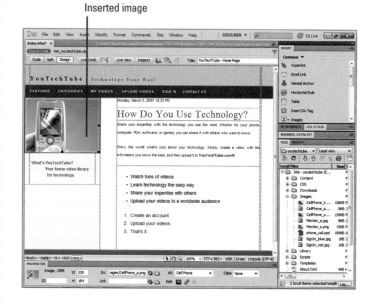

Inserting Images from Photoshop

After you create or modify images in Adobe Photoshop in the PSD format, you can quickly copy and paste all or part of a multi-layered or multi-sliced image or insert the entire PSD file directly into Dreamweaver. Dreamweaver handles the integration and optimizes them as Web-ready images in the selected format (GIF, JPEG, or PNG formats). Before you insert a PSD (or any other image) into a Web page, you should store the file along with the site files, so the link (relative path) to the file is always available and the file gets published when the time comes. When you insert the entire PSD file, Dreamweaver creates a Smart Object that maintains a live connection with Photoshop. This live connection allows you to update changes from the original image with the click of a button in Dreamweaver. When you copy and paste, a live connection is not maintained. Any changes to the original need to be manually updated again. However, Dreamweaver does remember your optimization setting when you re-paste it or use the Edit button in the Properties panel.

Create a Smart Object from a Photoshop File

1. Open a Web page you want to insert an image.

2. Click within the document where you want the image inserted.

3. Click the **Insert** menu, and then click **Image**.

   ◆ You can also drag the PSD file from the Files panel (if available) to the Web page.

4. Navigate to and select the PSD image you want, and then click **OK** (Win) or **Open** (Mac).

5. Click the **Options** tab, and then specify the format, quality, and smoothing options you want.

6. Click the **File** tab, and then specify the scale options you want.

7. Click **OK**.

8. If prompted, locate the Images folder on your local root site, save the image, and then specify Input Accessibility options.

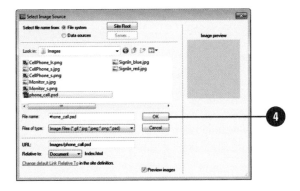

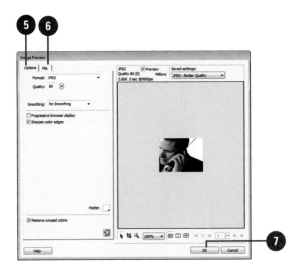

Copy and Paste All or Part of an Image from Photoshop

① Open the image you want to copy in Photoshop (PSD format).

② Select the image, layer, or slice.

③ Click the **Edit** menu, and then click **Copy**.

④ Exit Photoshop.

⑤ Open a Web page in Dreamweaver that you want to insert an image.

⑥ Click within the document where you want the image inserted.

⑦ Click the **Edit** menu, and then click **Paste**.

The Image Preview dialog box opens.

⑧ Click the **Options** tab, and then specify the format, quality, and smoothing options you want.

⑨ Click the **File** tab, and then specify the scale options you want.

⑩ Click **OK**.

⑪ If prompted, locate the Images folder on your local root site, save the image, and then specify Input Accessibility options.

⑫ To edit the pasted image, select it, and then click the **Edit** button in the Properties panel.

Did You Know?

You can change Image Preview optimization settings. If you want to change optimization settings after you insert an image, you can use the Edit Image Settings button in the Properties panel to open the Image Preview dialog and make the changes you want.

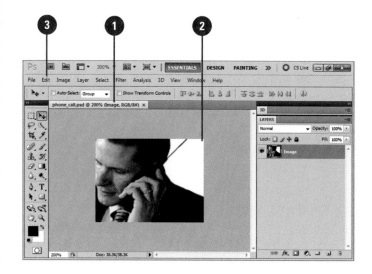

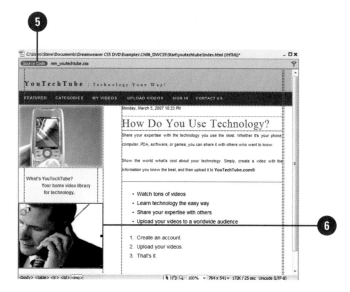

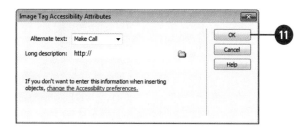

Updating Images from Photoshop

After you insert a Photoshop (PSD) file into a Web page, Dreamweaver creates a Smart Object that maintains a live connection with the original file in Photoshop. This live connection allows you to update changes from the original image with the click of a button in Dreamweaver. Any changes you make in Dreamweaver to the Smart Object do not affect the original Photoshop file. When you create a Smart Object from Photoshop, Dreamweaver displays an icon in the upper-left corner of the image. When the object in Dreamweaver and the original file in Photoshop are the same, both of the arrows in the icon are green. When the original file in Photoshop is different than the Smart Object in Dreamweaver, one of the arrows in the icon changes to red, which indicates you need to update it.

Update a Smart Object from a Photoshop File

1. Open a Web page in Dreamweaver that contains text.

2. Select the Smart Object image derived from a Photoshop PSD file.

3. Click **Edit Image** in the Properties panel.

   Dreamweaver opens the source file in Photoshop.

4. Make the changes you want, save the file, and then exit Photoshop.

   NOTE *If you're getting a PSD file from another person and don't have Photoshop installed on your computer, you can still make the update from Dreamweaver.*

5. Select the Smart Object.

   A red icon appears in the upper-left corner of the Smart Object.

6. Click the **Update from Original** button in the Document window.

   The red icon turns to green, indicating the Photoshop file and the Smart Object are the same.

Update Smart Object

Update Multiple Smart Objects

① In Photoshop, open the linked images (PSD) that you want to update in Dreamweaver, make changes to the files, save them, and then exit Photoshop.

② Open a Web page in Dreamweaver that you want to insert an image.

③ Open the **Files** panel, and then click the **Assets** tab to view the site assets.

④ Click the **Images** button to display Images view.

⑤ Select the image assets in the Assets panel that you want to update. You can use Control-click to select multiple filenames.

The Smart Objects display an icon in the upper left corner.

⑥ Right-click (Win) or option-click (Mac) one of the selected filenames, and then click **Update from Original**.

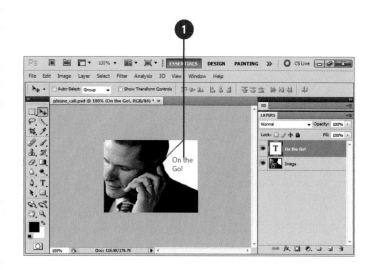

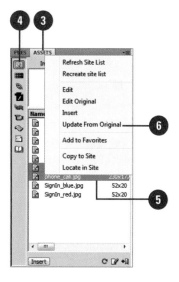

Updated Smart Object

Inserting Images from Fireworks

After you create or modify images in Adobe Fireworks in the PNG format, you can quickly copy and paste or insert them directly into Dreamweaver. Dreamweaver handles the integration and optimizes them as Web-ready images in the selected format (GIF, JPEG, or PNG formats). You can also paste images into a Web page. After you insert images into a Web page, you can edit the source image in Fireworks and update the image in Dreamweaver.

Copy and Paste Images from Fireworks

① Open the image you want to copy in Fireworks (PNG format).

② Select the image, layer, or slice.

③ Click the **Edit** menu, and then click **Copy**.

④ Exit Fireworks.

⑤ Open a Web page in Dreamweaver that you want to insert an image.

⑥ Click within the document where you want the image inserted.

⑦ Click the **Edit** menu, and then click **Paste**.

The Image Preview dialog box opens.

⑧ Click the **Options** tab, and then specify the format, quality, and smoothing options you want.

⑨ Click the **File** tab, and then specify the scale options you want.

⑩ Click **OK**.

⑪ If prompted, locate the Images folder on your local root site, and save the image, and then specify Input Accessibility options.

The image is inserted into the document with the specified format and settings.

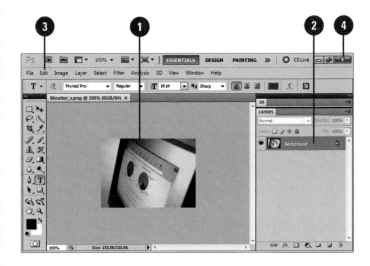

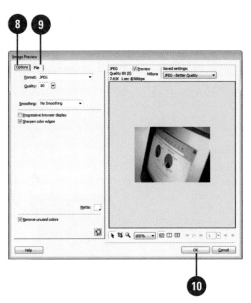

Insert Images from Fireworks

1. Open a Web page you want to insert an image.

2. Click within the document where you want the image inserted.

3. Click the **Insert** menu, and then click **Image**.

4. Navigate to and select the image you want (.PNG), and then click **OK** (Win) or **Open** (Mac).

5. Click the **Options** tab, and then specify the format, quality, and smoothing options you want.

6. Click the **File** tab, and then specify the scale options you want.

7. Click **OK**.

8. If prompted, locate the Images folder on your local root site, and save the image, and then specify Input Accessibility options.

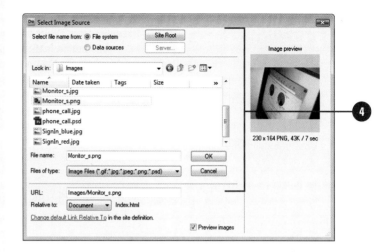

Update Images from Fireworks

1. Open a Web page in Dreamweaver that contains text.

2. Select the image derived from a Fireworks PNG file.

3. Click **Edit Image** in the Properties panel.

    Dreamweaver opens the source file in Fireworks.

4. Make the changes you want, and then save the file.

5. Select all or part of the image, copy it to the Clipboard, and then exit Fireworks.

    The image is optimized and updated.

Optimizing Images Using Fireworks

If you have Adobe Fireworks installed on your computer, you can use the program to optimize an image in a Web page from within Dreamweaver. When you select an image, you can use the Optimize In Fireworks button in the Properties panel or the Fireworks command on the Image submenu on the Modify menu.

Optimize an Image Using Fireworks

1. Open a Web page with the image you want to optimize.

2. Select the image you want.

3. Click the **Window** menu, and then click **Properties** to display the Properties panel.

4. Click the **Optimize In Fireworks** button in the Properties panel, or click the **Modify** menu, point to **Image**, point to **Edit With**, and then click **Fireworks**.

5. Confirm whether to optimize as a PNG file or use the open image file.

6. Edit the image file.

7. Click **Done**.

8. Click **Update**.

9. Click the **File** menu, and then click **Save**.

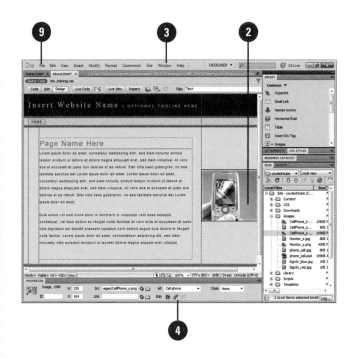

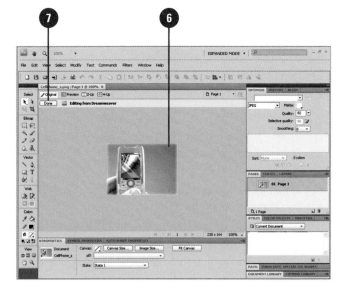

Using Low Source Images

Loading graphics onto a Web page has a good and a bad side. The good side is that images spice up an otherwise dull and drab Web site. The bad side is that images take up file space and increase download times. It's a catch-22 situation; your visitors expect lots of graphics and cool stuff and, at the same time, expect the page to load fast. The current rule on the Internet is called the 8-second rule (it used to be the 10-second rule). In other words if your page doesn't load within 8 seconds, many of your visitors will go elsewhere. One way to make a page load quicker is to specify low source images for your graphics. Low source images are copies of the original image, but severely compressed. For example, you have an image on your Web site of the Colorado Rocky Mountains and it's 150 k. You really want to use the image; however, you know on the average browser it takes 20 seconds to download the image. So, you open a copy of the photograph in an image-editing application like Adobe Photoshop or Fireworks, and you compress the copy to the max, and you save it. In Dreamweaver, you use the image for the low-source. When the page opens in the visitor's browser, the low source image quickly loads first, and then after the page opens, the higher-quality image loads over the other image.

Use a Low Source Image

1. Open the Web page that contains the image you want to apply the low source.

2. Select the image.

3. Click the **Window** menu, and then click **Properties** to display the Properties panel.

4. Click in the **Src** box, and use one of the following options:

   - Enter the name and path of the low source image.

   - Click the **Browse For File** button, and locate the file in the Select Image Source dialog box.

   - Click the **Point To File** button, and drag over to the Assets panel. Release the mouse when you're hovering over the low source image file name.

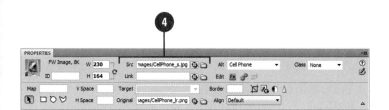

Modifying Images

Once an image is placed into a Web page, Dreamweaver gives you the ability to modify the document in two ways: temporary and permanent. For example, you can adjust the size of the image temporarily by adjusting the width and height statements in the Properties panel or by directly accessing the <img> tab. You can even select the image, and click and drag the image at a selection handle to change its relative size. Unfortunately, while the size of the file on the page might change, an image saved on the hard drive does not. This causes problems with the download of the image to the visitor's site, as well as displaying the image within the visitor's browser. The best way to modify an image is to plan out what you need ahead of time, and then place the image into the Web page. That's a nice plan; however, many times, designs change during the course of the creation process, and what worked for an image yesterday might not work today. With that in mind, Dreamweaver gives you the ability to modify the image whenever necessary. After you resize an image, you can reset the size or resample it to add and subtract pixels to match the appearance of the resized image.

Resize an Image

1. Open a Web page, and then select the image you want to modify.

2. Click the **Window** menu, and then click **Properties** to display the Properties panel.

3. Use any of the following resize methods:

   ◆ **Width or Height.** Drag a selection handle.

   ◆ **Proportions.** Shift-drag a corner selection handle.

   ◆ **Specific Size.** Click in the **W** and **H** boxes to change the size of the image width and height (in pixels).

4. To resample a resized image, click the **Resample** button in the Properties panel.

5. To return a resize image to its original size, click the **Reset Size** button in the Properties panel or delete the values in the W and H boxes in the Properties panel.

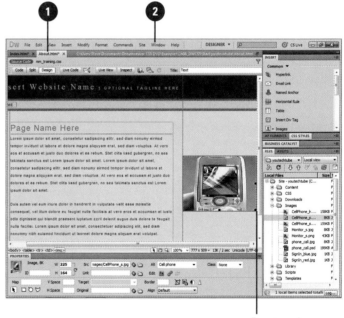

Drag to resize

Modify an Image Using the Properties panel

1. Open a Web page, and then select the image you want to modify.

2. Click the **Window** menu, and then click **Properties** to display the Properties panel.

3. Click in the **Border** box to add a border to the active image, as measured in pixels.

4. Click in the **V Space**, and **H Space** boxes to offset your images by adding vertical or horizontal white space (in pixels).

5. Click in the **Image Name** box to give the image a specific name. This is useful when calling the image using JavaScript.

6. Click in the **Alt** box to give the image the alternate text used by reader applications for the visually impaired.

    NOTE *In some browsers the Alt text is displayed in the empty box defined by the browser as the image loads.*

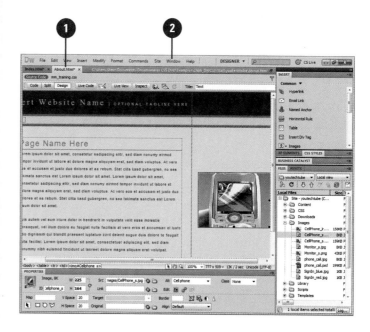

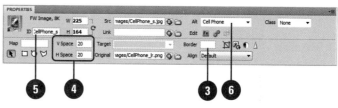

Did You Know?

You can edit image accessibility options. Edit the appropriate image attributes in Code view, edit the Alt box in the Properties panel, or right-click (Win) or control-click (Mac) the image, and then click Edit Tag.

Aligning Images

When you place an image into a Dreamweaver document, the default placement of the image is to the left and middle of the container area, which is a blank Web page, a table cell, or layer. Not only is alignment performed on images isolated within a container; they're also aligned according to adjacent images, or text.

Align an Image Using the Properties panel

① Open a Web page, and then select the image you want to modify.

② Click the **Window** menu, and then click **Properties** to display the Properties panel.

③ Click the **Align** list arrow, and then select one of the following align options:

♦ **Browser Default.** No alignment attribute is included in the <img> tag. Most browsers use the baseline as the alignment default.

♦ **Baseline.** The bottom of the image is aligned with the baseline of the surrounding text.

♦ **Top.** The top of the image is aligned with the top of the tallest object in the current line.

♦ **Middle.** The middle of the image is aligned with the baseline of the current line.

♦ **Bottom.** The bottom of the image is aligned with the baseline of the surrounding text.

♦ **Text Top.** The top of the image is aligned with the tallest letter or object in the current line.

♦ **Absolute Middle.** The middle of the image is aligned with the middle of the tallest text or object in the current line.

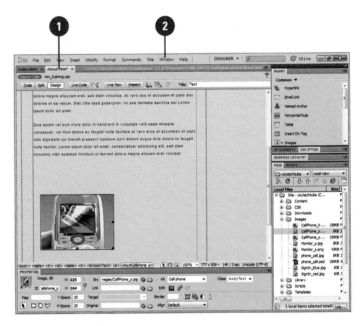

◆ **Absolute Bottom.** The bottom of the image is aligned with the descenders (as in y, g, p, and so forth) that fall below the current baseline.

◆ **Left.** The image is aligned to the left edge of the browser or table cell, and all text in the current line flows around the right side of the image.

◆ **Right**. The image is aligned to the right edge of the browser or table cell, and all text in the current line flows around the left side of the image.

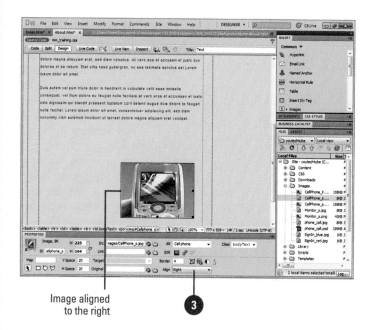

Image aligned to the right

Editing Images

When you place an image into a Dreamweaver document, there's a good chance that the image was first processed in another application. For example, you might use Adobe Fireworks or Photoshop to prep photographs. If you planned out the Web project, you'll be able to drop that image into the Web page, and it will fit like the proverbial glove. Unfortunately, you might not be the one creating the images; or it's possible that you need to make a change. While it's always desirable to edit an image in the originating application, Dreamweaver gives you the ability to make minor changes to the image. For example, you can use Dreamweaver's new optimize feature (Hint: If you've ever used Photoshop's and Illustrator's Save For Web feature, you're halfway there). In addition, you can resize the image to fit a specific width and height. When you edit an image in Dreamweaver, you're actually making permanent changes to the original, and Dreamweaver lets you know as you work.

Use Optimize

1. Open the Web page with the image you want to edit.

2. Select the image you want to modify.

3. Click the **Modify** menu, point to **Image**, and then click **Optimize**.

4. Click the **Options** tab to utilize the following options:

   ◆ Format. Click the **Format** list arrow, and then select a format from the available options.

   ◆ Palette. Click the **Palette** box, and then select a color palette from the available options.

   ◆ Loss. Set to zero by default (not applicable PNG-8 images).

   ◆ Dither. Select the **Dither** check box, and then set the dither percentage you want from zero to 100 percent. The dither option helps to visually approximate colors that are not in the original image.

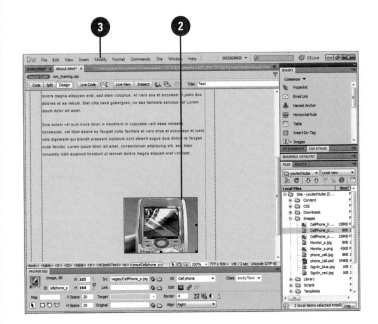

- **Color Value.** Enter a value that represents the maximum number of colors in the image (2-256), and then adjust the colors (optional) in the color box.

- **Transparency.** Click the **Transparency** list arrow, and then click **No Transparency**, **Index Transparency** (based on available colors), or **Alpha Transparency** (based on an alpha mask).

- **Eyedropper.** Click the **Select Transparent Color** button, and then click in the Index Color box to choose the image colors to be made transparent. You can also use the other eyedropper buttons to add or remove a color from the transparency.

- **Remove Unused Colors.** Select the **Remove Unused Colors** check box to remove any unused colors from the color box.

- **Interlaced Browser Display.** Select the **Interlaced Browser Display** check box to display (load) images in the client browser at low resolution and then progressively increases to full resolution.

- **Optimize To Size.** Click the **Optimize To Size** button to specify the desired size of the image. In turn, Dreamweaver attempts to optimize the image to the selected size.

Continue Next Page

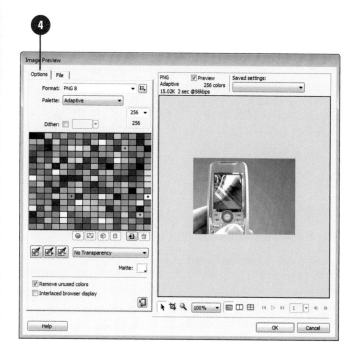

For Your Information

Preparing Images for the Web

There are several differences between preparing images for the Web and for print documents. The major differences include: (1) Web images are typically saved at 72 dpi (dots per inch), while print images are generally saved at 300 dpi, (2) Web images are saved using the RGB (Red, Green, Blue) color system, while print images are CMYK (Cyan, Magenta, Yellow, Black) color mode, and (3) Web images are saved to JPEG, GIF, or PNG format (which you can create or modify in Photoshop, Illustrator, and Fireworks), while print images are typically saved in the TIFF format.

Continued from Previous Page

5️⃣ Click the **File** tab to utilize the
following options:

◆ **%.** Enter a value from 2 to 200
percent, or drag the slider to
change the size of the image,
based on a percentage value.

◆ **W and H.** Enter a value (in
pixels) to change the width and
height of the image.

◆ **Constrain.** Select the **Constrain**
check box to keep the width
and height in proportion.

◆ **Export Area.** Select the **Export
Area** check box to crop the
image using x and y, or w
(width) and h (height) values.
Alternately, you can click on
the image in the Preview
window, and use the corner
and side anchor points to the
manually adjust the image.

6️⃣ Select from the following Preview
options:

◆ **Preview.** Select the **Preview**
check box to toggle the
preview of the image.

◆ **Saved Settings.** Click the **Saved
Settings** list arrow, and then
select from the preset
optimization options.

◆ **Select.** Click the **Pointer** button
to select and move a cropped
image in the Preview window.

◆ **Crop.** Click the **Export Area**
button to crop the active image.
Use the Hand cursor to specify
the area you want.

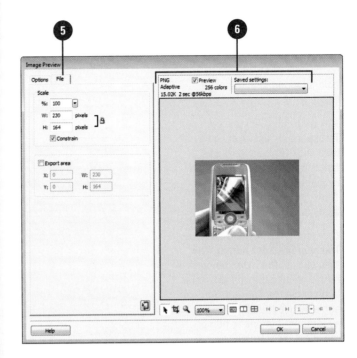

◆ **Zoom.** Click the **Zoom in/out** button, and then click the image to zoom the preview of the active image in (plus sign in magnifying glass) or press Alt (Win) or Option (Mac) and click the image to zoom the preview of the active image out (minus sign in magnifying glass), or click the **Zoom** list arrow, and then select a preset zoom value.

◆ **Preview Display.** Click a button to change the view to display 1, 2 or 4 images.

◆ **Image display.** Click a button to control the view of multiple images used in animations.

NOTE *When you click the Options tab and select a different format, you see new options based on the selected format. In this example, the options displayed reflected the modification of a GIF image.*

7 Click **OK**.

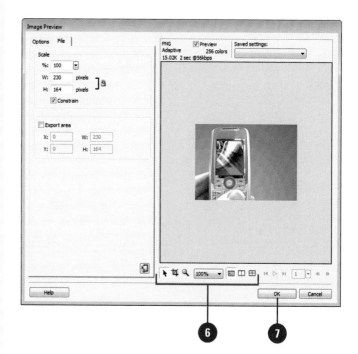

Changing Image Brightness and Contrast

And if that were not all, you can change the brightness and contrast of the image, and increase its sharpness. Once you have inserted an image into a Web page, you can adapt them to meet your needs. Perhaps you don't quite like the colors it uses. You can increase or decrease the brightness of the image, as well as the color contrast. The Brightness/Contrast adjustment changes an image by an overall lightening or darkening of the image pixels. While good for special effects, its linear way of changing an image's brightness and contrast do not lend themselves to photo restoration.

Change Image Brightness and Contrast

1. Open the Web page with the image you want to modify.

2. Select the image you want to modify.

3. Click the **Modify** menu, point to **Image**, and then click **Brightness/Contrast**.

    TIMESAVER *Click the Brightness and Contrast button in the Properties panel.*

4. Select from the following options:

    ◆ **Brightness.** Click and drag the slider to change the overall brightness of the selected image (-100 - 100).

    ◆ **Contrast.** Click and drag the slider to change the overall contrast of the selected image (-100 - 100).

    ◆ **Preview.** Select to toggle the preview of the image in the display window.

5. Click **OK**.

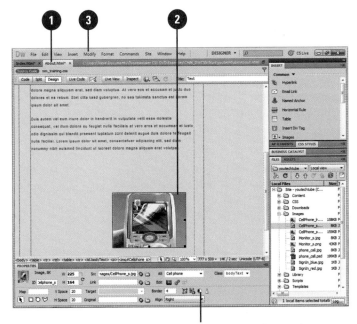

Brightness and Contrast button

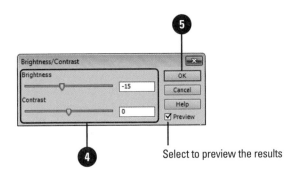

Select to preview the results

Changing Image Sharpness

If you have an image that looks a little fuzzy in spots, you can use the Sharpen command to create more image definition. Sharpening increases the contrast of pixels around the edges of objects in an image to increase the image's definition or sharpness. If you don't like the sharpening effect applied to an image, you can use the Undo command on the Edit menu before you save the image to revert the image back to the original.

Change Image Sharpness

1. Open the Web page with the image you want to modify.

2. Select the image you want to modify.

3. Click the **Modify** menu, point to **Image**, and then click **Sharpen**.

   TIMESAVER *Click the Sharpen button in the Properties panel.*

   NOTE *An alert may appear warning you that the changes you are about to make are permanent. Click OK to continue.*

4. Select from the following options:

   ◆ **Sharpen.** Click and drag the slider to increase the sharpness of the active image (0-10).

   ◆ **Preview.** Select to toggle the preview of the image in the display window.

5. Click **OK**.

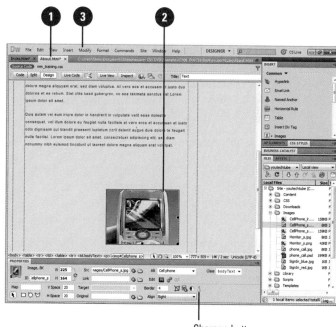

Sharpen button

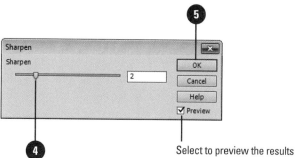

Select to preview the results

Cropping an Image

Cropping is the process of framing a portion of a photo and eliminating any unnecessary visual elements. If, for example, you have a photo that is not centered properly, you can crop out the side to center it. You can use the Crop button in the Properties panel to drag a resize handle on a graphic to crop out part of the image. The graphic remains unchanged and you can uncrop it at any time.

Crop an Image

1. Open the Web page with the image you want to modify.

2. Select the image you want to modify.

3. Click the **Modify** menu, point to **Image**, and then click **Crop**.

    TIMESAVER *Click the Crop button in the Properties panel.*

    NOTE *An alert may appear warning you that the changes you are about to make are permanent. Click OK to continue.*

4. Crop the image by clicking and dragging any of the 4 corners, or 4 side control points.

5. Click in the middle of the image and drag to move the crop window.

6. Double-click the image or press Enter (Win) or Return (Mac) to set the crop, or press the Esc (Escape) key to cancel.

    NOTE *Although the cropping function is permanent, you can always click the Edit menu, and then click Undo to return the image back to its original state.*

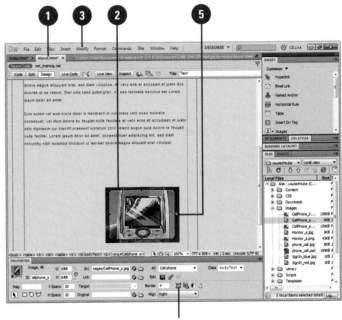

Crop button

Using an External Editor

Dreamweaver may give you some new and improved ways to edit an image; however, there's no substitute for the real thing. The two most powerful image-editing applications for raster-based (resolution dependent) images are Adobe Photoshop and Fireworks. You might recall an application that came bundled with Photoshop called ImageReady... well, that application is no longer part of the Adobe family, being replaced by Fireworks. While Adobe would prefer that you use one of these two applications to edit your images, they know full well that there are other fish in the sea, so they not only give you the ability to edit images in Photoshop or Fireworks, they give you the ability to choose any application you want.

Edit an Image in an External Editor

1. Open the Web page with the image you want to edit.

2. Select the image you want to edit.

3. Click the **Modify** menu, point to **Image**, point to **Edit With**, and then select one of the following options:

   ◆ **Photoshop.** Opens the selected image in Adobe Photoshop.

   ◆ **Fireworks.** Opens the selected image in Adobe Fireworks.

   ◆ **Browse.** Opens an Explorer (Win) or Finder (Mac) window and allows you to select the application to use.

   TIMESAVER *Double-click the image you want to edit using the default external image editor.*

4. Make the changes to the image, based on the selected application.

5. Click the **File** menu, and then click **Save**.

6. Click the **Close** button in the editing program and return to Dreamweaver.

   The changes are permanently applied to the image in Dreamweaver, which cannot be undone.

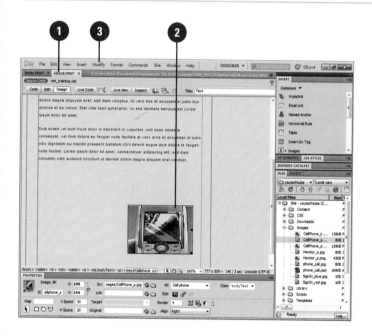

Setting File Types/ Editors Preferences

You can use the File Types/Editors section of the Preferences dialog box to choose the external image editor you want to use for specific file types. Setting specific external image editors for specific file types makes it quick and easy to edit images. All you need to do is double-click the image and the external image editor automatically opens. Any changes you make and save in an external image editor are displayed when you return to Dreamweaver. You can set different file types to open in different external editors, including Dreamweaver for script files. In addition, you can set Fireworks as your primary external editor for those extensions not specified.

Set File Type and Editor Preferences

1. Click the **Dreamweaver** (Mac) or **Edit** (Win) menu, and then click **Preferences**.

2. Click the **File Types / Editors** category.

3. Select the file extension you want to set an external editor, or add new extensions.

    ◆ Add Extension. Click the **Add** (+) button above the Extensions list, type an extension, and then press Enter (Win) or Return (Mac).

4. Select from the following options:

    ◆ Remove Editor. Select an editor, and then click the **Delete** (-) button above the Editors list.

    ◆ Add Editor. Click the **Add** (+) button above the Editors list, select the editor you want, and then click **Open**.

5. To make the editor the primary editor for the selected files, click **Make Primary**.

6. Click **OK**.

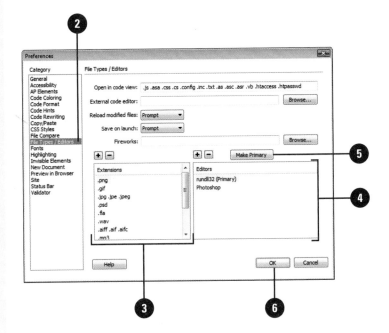

Set Other File Type and Editor Preferences

1. Click the **Dreamweaver** (Mac) or **Edit** (Win) menu, and then click **Preferences**.

2. Click the **File Types / Editors** category.

3. Click the **Reload Modified Files** list arrow, and then select the option you want: **Always**, **Never**, or **Prompt**.

4. Click the **Save On Launch** list arrow, and then select the option you want: **Always**, **Never**, or **Prompt**.

5. To set the primary external editor for file types not specified, click **Browse** next to the Fireworks box, select the Fireworks program, and then click **Open**.

6. To open script related files in Code view in Dreamweaver, enter the file types (separated by a space) in the Open In Code View box.

7. To open script related files in an external editor, click **Browse** next to the External Code Editor box, select the program you want, and then click **Open**.

8. Click **OK**.

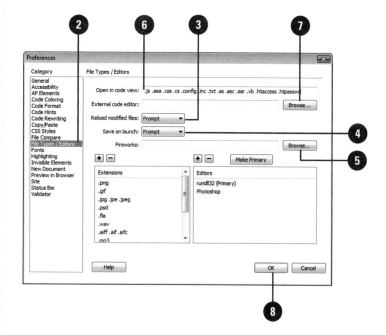

Creating Rollover Images

Dreamweaver makes the insertion and creation of rollover images a snap. A rollover is an image that—when viewed in a browser—changes when the pointer moves across or hovers over it. You need two separate images to create the rollover: a primary (the image that displays when the page first loads) and a secondary (the image that appears when the pointer moves over the primary). Both images in a rollover should be the same size; if the images are not the same size, Dreamweaver resizes the secondary image to match the width and height properties of the primary image. In reality, rollover images are set to respond to a onMouseOver event; although you can change what event triggers the action (for example, a mouse click). Rollover images are used extensively in the creation of user-friendly navigation buttons. For example, you have a button that returns the user to the site's home page; when they roll over the image, it changes from a gray button with the word, HOME, in white, to a gray button with the word, HOME, in yellow.

Create a Rollover Image

1. Open the Web page you want to insert a rollover image.

2. Click to place the insertion point where you want to create a rollover image.

3. Click the **Insert** menu, point to **Image Objects**, and then click **Rollover Image**.

   TIMESAVER *Click the Image button arrow on the Common tab on the Insert bar, and then click Rollover Image.*

4. Select from the following options:

   ◆ Image Name. The name of the rollover image. This is the image's JavaScript call name.

   ◆ Original Image. The image you want to display when the page loads. Enter the path in the text box, or click **Browse** to select the image.

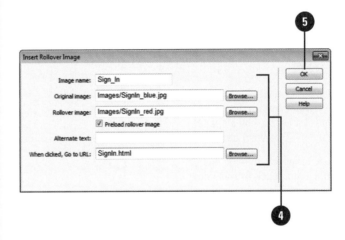

For Your Information

Customizing a Rollover Image

The Image Name is used when creating specific JavaScript routines; for example, you could create a JavaScript routine to change the look of the button based on the time of day. If you are not planning on creating a JavaScript routine, it's best to leave the name at its default value.

◆ **Rollover Image.** The image you want to display when the pointer rolls over the original image. Enter the path or click **Browse** to select the image.

◆ **Preload Rollover Image.** Select to preload the images in the browser's cache so no delay occurs when the user rolls the pointer over the image (recommended).

◆ **Alternate Text.** Text to describe the image for viewers using a text-only browser, or for the visually impaired (optional).

◆ **When Clicked Go to URL.** The file that you want to open when a user clicks the rollover image. Enter the path or click **Browse** and select the file.

⑤ Click **OK** to add the button to the active document.

NOTE *If you don't set a link for the image, Dreamweaver inserts a null link (#) in the HTML source code to which the rollover behavior is attached. If you remove the null link, the rollover image will not work.*

NOTE *You cannot see the effect of a rollover image in Design view.*

⑥ To see the effect in a browser, click the **File** menu, point to **Preview In Browser**, and then select the browser you to use.

Did You Know?

You can create buttons on the Web. Check out *www.cooltext.com* to create buttons with your own text. The buttons are free and you can download them in the .JPG format.

Rollover button

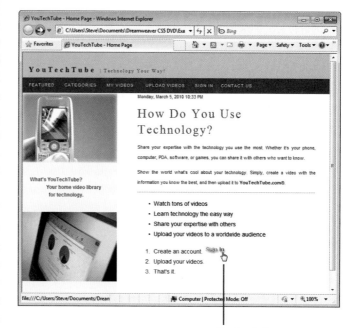

Preview in browser

Inserting an Image Placeholder

If you know you want to insert an image in a specific location, but the image is not created or ready yet, you can insert an image placeholder in its place. You can set the placeholder's size and color, and even add a text label to it. When you insert an image placeholder, the placeholder box appears, displaying the color, size, and label you selected. After you insert an image placeholder, you can use the Properties panel to change specific image related properties, such as name, width, height, alternative text description, alignment, and color. When you're ready to replace the image placeholder with an actual image, you can double-click the placeholder or use the Src box in the Properties panel to select the image.

Insert an Image Placeholder

1. Open the Web page you want to insert an image placeholder.

2. Click to place the insertion point where you want to place the image.

3. Click the **Insert** menu, point to **Image Objects**, and then click **Image Placeholder**.

   The Image Placeholder dialog box opens.

4. Specify the image placeholder options you want:

   ◆ Name. Enter the text you want to appear as a label (optional). Leave blank if you don't want a label.

   ◆ Width and Height. Enter the width and height (in pixels) to set the image size.

   ◆ Color. Click the **Color** box to select a color, or enter the hexadecimal value for the color.

   ◆ Alternate Text. Enter text to describe the image for viewers using a text-only browser or for the visually impaired who use speech synthesizers (optional).

5. Click **OK**.

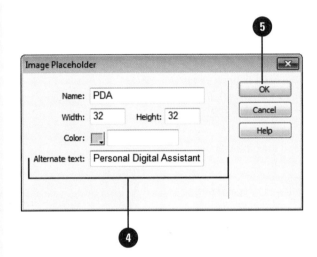

Set Image Placeholder Properties

1. Open a Web page, and then select the image you want to modify.

2. Click the **Window** menu, and then click **Properties** to display the Properties panel.

3. Specify the image placeholder related options you want:

   ◆ Name. Enter the text you want to appear as a label (optional). Leave blank if you don't want a label.

   ◆ W and H. Enter the width and height (in pixels) to set the image size.

   ◆ Src. Specify the source file for the image. Drag the **Point To File** button to a file in the Files panel or click the **Browse For Files** button to select a file.

   ◆ Link. Specify a hyperlink for the image placeholder. Drag the **Point To File** button to a file in the Files panel or click the **Browse For Files** button to select a file.

   ◆ Color. Click the **Color** box to select a color, or enter the hexadecimal value for the color.

   ◆ Alt. Enter text to describe the image for viewers using a text-only browser or for the visually impaired who use speech synthesizers (optional).

   ◆ Create. Click the **Create** button to start Fireworks to create a replacement image. The button is disabled if Fireworks is not installed on your computer.

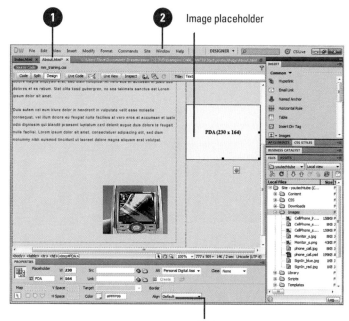

Image placeholder

Click to create an image in Fireworks.

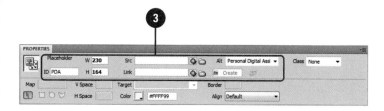

Linking Web Pages

Introduction

Static Web pages are composed of three basic elements: text, images, and links. Dynamic Web pages incorporate additional elements such as: video, animation, and/or audio. Of all of these elements, links are the primary building blocks of any Web page. If there were no links there would be no way for a visitor to control their journey through the maze of pages and sites that make up the World Wide Web. However, links are not just for moving a visitor from page to page, or site to site; in addition, links are used for transmitting emails, transferring data via FTP (file transfer protocol), and providing the ability to download data.

This chapter is devoted to creating links, modifying links, and attaching links to various outputs and URLs. Links are all about how you begin the process of making a Web page come alive.

Links come in all sizes and shapes; for example, a link can be as simple as an underlined section of text; for example, click here to go there, or it can be incorporated into a simple graphic, or even into a sophisticated JavaScript rollover. If your links are created using Flash, they can even include animation and sound.

The creation of a link is fairly straightforward... making that link intuitive to your visitor is the key to Web success. You don't want your visitors looking at a link and wondering if it is a link, or wondering what will happen if they click it.

What You'll Do

Understand Link Types

Understand Paths

Set the Relative Path

Add a Link

Add an E-mail Link

Link within a Web Page

Create Image Map Hotspots

Modify Image Map Hotspots

Create a Null or Script Link

Modify a Link

Remove a Link

Update Links

Test a Link

Change Links Sitewide

Understanding Link Types

Links come in all sizes and shapes; however, what they link to is more important than what they look like. Link types refer to the function of the link; for example, the most popular (and common) link is the standard http or HyperText Transfer Protocol. With this link you can access Web pages, images, animations, just about anything that a wandering Web visitor would like to see and experience. However, there is more to the World Wide Web then a simple jump from page to page. The following list illustrates the more common types of Web links and their usage.

telnet:// The telnet link allows a user to log onto a remote computer (called the host), and take over control. For example, computer troubleshooters, could take over control of your computer from a remote location, and fix the problem using the telnet link.

mailto: The mailto link allows a user to click and send email from a Web page. Basically, the mailto link opens a specified email application and automatically adds in the proper recipient's address.

news:// The news link connects the user to a specific newsgroup. Newsgroups are basically electronic bulletin boards; on various subjects… a newsgroup can be found for virtually any subject under the sun, and then some.

http:// The http, or HyperText Transfer Protocol, is the most common link type and allows the user to connect to any page on the Internet.

ftp:// The ftp, or File Transfer Protocol is used primarily for uploading or downloading large amounts of data. This is performed typically using an FTP server, and requires the user to have the correct username and password.

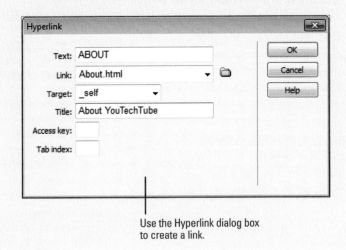

Use the Hyperlink dialog box to create a link.

Understanding Paths

When you create a link from one document to another, you need to specify the file path, or link path, to the linked document to make sure it works properly. There are three different ways to specify a link path: absolute, document-relative, and site root-relative.

An **absolute path** provides a complete URL (Uniform Resource Locator) to the linked document, including the protocol. For example, *http://www.perspection.com/books/od_books.htm.*

An absolute path is best used for linking to a document on another server. Think of an absolute path as a fixed location that doesn't change.

A **document-relative path** provides a partial path (the part not the same in URLs) to the linked document within the Web site. If you want to link to a document in the same folder, you only need to provide the file name of the linked document. You omit the part of the absolute path for both documents that are the same. For example, if you want to create a link from *http://www.perspection.com/books/od_books.htm* to *http://www.perspection.com/books/dwcs5.htm*, you can use the document-relative path *dwcs5.htm.*

If you want to create a link from the file *od_books.htm* to *http://www.perspection.com/books/download/download_dwcs5.htm*, you can use the document-relative path *download/download_dwcs5.htm*. Each slash (/..) indicates that you move down one folder level.

If you want to create a link from the file *od_books.htm* to *http://www.perspection.com/index.htm*, you can use the document-relative path *../index.htm*. Each slash (../) indicates that you move up one folder level.

A document-relative path is best used for linking to a document in the same folder or one relatively close and you don't plan on moving the documents.

A **site root-relative path** provides a path from the site's root folder to a document. A site root-relative folder starts with a forward slash (/), which indicates the root folder. For example, if you want to link to *od_books.htm*, you can use the site root-relative path */books/od_books.htm.*

A site root-relative path is best used for linking to a document on a large Web site that uses several servers or one server that hosts several sites, where the local root folder is equivalent to another remote root folder.

Setting the Relative Path

When you create a new link, you can specify the default relative path setting you want to use, either document or site root. If you already have links, setting this option doesn't convert existing links, it only applies to new links. By default, Dreamweaver sets links to use document-relative paths, which sets the path of a link relative to the current document. A site root-relative path sets links to use the complete HTTP address. If you select the Site Root option, you need to also specify the complete URL in the HTTP Address box to the site root folder on the remote site. For example, if the local root location is C:\Web Site\ and the site root location is http://www.website.com/Pub_Docs/, then the local root folder Web site is set to be equivalent to the remote root folder Pub_Docs. Content linked with a site root-relative path doesn't display when you preview pages in a browser unless you specify a testing server, or use the Preview Using Temporary File option in Preferences.

Set the Relative Path for New Links

1. Click the **Site** menu, and then click **Manage Sites**.

2. Click the site you want to change, and then click **Edit**.

3. Click the **Advanced Settings** category.

4. Click the **Local Info** category.

5. Click the **Document** or **Site Root** option.

6. For site root-relative paths, enter the Web site URL in the HTTP Address box with the equivalent root address on a remote server.

   ◆ To change the Web URL, click the **Change the Remote server's Web URL** link.

   Dreamweaver uses this address to make sure links work on a remote server.

7. Click **Save**.

8. Click **Done**.

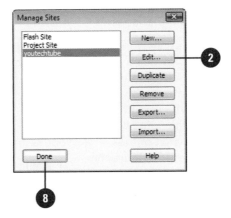

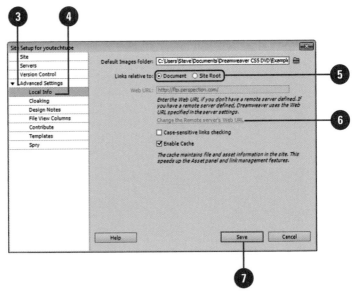

Set Preview in Browser to Use a Temporary File

1. Click the **Dreamweaver** (Mac) or **Edit** (Win) menu, and then click **Preferences**.

2. Click the **Preview In Browser** category.

3. Select the **Preview Using Temporary File** check box.

4. Click **OK**.

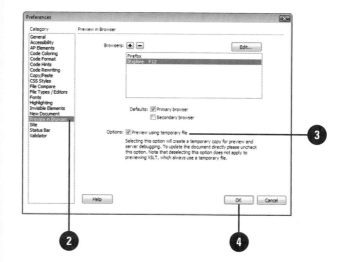

Adding a Link

Adding an http link to a Web page is a relatively simple and painless operation. You will need to decide what to use for the link (text, graphic, animation), what you are linking to (Web page, site, etc), and the correct path to the destination (URL or Uniform Resource Locator). Once you've answered those questions, it's a simple matter of opening Dreamweaver and getting to work. In this example, you're creating a simple text link that will connect the active Web page to the index page on another site.

Add a Text Link

① Open the Web page that you want to add the link.

② Enter or select the text that you want converted into a link, or click to place the insertion point where you want the link established.

③ Click the **Insert** menu, and then click **Hyperlink**.

④ Use the following options to convert the text into a link:

◆ Text. If you previously selected the text, it appears in this window. If you clicked in the document to add an insertion point, you need to add the text for the link.

◆ Link. Add the path and link document in the Link Input window, or click the **Browse** button to locate and add the link.

◆ Target. Click the **Target** list arrow, and then select from the following options:

◆ **_blank.** Opens the linked page in a new window.

NOTE *Be careful of this option because some spam blockers prevent the opening of additional windows.*

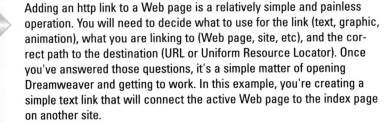

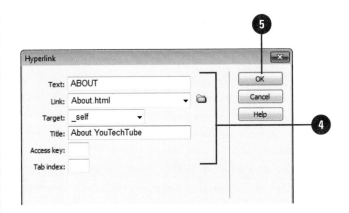

◆ **_parent.** Loads the linked document in the immediate frameset of the active document.

◆ **_self.** Loads the linked document in the same browser window (default).

◆ **_top.** Loads the linked document in the topmost window of a frameset.

◆ Title. Insert the title for the link.

◆ Access Key. Enter a keyboard stroke (one letter), to select the link in the browser (optional shortcut).

◆ Tab Index. Enter a numerical value to indicate the tab order of this link, as it relates to all other links on the page (optional).

5 Click **OK** to add the link to the page.

In Code view the link would look like this:

<a href="http://sitename.com" tabindex="3" title="Title Text" accesskey="f" target"_self">This is the link text<a/>

See Also

See "Modifying a Link" on page 178 for information on changing link settings in the Properties panel.

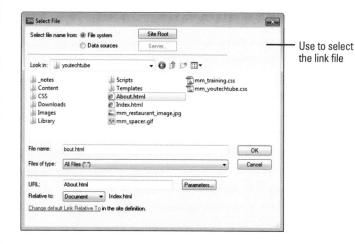

Use to select the link file

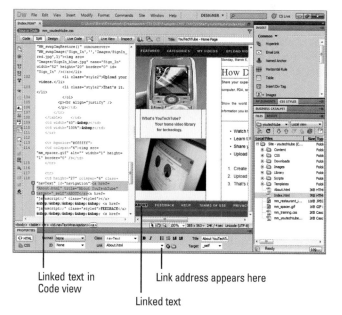

Linked text in Code view

Link address appears here

Linked text

Adding an Email Link

Where would we be without email... or at least that's a question that was posed to me by one of my students while I was teaching a class on communications. I will have to admit, e-mail is a big part of our communications structure. You see it everywhere you go: a patron in a restaurant emailing their spouse on the quality of the roast beef, kids emailing their friends, who happen to be sitting right next to them in class. Email is all around us, and Dreamweaver makes the creation of an email link a veritable piece of baklava, cake. Remember, clicking an email link requires that the person doing the clicking has a valid email application, and a connection to the Internet.

Add an Email Link

1. Open the Web page that you want to add an email link.

2. Enter or select the text that you want converted into an email link, or click to place the insertion point where you want the link established. In this example, the appropriate text is selected.

3. Click the **Insert** menu, and then click **Email Link**.

4. Create the link using the following options:

   - **Text.** If you previously selected the text, it will appear in this window. If you clicked in the document to add an insertion point, you will be required to add the text for the link.

   - **E-Mail.** Enter a valid email address.

5. Click **OK** to add the email link to the page.

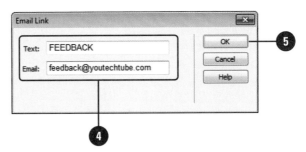

Modify an Email Link

① Select the email link in Design view.

② Click the **Window** menu, and then click **Properties** to display the Properties panel.

③ Modify the link using the following options:

◆ Link. Modify the name or path of the link by changing the link information, located within the Link box.

NOTE *If you remove the information in the Link box, you remove the link from the selected text.*

◆ Target. Since an email link opens another application; leave this field blank.

Linking within a Web Page

So far, the Web links created simply jump you from one page to another. When the selected document loads, it places you at the very top of the page. In most circumstances that's exactly what you want to happen; however, there are times when you want the page to load, and then start the visitor in the middle, or somewhere other than the very top. That's where named anchors come into play. **Named anchors** are internal navigation tools that let you select at what part of the page you want the visitor to start. This is extremely helpful in long scrolling documents where you can have the page stop at a particular chapter or paragraph. Named anchors are an HTML anchor tag pair (<a></a>) that includes a name attribute. The named anchor serves as a target for links. To create a named anchor, you first place a named anchor on your Web page, and then create a link that directs the browser to the specific tag. Named anchors are represented by a small book icon that appears in the position of the anchor. You can have as many named anchors as you need in your document and, of course, the corresponding links that direct the browser to the correct anchor.

Add a Named Anchor

1. Open the Web page that you want to add named anchors.

2. Click to place the insertion point where you want the named anchor established. This is where the named anchor is coded in HTML.

3. Select the **Insert** menu, and then click **Named Anchor**.

4. Enter the name for this specific anchor (i.e. chapter1, TOC, etc).

    IMPORTANT *Named anchors are case sensitive, and must be used only once within the document.*

5. Click **OK** to add the named anchor to the document.

6. Repeat this process to add as many named anchors as needed.

    NOTE *To change the name of an established anchor, simply click on the book icon and change the name using the Properties panel.*

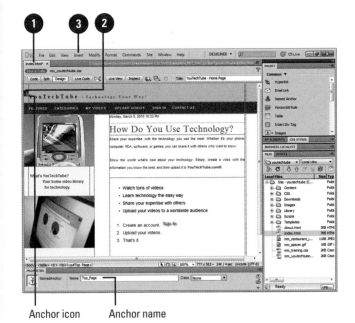

Anchor icon   Anchor name

Add Links to Named Anchors

① Select the text (or graphic) that you want to use as the link to a previously created named anchor.

② Click the **Window** menu, and then click **Properties** to display the Properties panel.

③ Click in the **Link** box.

④ Add the pound sign (#), followed by the name of the anchor (no spacing between the pound sign and the name of the anchor).

⑤ To test the links, click the **File** menu, point to **Preview In Browser**, and then select the browser you want to use.

TIMESAVER *If you're using a lot of anchors, it's not a bad idea to make a list of the anchors, and the order in which they appear within the document. That way you don't have to hunt for the name or, worse yet, guess.*

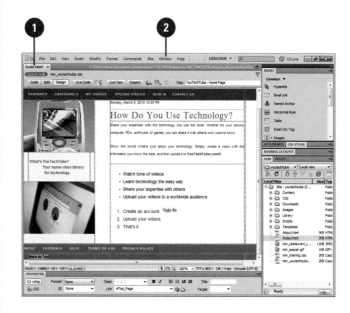

Did You Know?

You can use the Point To File button to create a link to a named anchor. You can use the Point To File button that appears to the right of the Link box to select an anchor (if it appears in Design view). Simply click the Point To File button, and then drag it over the book icon for the name anchor and release.

Creating Image Map Hotspots

Image maps are an image that has been sub-divided into regions (hotspots); when a user hovers and clicks within a hotspot, a predefined action occurs. For example, you could create a map of the United States with each State as a hot spot; clicking on a specific State would open another Web page and give you the current weather conditions. Dreamweaver allows you to create a client-side map, or a server-side map. Basically, client-side maps store the link information in the HTML document. Therefore, when a visitor clicks a hotspot in the image, the command is sent directly to the server. Server-side maps store the information on the server; while this allows the designer to modify a server-side map; in reality they're much slower, because every time the visitor clicks on a hot spot, the browser must go back to the originating server to map the response. Client-side maps are faster, because the server does not need to interpret where the visitor clicked. Since, in most cases, client-side maps are faster, easier for the visitor, and are supported by almost every browser your visitors are likely to have; it makes sense to include them into your Web pages.

Create a Client-Side Image Map

1. Open the Web page with the image you want to use to create an image map.

2. Place the image into the document that you want to use to create your image map.

3. Click the **Window** menu, and then click **Properties** to display the Properties panel.

4. Create an image map using the following tools:

   ◆ **Hotspot Tools.** Select the **Rectangular**, **Oval**, or **Polygon** hotspot tool, and draw an area on the selected image (this area represents the clickable link area for the visitor).

   ◆ **Pointer Tool.** Select the **Pointer** tool to select, move, or modify the hotspot.

5. Click **OK** to continue.

   Hotspot properties appear in the Properties panel.

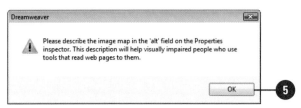

6 Enter the link for the active hotspot into the link box. Alternately, you can click the **Browse For File** button to select the link, or you can click the **Point To File** button, and drag to the link in the Files or Assets panel.

7 Click the **Target** list arrow, and then select from the following options:

◆ **_blank.** Opens the linked page in a new window.

◆ **_parent.** Loads the linked document in the immediate frameset of the active document.

◆ **_self.** Loads the linked document in the same browser window (default).

◆ **_top.** Loads the linked document in the topmost window of a frameset.

8 Enter the alternate text. Used by reader applications for the visually impaired, and for text-only browsers.

9 Continue using the hotspot tools until you have completed the client-side image map.

Hotspot

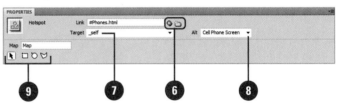

Modifying Image Map Hotspots

After you create some hotspots in an image map, you can modify them to create the links you want. Using the Pointer tool in the Properties panel, you can select one or more hotspots, move a hotspot area to a new location, resize a hotspot shape, or arrange the stacking order for overlapping hotspots in an absolutely-positioned element (AP element). If you want to duplicate a hotspot for use in the same image map or another one, you can copy and paste it. When you copy an image with one or more hotspots, the hotspots are copied along with the image.

Modify Image Map Hotspots

1 Open the Web page with the image map you want to change.

2 Click the **Window** menu, and then click **Properties** to display the Properties panel.

3 Click the **Pointer** tool.

4 Edit an image map using the following tools:

◆ **Select Multiple Hotspots.** Press and hold the Shift key, and then click each hotspot you want to select.

TIMESAVER *Press Ctrl+A (Win) or ⌘+A (Mac) to select all the hotspots.*

◆ **Move Hotspots.** Drag the hotspot to a new location.

TIMESAVER *Use the arrow keys to move a hotspot by 1 pixel. Use the Shift + arrow keys to move a hotspot by 10 pixels.*

◆ **Resize Hotspots.** Drag a hotspot selector handle.

◆ **Arrange Hotspots.** Select a hotspot, click the **Modify** menu, point to **Arrange**, and then click **Bring To Front** or **Bring To Back**.

◆ **Copy Hotspots.** Select the hotspot you want to copy, click the **Edit** menu, click **Copy**, click the **Edit** menu, and then click **Paste**.

Creating a Null or Script Link

A **null link** is an undesignated link, while a **script link** executes JavaScript code or a call to a JavaScript function. A null link is a useful way to activate a link without specifying a target. You can also use a null link to attach behaviors to objects or text on a page. A script link is useful for performing an action, such as performing calculations, without leaving the current Web page.

Create a Null or Script Link

1. Open the Web page that you want to create a link.

2. Select the text, an image, or an object you want to use to create a null or script link.

3. Click the **Window** menu, and then click **Properties** to display the Properties panel.

4. Use the following options to create a link:

   ◆ Null. Type **javascript:;** (the word javascript followed by a colon, followed by a semicolon) in the Link box.

   ◆ Script. Type **javascript:** (the word javascript followed by a colon) followed by JavaScript code or a function call. Do not type a space between the colon and the code or call.

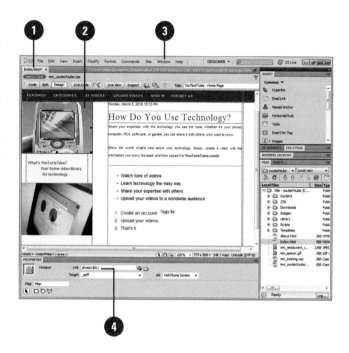

For Your Information

Attaching JavaScript Behaviors to Links

There are several commonly used behaviors you can attach to any link in a Web page. These include Set Text Of Status Bar, Open Browser Window, and Jump Menu. **Set Text Of Status Bar** allows you to display a text message in the status bar, which is useful for describing a link destination. **Open Browser Window** lets you to open a URL in a separate new window. **Jump Menu** provides a way to edit a jump menu.

Modifying a Link

As with any design application, things can change; including links. Say for example, you create a link to a specific site, and the original site owner changes its address. It's even possible that you created the link and mistyped the link... surely that could never happen. The good news is that just like any other computer application, mistakes are relatively easy to correct, and modifying a link is no exception.

Modify a Link

1 Select the link you want to change in the Design window.

2 Click the **Window** menu, and then click **Properties** to display the Properties panel.

3 Modify the link using the following options:

◆ Link. Modify the name or path of the link by changing the link information, located within the Link input box. Alternately, you can click the **Browse For File** button, and then locate the file, or you can click the **Point To File** button, and then drag over to the Files or Assets panel.

TIMESAVER *Right-click the link, click Change Link, select the file you want to link to, and then click OK.*

◆ Target. Click the **Target** list arrow, and then select from the following options:

◆ **_blank.** Opens the linked page in a new window.

◆ **_parent.** Loads the linked document in the immediate frameset of the active document.

◆ **_self.** Loads the linked document in the same browser window (default).

◆ **_top.** Loads the linked document in the topmost window of a frameset.

Removing a Link

Removing a link is a lot easier than creating one. As a matter of fact, it only takes a second or two of your precious time. There are several different ways to remove a link. You can delete the contents of the Link box in the Properties panel, use the Remove Link command, or delete the image or text and the link. Removing an entire link is simple, just select the graphic, or text that represents the link, and then press the Backspace (Win) or Delete (Mac) key.

Remove a Link

1 Select the text or graphic that contains the link.

TIMESAVER *Right-click the link, and then click Remove Link.*

2 Click the **Window** menu, and then click **Properties** to display the Properties panel.

3 Click in the **Link** box, and then erase all the text.

The link is now removed.

◆ To prevent a link error, enter the # (null) symbol in the Link box.

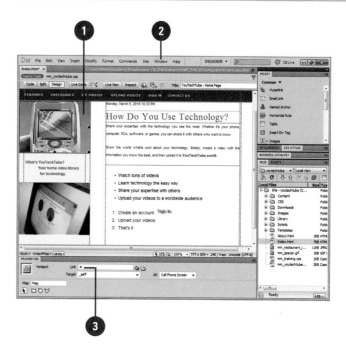

Updating Links

You can use the General section of the Preferences dialog box to specify how you want to update links in your Web pages. You can have Dreamweaver always update links, never update links, or prompt you when links change. Dreamweaver only updates links in your local root site. The remote site doesn't change until you update the files on the site. If the updating processing is taking too long, you can create a cache file to store information about all the links to speed up the process. The cache file is managed and maintained by Dreamweaver in the background while you work.

Set Preferences to Update Links Automatically

1. Click the **Dreamweaver** (Mac) or **Edit** (Win) menu, and then click **Preferences**.

2. Click the **General** category.

3. Click the **Update Links When Moving Files** list arrow, and then select one of the following:

    ◆ **Always.** Automatically updates all links when you move or rename a linked document.

    ◆ **Never.** Doesn't update any links when you move or rename a linked document.

    ◆ **Prompt.** Displays a dialog box listing all the linked documents you have changed. Click **Update** or **Don't Update** to update or leave the file unchanged.

4. Click **OK**.

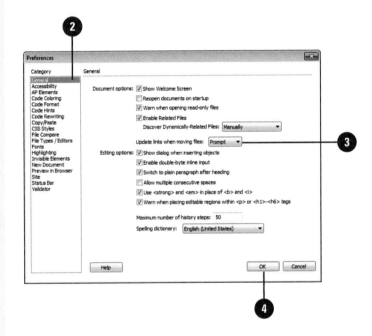

Create a Cache File

1. Click the **Site** menu, and then click **Manage Sites**.

2. Click the site you want to change, and then click **Edit**.

3. Click the **Advanced Settings** category.

4. Click the **Local Info** category.

5. Select the **Enable Cache** check box.

6. Click **Save**.

   The first time you change or delete links to files, Dreamweaver prompts you to load the cache.

7. Click **Yes** to load the cache and update all links to the file you changed, or click **No** to note the change for the future and not make any changes to the links.

8. Click **Done**.

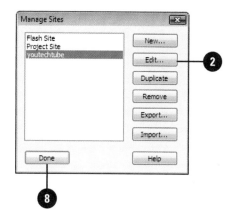

Did You Know?

You can re-create the cache. Click the Site menu, point to Advanced, and then click Recreate Site Cache.

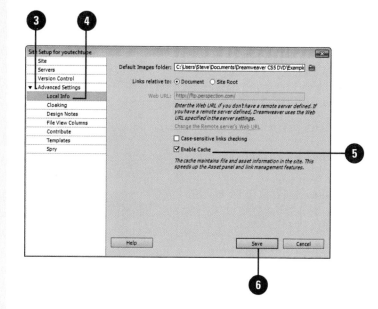

Testing a Link

After you create or change a link, it's important to test the link to make sure it works the way you want. You can test a link by previewing the Web page with a link in a browser or Live view (**New!**) in Dreamweaver, or by opening the linked page. When you want to test a link of any kind, the best way is to preview the page in a browser or Live view and click the link you want to test. When you use Live view to test a link, you can set options to follow links and show/use the Browser Navigation bar (**New!**) to browse between pages. If you want to test a link to another page and open the linked page, the best way is to open the linked page from within Dreamweaver.

Test a Link

1 Use any of the following methods:

- **Live View.** Click the **Live View** button on the Document toolbar.

- **Preview in Browser.** Click the **File** menu, point to **Preview In Browser**, and then select a browser to test the link.

2 To set Live view link options, click the **View** menu, point to **Live View Options**, and then click the following:

- **Follow Link (Ctrl+Click Link).** Select to follow links in Live view using Ctrl+click.

- **Follow Links Continuously.** Select to follow links in Live view using normal clicking.

- **Show Browser Navigation Bar.** Shows the Browser Navigation bar where you can navigate pages in Live view.

3 Move your mouse over the link (the cursor changes to a hand icon with extended index finger).

The link appears as blue underlined text.

4 Click the link to open it.

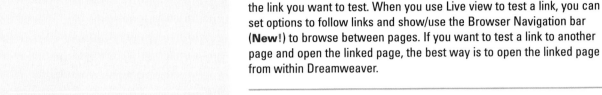

Live view button   Navigation bar in Live view

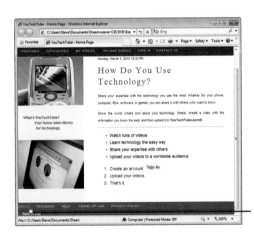

Preview in Browser

Open a Linked Page

◆ Select the link, click the **Modify** menu, and then click **Open Linked Page**.

◆ Press Ctrl (Win) or Command (Mac), and double-click the link.

See Also

See "Finding Broken Links" on page 452 for information on finding broken links or "Fixing Broken Links" on page 454 for information on changing links sitewide.

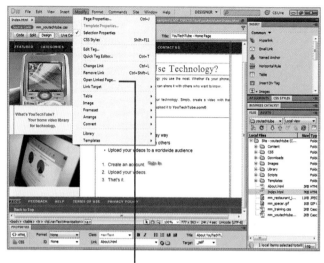

Click to open the linked page

Changing Links Sitewide

If you need to change a link across the entire site, you can use the Change Link Sitewide command to manually make the change you want. This command is useful when you want to delete a file other documents are linked to and redirect the link to another document. After you change a link sitewide, the selected file become an **orphan** (no documents link to it), which you can safely delete without breaking links.

Change a Link Sitewide

1 Open the Files panel, and then select the file you want to change in the Local view.

   NOTE *If you are changing an e-mail, FTP, null, or script link, you don't need to select a file.*

2 Click the **Site** menu, and then click **Change Link Sitewide**.

3 Select the options you want:

   ◆ Change All Links To. Click the **Browse For File** button to select the target file you want to unlink. If you are changing an e-mail, FTP, null, or script link, type the full text of the link you are changing.

   ◆ Into Links To . Click the **Browse For File** button to select the new file to link to. If you are changing an e-mail, FTP, null, or script link, type the full text of the replacement link.

4 Click **OK**.

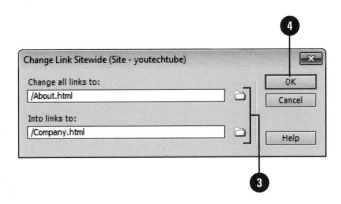

Working with Web Page Tables

Introduction

Although tables give designers control over the positioning of images and text on the page, tables were originally intended for displaying tabular data, not for use in page layout. Designers saw tables and thought that if they can hold, position and control tabular data, maybe they can hold other information. That started the use of tables for layout and design.

In recent years, tables are being phased out as design elements and returning to their original position of displaying tabular data. Tables for layout have been replaced by coding the placement and style of elements using Cascading Style Sheets.

This chapter will show you how to create and modify tables in Dreamweaver. Creating a table in Dreamweaver is basically a three-step process: Step one: insert the table, Step two: modify the table to fit the specific design requirements of the current page, and Step three: add the content (text, graphics, etc.) to the individual cells.

What You'll Do

Work with Tables

Switch Between Table Modes

Insert a Table in Standard Mode

Modify a Table

Add Content into a Table

Import and Export Table Data

Add Columns or Rows to Tables

Resize Columns and Rows

Split and Merge Cells

Sort Table Data

Change Table Properties

Change Cell, Row, or Column Properties

Use a Tracing Image

Create a Nested Table

Working with Tables

Tables are basically grids that allow the designer to precisely control the content of a Web page. The three main mechanisms of a table are rows, columns, and cells. A row extends across the entire table from left to right. Columns extend vertically from the top to the bottom of the table. A cell is the area where a row and column intersect. By default, table cells will expand to fit the content inserted into them.

If you're working in the design window, Dreamweaver will visually display the table, and allow you to expand or contract the table or individual rows or columns with a simple click and a drag.

Creating a table in Dreamweaver is basically a three-step process: Step one: insert the table, Step two: modify the table to fit the specific design requirements of the current page, and Step three: add the content (text, graphics, etc.) to the individual cells. Be advised, that since tables can display differently in different and older browsers, it's important to test your pages to make sure what you see is what you're visitors are seeing. The following examples illustrate how a Web page might appear in different browser windows.

Table

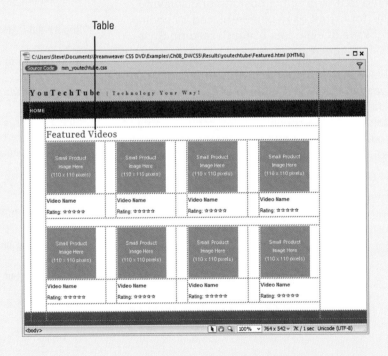

Switching Between Table Modes

You can create tables using two different modes: Standard and Expanded Tables. Each mode has its strengths and weaknesses. Standard mode is useful for creating and displaying a table as it will appear in a Web browser and adding and editing content. Expanded Tables mode adds cell padding and spacing to all the tables in a document and increases borders to make editing easier. For example, you might use Expanded Tables mode to position the insertion point to the left or right of an image, without inadvertently selecting the image or table cell, and then switch back to Standard mode to make your changes. By default, Dreamweaver starts you out in Standard mode.

Switch Between Table Modes

1. Create a new Web page or open the Web page you want to view.

2. Click the **View** menu, and then click **Design** or click the **Design** button to display the page in Design mode.

3. Click the **View** menu, point to **Table Mode**, and then select from the following modes:

   ◆ **Standard.** Use to display a table as it will appear in a Web browser and edit it.

   TIMESAVER *To quickly return to Standard mode, click the [Exit] link in Expanded Tables, located at the top center of the Document window.*

   ◆ **Expanded Tables.** Use to edit a table. This mode adds cell padding and spacing, and increases border.

   TIMESAVER *Press F6 to switch to Expanded Tables mode.*

   ◆ You can also click the **Standard** or **Expanded** button on the Layout tab on the Insert panel.

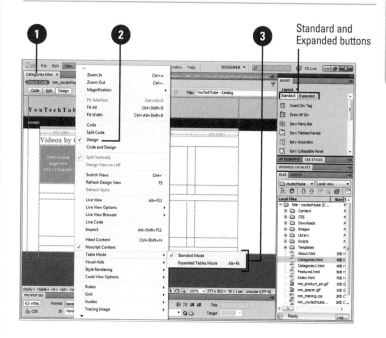

Standard and Expanded buttons

Inserting a Table in Standard Mode

When you insert a table using Standard mode, you get a very ordered table... think spreadsheet and you've got a pretty good idea of what I'm talking about. And once the table is created, you can, if you choose, to make changes in Standard or Expanded Table mode. You can add or subtract cells from the table design, add any type of information needed.

Insert a Table in Standard Mode

1. Open a Web page where you want to insert a table.

2. Click to place the insertion point for the new table.

3. Click the **View** menu, point to **Table Mode**, and then click **Standard Mode**.

   ◆ You can also click the **Standard Mode** button on the Layout tab on the Insert panel.

4. Click the **Insert** menu, and then click **Table**.

5. Create a table using the following options:

   ◆ **Rows.** Enter a value for the number of rows in the table.

   ◆ **Columns.** Enter a value for the number of columns in the table.

   ◆ **Table Width.** Enter a value (pixels or percent), for the initial width of the table.

   ◆ **Border Thickness.** Enter a value for the border width of the table.

   ◆ **Cell Padding.** Enter a value for the number of pixels between a cell's content and the cell boundaries.

   ◆ **Cell Spacing.** Enter a value for the number of pixels between adjacent table cells.

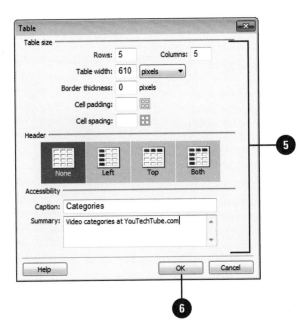

- ◆ **Header.** Select a position for a header area in the table: None, Left, Top, Both.

- ◆ **Caption.** Enter a table caption (displays outside of the table).

- ◆ **Align Caption.** Click to align where the table caption appears in relation to the table: default, top, bottom, left, right.

- ◆ **Summary.** Enter a table description. Screen readers read the summary text, but the text does not appear in the user's browser.

6 Click **OK**.

Table in Standard Mode

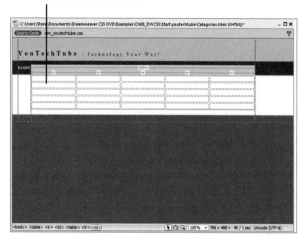

Did You Know?

You can change the highlight color for table elements. Click the Edit (Win) or Dreamweaver (Mac) menu, click Preferences, and then click Highlighting. To enable or disable highlighting for table elements, select or clear the Show check box for Mouse-Over. To change the highlighting color for table elements, click the Mouse-Over color box, and then select a color. When you're done, click OK.

Modifying a Table

After you create the initial table and cells, you can select, resize, move, or even delete the table and cells to fine tune it. When you move or resize a cell in a table, there are a few things you need to avoid. These include overlapping cells, crossing the boundaries of the table, and making the cell smaller than its contents. Before you can resize, move, or delete a table or cell, you need to select it first. You can select the table by clicking the table header arrow at the top or an outside table edge, or select a cell by clicking a cell edge. When you select the table or place the insertion point in the table, the widths of tables and cells appear at the top or bottom of the table in pixels or as a percentage of the page width. Next to the widths are arrows for the table and column headers you can use to display a menu with related commands. When you point to a table edge, Dreamweaver highlights it to make it easier to see.

Modify the Table and Cells

1. Open the Web page containing the table you want to modify.

2. Click the **Design** button to display the page in Design mode.

3. Click the **View** menu, point to **Table Mode**, and then click **Standard Mode** or **Expanded Tables Mode**.

   ◆ You can also click the **Standard** or **Expanded** button on the Layout tab on the Insert panel.

4. To modify the table:

   ◆ Select Table. Click in the table, click the **Modify** menu, point to **Table**, and then click **Select Table**, or click the table header arrow, and then click **Select Table**.

   TIMESAVER *Click in the table, and then press Ctrl+A (Win) or ⌘+A (Mac) to select it.*

   ◆ Resize Table. Select the table, and then drag the control points on the right table edge to expand or contract the table.

Table header arrow

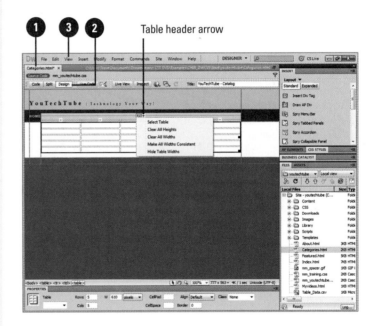

- **Delete Table.** Select the table, and then press the Backspace (Win) or Delete (Mac) key to remove the table.

5 To modify columns or rows:

- **Select Columns.** Click in the column, click the column header arrow, and then click **Select Column**.

- **Select Columns or Rows.** Click the left edge of a row or the top edge of a column, or drag to select multiple columns or rows.

- **Resize Columns or Rows.** Drag the border to change the size; for a column, the table keeps its width. To change change column width and keep column width, shift-drag the column border.

6 To modify the individual cells:

- **Select Cell.** Click on the edge of an active table cell, or Ctrl-click (Win) or ⌘-click (Mac) anywhere in the cell.

    To select more than one cell, drag from cell to cell, or Ctrl-click (Win) or ⌘-click (Mac) multiple cells.

- **Resize Cell.** Select the cell, and then drag any of the control points on the cell edges to expand or contract the size of the selected cell.

- **Delete Cell.** Select the cell, and then press the Backspace (Win) or Delete (Mac) key to remove the selected cell.

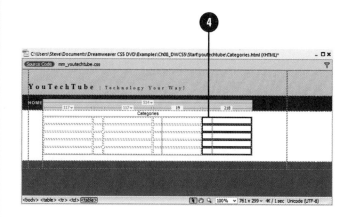

Column header arrow

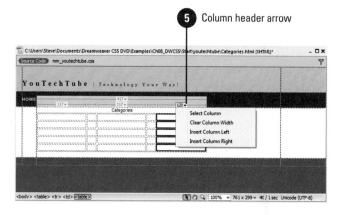

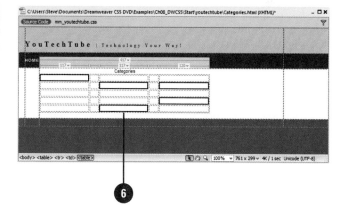

Adding Content into a Table

After you finishing creating the table layout and cells, you can insert content. You can add text, images, and other data in Standard or Expanded Table modes. Simply click in the cell where you want to add material, and then type, paste, or insert the content you want. If you have content available in the Assets or Files panel, you can drag it into the table; releasing your mouse when you're hovering over the right cell. You can only add content to layout cells; the empty grey area in a layout table is not available for content. When you add content to a cell, it automatically expands to accommodate the incoming content, which changes the size of the column and table.

Add Text or an Image to a Table

1 Open the Web page that contains the table you want to add content.

2 Click to place the insertion point in the layout cell where you want to add content.

3 To add text, type or paste the text you want.

   ◆ Press Enter (Win) or Return (Mac) to add a paragraph return.

   ◆ Press Shift+Enter (Win) or Shift+Return (Mac) to add a soft return.

   NOTE *By default, the text is left justified and centered within the cell, and soft wraps at the end of the table cell.*

4 To add an image, click the **Insert** menu, click **Image**, select the image file you want, and then click **OK**.

   The table expands to accommodate the text or image content.

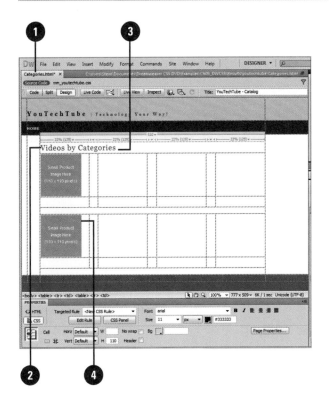

See Also

See "Importing Tabular Data" on page 93 for information on importing data and creating a layout table.

Modify Table Text

1. Select the table text you want to modify.

2. In the Properties panel, modify the text using the following options:

   ◆ **Format.** Click to change the basic HTML format of the text (heading and paragraph styles).

   ◆ **Style.** Click to work with CSS style sheets.

   ◆ **Alignment.** Click to change the justification of the text (Align Left, Align Center, Align Right, or Justify).

   ◆ **Bold/Italic.** Click to **bold** or *italicize* the selected text.

   ◆ **Font.** Click to change the default font of the selected table text.

   ◆ **Size.** Click to change the default size of the selected table text.

   ◆ **Color.** Click to change the color of the selected table text (black, default).

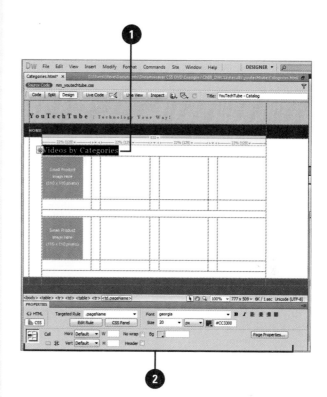

Did You Know?

You can sort rows in a table. If you don't have any merged cells in a table, you can sort the table. Select the table or click in any cell, click the Commands menu, and then click Sort Table. In the Sort dialog box, set the options you want, and then click OK. Some of the sort options include Sort By, Order, Sort Includes The First Row, Sort Header Rows, Sort Footer Rows, and Keep All Row Colors The Same After The Sort Has Been Completed.

Importing and Exporting Table Data

Instead of retyping data in a table that you have in another document, such as Microsoft Excel, you can import it into a table in Dreamweaver. The tabular data needs to be saved in a delimited text format with items separated by tabs, commas, colons, or semicolons. If you want to use data from a table in Dreamweaver in another document, you can export table data into a text file. When you export a table, the entire table is exported. You cannot export parts of a table. However, you can copy parts of a table and paste it into another document.

Export Table Data

1 Open the Web page with the table you want to format.

2 Click to place the insertion point in any cell of the table.

3 Click the **File** menu, point to **Export**, and then click **Table**.

4 Specify the following options:

  ◆ Delimiter. Specifies the character you want to separate items in the exported file.

  ◆ Line Breaks. Specifies the operating system in which you want to open the exported file.

    Different operating systems use different ways of indicating the end of a line break.

5 Click **Export**.

6 Navigate to the location where you want to save the file.

7 Enter a name for the file.

8 Click **Save**.

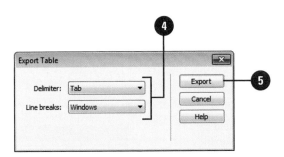

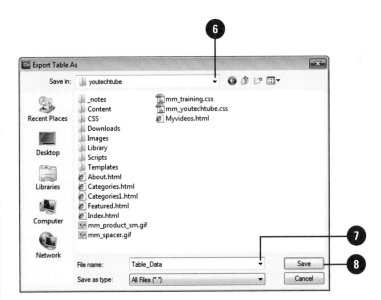

Import Tabular Data into a Table

1. Open the Web page with the table you want to use.

2. Click to place the insertion point in any cell of the table.

   If you click in an existing table, you'll create a nested table.

3. Click the **File** menu, point to **Import**, and then click **Tabular Data**.

4. Specify the following options:

   ◆ **Data File.** Enter the name of the file, or click **Browse** to select it.

   ◆ **Delimiter.** Specify the character used to separate items in the imported file. Select **Other** to enter a delimiter character.

   ◆ **Table Width.** Specifies the width of the table. Select **Fit to Data** to make each column wide enough to fit the data. Select **Set** to specify an exact width.

   ◆ **Cell Padding.** Specifies the number of pixels between a cell's content and the cell boundaries.

   ◆ **Cell Spacing.** Specifies the number of pixels between adjacent table cells.

   ◆ **Format Top Row.** Specifies the formatting applied to the top row.

   ◆ **Border.** Specifies the width in pixels of the table's border.

5. Click **OK**.

   Dreamweaver creates a new table with the tabular data from the imported file.

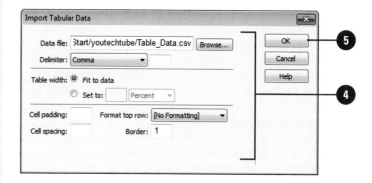

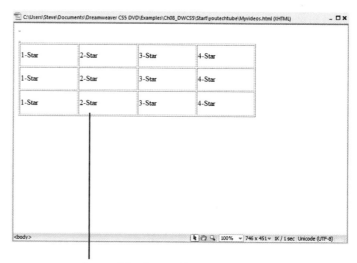

Imported data into a table

Adding Columns or Rows to Tables

As you begin to work on a table, you might need to modify its structure by adding more rows and columns to accommodate new text, graphics, or other tables. The table realigns as needed to accommodate the new structure. When you insert rows or columns, the existing rows shift down, the existing columns shift right, and you choose what direction the existing cells shift. Similarly, when you delete unneeded rows, columns, or cells from a table, the table realigns itself.

Add a Column or Row to a Table

1. Open the Web page with the table you want to modify.

2. Click to place the insertion point where you want to add a row or column.

3. To add a row or column, click the **Insert** menu, point to **Table Objects**, and then click **Insert Columns to The Left**, **Insert Column to The Right**, **Insert Row Above**, or **Insert Row Below**.

   TIMESAVER *Use buttons on the Layout tab on the Insert panel or the column header menu (arrow above a column) for columns.*

4. To add multiple rows or columns, click the **Modify** menu, point to **Table**, click **Insert Rows Or Columns**, enter the number of columns or rows you want to add to the table, and the related options, and then click **OK**.

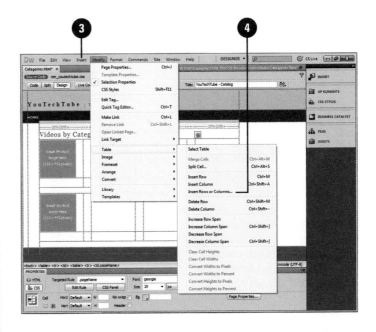

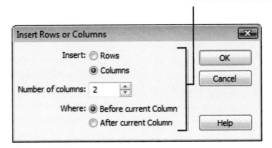

Enter number of columns or rows

Did You Know?

You can delete rows and columns in a table. Select the rows or columns you want to delete, click the Modify menu, point to Table, and then click Delete Row or Delete Column.

Resizing Columns and Rows

After you create a table, you can resize the columns and rows to fit your space and data needs. You can set a column to a variable, fixed or consistent width. If you see two numbers for a column's width, then the column width set in the HTML code doesn't match the columns width on the screen. You can make the width specified in the code match the visual width. After you insert content into the cell, you can clear the excess width and height of the cell.

Modify Column Widths and Row Heights

1 Open the Web page with the table you want to modify.

2 To change a columns width, use any of the following:

◆ **Change Column Width and Keep Table Width.** Drag the right border of the column to change it.

◆ **Change Column Width and Keep Other Column Widths.** Shift-drag the column border.

◆ **Clear Column Width.** Click the **Column Header Arrow**, and then click **Clear Column Width**.

3 To change a row height, drag the lower border of the row.

4 Click the **Table Header Arrow**, and then select any of the following options:

◆ **Clear All Heights** or **Clear All Widths.** Removes the excess empty space in a cell.

◆ **Make All Widths Consistent.** Makes all the column widths the same.

◆ **Hide Table Widths.** Hides the table widths at the top of the table.

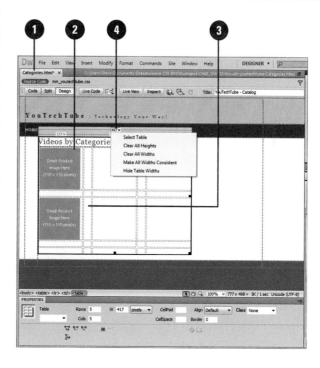

Splitting and Merging Cells

Cells can also be split or combined (also known as merged). Often there is more to modifying a table than adding or deleting rows or columns; you need to make cells just the right size to accommodate the text you are entering in the table. For example, a title in the first row of a table might be longer than the first cell in that row. To spread the title across the top of the table, you can merge (combine) the cells to form one long cell. Sometimes to indicate a division in a topic, you need to split (or divide) a cell into two.

Split a Cell into Two Cells

1. Open the Web page with the table you want to modify.

2. Select the cell or cells you want to split.

3. Click the **Split Cell** button in the expanded Properties panel.

   ◆ You can also click the **Modify** menu, point to **Table**, and then click **Split Cell**.

4. Click the **Columns** or **Rows** option.

5. Type the number of columns or rows you want.

6. Click **OK**.

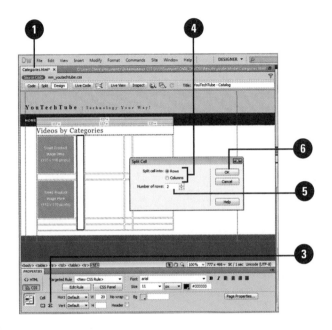

Merge Cells Together

1. Open the Web page with the table you want to modify.

2. Click a column, row, or group of adjacent cells, and then drag to select them.

3. Click the **Merge Cells** button in the expanded Properties panel.

   ◆ You can also click the **Modify** menu, point to **Table**, and then click **Merge Cells**.

   The cells merge into a single, larger cell.

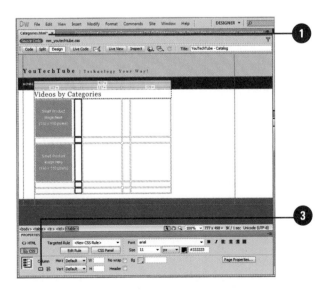

Sorting Table Data

If you have a table without merged cells you can sort the rows of a table based on one or more columns. You can table information by ascending order from A to Z, earliest to latest, or lowest to highest, or by descending order from Z to A, latest to earliest, or highest to lowest. In addition, you can set sort options to include the first row and header and footer rows, and keep all row colors the same after the sort has been completed.

Sort Table Data

1. Open the Web page with the layout table you want to modify.

2. Select the table or click in any table cell.

3. Click the **Commands** menu, and then click **Sort Table**.

4. Specify the following options:

   ◆ **Sort By.** Select the sort option.

   ◆ **Order.** Select the sort order (Alphabetically or Numerically), and then select the direction (Ascending or Descending).

   ◆ **Then By/Order.** Specify a secondary sort.

   ◆ **Sort Includes The First Row.** Select to include the first row in the sort.

   ◆ **Sort Header Rows.** Select to sort the header rows.

   ◆ **Sort Footer Rows.** Select to sort footer rows.

   ◆ **Keep All Row Colors The Same After The Sort Has Been Completed.** Select to keep all row colors the same after the sort has been completed.

5. Click **OK**.

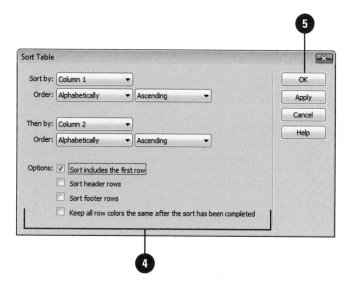

Changing Table Properties

When you create a table, it's not just about what you place into the individual table cells; it's how you format the table and the individual cells. When formatting tables, you can set properties for the entire table or for individual rows, columns, or cells in the table. You can set table properties to specify the number of rows and columns you want as well as the number of pixels between cells, either CellPad or CellSpace. When a property is set to one value for the whole table and another value for individual cells, cell formatting takes precedence over row formatting, which in turn takes precedence over table formatting. For example, if you set the alignment for a single cell to center align, then set the alignment of the entire table to left align, the center align cell does not change to left align, since cell formatting takes precedence over table formatting. It's all about priority.

Change Table Properties

1. Open the Web page with the table you want to format.

2. Select the table you want to change.

3. In the Properties panel, modify the table using the following options:

   - **Table ID.** Enter an ID for the table (used when calling from JavaScript).

   - **Rows.** Sets the number of rows in the selected table. Click to enter a new value.

   - **Cols.** Sets the number of columns in the selected table. Click to enter a new value.

   - **CellPad.** Sets the number of pixels between a cell's content and the cell boundaries.

   - **CellSpace.** Sets the number of pixels between adjacent table cells.

   - **Align.** Determines where the table appears, relative to other elements in the same paragraph, such as text or images. Click to change alignment from Left (default), Center, or Right.

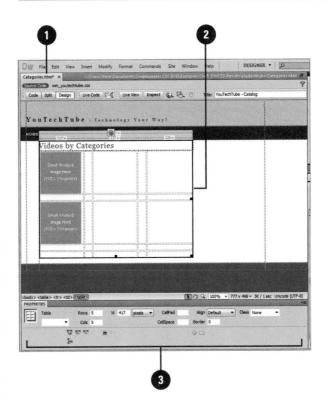

- ◆ **Border.** Sets the number of pixels for the border of the table. Click to enter a new value.

- ◆ **Class.** Used with CSS (Cascading Style Sheets) to help define the properties of the table. In this example, leave the box at None.

- ◆ **Clear Column Widths and Clear Row Heights.** Deletes all specified row height or column width values from the table.

- ◆ **Convert Table Widths To Pixels and Convert Table Heights To Pixels.** Sets the width or height of each column in the table to its current width in pixels (also sets the width of the whole table to its current width in pixels).

- ◆ **Convert Table Widths To Percent and Convert Table Heights To Percent.** Sets the width or height of each column in the table to its current width expressed as a percentage of the Document window's width.

- ◆ **Bi Color.** Sets the table's background color.

- ◆ **Brdr Color.** Sets the color for the table's borders.

- ◆ **Bi Image.** Specifies the source and path to a table background image. You can click the **Browse For File** or **Point To File** button to select the file.

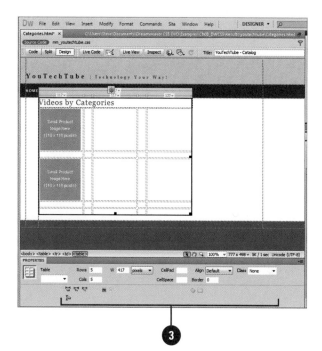

Changing Cell, Row, or Column Properties

Cells can contain colors or image backgrounds, and when placing text and graphics, you decide how the information appears within the table cells; however, there is a priority to how the cells are formatted. When a property, such as background color or alignment, is set to one value for the whole table and another value for individual cells, cell formatting takes precedence over row formatting, which in turn takes precedence over table formatting. It's all about priority. For example, if you set the background color for a single cell to green, then set the background color of the entire table to blue, the green cell does not change to blue, since cell formatting takes precedence over table formatting.

Change Cell, Row, or Column Properties

1. Open the Web page with the table you want to format.

2. Select the cells, rows, or columns you want to change.

3. In the Properties panel, modify the selection using the following options:

   ◆ **Horz.** Click to change the default (left) horizontal placement of items placed within the cell (Left, Center, Right).

   ◆ **Vert.** Click to change the default (middle) vertical placement of items placed within the cell (Default, Top, Middle, Bottom, Baseline).

   ◆ **W & H.** Enter a value for the width and height of selected cells in pixels, or as a percentage of the entire table's width or height. To specify a percentage, follow the value with a percent symbol (%).

   NOTE *To let the browser determine the proper width or height based on the contents of the cell and the widths and heights of the other columns and rows, leave the box blank (default).*

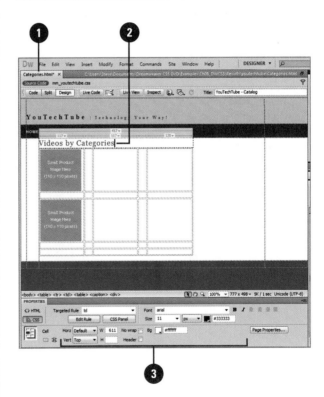

- **No Wrap.** Select if you do not want text to wrap between the left and right borders of the selected cell.

- **Header.** Select to format the selected cells as table header cells. The contents of table header cells are bold and centered by default.

- **Bi Image.** Enter the filename for the background image. You can click the **Browse For File** or **Point To File** button to select the file.

- **Bi Color.** Click to choose a background color for the selected cells (background color is independent of text color).

- **Brdr Color.** Click to choose a border color for the selected cells.

- **Merge Cells.** Click to combine selected cells, rows, or columns into one cell.

NOTE *Merging cells can only be accomplished if they form a rectangular or linear block.*

- **Split Cells.** Click to divide a cell, creating two or more cells. This option is disabled if you have more than one cell selected.

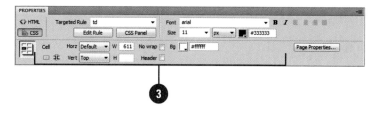

Split Cell button

Merge Cells button

Using a Tracing Image

You can use a tracing image as a guide to create a page design in Dreamweaver. For example, you can use Adobe Photoshop to create an exact replica of what you want your Web page to look like (i.e. headings, body text areas, navigation, etc), and then use that image as a tracing image to help design the actual Web page. A tracing image is a JPEG, GIF, or PNG formatted image that appears in the background of the Document window. In addition, a tracing image is visible only in Dreamweaver, not visible when you view the page in a browser. When the tracing image is visible, the page's real background image and color are not visible in the Document window; however, the background image and color is visible when the page is viewed in a browser.

Insert a Tracing Image

1 Open a Web page that you want to insert the tracing image.

2 Click the **View** menu, point to **Tracing Image**, and then click **Load**.

3 Navigate to the image you want to use, select it, and then click **OK**.

4 Drag the **Transparency** slider to adjust the transparency of the tracing image.

NOTE *If the chosen graphic file is not located in the current Site, Dreamweaver prompts you to save a copy within the active Site folder (recommended).*

5 Click **OK**.

The tracing image now appears in the background of the current Web document.

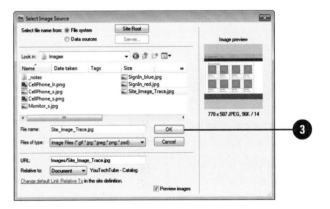

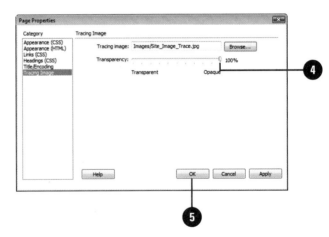

Modify a Tracing Image

1. Click the **View** menu, and then point to **Tracing Image**.

2. Select from the following options:

   - **Show.** Select to show or hide the tracing image.

   - **Align With Selection.** Select an element in the document window, and then use this option to align the upper-left corner of the tracing image with the upper left corner of the selected element (i.e. a table cell).

   - **Adjust Position.** Select to open a dialog box where you can precisely specify the position of the tracing image by entering coordinate values in the X and Y text boxes.

   - **Reset Position.** Select to return the tracing image to its default position, the upper-left corner of the Web document.

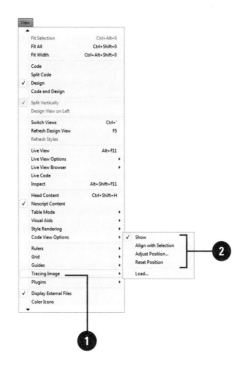

Tracing image aligned to selection

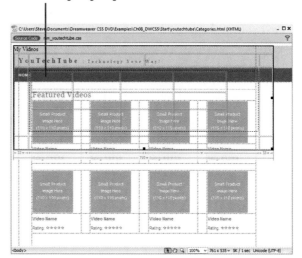

Creating a Nested Table

A **nested table** is a table inside a cell of another table. You can format a nested table as you would any other table; however, its width is limited by the width of the cell in which it appears. The cells inside a nested table are isolated from changes made to the outer table; for example, when you change the size of a row or column in the outer table, the cells in the inner table don't change size. The question arises as to why you might want to do something like this, and there are several answers to that. You might want to use a table to add design elements to a page, and at the same time use one of the cells for tabular data, or you have a picture and a related caption and you want them to remain stationary in relation to one another while text on the page flows according to the size of the browser window. In older browsers (pre 5.0) creating nested tables can slow down the load of the page. In Web design one of the things we have to do is balance page content to load speed. Make sure you keep things in balance.

Nest a Table in Standard Mode

1. Open the Web page containing a table, or create a new table.

2. Click the **Design** button to display the page in Design mode.

3. Click the **View** menu, point to **Table Mode**, and then click **Standard Mode**.

4. Select the cell you want to insert the nested table.

5. Click the **Insert** menu, and then click **Table**.

6. Choose the properties for the nested table you want from the Table dialog box.

7. Click **OK**.

   The nested table is inserted into the selected cell.

   NOTE *By default, the nested table is left justified and centered vertically within the cell. If you want to change the position of the nested table, select the cell that contains the table, and make your changes using the Properties panel.*

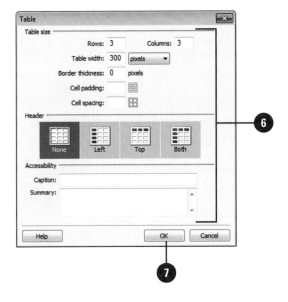

Nested table in Standard Mode

Working with Cascading Style Sheets

9

Introduction

Cascading Style Sheets are one of the greatest things to come along since the creation of the World Wide Web. A hard definition of CSS might go something like this: Cascading Style Sheets (CSS) are a collection of formatting rules that control the appearance of the content in a Web page.

Using CSS styles to format a page separates content from presentation. This gives you greater flexibility and control over the exact appearance of your Web pages. With CSS you can control text properties including specific fonts and font sizes; bold, italics, underlining, and text shadows; text color and background color, link color and underlining. With CSS controlling fonts, it ensures a more consistent treatment of your page layout and appearance in multiple browsers.

In this chapter you'll get an introduction to Cascading Style Sheets: what they are, and how to use them efficiently to create great Web content. You'll also learn how CSS functions, and how it's used to control multiple Web pages.

With Dreamweaver and Cascading Style Sheets we're getting closer and closer to the goal of What You See Is What You Get, and I can't wait.

Introducing Cascading Style Sheets

Cascading Style Sheets (CSS) are a revolution in the world of web design. Some of the benefits include:

◆ The layout of many documents from one single style sheet

◆ Precise control of layouts

◆ Application of different layout to different media-types (screen, print, etc.)

◆ Many advanced and sophisticated techniques

Many of the CSS properties are similar to those of HTML. Therefore, if you are comfortable designing Web pages using HTML code, you will most likely recognize many of the codes.

CSS Versus HTML

If you wanted to change the color of the background of a Web page, the HTML code would look like this:

```
<body bgcolor="#0000FF">
```

To write the same thing using CSS, would look like this:

```
body {background-color: #0000FF;}
```

Incidentally, the code, in both cases, is instructing the browser to paint the background in pure blue.

CSS Breakdown

Cascading Style Sheets are broken down into three sections: a selector, a property, and a value. In our example, body is the selector, background-color is the property, and #0000FF is the value.

Create CSS Styles

There are three ways you can apply CSS to an HTML document: Attributes, Tags, and External Style Sheets.

Attribute Styles

One way to apply CSS to HTML is by using the HTML attribute style. CSS used in this way is coded directly into the HTML document. For example, you can create your own named tags, and use them throughout the active document. Building on the above example, it can be applied like this:

```
<html>
  <head>
    <title>Attribute Style Example<title>
  </head>
  <body style="background-color: #0000FF;">
    <p>This page has a blue background</p>
  </body>
</html>
```

> **NOTE** *Attribute styles are a one-shot deal. That is, they are applied to single areas of an HTML document such as a background color, or a specific portion of text.*

Tag Styles

A second way to include CSS into an HTML document is to use the Tag Style method. In this method you control the formatting of standard HTML tags. For example, you could redefine the <H1> heading tag to always use a specific font, size and justification or, in this example, use the <body> tag to paint the background blue.

```
<html>
  <head>
    <title>Tag Style Example<title>
    <style type="text/css">
body {background-color: #0000FF;}
    </style>
  </head>
```

```
<body>
    <p>This page has a blue background</p>
</body>
</html>
```

NOTE *A Tag style changes all instances of an HTML tag throughout the active document, but will not impact other Web documents.*

External Styles

This is the recommended way to create styles. Using this method you create a text document (called a style sheet). This document contains all of the formatting information necessary to drive your Web page. This document is then attached to one or more Web pages, and when the page loads, it gets its formatting information from the external style sheet. The line of code must be inserted in the header section of the HTML code between the <head> and </head> tags. Like this:

```
<html>
  <head>
    <title>My document</title>
    <link rel="stylesheet" type="text/css"
href="style/style.css" />
  </head>
  <body>
<p>This page has a blue background</p>
  </body>
</html>
```

In the example, an external style sheet (basically, a text document) called style.css is used to format the active Web document.

Back to Basics

With all this talk of selectors, attributes, and values, you might assume that we're about to leave the Design mode of Dreamweaver and go back to the basics of straight HTML coding. Well, you can do that, if you choose; however, as you're about to find out, creating Cascading Styles Sheets is not difficult at all. As a matter of fact, Dreamweaver does most of the work for you. Now, isn't that nice of Adobe to provide us with so much help.

Style Types

There are four types of styles, and as you might guess, each one performs a specific function when using Cascading Style Sheets. The four types of Styles are as follows:

♦ **Class.** Creates a custom style that can be applied as a class attribute to a range or block of text.

   NOTE *Class names must begin with a period and can contain any combination of letters and numbers. If you don't enter a beginning period, Dreamweaver will enter it for you.*

♦ **ID.** Creates a style and attaches it to a current HTML tag that contains a specific ID attribute.

   NOTE *ID names must begin with a pound (#) sign and can contain any combination of letters and numbers. If you don't enter a beginning period, Dreamweaver will enter it for you.*

♦ **Tag.** Redefines a current style and attaches it to a current HTML tag. For example, changing the <body> tag so that each time it's applied the text is red.

♦ **Compound.** Defines specific formatting for a particular combination of tags or for all tags that contain a specific ID attribute. The selectors available from the pop-up menu are a:active, a:hover, a:link, and a:visited.

Creating a Web Page with a CSS Layout

If you're not sure where to start, you can create a Web page that already contains a CSS Layout. Dreamweaver includes over 30 different CSS layouts. The CSS layouts are divided into 4 categories based on the page's column width: Fixed, Elastic, Liquid, or Hybrid. Each of the built-in CSS layouts includes extensive comments that explain the layout, so beginning and intermediate designers can learn quickly. After you select a CSS layout, you need to select the location (add to HTML head, create new file, or link to existing file) for the layout's CSS style sheet. A CSS layout can also be a starting point to create your own custom template, which you can add to the list of layouts in the New Document dialog box.

Create a Web Page with a CSS Layout

1. Click the **File** menu, and then click **New**.

   The New Document dialog box opens.

2. Click the **Blank Page** category.

3. Select the Page Type you want.

4. Select from the following CSS Layouts:

   ◆ **Fixed.** Column width is fixed (in pixels) and remains the same in a browser.

   ◆ **Elastic.** Column width is set relative to the size of the text in a browser (in ems).

   ◆ **Liquid.** Column width is set based on the percentage of the browser's width.

   ◆ **Hybrid.** Columns are set to a combination of Fixed, Elastic, and Liquid.

5. Click the **DocType** list arrow, and select the option you want.

6. Click the **Layout CSS** list arrow, and select the option you want:

   ◆ **Add To Head.** Adds CSS for the layout to the head of the new page.

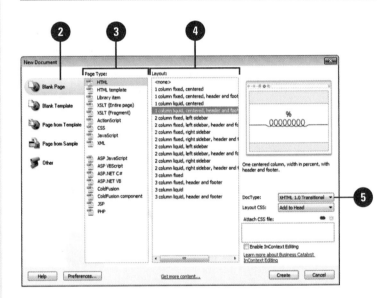

- ◆ **Create New File.** Add CSS for the layout to a new external CSS style sheet that attaches to the new page.

- ◆ **Link To Existing File.** Attaches an existing CSS file to the new page.

7 If you selected the Link To Existing File option in the Layout CSS menu, click the **Attach Style Sheet** icon, select the CSS file you want in the Attach External Style Sheet dialog box, and then click **OK**.

8 Click **Create**.

9 If you selected the Create New File option in the Layout CSS menu, enter a name for the new external file in the Save Style Sheet File As dialog box.

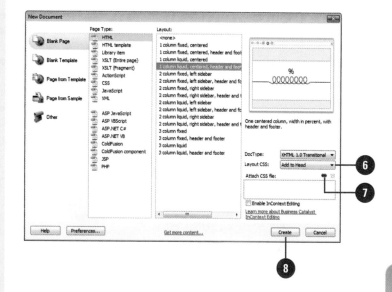

Create a CSS File

1 Click the **File** menu, and then click **New**.

The New Document dialog box opens.

2 Select from the following methods:

- ◆ **Blank.** Click the **Blank Page** category, and then click **CSS**.

- ◆ **Sample.** Click the **Page from Sample** category, click **CSS Style Sheet**, and then select the sample you want.

3 Click **Create**.

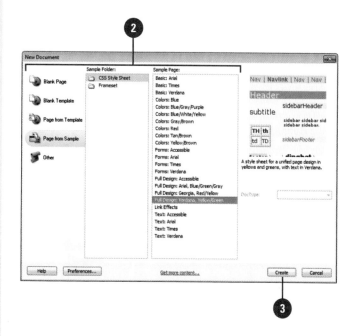

Creating CSS Styles

As mentioned in the last section, CSS can be applied to an HTML document in one of three ways: Attributes, Tags, or Externally. Although we will cover all three methods in this section, it's important to understand that the external method gives you the most control over the styles, once they've been created. In the other two methods, the CSS styles created only apply to that one specific page, and changes to the styles must be performed by reopening the page. The external method is like creating a text document of how you want a page or pages to display. Any changes to the formatting are performed to the text document. When the Web page opens, any changes made to the external document are immediately reflected in the active page... now that's what I call control.

Create an Attribute or Tag Style

① Open the Web page you want to create a CSS style.

② Click the **Format** menu, point to **CSS Styles**, and then click **New**.

③ Click the **Selector Type** list arrow and then select a CSS style type:

◆ **Attribute Style.** Select **Class**, click the **Name** arrow, and then select a style name, or type one in. Attribute style tags must begin with a period.

◆ **Tag Style.** Select **Tag**, click the **Name** arrow, and then select an HTML tag (in this example, body).

④ Click the **Define In** list arrow, and then click **(This Document Only)**.

⑤ Click **OK**.

⑥ Select a category, and then set the properties you want for the CSS style.

⑦ Click **OK**.

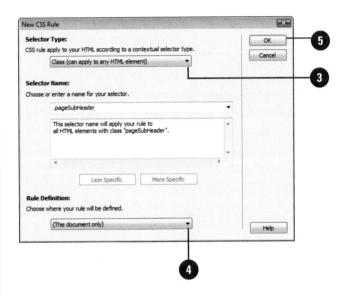

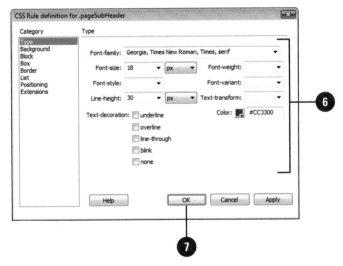

Create an External Style

1. Open the Web page you want to create an external CSS style.

2. Click the **Format** menu, point to **CSS Styles**, and then click **New**.

3. Click the **Class** or **Tag** option (in this example, tag).

4. Click the **Name** arrow, and then select an HTML tag (in this example, body.)

5. Click the **Define In** list arrow, and then click **New Style Sheet File**.

6. Click **OK**.

7. Enter the file name for the CSS style in the File Name input box.

8. Leave the other options at their default values, and then click **Save**.

   NOTE *Dreamweaver creates a folder in the active site called, CSS, and this is where all style sheets should be saved.*

9. Select a category, and then set the properties you want for the CSS style.

10. Click **OK**.

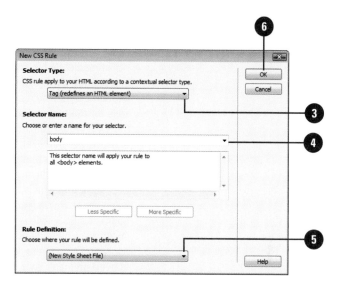

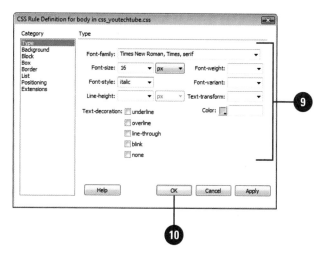

See Also

See "Setting CSS Properties" on page 222 for information on setting CSS properties for a rule.

Applying Internal CSS Styles

Cascading Style Sheets function and perform just like their counterparts in word-processing applications. For example, you could create a character style in Microsoft Word that specifies text be Garamond, 12 point, bold, and the color black. When the style is applied to the text it will immediately take on those characteristics. If you access the style and change it (for example, change the color to red), all text associated with that style would change. CSS works the same way: You create a style for the text and apply the style to the Web document. Changing the style would subsequently change all text associated with that particular style. However, the difference between word-processing styles and CSS styles is that paragraph and character styles are one in the same. For example, if you select a word or group of words and apply a CSS style, the style is applied only to the selected text (also called an inline style). However, if you click within a paragraph (add an insertion point), the CSS style is applied to the entire paragraph. Generally, inline styles are frowned upon because of the amount of effort it takes to apply and modify the items on an item-by-item basis. Instead, you can convert an inline style to a CSS rule located in the head of the page or in an external style sheet, which is cleaner and easier to use.

Apply a Paragraph Style

1. Open the Web page you want to apply a paragraph style.

2. Click within a specific paragraph, to create an insertion point.

   NOTE *Do not select any text.*

3. Click the **Format** menu, point to **CSS Styles**, and then select a user-defined CSS style.

   TIMESAVER *In the Properties panel, click CSS, click the Targeted Rule list arrow, and then select the CSS style you want.*

   The CSS style is applied to the entire paragraph.

   NOTE *A paragraph is defined as the information contained between two carriage returns.*

Click the Targeted Rule list arrow, and then select a style.

Apply a Character (Inline) Style

1. Open the Web page you want to apply a character style.

2. Select a word or words within the text document.

3. Click the **Format** menu, point to **CSS Styles**, and then select a user-defined CSS style.

   The CSS style is applied to the selected text.

See Also

See "Moving CSS Rules" on page 226 for information on moving CSS rules to a style sheet.

Convert Inline CSS to a CSS Rule

1. Open the Web page with the style you want to change.

2. Click the **View** menu, and then click **Code**.

3. Select the entire <style> tag that contains the inline CSS you want to convert.

4. Right-click (Win) or Control-click (Mac) the selection, point to **CSS Styles**, and then click **Convert Inline CSS To Rule**.

5. Click the **Convert to** list arrow, select a convert type, and then enter a class name for the new rule.

6. Specify a style sheet or select the head of the document as to where you want the new CSS rule.

7. Click **OK**.

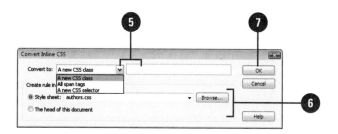

Applying and Modifying External CSS Styles

When you start to modify an external style sheet, you really begin to see the awesome power of using CSS. An external style sheet normally contains all of the formatting options for one or more Web pages. When you attach the style sheet to the document, the style sheet controls the formatting of the document. For example, if you had a style sheet that modified the <body> tag to use the Helvetica font, centered, and 12 point, when the style sheet was attached to the HTML document, all text defined by the <body> tag would change, according to the rules set up by the style sheet. Since the style sheet is only a text document it's easy to make changes (they can even be made in a text editor). For example, you could access the style sheet and change the formatting of the text from centered to left, and then save the style sheet. The next time the Web page opens, all the <body> tag text will be left justified. In addition to this power, you can use more than one style sheet within a Web page. For example, you can have a style sheet that defines all your headings, one that defines the look of the page, and another that defines body text. Cascading Style Sheets separate the page content from the formatting, and give you total control over your designs.

Attach an External Style Sheet

1. Open the Web page you want to attach an external style sheet.

2. Click the **Format** menu, point to **CSS Styles**, and then click **Attach Style Sheet**.

3. Select from the following options:

   ◆ File/URL. Enter the path and file name of the external style sheet, or click **Browse** to select a file.

   ◆ Add As. Click the **Link** option to create a link from the page to the external style sheet (recommended), or click the **Import** option to write the style sheet directly into the page.

   ◆ Media. Click the **Media** arrow to select the media type associated with this particular page (Default: All).

   ◆ Preview. Click **Preview** to view the effects of the external style sheet on your page.

4. Click **OK**.

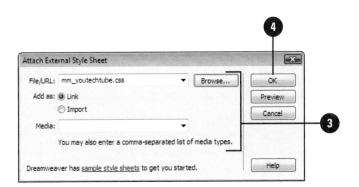

Open and Modify an External Style Sheet

1 Open the Web page you want to modify an external style sheet.

Any associated files, such as an external style sheet and scripts, with the main document are automatically available on the Related Files toolbar.

2 Click the external style sheet file on the Related Files toolbar.

3 Modify the document to reflect the changes required.

4 Click the **File** menu, and then click **Save**.

5 To view the main document, click **Source Code** on the Related Files toolbar.

When you display the main document, the formatting reflects the changes made to the attached style sheet.

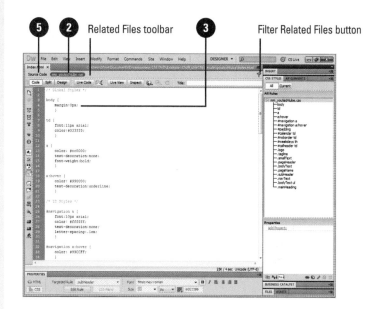

Related Files toolbar   Filter Related Files button

Did You Know?

You can use a Dreamweaver sample style sheet. Dreamweaver provides sample style sheets you can apply to your Web pages or use it as a starting point to create your own style sheet. Click the Window menu, click CSS Styles, click the Attach Style Sheet button, click the Sample Style Sheets link, select the sample style sheet you want, click Preview to apply it to the current Web page, and then click OK.

For Your Information

Filtering Files on the Related Files toolbar

The Related Files toolbar displays static and dynamically-related files for a Web page. Status files appear first starting from the left, followed by external files (such as .css and .js), and concluding with dynamic path server included files (such as .php, .inc, and .module). When the Related Files toolbar contains too many files to fit on the toolbar, scroll arrows appear to access files. To help you reduce the number of files on the toolbar, you can filter files by type to hide the ones you don't want to display. Click the Filter Related Files button (**New!**) on the Related Files toolbar, and then select the file types you want to filter (checked to show or unchecked to hide) or click Show All File Types to show all files. The list of file types on the menu is built based on the file types connected to the current open document, which varies. You cannot filter out all the file types. When you get to the last file type, it will be grayed out in the menu. When you close a document, the filter settings are not saved.

Removing Internal Styles

You can remove a style from any tag, you can delete the redefined tag, or you can even edit the existing style to reflect different formatting. Once again this reflects the versatility of using style sheets over standard HTML coding. When you remove a style from a Web document the item or text will revert back to its original formatting. For example, if you remove a style from a section of body text, the text will revert back to the default for that particular tag. If, however, you have an external style sheet attached to a document, and you have applied a local class or attribute (internal) style to the text, when you remove the localized style, the text will revert back to the rules supplied by the external style sheet.

Remove an Internal Style

1. Open the Web page you want to remove an internal style.

2. Select the stylized text, or place the insertion point in a paragraph containing stylized text.

3. Click the **Format** menu, point to **CSS Styles**, and then click **None**.

   TIMESAVER *In the Properties panel, click CSS, click the Targeted Rule list arrow, and then click None.*

   The CSS style is removed from the selected text.

Did You Know?

You can rename a CSS class style. Click the Window menu, click CSS Styles, right-click (Win) or control-click (Mac) the CSS class style you want to rename in the CSS Styles panel, click Rename Class, enter a new name, and then click OK.

Using the CSS Styles Panel

Dreamweaver gives you complete control over internal and external styles with the CSS Styles panel. The CSS Styles panel lists all the internal and external styles attached to the active Web page. In addition to displaying the styles, known as rules, the CSS Styles panel gives you the ability to attach style sheets, modify existing styles (internal or external), disable or enable CSS properties (**New!**), and even remove styles.

Use the CSS Styles Panel

1. Open the Web page that contains the stylized text you want to view.

2. Click the **Window** menu, and then click **CSS Styles** or click the **CSS** button in the Properties panel.

3. The following options are available on the CSS Styles panel:

   ◆ **All or Current.** Shows all of the active document's style rules, or the currently selected rule.

   ◆ **Rules Window.** Displays a list of the active document's rules.

   ◆ **Properties Window.** Displays a list of the properties for the rule selected in the Rules window.

   ◆ **Show Category View.** Displays the properties for the selected rule by categories.

   ◆ **Show List View.** Displays the properties for the selected rule in List view (color, font, etc.).

   ◆ **Show Only Set Properties.** Displays only set properties.

   ◆ **Attach Style Sheet.** Attaches an external style sheet.

   ◆ **New CSS Rule.** Creates a new CSS rule.

   ◆ **Edit Style Sheet.** Opens a dialog box to edit styles.

   ◆ **Disable/Enable CSS Property.** Disables or enables the selected CSS property (**New!**).

   ◆ **Delete CSS Style Sheet.** Deletes the selected rule or property.

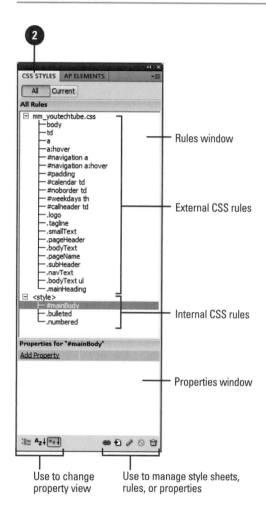

Rules window

External CSS rules

Internal CSS rules

Properties window

Use to change property view

Use to manage style sheets, rules, or properties

Editing CSS in the Properties Panel

The CSS Styles panel lists all the internal and external styles attached to the active Web page. Dreamweaver allows you to edit the internal and external styles with the CSS Styles panel and the Properties panel. If you only want to work with the CSS style for the currently selected text, you can use the Properties panel. From the Properties panel, you can display or change the selected target rule, edit the rule definition, access the CSS Styles panel, and change text style formatting. When you change CSS rules, the rule properties are updated in the head of the document or to an external style sheet. You can quickly toggle back and forth between CSS rule properties and HTML formatting properties on the Properties panel.

Edit CSS in the Properties Panel

1. Open the Web page that contains the stylized text you want to view.

2. Click the insertion point inside the block of text with the CSS rule that you want to edit.

3. Click the **CSS** button in the Properties panel.

4. The following options are available on the Properties panel:

   ◆ **Targeted Rule.** Displays the selected rule. You can use the list arrow to create new CSS rules, in-line styles, or apply existing classes to selected text.

   ◆ **Edit Rule.** Opens the CSS Rule Definition dialog box for the selected rule.

   See "Setting CSS Properties," on page 222 for information on available options in the CSS Rule Definition dialog box.

   ◆ **CSS Panel.** Opens the CSS Styles panel and displays properties for the selected rule.

   ◆ **Font.** Sets the font family to the selected rule.

   ◆ **Size.** Sets the font size to the selected rule.

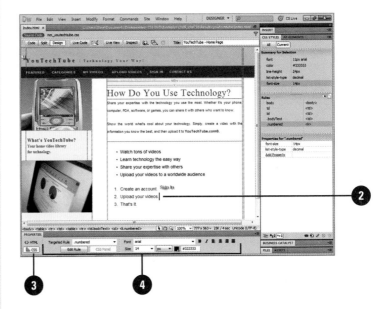

- ◆ **Text Color.** Sets the font color to the selected rule.

- ◆ **Bold.** Adds bold to the selected rule.

- ◆ **Italic.** Adds italic to the selected rule.

- ◆ **Left, Center, and Right Align.** Adds alignment to the selected rule.

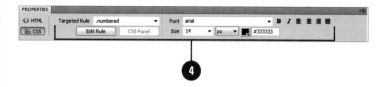

Set HTML Formatting in the Properties Panel

1. Open the Web page that contains the stylized text you want to view.

2. Select the text you want to format.

3. Click the **HTML** button in the Properties panel.

4. The following options are available on the Properties panel:

- ◆ **Format.** Sets the paragraph style.

- ◆ **ID.** Assigns an ID to the selection.

- ◆ **Class.** Displays the class style.

- ◆ **Bold.** Applies <b> or <strong>.

- ◆ **Italic.** Applies <i> or <em>.

- ◆ **Unordered or Ordered List.** Creates a bulleted or numbered list.

- ◆ **Indent and Outdent.** Adds or removes an indention.

- ◆ **Link.** Creates a hyperlink.

- ◆ **Target.** Specifies the frame or window in which the linked document loads.

Setting CSS Properties

After you create a new CSS rule, you can alter properties for it. The CSS Rule Definition dialog box lets you select the CSS properties you want to define a CSS rule. You can set CSS properties for any of the following categories: Type, Background (image and color), Block (spacing and alignment), Box (placement), Border (width, color, and style), Lists (bullets or numbers), Positioning (on page), and Extensions (filters, page breaks, and pointers).

Set CSS Properties

1. Open the Web page that contains CSS styles (internal or external) you want apply properties.

2. Open the CSS Styles panel.

3. Double-click the rule or property you want to define.

   TIMESAVER *Select the rule or property, and then make changes to the available attributes in the lower panel in the CSS Styles panel. Use the Show buttons at the bottom of the CSS Styles panel to display different attributes.*

4. Specify the options you want in the CSS Rule Definition dialog box:

   ◆ **Type and Font.** Click the **Type** category, and then specify the following options: Font, Size, Style, Line Height, Decoration (underline, overline, line-through, or blink), Weight (boldface), Variant (small caps), Case (first letter, uppercase or lowercase), or Color.

   ◆ **Background Image and Color.** Click the **Background** category, and then specify the following options: Background Color, Background Image, Repeat, Attachment, or Horizontal Position and Vertical Position.

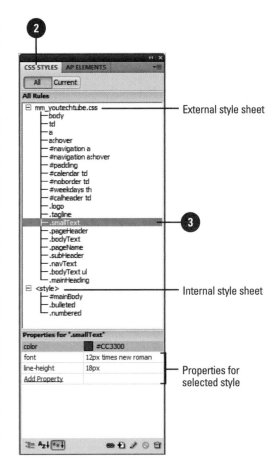

External style sheet

Internal style sheet

Properties for selected style

- ◆ **Spacing and Alignment.** Click the **Block** category, and then specify the following options: Word Spacing, Letter Spacing, Vertical Alignment, Text Align, Text Indent, Whitespace (*Normal* collapses white space, *Pre* works like the pre tag, or *Nowrap* only with br tag), or Display.

- ◆ **Placement.** Click the **Box** category, and then specify the following options: Width and Height, Float, Clear, Padding, Same For All (padding), Margin, or Same For All (margins).

- ◆ **Border Width, Color, and Style.** Click the **Border** category, and then specify the following options: Style, Same For All (style), Width, Same For All (width), Color, or Same For All (color).

- ◆ **Bulleted and Numbered Lists.** Click the **List** category, and then specify the following options: Type, Bullet Image, or Position.

- ◆ **Page Positioning.** Click the **Positioning** category, and then specify the following options: Type (*Absolute, Relative, Fixed,* or *Static*), Visibility (*Inherit, Visible,* or *Hidden*), Z-Index, Overflow, Placement, or Clip.

- ◆ **Filters, Page Breaks, and Pointers.** Click the **Extensions** category, and then specify the following options: Pagebreak, Cursor, or Filter.

5 Click **OK**.

Click the Current button to display the style for the selected text.

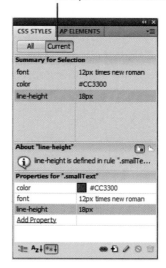

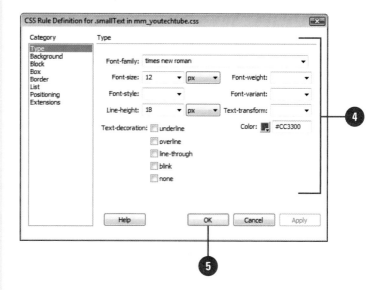

Working with CSS Rules

A CSS rule consists of two parts: selector and declaration. The **selector** identifies the formatted elements (such as p, body, or h1), while the **declaration** defines the style properties. The declaration is a collection, known as a block, of properties and values. For example, font-family: Arial; defines the text style as the Arial font. The declaration is everything between the braces ({}). After you create a CSS rule, you can use the CSS Styles panel to modify and customize it to better suit your needs. If you no longer need a CSS rule, you can remove it.

Modify an Existing Rule

1. Open the Web page that contains CSS styles with the rule you want to apply a property.

2. Open the CSS Styles panel.

3. Select a rule from the available options in the All Rules pane (All mode) or select a property in the Summary for Selection pane (Current mode).

4. Use any of the following methods:

   ◆ Double-click a rule or property to open the CSS Rule Definition dialog box. Make changes to the rule, and then click **OK** to save the changes.

   ◆ Click the **Show Only Set Properties** button, click the **Add Properties** link, and then fill in a value for the property in the Properties panel.

   ◆ Click the **Show Category View** or **Show List View** button, and then fill in a value for the property in the Properties panel.

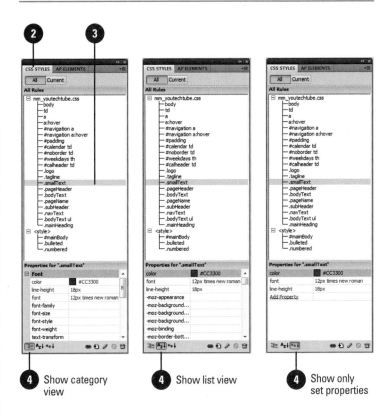

4 Show category view

4 Show list view

4 Show only set properties

Delete an Existing Rule

1. Open the Web page that contains CSS styles with the rule you want to delete.

2. Open the CSS Styles panel.

3. Select a rule from the available options.

4. Click the **Delete** button in the CSS Styles panel.

   NOTE *The rule will be deleted and all text the rule was attached to will revert back to their default format.*

Did You Know?

You can edit a CSS style sheet. Instead of editing individual rules, you can edit the entire style sheet. Click the Window menu, click CSS Styles to open the CSS Styles panel, click the All button, double-click the name of the style sheet you want to edit, modify the style sheet in the Document window, and then save your changes.

You can change the name of a CSS selector. Open the CSS Styles panel, click the All button, click the selector you want to change, click it again to make the name editable, change the name, and then click Enter (Win) or Return (Mac).

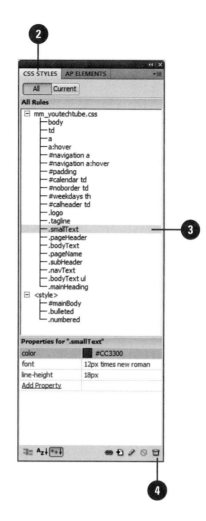

Moving CSS Rules

After you create a set of CSS rules that you like, you can move them from one document to another, from the head of a document to an external style sheet, and between different external CSS files. If a conflict arises when you move a CSS rule from one place to another, you can specify how you want Dreamweaver to handle it.

Move CSS Rules to a New Style Sheet

1. Open the document with the CSS rules you want to move.

2. Open the CSS Styles panel or display Code view.

3. Select the rule or rules you want to move.

   ◆ To select multiple rules, Ctrl-click (Win) or ⌘-click (Mac) the rules you want to select.

4. Right-click (Win) or Control-click (Mac) the selection, point to **CSS Styles**, and then click **Move CSS Rules**.

5. Select the **A New Style Sheet** option.

6. Click **OK**.

7. Enter a name for the new style sheet.

8. Click **Save**.

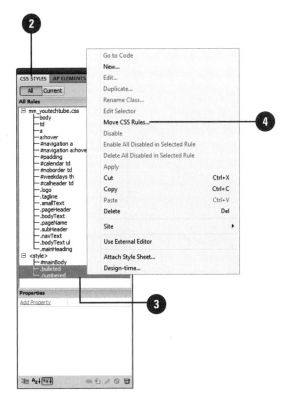

Move CSS Rules to an Existing Style Sheet

1 Open the document with the CSS rules you want to move.

2 Open the CSS Styles panel or display Code view.

3 Select the rule or rules you want to move.

◆ To select multiple rules, Ctrl-click (Win) or ⌘-click (Mac) the rules you want to select.

4 Right-click (Win) or Control-click (Mac) the selection, point to **CSS Styles**, and then click **Move CSS Rules**.

TIMESAVER Drag a rule in the CSS panel to a new position. For example, you can drag a rule from the internal document to the external document.

5 Click the **Style Sheet** option, and then select an existing style sheet already linked to the document from the menu or click **Browse** to select an existing style sheet.

6 Click **OK**.

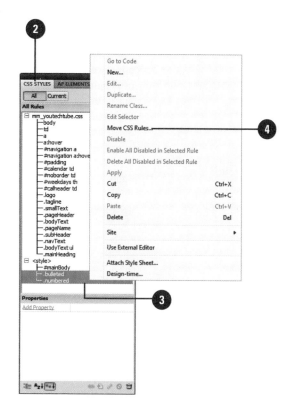

Did You Know?

You can rearrange or move CSS rules by dragging. Open the Styles panel, click the All button, select the rules you want to move, and then drag them to the new location. You can move a rule to another style sheet or the document head or rearrange rules within a style sheet.

Disabling or Enabling CSS Rules

Instead of deleting a CSS rule that you might want to use in the future, you can disable one or more rule properties (**New!**). When you need it again, you can enable it. When you disable a CSS rule property, Dreamweaver wraps the CSS code as a comment. In the CSS Styles panel, you can use the Disable/Enable CSS Property button to disable or enable individual properties. When you disable a property, the red universal no sign (circle with a line thru it) appears next to it in the CSS Styles panel and Code Navigator. If you assign a new value to a disabled property, Dreamweaver automatically enables it.

Disable or Enable CSS Rule Property

1 Open the document with the CSS properties you want to disable/enable.

2 Open the CSS Styles panel.

3 Select the rule with the property you want to disable/enable.

4 Select the CSS property you want to disable/enable.

5 Click the **Disable/Enable CSS Property** button.

TIMESAVER *Point to the left of the property name in the CSS Styles panel, and then click a blank area to disable a property or click a Disable icon to enable a property.*

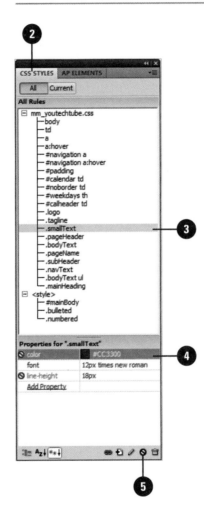

Did You Know?

You can enable all disabled properties in a selected rule. In the CSS Styles panel, select the rule, click the Options menu, and then click Enable All Disabled In Selected Ruler (**New!**).

You can delete all disabled in a selected rule. In the CSS Styles panel, select the rule, click the Options menu, and then click Delete All Disabled In Selected Ruler (**New!**).

Inspecting CSS Code

CSS Inspect works together with Live View to quickly identify HTML elements and their associated CSS styles to give you immediate feedback (**New!**). In Live View, you can click the Inspect button on the Document toolbar to enable the feature. With CSS Inspect enabled, you can move the mouse over elements on your page to see the CSS box model attributes for any block level element. When an element is highlighted in Live View, the corresponding HTML code is selected in Code or Split view. You can also view the CSS styles and properties for the selected element in the CSS Styles panel. CSS Inspect works best with the CSS Styles panel open in Current mode, and the Document window in Split Code/Live View and Live Code. If the workspace is not in this set up, the Info bar appears, asking you to switch to it.

Inspect CSS Styles

1 Open the Web page you want to view.

2 Switch to Design, Split, or Code view.

3 Click the **Live View** button.

4 Click the **Inspect** button.

5 If the Info bar opens asking you to switch to the best workspace, click the **Switch now** link.

The CSS Styles panel opens in Current mode, and the view changes to Split Code and Live Code view.

6 Point to HTML elements on the page to display CSS styles in the CSS Styles panel.

7 Click the **Refresh** button in the Document toolbar or press F5 to view any changes.

8 If you want, make CSS changes, select the element, and then make the changes you want in the CSS Styles panel.

9 To return back to Design view, click the **Live View** button again.

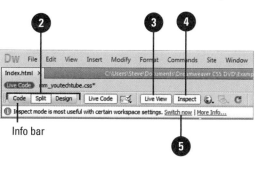

Info bar

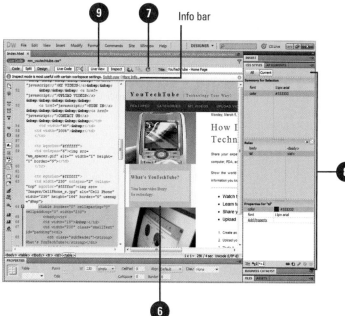

Info bar

Using the Relevant CSS Tab

Understanding Inheritance

With CSS, certain properties can be inherited from parent elements, making it easy to style one element and have all the descendent elements display the same style. This reduces the size of your CSS code and makes it easier to read, debug, and maintain. When you apply a style to an element, any property that can be inherited is passed to any child, or nested, elements. For example, if you apply the font properties of Times New Roman and 14px to the <p> tag, any nested <em> element would also be Times New Roman at 14 px. If styles conflict, the style closes to the element is applied. You can use the Relevant CSS tab to help you determine which style is in control and make any adjustments that you want.

Using the Relevant CSS Tab

The Relevant CSS tab lets you track the CSS rules affecting the currently selected text element as well as modifying the rule's properties. The Relevant tab is located in the Tag Inspector. Click the Window menu, and then click Tag Inspector. The Relevant CSS tab consists of two sections:

◆ The upper portion of the Relevant CSS tab shows the rules affecting the current selection and the tags that they affect.

◆ The lower portion of the Relevant CSS tab displays the properties of the currently selected element in an editable grid.

The properties are arranged alphabetically, with the set properties sorted to the top of the tab. Set properties are displayed in blue; properties irrelevant to the selection are displayed with a red strike through line. Hovering over a rule that is irrelevant displays a message explaining why the property is irrelevant. Typically, a property is irrelevant because it is overridden or not an inherited property.

You can also use the lower panel of the Relevant CSS tab to modify the properties of a selection. The editable grid lets you change the values for any of the displayed properties. Any changes you make to a selection are applied immediately, letting you preview your work as you go.

Working with ID Selectors

CSS Advanced styles redefine the formatting for a particular combination of elements, or for other selector forms as allowed by CSS (for example, the selector td h2 applies whenever an h2 header appears inside a table cell).

This is accomplished through the association of styles to HTML tags through ID attributes and ID selectors. ID attributes in HTML tags uniquely identify that tag with a name. Styles can be linked to that ID just like they can with classes. The big difference is that ids cannot be used on more than one tag. This also means that style definitions for ids only relate to one tag per page. You should never run into the need to apply an ID selector more than once. Should you need to use an ID selector on more then one occasion in any given page, you will need to re-plan your CSS.

For example, an ID can be applied to the h1 tag of a document containing heading text. The tag will be given the ID "master-heading" indicating that it is the sole and primary heading of the page. As such it will also receive a unique style.

Advanced styles can also redefine the formatting for tags that contain a specific id attribute (for example, the styles defined by #myStyle (user defined) apply to all tags that contain the attribute-value pair id="myStyle").

The following example is an ID selector:

```
#MyID {
  color: #0033ff;
}
```

The primary difference between a Class and ID selector is that the first character is a hash or pound sign (#).

Creating advanced styles also helps when Web pages are converted into text documents. For example, if ID's are selected for various heading, body, and sub text, these unique names can be used to help convert the Web text to print text.

In addition to ID selectors, CSS specifications refer to link styles as Pseudo-classes. These are special classes that describe styles for elements that only apply under certain circumstances. For example, the four default pseudo-classes you will find in the Advanced menu are:

- **a:link.** Describes any hyperlink that has not been visited by the user's browser. In other words, the page linked to is not present in the browser's local memory.

- **a:visited.** Describes any hyperlink that has been visited and is present in the browser's local memory.

- **a:hover.** Describes a hyperlink while the user's mouse happens to be hovering over it. This class is recognized by all version 4 and higher browsers, except Netscape 4.

- **a:active.** Describes a hyperlink that has been clicked but not yet released.

NOTE *The hover class is recognized by all version 4 and higher browsers, except Netscape.*

Creating and Applying an ID Selector

If you want to define the formatting for a combination of tags, you can use the Advanced option to create an ID selector. You can specify one or more HTML tags to create an ID selector or select one from the menu, which includes a:active, a:hover, a:link, and a:visited. After you specify the tags you want to use, you can define the formatting associated with it. When you're done, you can apply the ID selector to other elements.

Create an ID Selector

1. Open the Web page you want to create an ID selector.

2. Click the **Format** menu, point to **CSS Styles**, and then click **New**.

3. Click the **Select Style** list arrow, and then click **ID**.

4. Enter a style name in the Selector Name box (in this example, #mainBody), or select one from the list. IDs must begin with a pound (#) sign.

5. Click the **Define In** list arrow, and then select a new or existing external style sheet or **(This Document Only)**.

6. Click **OK**.

7. Click the **Type** category, and make the modifications you want. Some include the following:

   ◆ Font. Click the arrow button, and then select a font (in this example, click Verdana, Arial, Helvetica, sans-serif).

   ◆ Size. Click the arrow button, and then select a size (in this example, enter 24 pixels).

   ◆ Variant. Click the arrow button, and then select an option (in this example, click small-caps).

   ◆ Color. Click the arrow button and then select a color (in this example, click Blue (#0000FF)).

8. Click **OK**.

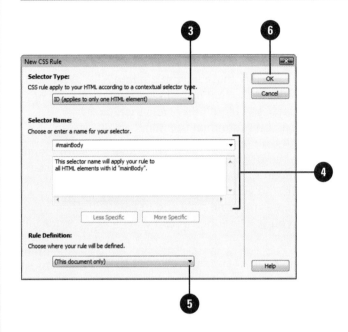

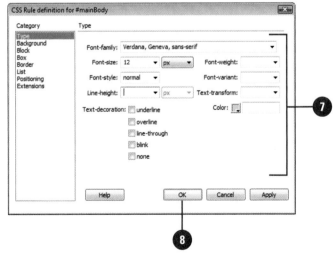

Apply an ID Selector

1 Click to place the insertion point into a portion of the text that you want to apply the ID selector.

2 Right-click one of the tags in the quick tag selector (in this example, the <p> tag).

3 Point to **Set ID**, and then select from the available ID selector options (in this example, paragraphText).

The selected paragraph now changes to the modifications made to the #paragraphText ID selector.

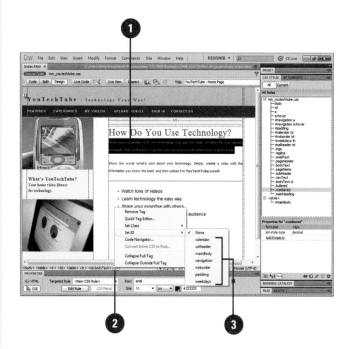

Checking for CSS Browser Compatibility

The Browser Compatibility Check (BCC) analyzes the HTML and CSS on the open page and determines whether it has problems in certain browsers. Browser targeting checks your pages for all popular platforms and browsers, including Firefox, Internet Explorer (Mac and Win), and Safari. When you run the BCC, it scans the open page and reports any potential CSS problems in the Results panel. Each potential problem is given a confidence rating, a circle. The amount of the circle filled in—quarter, half, three-quarters, or full—determines the occurrence probability level of the problem. Browser problems fall into three categories: serious (visible problem), warning (not supported), and informational (no visible effect). A direct link to documentation and solutions related to the problem is also provided on the Adobe CSS Advisor Web site.

Check for CSS Browser Compatibility Issues

1. Click the **File** menu, point to **Check Page**, and then click **Browser Compatibility**.

   The Results panel appears with the Browser Compatibility Check tab, indicating any problems.

2. Double-click an issue to select it.

   Information about the potential problem appears to the right in the Results panel.

3. To display the issue in the code, click the **Check Page** button on the Document window, and then click **Next Issue** or **Previous Issue**.

4. To open the Adobe CSS Advisor Web site, click the link at the bottom right of the Results panel.

5. To exclude an issue from future checking, right-click the issue in the Results panel, and then click **Ignore Issue.**

   ◆ To edit the Ignore Issues list, click the green arrow in the Results panel, click **Edit Ignored Issues List**, delete the issue from the Exceptions.xml file, and then save and close the file.

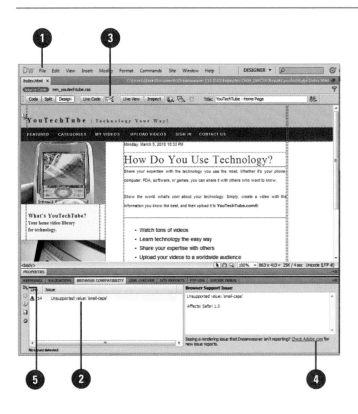

Select Browsers to Check

1 Click the **Check Page** button on the Document window, and then click **Settings**.

The Target Browsers dialog box opens.

2 Select the check boxes next to the browsers you want to check and clear the ones you don't want to check.

3 Click the **Version** list arrow for each browser to select the version you want.

4 Click **OK**.

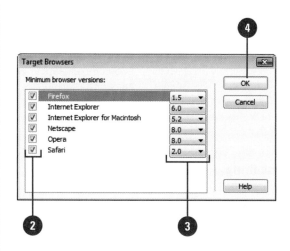

View and Save a BCC Report

1 Click the **File** menu, point to **Check Page**, and then click **Browser Compatibility**.

◆ You can also click the **Window** menu, point to **Results**, and then click the **Browser Compatibility**.

The Results panel appears with the Browser Compatibility Check tab, indicating any potential problems.

2 To view the report, click the **Browse Report** button in the Results panel.

3 To save the report, click the **Save Report** button in the Results panel.

Formatting CSS Code

You can use the Code Format section of the Preferences dialog box to access CSS source formatting options. You can set options to indent properties, and insert separator lines to make it easier to work with CSS code. As you make formatting option changes, a preview of the CSS code appears in the dialog box. If you like the preview results, you can accept the options. Otherwise, you can continue to make option changes. After you set CSS code formatting preferences, you can apply them to an entire document (in a CSS style sheet) or the head of the document only (embedded CSS code).

Set CSS Code Formatting Preferences

1 Click the **Dreamweaver** (Mac) or **Edit** (Win) menu, and then click **Preferences**.

2 Click the **Code Format** category.

3 Click the **CSS** button.

4 Select from the following CSS source code format options:

◆ **Indent Properties With.** Sets the indent number and type (Tabs or Spaces) for properties within a rule.

◆ **Each Property On Separate Line.** Places each property within a rule on a separate line.

◆ **Opening Brace On Separate Line.** Places the opening brace for a rule on a separate line from the selector.

◆ **Only If More Than One Property.** Places the single-property rules on the same line as the selector.

◆ **All Selectors For A Rule On Same Line.** Places all selectors for the rule on the same line.

◆ **Blank Line Between Rules.** Inserts a blank line between each rule.

5 Click **OK**.

6 Click **OK**.

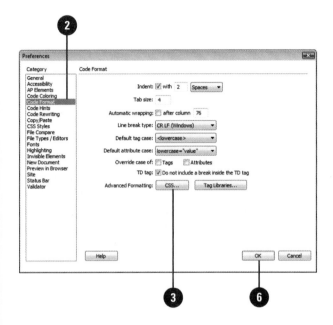

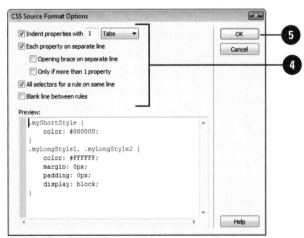

Format CSS Code in a CSS Style Sheet Manually

1. Display the CSS style sheet you want to format. Click the CSS style sheet name on the Related Files toolbar.

2. Click the **Commands** menu, and then click **Apply Source Formatting**.

   The formatting options set in CSS code formatting preferences are applied to the entire document.

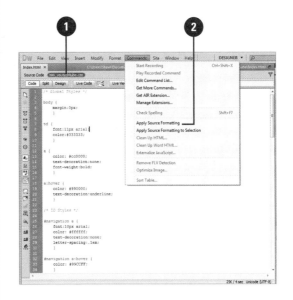

Format Embedded CSS Code Manually

1. Display the HTML page that contains CSS embedded in the head of the document. Click **Source Code** on the Related Files toolbar.

2. Select any part of the CSS code.

3. Click the **Commands** menu, and then click **Apply Source Formatting To Selection**.

   The formatting options set in CSS code formatting preferences are applied to all CSS rules in the head of the document only.

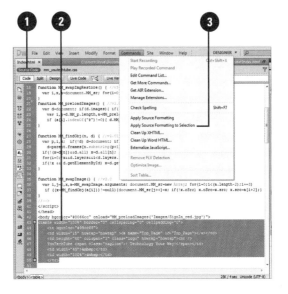

Setting CSS Styles Preferences

You can use the CSS Styles section of the Preferences dialog box to control the way Dreamweaver writes the code that defines CSS styles. You can specify the properties—including font, background, margin and padding, border and border width, or list-style—you want Dreamweaver to write in shorthand, determine whether Dreamweaver edits existing styles in shorthand, and select the editing tool you want to use to modify CSS rules. Shorthand CSS is an abbreviated syntax that allows you to create styles.

Set CSS Styles Preferences

1. Click the **Dreamweaver** (Mac) or **Edit** (Win) menu, and then click **Preferences**.

2. Click the **CSS Styles** category.

3. Select from the following CSS style options:

   ◆ **When Creating CSS Rules Use Shorthand For.** Select the check boxes for the properties you want Dreamweaver to write in shorthand.

   ◆ **When Editing CSS Rules Use Shorthand.** Select the font and size you want to use to display text within pre, code, and tt tags.

   ◆ **When Double-clicking In CSS Panel.** Select the option with the editing preference you want to use: CSS dialog, Properties panel, or Code view.

4. Click **OK**.

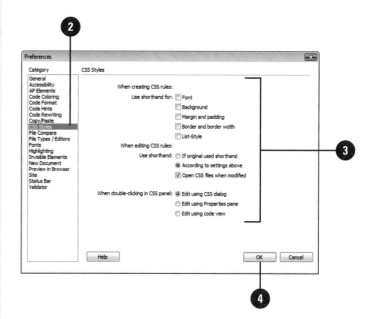

Using Design-Time Style Sheets

In Dreamweaver, you can use design-time style sheets to show or hide designs applied by a CSS style sheet as you work on a Web page. This is useful when you want to include or exclude the effect of a style sheet as you design a page. Design-Time style sheets only apply while you are working on a page. When the page displays in a browser, only the styles that are actually attached to or embedded in the page appear.

Use Design-Time Style Sheets

① Open the Web page you want to create a CSS style.

② Click the **Format** menu, point to **CSS Styles**, and then click **Design-Time.**

③ Select from the following CSS style options:

◆ Show. Click the **Plus** (+) button above Show Only At Design-Time, select the CSS style sheet you want to show, and then click **OK**.

◆ Hide. Click the **Plus** (+) button above Hide At Design-Time, select the CSS style sheet you want to hide, and then click **OK**.

◆ Remove. Click the style sheet you want to remove, and then click the appropriate **Minus** (-) button.

④ Click **OK**.

The CSS Styles panel displays an indicator, either "hidden" or "design" that reflects the current status of the style sheet.

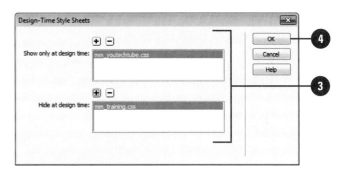

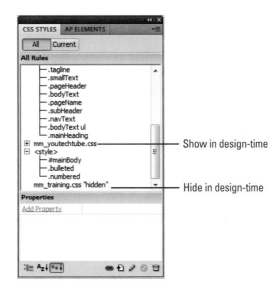

Show in design-time

Hide in design-time

Optimizing Web Pages

Page weight is a measurement of the file size of a Web page that includes the combined size of all the elements of the page. The elements images, audio or video files, associated style sheets, multiple HTML files loaded within frames, and so on.

Page weight can be used to determine the download time for a given page on a variety of Internet connection speeds. At high speeds (DSL and cable connections), most reasonably sized pages will download relatively quickly. However, at slower speeds (including faster dial-up speeds), even medium-sized pages can take ten seconds or more to download.

You can reduce page weight by doing some things and not doing others. Here is a brief list of different ways to reduce page weight:

- **Use CSS (Cascading Style Sheets).** CSS can be a very effective way to reduce the load time of your overall site.

  CSS reduces file size because it decreases the amount of markup in the HTML. CSS eliminates the need for page elements such as one-pixel spacer images, multiple font tags, nested tables, and similar items.

  Using an external style sheet also allows for the caching of the styles so that the browser doesn't have to reload it with each new page, thus reducing the time for subsequent pages (after the first) to load. Change a single property in the external file and it changes the appearance of that element for the entire website.

- **Remove inessential elements of your pages.** This is especially true of sound and video files, but also extends to unnecessary graphics and even extraneous text.

- **Avoid frames.** Not only do framed pages load more slowly, some search engines still do not index framed pages correctly.

- **Avoid nested tables.** Inexperienced Web designers will often utilize tables inside of tables in order to get the page layout just right. This can be avoided by using a single, well-thought-out table for page layout.

- **Compress your images.** Uncompressed JPEGs and GIFs often contain extra data not necessary for their correct display.

- **Remove extra "whitespace" in your code.** Every space, tab, and "newline" character in your HTML code requires extra data in the page. Thus, limit their use and pay attention to what extra space is inserted by your design software.

- **Break up long copy.** While long copy can often be an effective means of marketing your products or services, long-copy pages taken to the extreme may take so long to load that they will lose visitors during the wait. Consider breaking up very long copy to multiple pages.

- **Clean up your code with tools.** A number of free and commercial tools are available online that will clean up your website code, reducing page weight without affecting how your page is displayed.

Creating Page Layouts Using CSS-P

10

Introduction

Cascading Style Sheets-Positioning (CSS-P) is more than the perfect positioning of words and objects on a Web page, in addition, layers technology lets you create movable containers (called **AP elements**, formerly known as layers) that allow you to precisely position Web text and objects, even going so far as to stack one AP element on top of another, or to use JavaScript to show or hide AP elements. For example, you could have several AP elements containing thumbnails of images and when you hover over a particular AP element, a JavaScript would show a previously hidden AP element with information about the image. The incorporation of AP elements into a Web page gives the designer, for the first time, the use of all three dimensions: width, height, and even depth (stackable AP elements).

There is, of course, in all things a good news/bad news scenario. The good news is that AP elements and CSS-P are awesome tools for the creative designer to use. The bad news is that they do not work in earlier browsers (pre 4.0). Fortunately, Dreamweaver turns that bad news on its head by giving you the ability to convert AP elements into a more compatible tables document and vise versa.

This chapter covers the use of AP elements and CSS-P for the creation and implementation and total control of the design of Web pages. We'll focus in on how to create CSS-P design, and why you might want to use it.

What You'll Do

Introduce CSS Layouts and AP Elements

Create AP Elements

Nest AP Elements

Set AP Element Preferences

Use CSS Positioning

Apply a CSS-P Style

Modify CSS-P Properties

Work with AP Elements

Create a Rollover Using AP Elements

Convert AP Elements to Tables

Introducing CSS Layouts and AP Elements

In the beginning, support for Cascading Style Sheets (CSS) was a bit sketchy; however, as time when on, and CSS caught on, more and more browsers came on board. In response, Dreamweaver began giving Cascading Style Sheets complete support.

Cascading Style Sheets is all about the control of the Web page, and are a designer's dream come true. Not only do you have the ability to specify and apply specific font characteristics; in addition you can precisely place elements on the page. Basically CSS are a set of rules encased within a style sheet. The rules are customized styles, or modified HTML tags that define the look, position, and feel of the Web page. In the previous chapter, you learned about the syntax of CSS. In this chapter you'll learn how to use CSS to control and format Web pages, using AP elements, formally known as layers. An AP element is a movable container that allows you to precisely position Web text and objects

Web designers have always wanted the type of control over text and graphic elements that page designers have had, and with the advent of CSS, and the incorporation of AP elements, that day has finally arrived.

CSS and AP elements give you the ability to precisely position elements on a Web page, and let you stack AP elements over each other. This addition of the third dimension is not only a new concept in Web design, but it is exactly why CSS absolute position is called AP elements. Not only can Web designers position elements using x and y (width and height) positioning, they now have z indexing (depth)... and that's what I call control.

The Code

When you use Dreamweaver to create an AP element, the HTML code looks something like the following:

```
<div id="Layer4" style="position:absolute; visibility:inherit; width:200px; height:175 px; z-index:6">
</div>
```

Although it's not the only way to create the code, AP elements are usually placed between <div> ...</div> or ... tags.

Creating AP elements in Dreamweaver's design window (the most common method) is as simple as a drag and release. The visible result is the creation of a square or rectangle, which becomes a floating element on the Web page. This element can be populated with text, images or any combination thereof. Think of an AP element as a floating, independent table cell, and you have the picture. To move an AP element to a different position on the Web page, the designer has only to click and drag.

In addition to creating and moving the AP elements about the Web page, you have the ability to stack AP elements in the third dimension. By default every AP element is assigned a z-index, or stacking order. The first AP element is assigned the stacking order of 1, and each new AP element follows the progression 2, 3, 4, etc. Therefore, when two AP elements interact, they can actually slide over each other; creating Web designs that would have been impossible in straight HTML.

If you've ever used AP element-intensive applications, such as Adobe Photoshop, Illustrator, or InDesign, you're ready to get started designing CSS AP elements in Dreamweaver.

Creating AP Elements

An AP element is an HTML page element that has absolute position assigned to it. An AP element can contain text, images, or other HTML body content. You can create AP elements by using styles and rules, or by drawing them on the page manually using the Draw AP Div tool. When you manually create AP elements, they are not attached to any particular style, and therefore stand on their own. If you want to change all the AP elements attached to a style, all you need to do is change the style. If you want to change all the manually created AP elements, you need to modify each one independently. While this does not impair the display of the AP element in the browser window, it does mean that creating AP elements with styles (discussed later in this chapter) helps to make modifications quick and easy.

Create an AP Element Manually

1. Open the page you want to add an AP element.

2. Click the **Layout** tab on the Insert panel, and then click the **Draw AP Div** button.

3. Click in the Document window in Design view, and then use one of the following methods:

   ◆ **Draw An AP Element.** Drag to create the AP element the size you want. You can also use Ctrl+drag or ⌘+drag to draw multiple AP elements. Release the Ctrl or Command key when you're finished drawing.

   ◆ **Insert An AP Element.** Click the **Insert** menu, point to **Layout Objects**, and then click **AP Div**.

4. Click the edge of the AP element to select it.

   Selection handles appear around the edges of the AP element.

5. To adjust the width and height of the new AP element, drag one of the selection handles.

6. To adjust the position of the AP element, drag the AP element handle (tab in the upper-left corner) or the edge of the AP element.

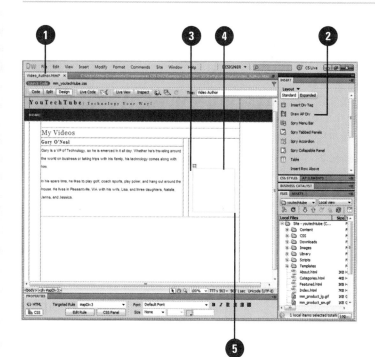

Nesting AP Elements

If you thought that creating an AP element was the greatest thing since sliced bread, then you're going to love that fact that you can nest AP elements. When you nest an AP element, you're placing an AP element within an AP element. Each AP element has its own formatting controls and gives you precise control over its position, for example, of text and graphics. Since the nested AP elements will be positioned based on the current position of the parent AP element, it's considered to have relative positioning concerning the page, and absolute or relative positioning within the nest.

Nest an AP Element

1. Open the page you want to add an AP element.

2. Click the **Layout** tab on the Insert panel, and then click the **Draw AP Div** button (formally called the Layer button).

3. Create an AP element in the Design view window of the current document.

4. Click the **Draw AP Div** button a second time; hold down Alt (Win) or Option (Mac) and drag to create another AP element within the first AP element.

5. Drag the parent AP element and the nested AP element moves at the same time.

6. To reposition the nested AP element relative to the parent AP element, drag the nested AP element.

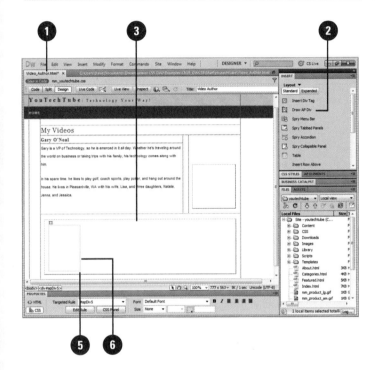

Did You Know?

You can show or hide AP element borders. To show AP element borders, click the View menu, point to Visual Aids, and then select either AP Div Outlines or CSS Layout Outlines. To hide AP element borders, click the View menu, point to Visual Aids, and then deselect AP Element Outlines and CSS Layout Outlines.

Setting AP Element Preferences

You can use the AP Element section of the Preferences dialog box to specify the default settings you want for new AP elements. Whether you create a new AP element using the Draw AP Div button on the Layout tab on the Insert panel or the AP Div command on the Layout Objects submenu on the Insert menu, Dreamweaver uses the default options you set in the Preferences dialog box for visibility, width and height, and background color options to create a new AP element.

Set AP Element Preferences

1 Click the **Dreamweaver** (Mac) or **Edit** (Win) menu, and then click **Preferences**.

2 Click the **AP Elements** category.

3 Select from the following AP Elements style options:

◆ **Visibility.** Select the default option to show or hide AP elements: Default, Inherit, Visible, Hidden.

◆ **Width and Height.** Enter the default width and height (in pixels) when you use Insert > Layout Objects > AP Div.

◆ **Background Color.** Select a default background color.

◆ **Background Image.** Select a default background image.

◆ **Nesting: Nest When Created Within An AP Div.** Select to create a nested AP Div when you draw within an existing AP Div.

4 Click **OK**.

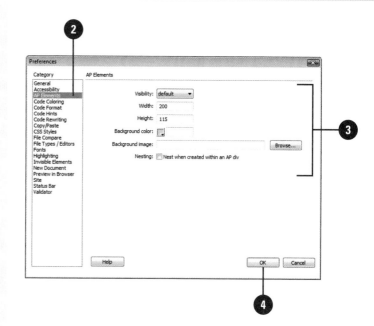

Using CSS Positioning

Cascading Style Sheets Positioning, or CSS-P, allows for specific positioning in HTML of Web elements. You can apply CSS-P to a block of text, a block element, an image, or an AP element. There are two ways to apply positioning: One is to create a style class and apply it to selections of text blocks on the page (this basically converts the object to an AP element, automatically), the second way is to create an AP element, and modify it independently of creating a style. In the end, you have a fully controllable CSS-P AP element. Once an AP element is established, it is controlled using absolute or relative positioning. **Relative positioning** means that AP elements are given a position relative to the top-left corner of the parent container, and is considered to be part of the flow of the page, such as a normal inline element within a text flow, or an AP element, nested with another AP element. **Absolute positioning** means that the AP element is positioned outside the flow of the Web page. In other words, nothing can make it move or change position. Setting the absolute positioning of the AP element does not impact the positioning of elements within the AP element. You can use the Properties panel to position and place AP elements where you want.

Change CSS-P Positioning Manually

① Open the Web page that contains the AP elements you want to modify.

② Select the AP element you want to change.

③ Open the Properties panel, and then modify the AP element's absolute position using the following options:

 ◆ **L.** Enter a value (in pixels) to position the AP element from the Left side of the Web page.

 ◆ **T.** Enter a value (in pixels) to position the AP element from the Top of the Web page.

 ◆ **Z-Index.** Enter a numerical value to indicate the AP element's stacking position when two or more AP elements overlap each other (higher numbers indicate a higher position within the stacking order of the active Web page).

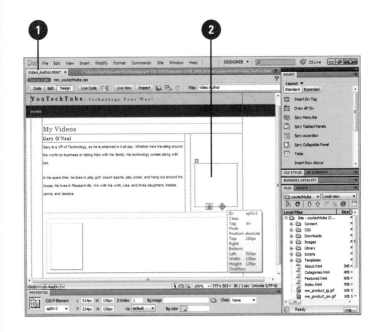

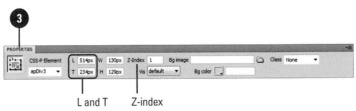

L and T   Z-index

Create a CSS-P Style

1. Open the Web page you want to create an AP element style.

2. Click the **Format** menu, point to **CSS Styles**, and then click **New**.

3. Click the **Select Type** list arrow, and then click **Class**.

4. Enter a name for your new class. The style name must begin with a period.

5. Click the **Define In** list arrow, and then click **(This Document Only)** or select an attached style sheet.

6. Click **OK**.

7. Click the **Positioning** category.

8. Specify AP element positioning using the following options:

   ◆ **Position.** Click the **Position** list arrow, and then select an option: **Absolute**, **Relative**, **Fixed**, or **Static**.

   The Static option is used when you do not wish to add content to an AP element.

   ◆ **Width.** Enter a Width (in pixels) for the new AP element.

   ◆ **Height.** Enter a Height (in pixels) for the new AP element.

   ◆ **Placement.** Enter a value (in pixels) for the absolute position of the AP element box in relation to the Web page.

   ◆ **Clip.** Enter a value (in pixels) for the absolute position of the AP element content in relation to the Web page.

   ◆ **Overflow.** Click the **Overflow** list arrow, and then select an option when content exceeds the container.

9. Click **OK** to add the embedded style to the active Web page.

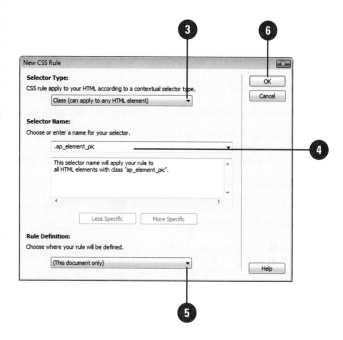

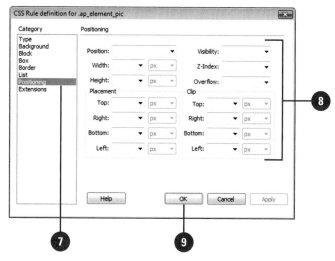

Applying a CSS-P Style

Once you've created one or more styles with AP elements, it's a simple matter to apply those styles to existing elements within a Web page. For example, you can create a navigational system, and then attach an AP element style that would control the element's position, width, height, and Z-index. You can apply AP element styles to text, groups of text, images, or virtually anything on a standard Web page. Not only can the dimensions and position of an AP element be controlled by CSS-P styles; in addition there are options for controlling fonts, sizing, styles; even the insertion of a color or background image into the AP element.

Apply a CCS-P Style

① Open the Web page that contains text and/or graphics you want to apply an AP element style.

② Select a group of text, or a graphic element on the page.

③ Click the **Format** menu, point to **CSS Styles**, and then select the appropriate style you want.

The selected CSS-P style is applied to the selected Web object.

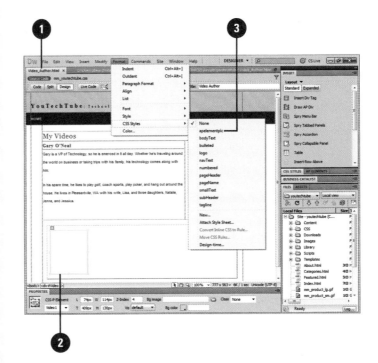

Did You Know?

You can create styles by using the ID of the AP element. You can name an AP element HeadLine (AP elements' IDs are changed in the Properties panel), and then create a customized style named, #HeadLine (remember to begin the name of the style with the # sign). Any AP elements with the name HeadLine (case is important) takes on the style of the #HeadLine CSS-P style.

Apply a Z-Index to an AP Element

①　Open the Web page that contains multiple AP elements you want to modify.

②　Open the Properties panel.

③　Select one of the AP elements, and then enter a value of 1 into the Z-index box in the Properties panel.

④　Select another AP element, and then enter a value of 2 into the Z-index box in the Properties panel.

⑤　Drag one of the AP elements so that it overlaps the other AP element.

　　The AP element with the higher Z-index is positioned on the top of the other AP element.

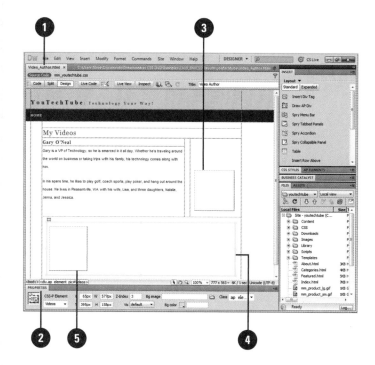

Did You Know?

The Z-index option works only when AP elements overlap. A single Web page can contain any number of AP elements. So long as the AP elements do not overlap, the Z-index is not utilized. However, when they overlap, the Z-index determines what AP element is on top of another.

Modifying CSS-P Properties

After you create a style, it's not locked in stone. For example, you might create a style using a particular font, and later change your mind. Or you might create a style using a color or background for the AP element, and later wish to change the style. Editing CSS-P styles is a snap in Dreamweaver, mainly because Adobe knows that sometimes you want to change your mind. The easiest way to change the properties of the style is through the CSS Styles panel, and that's exactly where we're headed. When you change a style, all elements currently assigned that style change to reflect the modifications.

Modify CSS-P Properties

1. Open the Web page that contains one or more styles you want to modify.

2. Open the CSS Styles panel.

3. Click the **All** button.

4. Select the style you want to modify.

5. Click the **Edit Style** button.

   TIMESAVER *Double-click the style you want to modify in the CSS Styles panel.*

6. Use the categories to change the following options:

   ◆ Type. Click the **Type** category to define basic font and type settings for a CSS style.

   ◆ Background. Click the **Background** category to define background settings for a CSS style.

   ◆ Block. Click the **Block** category to define spacing and alignment settings for tags and attributes.

   ◆ Box. Click the **Box** category to define settings for tags and attributes that control the placement of elements on the page. You can change width and height, float, clear, padding, and margins.

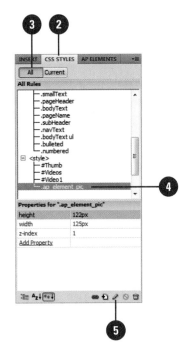

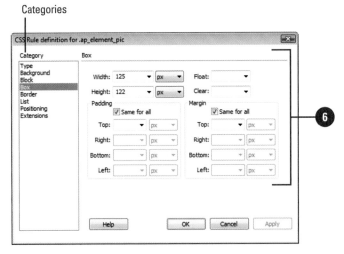

Categories

- ◆ **Border.** Click the **Border** category to define settings, such as width, color, and style, for the borders around elements.

- ◆ **List.** Click the **List** category to modify list settings, such as bullet size and type, for list tags.

- ◆ **Positioning.** Click the **Positioning** category to modify the tag or block of selected text into a new AP element using the default tag for defining AP elements as set in the AP Elements preferences.

- ◆ **Extensions.** Click the **Extensions** category to modify filters, page break, and pointer options, most of which aren't supported in any browser or are supported only in Internet Explorer 4.0 and above.

7 Click **OK** to save the changes, or click **Apply** to view how the changes impact the style before saving.

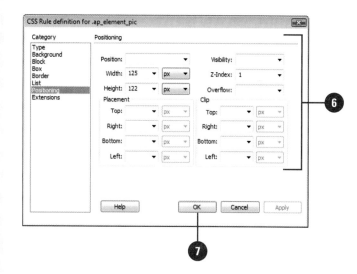

Did You Know?

It's important to preview AP element positioning. Dreamweaver only previews relative positioning when you're working with a nested AP element or have not set any top or left attributes. Therefore, always preview your pages to visually verify that the positioning is accurate.

For Your Information

Using the CSS Box Model for Page Layout

The CSS Box model says that every HTML element in a document is a rectangle box. You can create CSS styles that make boxes, one inside the other by using the Box category in the CSS Rule Definition dialog box. This allows you to create a web page layout (multi-column) independent of tables. Each box controls display properties, including Width and Height, Float, Clear, Padding, and Margins. The Float property moves an element left or right and wraps content around it, while the Clear property prevents an element from wrapping. The Padding property is the gap that separates the content of the style, such as space between an image and its border. The Margin property is the outer space surrounding an element.

Working with AP Elements

After you create the AP elements you want, you can use the AP Elements panel and other commands to manage and work with AP elements. You can change the stacking order and place one AP element in front or behind another, hide some AP elements while showing others, move and align AP elements across the screen, and resize them individually or together.

Work with AP Elements in the AP Elements Panel

1. Open the Web page that contains one or more AP elements you want to modify.

2. Click the **Window** menu, and then click **AP Elements** to display the AP Elements panel.

3. Use the AP Elements panel to change the following options:

   ◆ **Show or Hide.** Click the Eye icon column to show (open eye) and hide (closed eye) elements.

   TIMESAVER *Click the header Eye icon at the top of the column to show or hide all the elements.*

   ◆ **Stacking Order.** Drag an element up or down in the list. A line appears as you drag to indicate the position.

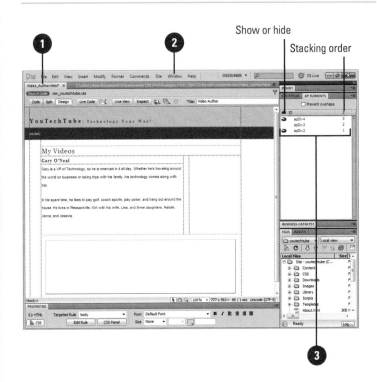

Show or hide

Stacking order

Did You Know?

You can prevent AP elements from overlapping. Select the Prevent overlaps check box in the AP Elements panel or click the Modify menu, point to Arrange, and then click Prevent AP Element Overlaps to select it.

Move, Resize, and Arrange AP Elements

1. Open the Web page that contains one or more AP elements you want to modify.

2. Select the AP element you want.

3. Use the AP Elements panel to change the following options:

   ◆ **Move.** Drag the AP element handle (tab in the upper-left corner) or the edge of the AP element.

   TIMESAVER *Use the arrow keys to move an AP element one pixel at a time.*

   ◆ **Resize.** Drag one of the selection handles or type values for width (W) and height (H) in the Properties panel.

   TIMESAVER *Use Ctrl (Win) or Option (Mac) and the arrow keys to resize an AP element one pixel at a time. Use Shift+Ctrl (Win) or Shift+Option (Mac) and the arrow keys to resize by the grid snapping increment.*

   ◆ **Make Same Width or Height.** Select two or more AP elements, click the **Modify** menu, point to **Arrange**, and then click **Make Same Width** or **Make Same Height**.

   ◆ **Align.** Select two or more AP elements, click the **Modify** menu, point to **Arrange**, and then select an alignment option. All the AP elements align themselves to the last selected AP element.

   ◆ **Stacking Order.** Click the **Modify** menu, point to **Arrange**, and then click **Bring To Front** or **Send To Back**.

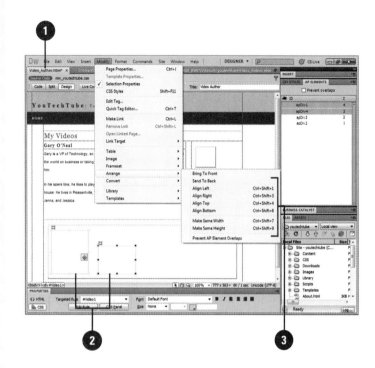

Creating a Rollover Using AP Elements

AP Elements have several unique properties that let you design way beyond the static text and graphic Web pages of the past. You can show and hide AP elements to create effects. For example, you can create a drop-down menu, or you can display the larger version of an image when you point to, or rollover, the small thumbnail version. In this example, Dreamweaver shows or hides the AP elements with the different images.

Create a Show/Hide Rollover

1. Create a new Web page.

2. Click the **Layout** tab on the Insert panel.

3. Click the **Draw AP Div** button, and then create two AP elements.

   ◆ An AP element 60 by 60 pixels, which contains a small thumbnail graphic. Name the AP element in the Properties panel, Thumb.

   ◆ An AP element 300 by 300 pixels, which contains the larger image. Name this AP element, Main.

4. Move the Thumb AP element to the left in the document window, and then move the Main AP element to the right.

5. Drag an image to the Thumb AP element, and an image to the Main AP element (the images should have the same width and height as the AP elements).

6. Open the Properties panel.

7. Select the **Main** AP element and change the Visibility of the AP element to **Hidden**.

8. Click the **Window** menu, and then click **Behaviors** to display the Behaviors panel.

9. Select the Thumb AP element.

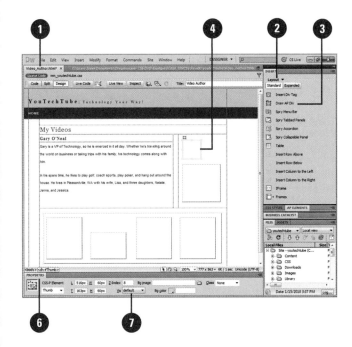

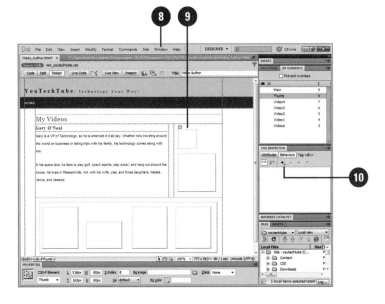

10. Click the **Add Behavior** button, and then click **Show-Hide Elements**.

11. Select div "Main" from the available elements.

12. Click the **Show** button.

13. Click **OK**.

14. Click the **Event** list arrow, and then click **onMouseOver**.

15. Click the **Add Behavior** button, and then click **Show-Hide Elements**.

16. Select div "Main" from the available elements.

17. Click the **Hide** button.

18. Click **OK**.

19. Click the **Event** list arrow, and then click **onMouseOut**.

20. Click the **File** menu, point to **Preview In Browser**, and then select a browser.

When the Web page displays, rolling over the smaller thumbnail of the image causes the larger image to display. When you roll out of the thumbnail AP element, the larger image disappears... like magic.

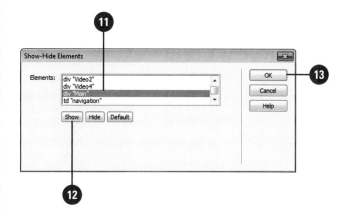

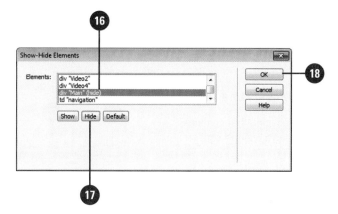

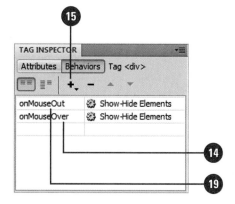

Converting AP Elements to Tables

While the advantage to designing with AP elements is the greater flexibility it affords, one of the greatest disadvantages of using AP elements is that they are viewable in only the most recent generation of browsers. Dreamweaver enables you to get the best of both worlds by making it possible for you to use AP elements to design complex page layouts, and then to transform those AP elements into tables that can be viewed in earlier browsers. For example, you might need to convert your AP elements to tables if you need to support browsers before version 4.0. Nevertheless, Dreamweaver's capability to convert AP elements to tables enables you to create complex layouts with ease. Designing this way has some limitations—you can't, for example, overlap AP element items on top of one another. If you have any overlapping AP elements within the document, Dreamweaver does its best to reposition the AP elements side by side. However, it's best if you make those corrections manually before performing the conversion. In addition, instead of using tables or Layout mode to create a document, some Web designers prefer to work with AP elements. If you need to convert a table back to AP elements, you can do it in Dreamweaver.

Convert AP Elements to a Table

1. Open the Web page that contains AP elements you want to convert to a table.

   ◆ Make sure you don't have any overlapping AP elements.

2. Click the **Modify** menu, point to **Convert**, and then select **AP Divs To Tables**.

3. Select from the following table layout options:

   ◆ **Most Accurate.** Attempts to convert the AP element document as close to the original as possible.

   ◆ **Smallest.** Choose to collapse smaller than a user-defined size.

   ◆ **Use Transparent GIFs.** Select this option to allow the use of transparent GIF files in empty cells.

   ◆ **Center On Page.** Select this option to center the table on the active Web page.

4. Select from the following layout tools options:

* **Prevent Overlaps.** Select to prevent cells from overlapping.

* **Show AP Elements Panel.** Select to show the AP Elements panel (displays when you click the OK button).

* **Show Grid.** Select to display a grid in the document window.

* **Snap To Grid.** Select to force the newly created table to snap to the existing grid.

5. Click **OK**.

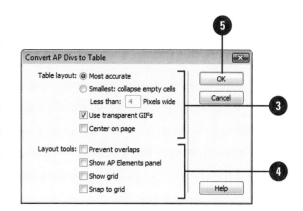

Convert Table to AP Elements

1. Open the Web page that contains a table you want to convert to AP elements.

2. Click the **Modify** menu, point to **Convert**, and then click **Tables To AP Divs**.

3. Select from the following table layout options:

* **Prevent Overlaps.** Select to prevent AP elements from overlapping.

* **Show AP Elements Panel.** Select to show the AP Elements panel (displays when you click the OK button).

* **Show Grid.** Select to display a grid in the document window.

* **Snap To Grid.** Select to force the newly created table to snap to the existing grid.

4. Click **OK**.

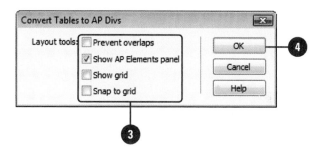

Creating Frames

Introduction

When it comes to Web design, frames have been around for quite a long time. In that time they have constantly fallen in and out of favor. Some Web designers can't live without them, and some designers would never in a million years use them. However, whether you love them or dislike them, frames are here to stay... at least for today.

Frames are an interesting way to design a Web document. Think of a window with separate panes of glass. Now, think of that window as a Web page, and each one of those separate panes of glass as a separate HTML document, and you've got a pretty good visualization of a Web page containing frames. For example, you can have a two-frame page with one frame containing the navigation for the site, and the other frame the contents. When you click on a link in the navigation frame, the content frame displays another HTML document, and the frame containing the navigation never changes.

There's a certain beauty in being able to change one area of a Web page and leave another area static. Good Web designers with a good sense of how to utilize frame technology can create some pretty awesome Web sites.

A framed document is composed of a frameset page (called so because it uses the <frameset> tag), and two or more HTML documents. When the frameset page loads on the visitor's browser, it calls and loads the HTML documents, and displays the page.

Dreamweaver makes the coding and managing of frames easy with a point-and-click interface. You control the commands for modifying the properties of the overall frames, and each individual frame. This chapter will give you the essentials of creating frames, and information for inserting and modifying frames and framesets, as well as how you might apply them in your own Web designs.

What You'll Do

Introduce Frames

Create a New Frame

Open a Web Page in a Frame

Provide Information for No Frame Support

Select Frames and Framesets

Add Frameset Information

Save a Frameset

Modify Frames

Change Frame Properties

Change Frameset Properties

Target Links

Create Quick and Easy Frame Links

Introducing Frames

Frame documents use a <frameset>... </frameset> tag set to create documents in multiple views. The multiple view nature of frame documents lets designers keep certain information visible, while other windows within the frame are scrolled or replaced. For example, within the same window, one frame might display a static banner, a second a navigation menu, and a third the main document that can be scrolled through or replaced by navigating in the second frame.

If you were to design a Frame page directly in HTML, it might look something like this:

```
<!DOCTYPE HTML PUBLIC "-//W3C//DTD HTML 4.01
Frameset//EN"

    "http://www.w3.org/TR/html4/frameset.dtd">

<html>

<head>

<title>A frameset </title>

</head>

<frameset cols="20%, 80%">

  < frameset rows="100, 200">

     <frame src="doc1.html">

     < frame src="doc2.gif">

  </ frameset >

  < frame src="doc3.html">

</ frameset >

</html>
```

Image

Frames divide a browser window into two or more document windows, each displaying a different document, or a different part of the same document. Frames in an HTML document cause a web page to look as if it's divided into multiple, scrollable regions. Each separate frame has a distinct name, which the frameset uses to load specific HTML documents.

Frames in HTML documents are created and controlled through three distinct element types: FRAMESET, FRAME and NOFRAMES.

The Frameset Element

A frameset divides the browser window into two or more rectangular regions. For example the following HTML code describes a basic frameset:

```
<frameset cols="30%,30%,40%">
```

This code describes a frame set divided vertically into three regions, and each region is a percentage of the width of the browser window (30%, 30%, and 40%). Since the rows attribute was not used, this frameset does not include rows.

The Frame Element

The Frame element defines a single frame in a frameset, and can include up to seven attributes: src, name, frameborder, margin-width, marginheight, scrolling, and noresize. Since the frame tag is not defined as a container, it has no matching end tag. The following is an example of a frame element:

```
<html>

<frameset rows="20%,80%">

        <frame src="http://www.power.com/">

        <frameset cols="60%,40%">

                <frame
src="http://www.andy.com/">

                <frame
src="http://www.steve.com/">

        </frameset>

</frameset>

</html>
```

The <noframes> Tag

The noframe element contains content that should only be rendered when frames are not displayed. Noframe is typically used in a Frameset document to provide alternate content for browsers that do not support frames or have frames disabled. The following is an example of the noframes tag.

```
<noframes>

    <p>The Frameset contains:

    <ul>

        <li><A href="contents_of_frame1.html">content_1</A>

            <li><img src="image.gif">

            <li><A href="noframes.html">Some other neat contents</A>

        </ul>

    </noframes>
```

Creating a New Frame

Most of the framesets on the Web today use two or three frames. For example, a common setup is to have one narrow frame spanning the top of the page to hold a banner and some site navigation; a lower-left frame to hold a table of contents or additional navigation; and a large lower-right frame to hold the content of the site. Or it can be as simple as two frames: one small frame for navigation, and a larger frame for the main body of information. You can create a new document with frames using samples from the New Document dialog box or add frames to an existing document using the Frames button or dragging a frame border. After you create a frameset, you can enter text, images, and other content in each of the frames, as you would for any normal HTML document, or you can instruct the frame to load a previously created HTML document.

Create a Frameset from a Sample

1. Click the **File** menu, and then click **New**.

2. Click the **Page from Sample** category.

3. Click **Frameset** in Sample Folder options.

4. Select a Sample Page.

   TIMESAVER *Click the Get more content link to add more templates to the New Document dialog box.*

5. Click **Create**.

   The Frame Tag Accessibility Attributes dialog box opens.

6. Click the **Frame** list arrow, select a frame, and then enter a name (one word, start with a letter, and case-sensitive) for each frame in the document.

7. Click **OK**.

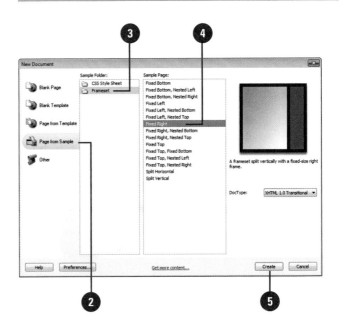

Did You Know?

You can use a grid to help layout a frame document. Click the View menu, point to Grid, and then click Show Grid to show the grid.

Insert a Frameset

1. Create a new HTML document, or open an existing one.

2. Click the **Layout** tab on the Insert bar.

3. Click the **Frames** button, and select a frameset from the available options (in this example, Left Frame).

   The Frame Tag Accessibility Attributes dialog box opens.

4. Click the **Frame** list arrow, select a frame, and then enter a name (one word, start with a letter, and case-sensitive) for each frame in the document.

5. Click **OK**.

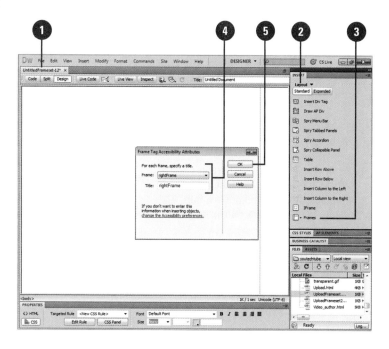

Create a Frameset with Click and Drag

1. Create a new HTML document, or open an existing one.

2. Click the **View** menu, point to **Visual Aids**, and then click **Frame Borders**.

   Dreamweaver creates a heavy outline around the edges of the document window.

3. Position the cursor over one of the borders until it turns into a double-headed arrow, and then drag to create a new frame.

4. Continue dragging from the vertical or horizontal border until you have the frames you want.

   TIMESAVER *Hold down Alt (Win) or Option (Mac) while you drag an existing frame border to create a new frame instead of moving it.*

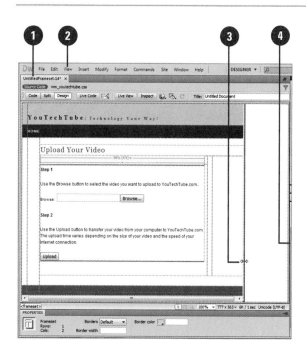

Opening a Web Page in a Frame

After you create a frame, you can specify the content you want to appear in it. You can insert new content in a frame the same way you insert other content, such as text or images, into a Web page or open an existing HTML Web page in a frame. If you consistently use the same Web page in a frame, you can make the page the default document when the frameset appears in a browser.

Open an Existing Web Page in a Frame

1. Open the Web page with frames you want to modify, and then click to place the insertion point in the frame where you want to insert a Web page.

2. Click the **File** menu, and then click **Open in Frame**.

   TIMESAVER *Press Ctrl+Shift+ O (Win) or ⌘+Shift+O (Mac).*

3. Navigate to the drive and folder location where you want to open the Web page.

4. Click the **Files of Type** list arrow (Win) or **popup** (Mac), and then select the type of file you want to open.

5. Select the page you want to open from the page list in the working folder, or type the URL of the page you want.

6. Click **OK**.

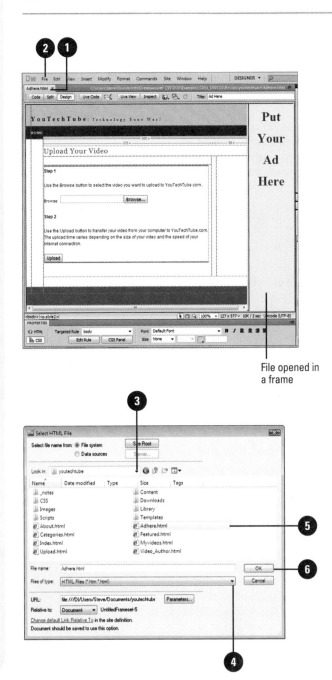

File opened in a frame

Providing Information for No Frame Support

If a browser doesn't support frames, you can provide information to visitors instead of leaving them hanging with nowhere to go. When a browser that doesn't support frames loads the frameset document, the browser displays the information you provide in a noframes tag. The Edit NoFrames Content command makes it easy to add the information you want without inserting HTML code. However, if you are comfortable entering code, you can certainly enter the information in the noframes tag.

Provide Information for Browsers with No Frame Support

1. Open the Web page with the frameset you want to modify.

2. Click the **Modify** menu, point to **Frameset**, and then click **Edit NoFrames Content**.

   The Design view clears, and the words "NoFrames Content" appears at the top of the Document window.

3. Type the information you want visitors to see when their browsers don't support frames.

   ◆ You can also click the **Window** menu, click **Code Inspector**, and then type the HTML code for the text you want to display in the body tags inside the noframes tags.

4. Click the **Modify** menu, point to **Frameset**, and then click **Edit NoFrames Content**.

   The normal view of the frameset document appears.

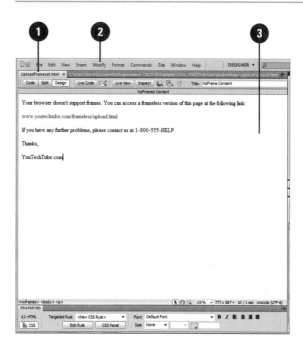

Selecting Frames and Framesets

Before you can make any changes to a frame or frameset, you need to select it first. You can select a frame or frameset directly in the Document window, by using keyboard shortcuts, or by using the Frames panel. The Frames panel shows you the frames within a frameset. A frameset appears with a thick border and each frame appears with a thin gray link along with a frame name, which makes them easier to view and select. When a frame is selected in the Document window, the frame border appears outlined with a dotted line. When a frameset is selected, all the frame borders appear with a light dotted line.

Select Frames and Framesets

◆ **Frames Panel.** Click the **Window** menu, click **Frames** to display the Frames panel, and then use any of the following:

  ◆ **Frame.** Click the frame.

  ◆ **Frameset.** Click the border around the frameset.

◆ **Document Window.** Display the Web page with frames in Design view, and then use any of the following:

  ◆ **Frame.** Alt-click (Win) or Option-Shift-click in a frame.

  ◆ **Frameset.** Click one of the frameset's internal borders.

◆ **Different Frames or Framesets.** Use the Arrow keys to select frames or framesets.

  ◆ **Next or Previous.** Press Alt+Left Arrow or Alt+Right Arrow (Win) or ⌘+Left Arrow or ⌘+Right Arrow (Mac).

  ◆ **Parent Frameset.** Press Alt+Up Arrow (Win) or ⌘+Up Arrow (Mac).

  ◆ **First Child Frame or Current Frameset.** Press Alt+Down Arrow (Win) or ⌘+Down Arrow (Mac).

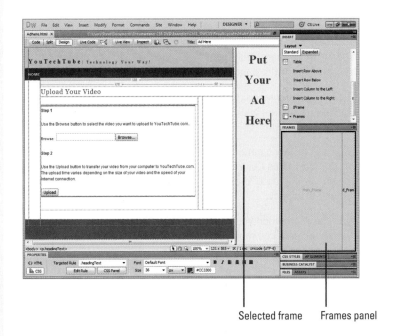

Selected frame   Frames panel

Adding Frameset Information

A frameset document consists of separate frames. As a matter of fact, each one of the frames is simply a small HTML document. Frames can contain any normal HTML information, including text, tables, images, multimedia, objects, and even nested frames. When you create a Frameset document, you're actually creating several separate documents. You have the frameset HTML document, and a separate HTML document for each of the frames. For example, if you create a frameset with two frames, you're actually saving three separate documents: one for the frameset and one for each of the frames within the document.

Add Frameset Information

1. Create a new Web page with a frameset, or open an existing one.

2. Click in a frame where you want to add some information.

3. Add or insert the text and graphics you want until the frames are filled with the specified information (in this example, a graphic).

Drag graphic from Files panel

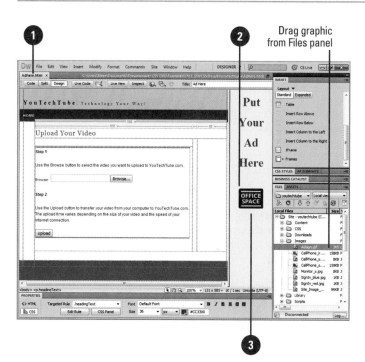

Saving a Frameset

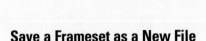

When you create a frameset with two frames, you're actually saving three separate documents: one for the frameset and one for each of the frames within the document. You can save the frameset and each document in a frame individually or you can save them all at once. Before you can preview a frameset in a browser, you need to save the frameset and all frame document first. Once the frame documents have been saved, they can be opened independently of the frameset and modified just like regular HTML documents; any changes to the page will be reflected when it's reopened in the frameset. When you reopen the frameset document, it locates and reopens the associated pages and place them into the proper frames.

Save a Frameset as a New File

1. Select the frameset you want to save.

2. Click the **File** menu, and then click **Save Frameset As**.

   TIMESAVER *Press Ctrl+Shift+S (Win) or ⌘+Shift+S (Mac).*

   NOTE *Dreamweaver prompts you to save your document in the active site folder (strongly recommended).*

3. Navigate to the location where you want to save the frame document.

4. Enter a name for the frameset document.

5. Click **Save**.

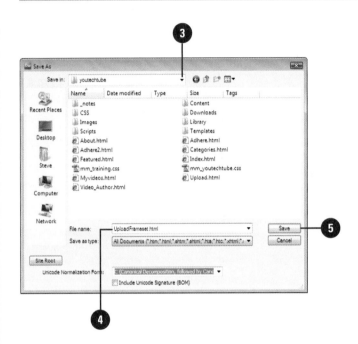

Did You Know?

You can save the frameset and all frame documents at the same time. Click the File menu, and then click Save All.

Save a Frame as a New File

① Click in the frame you want to save.

② Click the **File** menu, and then select **Save Frame As**.

TIMESAVER *Press Ctrl+Shift+S (Win) or ⌘+Shift+S (Mac).*

NOTE *Dreamweaver prompts you to save your document in the active site folder (strongly recommended).*

③ Navigate to the location where you want to save the frame document.

④ Enter a name for the new frame document.

⑤ Click **Save**.

Did You Know?

You can quickly save a frameset or frame previously saved as a file.
Select the frameset or frame you want to save, click the File menu, and then click Save Frameset or Save Frame. You can also press Ctrl+S (Win) or ⌘+S (Mac).

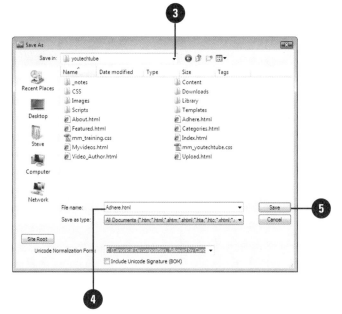

Modifying Frames

Once a frameset is created, it's possible, and quite likely, that you will want to modify the dimensions of the frames to fit a specific design need. Remember that the frame within a frameset functions as a container for a specific HTML document. If this document is not set up correctly, you may experience problems with unwanted reformatting of the information when it displays in the browser window. Therefore, it's important to modify the frames to give your document the best look and feel for the visitor.

Resize a Frame

1. Open the Web page with the frameset you want to modify.

2. To display visual frame borders, click the **View** menu, point to **Visual Aids**, and then click **Frame Borders**.

3. Mouse over one of the borders until your cursor turns into a double-headed arrow.

4. Drag a frame border to modify its position and size.

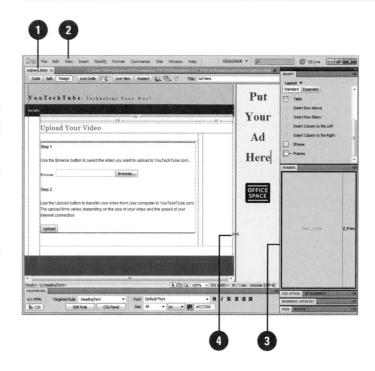

Did You Know?

You can edit accessibility values for a frame. Click the View menu, and then click Code or Code and Design, click the Window menu, click Frames to display the Frames panel, click to place the insertion point in a frame, right-click (Win) or ⌘-click (Mac) in the code, and then click Edit Tag, make the changes you want, and then click OK.

Add a Frame

① Open the Web page with the frameset you want to modify.

② To display visual frame borders, click the **View** menu, point to **Visual Aids**, and then click **Frame Borders**.

③ Holding down Alt (Win) or Option (Mac) and drag one of the borders.

④ Release your mouse to add the new frame to the document.

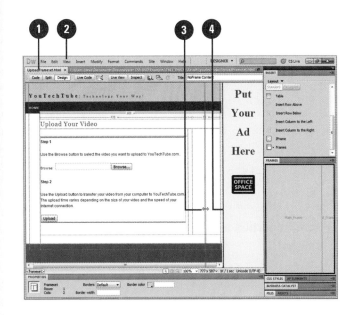

Delete a Frame

① Open the Web page with the frame you want to modify.

② To display visual frame borders, click the **View** menu, point to **Visual Aids**, and then click **Frame Borders**.

③ Click the frame border and drag it into the border of the enclosing or parent frame.

> **NOTE** *If no parent frame is present, drag the frame border to the edge of the page.*

④ Release the mouse and the frame is removed.

If the deleted frame contains unsaved content, Dreamweaver asks if you want to save the file before closing it.

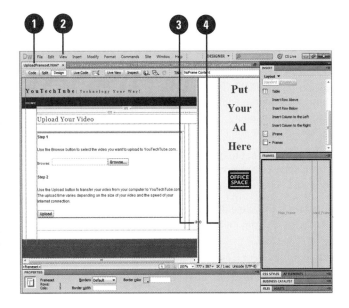

Changing Frame Properties

As mentioned before, frameset documents are simply individual HTML documents, with all the rights and privileges of any other HTML document. They can have any content; including tables and layers, and they have the same properties of any other HTML document, such as: backgrounds, margins, headings, etc. You can change the properties of a HTML document destined to be displayed within a frameset in one of two ways. The first is to open the document directly in Dreamweaver, make any changes, and then save the document. When it's opened within the frameset, the changes to the properties will be displayed as ordered by you. The second way is to change their properties while viewing the document within the frameset (recommended). Since the procedure is basically the same, we'll examine the changing of page properties while viewing the document in the frameset.

Change Page Properties for a Frame Document

① Open the Web page with the frameset you want to modify.

② Right-click (Win) or Control-click (Mac) the HTML frame document that you want to modify, and then click **Page Properties**.

③ Select from the following Page Properties options:

◆ **Appearance (CSS)** or **Appearance (HTML).** Select to change the overall appearance of the page; including background, text and margins.

◆ **Links (CSS).** Select to change linking information; link colors and fonts and underlining.

◆ **Headings (CSS).** Select to modify the heading font, color and size.

◆ **Title/Encoding.** Select to modify the title and encoding of the page (this information is used by browsers to help properly display the page).

◆ **Tracing Image.** Select to add or modify a tracing image.

④ Click **OK**.

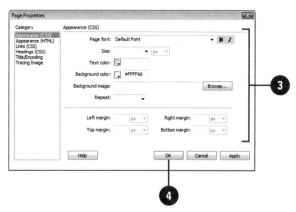

Change Frame Properties

1 Open the Web page with the frameset you want to modify.

2 Select the frame you want to modify in the Frames panel or Shift-Alt-click (Win) or Shift-Option-click (Mac) the frame in Design view.

◆ You can also click a frame in the Frames panel.

3 Open the Properties panel.

4 Select from the following Frame Properties options:

◆ **Frame Name.** Enter the name you want used by a link's target attribute or by a script to refer to a frame. A frame name must start with a letter and it's case-sensitive.

◆ **Scr.** Specifies the source document to display in the frame.

◆ **Scroll.** Click to select a scroll display option: No (hide), Yes (show), Auto (only when needed), or Default (dictated by browser).

◆ **No Resize.** Select to prevent visitors from dragging frame borders in a browser.

◆ **Borders.** Click to select a border display option: No (hide), Yes (show), or Default (dictated by browser).

◆ **Border Color.** Click to select a color for the frame borders.

◆ **Margin Width.** Specify the width in pixels of the left and right margins.

◆ **Margin Height.** Specify the height in pixels of the top and bottom margins.

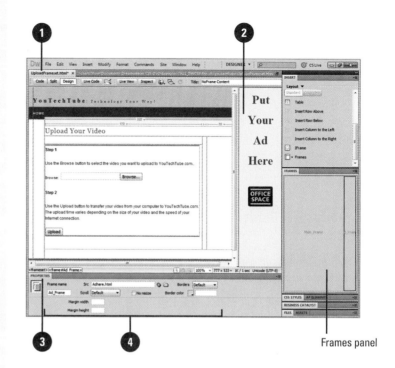

Frames panel

Changing Frameset Properties

In addition to setting properties for the individual frames and frame documents, you can also set properties for the frameset. After you select the frameset, you can use the Properties panel to view and set frameset properties. The available options allow you to change border and frame sizes. You can show or hide borders, change border width and color, and set the frame sizes for rows and columns of the frameset. The RowCol Selection area in the Properties panel provides tabs on the left side and top to select a frame. After you select a frame, you can set the frame height and width you want in the Value box and how much space the browser allocates to each frame in the Units list arrow. You can set these options for each frame you select. In the Document window, you can also change the frameset title.

Modify Frameset Border Properties

1. Open the Web page with the frameset you want to modify.

2. Click the **View** menu, point to **Visual Aids**, and then click **Frame Borders** to display visual borders.

3. Open the Properties panel, and then expand it.

4. Click one of the frame borders to select the frameset.

5. Modify the frames using the options in the Properties panel:

   ◆ **Border Window.** Click to select the specific frame (row/column) you want to modify.

   ◆ **Borders.** Click to select border displays option you want: No (hide border), Yes (show border), or Default (dictated by browser).

   ◆ **Border Width.** Enter a value (in pixels) for the width of the borders.

   ◆ **Border Color.** Click to select a color for the borders.

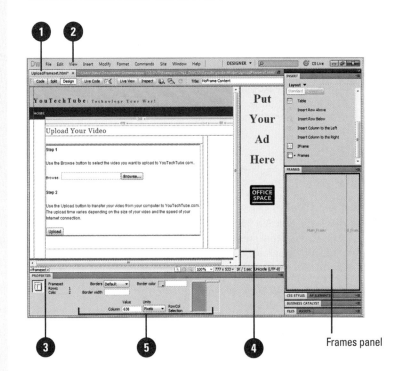

Frames panel

Modify Frameset Size Properties

1 Open the Web page with the frameset you want to modify.

2 Click the **View** menu, point to **Visual Aids**, and then click **Frame Borders** to display visual borders.

3 Open the Properties panel, and then expand it.

4 Click one of the frame borders to select the frameset.

5 Click a tab on the left side or top of the Row/Col Selection area to select the frame you want to set the Value and Units below.

6 Enter a value to determine the height or width of the frame.

7 Click the **Units** list arrow, and then select the measurement units for the Row/Column value you want:

◆ **Pixels.** Sets the size of the column or row to an absolute value. Typically used with a left-side frame.

◆ **Percent.** Sets the column or row to be a percentage the total width or height of its frameset.

◆ **Relative.** Allocates the available space after Pixels to the selected column or row. Typically used with a right-side frame.

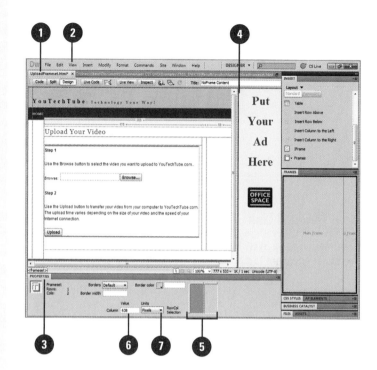

Did You Know?

You can set the title for a frameset page. Open the page, select the frame-set in Design view, and then type a name for the frameset in the Title box on the Document toolbar. When a visi-tor opens the frameset page in a browser, the title appears in the browser's title bar.

Targeting Links

Thus far, this chapter has dealt with the creation of frameset documents, and the adding and saving of Web data on the individual HTML pages. However, the real power of frames is their ability to load new pages into selected frames, based on an available link. For example, you could be a photographer that wants people to see your images (and hopefully buy them). You create a two-framed Web document that has links to your images on the left. When you click on a link, the frame on the right changes to display a large example of your photographic talent. To use a link in one frame to open a document in another frame, you need to set a target for the link. The target instructs the browser into which frame to place the new document. When a visitor clicks the link, the specified content opens in the specified frame.

Create a Targeted Link

1. Open the Web page with the frameset you want to create a targeted link.

2. Select the object or text to be converted into a targeted link.

3. Open the Properties panel.

4. Create the link to the new document using one of the following methods:

    ◆ Click the **folder** icon, and then select the **link file**.

    ◆ Drag the **Point to File** icon to the Files panel to select the link file.

5. Click the **Target** list arrow, and then select the target frame name (at the bottom of the list), or select from the following options.

    ◆ **_blank.** Opens the linked document in a new browser window, leaving the current window untouched.

    ◆ **_parent.** Opens the linked document in the parent frameset of the frame the link appears in, replacing the entire frameset.

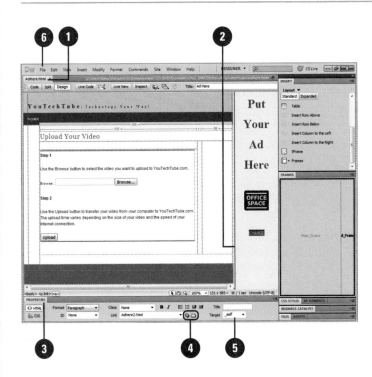

- **_self.** Opens the link in the current frame, replacing the content in that frame.

- **_top.** Opens the linked document in the current browser window, replacing all frames.

IMPORTANT *Frame names appear when you're editing the document within a frameset. When you edit a document in its own window, frame names do not appear in the Target menu. If you're editing a document outside of the frameset, you can type the target frame's name in the Target text box.*

6 Click the **File** menu, point to **Preview In Browser**, and then select a browser of your choice to test the document.

Preview in a browser; click to test link.

Creating Quick and Easy Frame Links

This method is great for those Web sites that contain a lot of links to a lot of boring text documents. To make this process work, the name of the HTML document should be the name you want for the link; for example, formatting.html, or frame_help.html. The documents are the standard HTML type: graphics, text... the whole nine yards. You just want to create a simple, almost file folder kind of page, where a visitor clicks on a link, and it loads the appropriate page in another frame.

Create Quick and Easy Frame Links

1 Create a frameset document with two frames: one for the links, and one for the documents. Name them links and documents.

2 Open the Files panel and display all the HTML documents that you want to use as links.

3 Drag and drop one of the files from the Files panel into the links frame (it appears as an underlined link).

NOTE *If the original name of the HTML document is document_1.html, the linked text will be document_1, without the HTML extension.*

4 Select the linked text.

5 Click the **Target** list arrow in the Properties panel, and then select the content frame name as the target for this file.

6 Repeat steps 3-5 until you have all your documents displayed as links.

7 Click the **File** menu, point to **Preview In Browser**, and then select a browser of your choice to test the document.

NOTE *If you don't like the file name as the link name, you can always select the file name in the links frames and change it. The change in name will not affect the link to the file.*

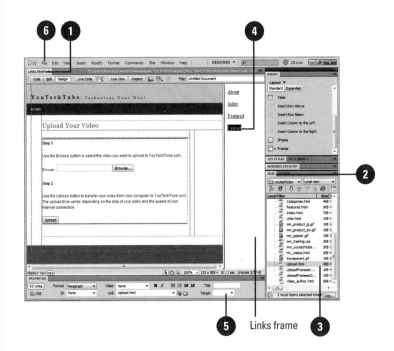

Links frame

Working with Multimedia and Online Tools

Introduction

It almost seems that every page you visit on the Web uses Flash or other multimedia in some way or another. Whether it's an intro movie, or animated buttons, it's everywhere. However, if you don't have applications such as Flash, does that mean you can't create multimedia? If you have Dreamweaver it's a snap to quickly add Flash and other multimedia to your Web pages.

In addition to Flash elements such as text and buttons, Dreamweaver lets you add user-defined Flash movies, Java Applets (Java programs used on Web pages to operate animation, calculators, and other tasks), and ActiveX Controls (can be used to add specialized functionality, such as animation, pop-up menus, or Web pages). Most multimedia is controlled by specific plug-ins. For example, the Flash plug-in allows you to play flash movies, just as the QuickTime plug-in allows you to play QuickTime movies. Plug-ins are a part of the open application architecture of Web browsers. Without the ability to use plug-ins, the only way you would be able to use some of the current multimedia would be if the players were actually coded into the browsers, which would be unreasonable and not very practical.

This chapter will introduce you to multimedia and how to incorporate it into your Web design. As with anything in design, the important thing is to use multimedia to support your message, not just to fill space.

What You'll Do

Introduce Flash File Types

Insert a Flash or Shockwave Movie

Change Flash or Shockwave Movie Properties

Insert a Flash Video

Link or Embed Sound

Use Java Applets

Use ActiveX Controls

Use Plug-ins

Check for Plug-ins

Explore CS Live Services

Share My Screen

Introducing Flash File Types

Adobe Flash allows you to create a variety of file types—FLA, SWF, SWT, SWC, and FLV—for different purposes. The Flash file (.fla) is the source file format for the Adobe Flash program. This file format cannot be opened in Dreamweaver; you can only open this file format in Flash. You use the source Flash file (.fla) to create the other Flash file formats.

You can insert the following Flash file formats into a Web page in Dreamweaver:

◆ **Flash SWF (.swf).** This file format creates a compressed movie of the Flash (.fla) file.

◆ **Flash Template (.swt).** This file format creates a SWF file you can customize with your own text or links, such as a Flash button or Flash text.

◆ **Flash element file (.swc).** This file format creates a SWF file you can create Rich Internet applications with customizable parameters.

◆ **Flash Video file (.flv).** This file format creates a video file with audio and video encoding you can play in the Flash Player.

If you have Adobe FlashPaper 2 or later, you can convert printable files into Flash documents or Adobe PDF files, which you can insert into Dreamweaver.

You don't need to have Adobe Flash installed on your computer to insert these file formats into pages in Dreamweaver. However, when you do have Adobe Flash installed on your computer, you can make changes to the source Flash files (.fla), and then create the file format you want to use in Dreamweaver.

You can use the Media button on the Common tab on the Insert panel, or use the Media submenu on the Insert menu to add different Flash file types into a page in Dreamweaver.

Inserting a Flash or Shockwave Movie

Flash can create all types of multimedia content. From a lead-in page (called a splash screen), to animated banners, to cool-looking, as well as functional menus, Flash is leading the way in Web based multimedia content. Flash utilizes resolution independent vector graphics, streaming audio, and even raster images to create fast-loading Web content. Flash is so popular that according to the World Wide Web Consortium, over 90 percent of people surfing the Web have browsers that can view Flash content. And since version 4, Flash has its own scripting language to help designers take designs into the Stratosphere. Dreamweaver does not create Flash movies; however, it makes it very easy to add them to your Web pages. Once inserted, the Properties panel will give you access to controls that instruct the browser exactly what to do when the movie loads.

Insert and Preview a Flash or Shockwave Movie

1. Open the Web page you want to insert a movie.

2. Click to place the insertion point where you want the movie.

3. Insert the movie using one of the following options:

   ◆ Click the **Common** tab on the Insert panel, click the **Media** arrow button, and then click **SWF** or **Shockwave**.

   ◆ Click the **Insert** menu, point to **Media**, and then click **SWF** or **Shockwave**.

4. Navigate to the location with the Flash file (extension .swf or .swc), and then select it.

5. Click **OK**.

6. Enter the accessibility attributes (title, access key, and tab index) you want.

7. Click **OK**.

8. To view the Flash content, click the Flash placeholder icon, and then click the **Play** button in the Properties panel to begin the preview. Click **Stop** to end the preview.

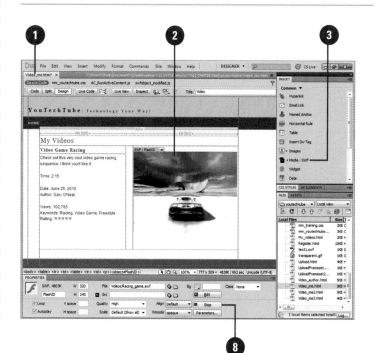

Changing Flash or Shockwave Movie Properties

After you insert a Flash or Shockwave movie into your page in Dreamweaver, you can use the Properties panel to set or change movie properties. You can use the Properties panel to adjust the movie size and scale, set loop and autoplay options, show or hide a border, align the movie on the page, and specify a background color for the movie area. If you have the Flash program installed on your computer, you can even edit the source Flash file (.fla) associated with the SWF file directly from the Properties panel.

Change Flash Movie Properties

1. Open the Web page with the movie you want to change properties.

2. Select the Flash SWF file or a Shockwave movie.

3. Click the **Window** menu, and then click **Properties** to display the Properties panel.

4. To view all Flash options, double-click a blank area of the Properties panel.

5. Set any of the following options to control a Flash or Shockwave movie:

   ◆ **Name.** Enter a name to identify the movie for scripting.

   ◆ **W and H.** Enter the width and height of the movie (in pixels).

   ◆ **File.** Enter the path to the Flash or Shockwave file. Or click the folder icon to browse to a file, or type a path.

   ◆ **Src.** Specifies the path to a Flash source document (FLA) (when Dreamweaver and Flash are both installed on your computer).

   ◆ **Edit.** Click to locate and update a FLA file; the option is grayed out if the Flash program is not installed on your computer.

   ◆ **Reset Size.** Click to return the selected movie to its original size.

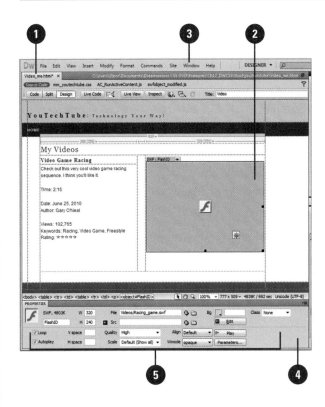

- ◆ **Loop.** Select to make the movie play continuously.

- ◆ **Autoplay.** Select to automatically play the movie when the page loads.

- ◆ **V Space and H Space.** Specify the number of pixels of white space above, below, and on both sides of the movie.

- ◆ **Quality.** Controls anti-aliasing during playback of the movie.

- ◆ **Scale.** Controls how the movie fits into the dimensions set in the width and height text boxes.

- ◆ **No Border.** Select to fit the movie into the set dimensions so that no borders show and it maintains the original aspect ratio.

- ◆ **Exact Fit.** Select to scale the movie to the set dimensions, regardless of the aspect ratio.

- ◆ **Align.** Controls how the movie is aligned on the page.

- ◆ **Bg.** Defines a background color for the movie area.

- ◆ **Parameters.** Opens a dialog box for entering additional parameters to pass to the movie.

Did You Know?

You can preview all Flash content in a page. Press Ctrl+Alt+Shift+P (Win) or Shift+Option+⌘+P (Mac) to set all Flash objects and SWF files to play.

Inserting a Flash Video

When you create a Flash video (.flv) file using Adobe Flash, you insert the Flash video component in Dreamweaver. When you view the page in a browser, the component displays the Flash video and playback controls. You can deliver the Flash video in two delivery formats: Progressive Download Video or Streaming Video. **Progressive Download Video** downloads the FLV file to the visitor's computer and then plays it. The video starts to play before the download is complete to speed up the process. On the other hand, **streaming video** buffers the video on the Web server with Adobe Flash Media Server, and then plays it.

Insert a Flash Video

1. Open the Web page you want to insert a Flash video.

2. Click to place the insertion point where you want the Flash video.

3. Insert the Flash video using one of the following options:

   ◆ Click the **Common** tab on the Insert panel, click the **Media** arrow button, and then click **FLV**.

   ◆ Click the **Insert** menu, point to **Media**, and then click **FLV**.

4. Click the **Video Type** list arrow, and then click **Progressive Download Video** or **Streaming Video**.

5. Select from the following Flash video options:

   ◆ URL (Progressive). Specifies a relative or absolute path to the FLV file.

   ◆ Server URI (Streaming). Specifies the server name, program name, and instance name.

   ◆ Stream Name (Streaming). Specifies the name of the FLV file; .flv extension is optional.

   ◆ Skin. Click the **Skin** list arrow, and then select the appearance of the Flash Video component.

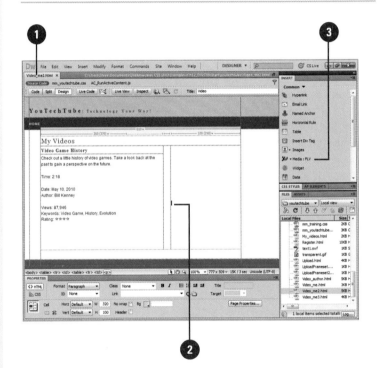

- ◆ **Width and Height.** Specifies the width and height of the FLV video (in pixels).

- ◆ **Constrain.** Select to maintain the same aspect ratio between the width and height.

- ◆ **Live Video Feed (Streaming).** Select to play the streaming live video content from the Flash Media Server.

- ◆ **AutoPlay.** Select to play the video when the page opens.

- ◆ **Auto Rewind.** Select to return the playback to the beginning.

- ◆ **Buffer Time (Streaming).** Specifies the time (in seconds) needed to buffer before the video starts to play.

6 Click **OK**.

Did You Know?

You can remove the code that detects the Flash Player version. Click the Commands menu, and then click Remove Flash Video Detection.

You can delete the Flash Video component. Select the Flash Video component, and then press Delete.

You can edit the Flash Video component. Select the Flash Video component placeholder, open the Properties panel, and then make your changes.

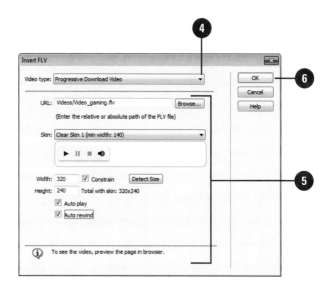

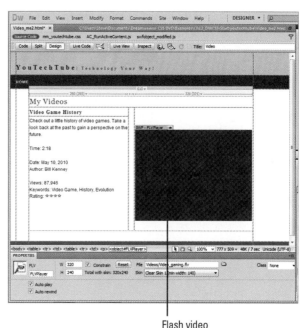

Flash video

Linking or Embedding Sound

If you want to add some life to a Web page, you can add sound to it. Dreamweaver allows you to add a variety of sounds formats, including WAV, MIDI, MP3 (MPG), AIF, RA (Real Audio), MOV (QuickTime). Some audio formats require visitors to download and install a plug-in to play the sound. Some plug-ins include QuickTime, Windows Media Player or RealPlayer. You can add a sound to a page by linking the audio file to text or an image or by embedding the audio file directly into the page. When you link an audio file, the visitor needs to click the link to play the sound. When you embed an audio file, the sound plays when you load a page with a background sound, or when you trigger an event. When you add sounds to one or more pages, use careful judgement and discernment. The old adage "less is more" seems to be a good rule of thumb. It's always a good practice to provide a way for visitors to turn off the sound.

Link to a Sound File

1 Open the Web page you want to create a link to an audio file.

2 Select the text or image you want to use as the link to the audio file.

3 Open the Properties panel.

4 Click the **Browse For File** button next to the Link box to select the audio file, or enter the file's path and name.

Did You Know?

You can link to or embed other videos (AVI or MPEG). Instead of using a sound file, you can use the same steps to link to a video file or embed a video file.

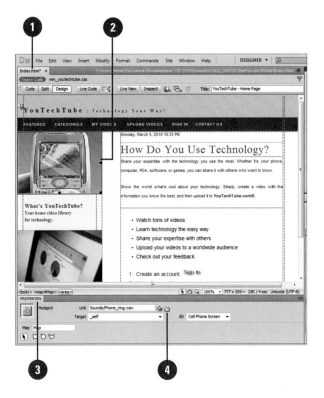

Embed a Sound File

1. Open the Web page you want to embed a sound file.

2. Click to place the insertion point where you want to embed a sound file.

3. Embed a sound file using one of the following options:

   ◆ Click the **Common** tab on the Insert panel, click the **Media** arrow button, and then click **Plugin**.

   ◆ Click the **Insert** menu, point to **Media**, and then click **Plugin**.

4. Open the Properties panel.

5. Click the **Browse For File** button next to the Src box to select the audio file, or enter the file's path and name.

6. Enter the width and height for the placeholder, or drag to resize it.

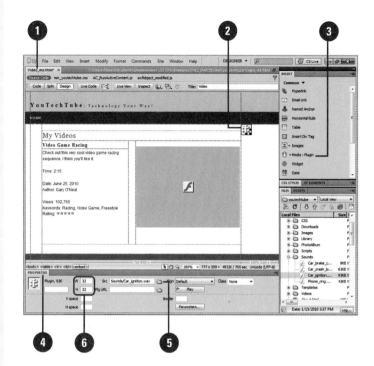

Using Java Applets

You can insert a Java applet into an HTML document using Dreamweaver. Java is a programming language that allows the development of lightweight applications (applets) that can be embedded in web pages. Java applets are executed in a secure area (called a sandbox) by most Web browsers, preventing them from accessing local data. The code of the applet is downloaded from a Web server and the browser embeds the applet into a Web page. In order for an applet to run, it requires the Java plug-in, which isn't available by default on all browsers. It is considered more difficult to build and design a good user interface with Java than other technologies such as DHTML and Flash. It is, however, still a very popular system for the design of Web navigational systems, games, and audio and text effects.

Insert a Java Applet

1. Open the Web page you want to insert a Java applet.

2. Click in the Document window to place the insertion point.

3. Insert the Java applet using one of the following options:

   ◆ Click the **Common** tab on the Insert panel, click the **Media** arrow button, and then click **Applet**.

   ◆ Click the **Insert** menu, point to **Media**, and then click **Applet**.

4. Navigate to the location with the file containing a Java applet.

5. Select a file containing a Java applet.

6. Click **OK**.

7. Enter the accessibility attributes (title, access key, and tab index) you want.

8. Click **OK**.

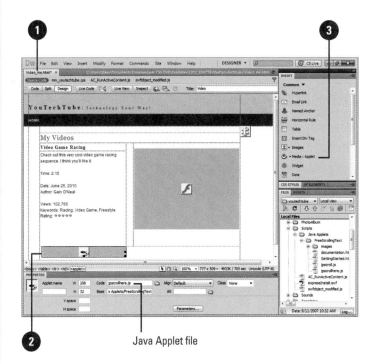

Java Applet file

Modify Java Applet Preferences

1. Open the Web page you want to modify settings for a Java applet.

2. Open the Properties panel, and then double-click a blank area of the panel to display all properties.

3. Select the Java applet for which you want to modify settings.

4. Select from the following Java Applet options:

   ◆ **Name.** Enter a name to identify the applet for scripting.

   ◆ **W and H.** Enter the width and height of the applet, in pixels.

   ◆ **Code.** Enter the file containing the applet's Java code, or click the folder icon to browse to a file.

   ◆ **Base.** Displays the folder containing the selected applet (this text box is filled automatically, when you select an applet).

   ◆ **Align.** Controls the alignment of the applet on the page.

   ◆ **Alt.** Specifies alternative content (usually an image) to be displayed if the user's browser doesn't support Java applets or has Java disabled.

   ◆ **V Space and H Space.** Specify the amount of white space in pixels above, below, and on both sides of the applet.

   ◆ **Parameters.** Opens a dialog box for entering additional parameters to pass to the applet.

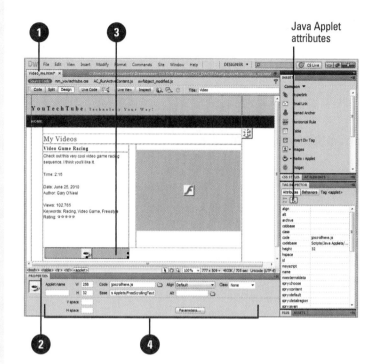

Java Applet attributes

Using ActiveX Controls

You can insert an ActiveX control in your page. ActiveX controls (formerly known as OLE controls) are reusable components, somewhat like miniature applications, that can act like browser plug-ins. They run in Internet Explorer with Windows, but they don't run on the Macintosh or in Netscape Navigator. The ActiveX object in Dreamweaver lets you supply attributes and parameters for an ActiveX control in your visitor's browser.

Insert an ActiveX Control

1. Open the Web page you want to insert an ActiveX control.

2. Click to place the insertion point where you want to insert an ActiveX control.

3. Insert the ActiveX control using one of the following options:

   ◆ Click the **Common** tab on the Insert panel, click the **Media** arrow button, and then click **ActiveX**.

   ◆ Click the **Insert** menu, point to **Media**, and then click **ActiveX**.

4. Enter the accessibility attributes (title, access key, and tab index) you want.

5. Click **OK**.

   An icon marks where the ActiveX control appears on the page in Internet Explorer.

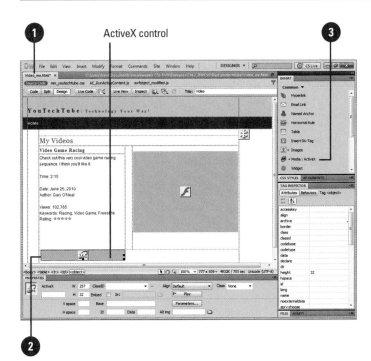

ActiveX control

Modify ActiveX Properties

1. Open the Web page you want to modify ActiveX control properties.

2. Select the ActiveX icon in the Document window.

3. Open the Properties panel, and then double-click a blank area of the panel to display all properties.

4. Select from the following options:

   ◆ **Name.** Enter a name to identify the ActiveX object for scripting.

   ◆ **W and H.** Enter the width and height of the object (in pixels).

   ◆ **Class ID.** Identifies the ActiveX control to the browser (enter a value or select one).

   ◆ **Embed.** Inserts an embed tag within the object tag for the ActiveX control.

   ◆ **Align.** Aligns the object.

   ◆ **Parameters.** Select to enter additional parameters to pass to the ActiveX object.

   ◆ **Src.** Defines the data file used for a Netscape Navigator plug-in if the Embed option is on.

   ◆ **V Space and H Space.** Enter the amount of white space (in pixels) above, below, and on both sides of the object.

   ◆ **Base.** Displays the URL containing the ActiveX control.

   ◆ **Alt Img.** Enter an image to be displayed if the browser doesn't support the object tag.

   ◆ **Data.** Enter a data file for the ActiveX control to load.

5. Click the **File** menu, point to **Preview In Browser**, and then select a browser to preview the ActiveX control.

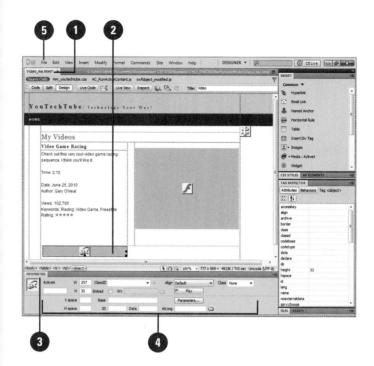

Using Plug-ins

You can include content on a page that runs in a Netscape Navigator plug-in, such as a QuickTime or RealPlayer movie, in the user's browser. After you insert content for a Netscape Navigator plug-in, you can use the Properties panel to set options and parameters for the selected element. When you're ready to preview the content, you can play all the plug-in elements at once or play them individually. If you want to play movies in Design view, the proper plug-ins must be installed on your computer.

Insert Plug-in Content

1. Open the Web page you want to insert a plug-in content.

2. Click to place the insertion point where you want to insert Plug-in content.

3. Insert the Plug-in using one of the following options:

   ◆ Click the **Common** tab on the Insert panel, click the **Media** arrow button, and then click **Plugin**.

   ◆ Click the **Insert** menu, point to **Media**, and then click **Plugin**.

4. Navigate to the location with the Plug-in file, and then select it.

5. Click **OK**.

   An icon marks where the Plug-in control appears on the page in Netscape Navigator.

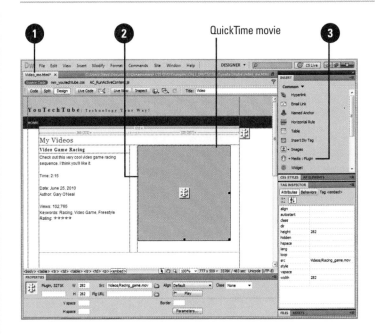

QuickTime movie

Play the Plug-in

1. Open the Web page with the plug-in you want to play.

2. Use any of the following options to play a Plug-in:

   ◆ **Selected Elements.** Select the media elements, click the **View** menu, point to **Plugins**, and then click **Play**, or click the **Play** button in the Properties panel.

   ◆ **All Elements.** Click the **View** menu, point to **Plugins**, and then click **Play All**.

3. Use any of the following options to stop a Plug-in:

   ◆ **Selected Elements.** Click the **View** menu, point to **Plugins**, and then click **Stop**, or click the **Stop** button in the Properties panel.

   ◆ **All Elements.** Click the **View** menu, point to **Plugins**, and then click **Stop All**.

Use to play or stop the plug-in movie

Use button to play and stop the plug-in movie

For Your Information

Troubleshooting Plug-ins

If you have followed the steps to play plug-in content in the Document window, but some of the plug-in content does not play, try the following: (1) Make sure the associated plug-in is installed on your computer, and the content is compatible with the plug-in version; (2) Open the file Configuration/Plug-ins/UnsupportedPlug-ins.txt in a text editor and look to see if the problematic plug-in is listed. This file keeps track of plug-ins that cause problems in Dreamweaver and are therefore unsupported. If you experience problems with a particular plug-in, consider adding it to this file; or (3) Check to see if you have enough memory. Some plug-ins require an additional 2 to 5 MB of memory to run.

Checking for Plug-ins

Use the Check Plugin action to send visitors to different pages depending on whether they have the specified plug-in installed. For example, you might want visitors to go to one page if they have Shockwave and another page if they do not. The Check Plugins action is an excellent tool for making your visitor's experience a pleasant one.

Use the Check Plug-in Action

1. Open the Web page you want to use.

2. Select an object (for an element) or click the <body> tag in the tag selector (for an entire page).

3. Open the Behaviors panel.

4. Click the **Plus** (+) button, and then click **Check Plugin** from the Actions menu.

5. Select a plug-in from the **Plugin** list arrow, or type the exact name of the plug-in in the adjacent text box.

6. Configure Check Plug-in using the following options:

   ◆ **If Found, Go To URL.** Enter a URL for visitors who have the plug-in.

   NOTE *To cause visitors with the plug-in to stay on the same page, leave this field blank.*

   ◆ **Otherwise, Go To URL.** Enter an alternative URL for visitors who don't have the plug-in.

   NOTE *To cause visitors without the plug-in to stay on the same page, leave this field blank.*

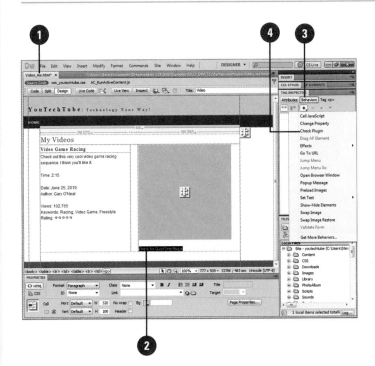

◆ **Always Go To First URL If Detection Is Not Possible.** In general, if the plug-in content is integral to your page, select this option; visitors without the plug-in will often be prompted by the browser to download the plug-in. If the plug-in content is not essential to your page, leave this option deselected.

NOTE *This option applies only to Internet Explorer; Netscape Navigator can always detect plug-ins.*

⑦ Click **OK**.

⑧ Select an event from the list menu.

⑨ Click the **File** menu, point to **Preview In Browser**, and then select a browser to test the page from the available options.

IMPORTANT *Plug-in detection is not possible in Internet Explorer on the Macintosh, and most plug-ins cannot be detected in Internet Explorer on Windows.*

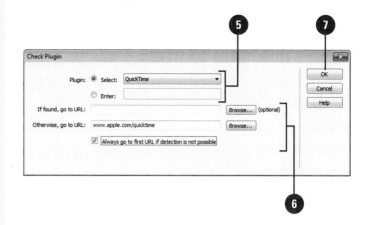

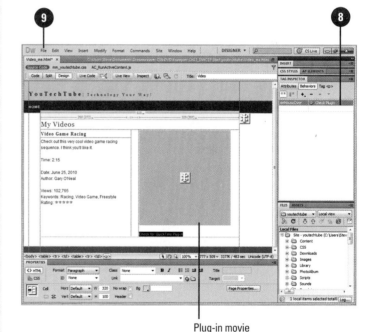

Plug-in movie

Exploring CS Live Services

Adobe CS Live (**New!**) is an online service that allows you to set up or manage (sign in and out) an Adobe account, access Adobe Browserlab from a panel, learn about reviewing CS5 documents online, view netaverages from SiteCatalyst, access the Acrobat.com subscription-based Web site or the Adobe ConnectNow Web site where you can collaborate with others, display CS news and resources in a panel, and access an Adobe Web site with information about CS Live Services. You can access these options directly from the CS Live menu on the right side of the menu bar next to the Search bar. When the CS Live menu icon includes a bulls eye, you are signed in to the online services.

Explore CS Live Services

1. Click the **CS Live** menu (**New!**), and then select any of the following:

   - **Set Up Your Access To Adobe CS Live Online Services**, **Sign In**, or **Sign Out**. Select to set up, sign in, or sign out of the CS Live online service.

   - **BrowserLab**. Accesses an online tool from a panel to view how different operating systems and browsers render Web pages.

   - **CS Review**. Learn how to review CS5 documents online.

   - **SiteCatalyst NetAverages**. View the latest NetAverages using SiteCatalyst from Omniture.

   - **Acrobat.com Home**. Opens the Acrobat.com subscription-based Web site that allows you to work and collaborate with others.

   - **Share My Screen**. Opens the Adobe ConnectNow Web site where you can collaborate on design projects online.

   - **CS News and Resources**. Opens the CS News and Resources panel with news and resources.

   - **Manage My Account**. Opens a secure Web site to manage your Adobe account information.

   - **Explore CS Live Services**. Opens an Adobe Web site that describes CS Live Services.

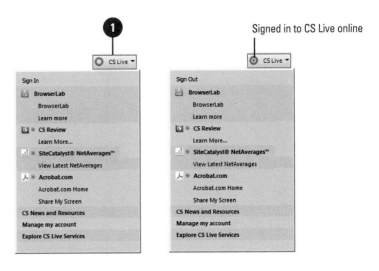

Signed in to CS Live online

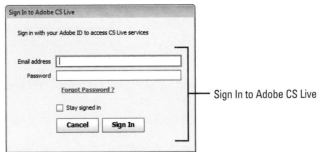

Sign In to Adobe CS Live

Use Adobe BrowserLab

① Open the Web page you want to view in a Design view or Live View.

② To find out more about BrowserLab online, click the **CS Live** menu, and then click **Learn More** (under BrowserLab).

③ Click the **CS Live** menu, and then click **BrowserLab**.

◆ You can also click the **Window** menu, point to **Extensions**, and then click **Adobe BrowserLab**.

④ Click the **Location** list arrow, and then click **Local** or **Server**.

⑤ Click **Preview**.

◆ You can also click the **File** menu, point to **Preview In Browser**, and then click **Adobe BrowserLab**.

⑥ If prompted, click **Yes** to update the file on the server.

Your browser opens, displaying the Adobe BrowserLab Web site.

⑦ If prompted, enter your Adobe ID and password.

⑧ Click the **Browser** list arrow, and then select the browser you want to use.

⑨ To view the page using multiple browsers, click the **View** list arrow, and then click **1-up View**, **2-up View**, or **Onion Skin**.

Check the page display and links.

⑩ When you're done, close your browser.

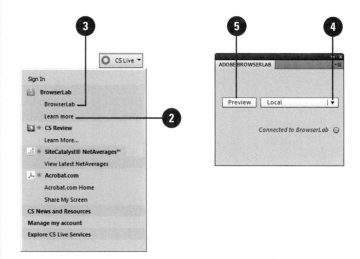

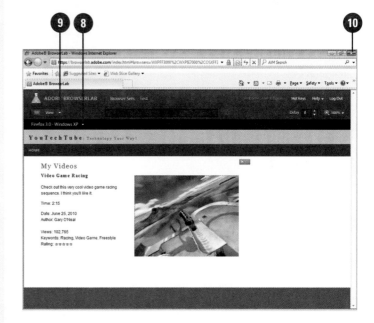

Sharing My Screen

The Share My Screen command on the File or CS Live (**New!**) menu allows you to connect to Adobe ConnectNow, which is a secure Web site where you can start an online meeting and collaborate on any design project across platforms and programs. You can share and annotate your computer screen or take control of an attendee's computer. During the meeting, you can communicate by sending chat messages, using live audio, or broadcasting live video. In addition, you can take meeting notes, and share files.

Share My Screen

1. Click the **File** or **CS Live** (**New!**) menu, and then click **Share My Screen**.

2. Enter your Adobe ID and password.

   ◆ If you don't have an Adobe ID and password, click the Create a Free Adobe ID link, and then follow the online instructions.

3. Click **Sign In**.

   ◆ If prompted, sign in to ConnectNow.

4. To share your computer screen, click the **Share My Computer Screen** button.

5. Use the ConnectNow toolbar to do any of the following:

   ◆ **Meeting.** Use to invite participants, share my computer screen, upload a file, share my webcam, set preferences, end a meeting, and exit Adobe ConnectNow.

   ◆ **PODS.** Use to show and hide pod panels.

   ◆ **Help.** Use to get help, troubleshoot problems, and set account and Flash Player settings.

6. Click the participant buttons at the bottom to specify roles, remove a user, or request control of a user's computer.

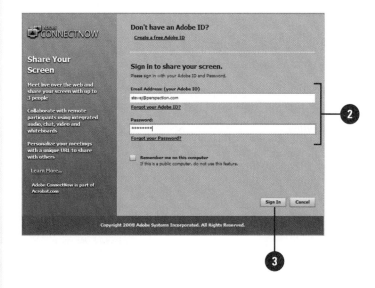

Creating Forms

Introduction

Forms are all around us... You fill out forms to get your driver's license, apply for a job; even to get married. A simple definition of a form would be some method for extracting information on a particular subject. For example, to fill out a job application form, you would have to enter your pertinent information on who you are (name, address), recent jobs, why you're experienced enough to apply for the job, and government stuff, like your social security number. An even simpler definition would be to say that forms collect information... it's how you collect that information that makes all the difference.

For example, you might design your form on paper, and the person filling out the form is required to write the information down with a pen or pencil. The information is collected by another person, and along with other forms, compiled (by hand) into a final readable product. Not very efficient; however, that's the way it was done, many long years ago.

Today forms are filled out on a computer screen; the data is validated and compiled into a readable final product, along with relevant statistics and averages. What I'm describing is creating electronic forms, designed, implemented, and finished, all with the help of Adobe Dreamweaver.

Adobe Dreamweaver simplifies the process of creating and implementing forms of any size and complexity. In this chapter you learn how to create basic forms, and populate the forms with all the goodies, such as: check boxes, radio buttons, text input fields; even drop-down menus.

Once a form is created, it can deposit that information into an appended database, where other statistical applications can massage the data into any structure desired by the final user.

What You'll Do

Understand Forms

Create a Form

Insert Form Objects

Modify Text Fields and Text Areas

Modify Radio Buttons and Check Boxes

Modify Lists and Menus

Modify Buttons

Insert an Image Button

Make Form Objects Dynamic

Use Tables to Control Forms

Validate Forms

Create and Edit a Jump Menu

View Example Code for Forms

Understanding Forms

As mentioned in the previous section, forms are all about the collection and eventual processing of information. Considering the information-based society that we live and work in, without forms the entire world would probably fall apart in a matter of days. Well, maybe that's a bit exaggerated; however, forms collect information, information drives our lives, and Dreamweaver makes the creation of those forms a virtual snap.

Beyond Dreamweaver

It's important to understand that although Dreamweaver will make the overall creation of a form easy (buttons, check boxes, input fields, etc), it does not include the backend tools that make the form functional. For that you will need to install a form handler on your server. In many cases someone in the IT department performs this function. Understand that until the form handler is installed, your visitors will not be able to send you any data; no matter how many times they click the Submit button.

While the scope of the book is not to teach you how to write form handler code, there are many sites that offer free form-handler scripts. These sites typically provide scripts for collecting simple and predictable form data; for more complex scripts the services of an engineer might be required.

Form Elements

Forms can be populated with any number of elements. For example, you could create a simple bio form that asks for information such as name, address, phone number, sex, age, social security number, etc. Because of all this information, it's a good idea to sketch out the general look and feel of the form on a piece of paper, and then use that as a visual guide to the creation of the form in Dreamweaver. When you create an interactive field, Dreamweaver inserts the code necessary to display the field in the browser.

Dynamic Form Elements

A dynamic form element is a form object that gets its initial value by the Web server where the Web site is stored. When a visitor opens a form page in a browser, the dynamic form objects get information directly from the Web server before the page appears on the screen. When form objects are dynamic, it makes updating a snap. In order to use dynamic form objects, you need to have a data source set up and available on your Web server.

Form Validation

Once the various form elements are ironed out, you can look at the possibility of validating some of the fields. For example, it might be difficult to create a validation for a name field; however, you at least check to see that the field is not blank. In addition, you could check to see if all zip code fields contain five numbers and not alphabetic characters. Options that require specific answers, such as sex (male/female) could be placed as a pop-up with the correct choices, and other options could be designed using check boxes or radio buttons. In most cases, using check boxes allows the user to choose more than one option (check all that apply), and radio button typically allow for a single choice from a group (choose only one). When you choose form validation, Dreamweaver creates a script that instructs the browser how to handle the input.

Forms tab with form related buttons

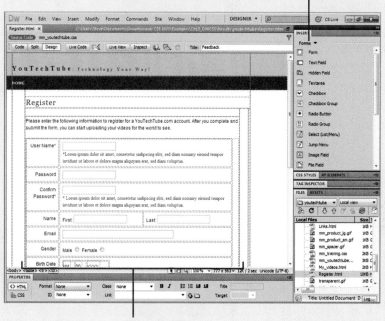

Form elements

Creating a Form

Just because Dreamweaver makes the initial creation of the form easy for you, it doesn't mean that you shouldn't think about its construction. One of the rules in creating forms is that you're designing the form for the person who is filling it out... not for you. The form should be as simplistic as possible with easy to understand instructions. When they make a mistake (not filling in a field), there should be a way to tell that person a mistake was made, and what to do to correct it. Studies show that the more difficult the form, the less likely that people are going to spend the time to fill it out. There are two stages in the creation of a form: The initial insertion of the form, and then populating the form with text and form objects.

Create a Form

1. Create a new HTML document, or open an existing one.

2. Click to place the insertion point where you want to insert a form.

3. Insert the form using one of the following options:

   - Click the **Forms** tab on the Insert panel, and then click the **Form** button.

   - Click the **Insert** menu, point to **Form**, and then click **Form**.

   An empty form appears with a dotted red outline.

   TROUBLE? *If you don't see the outline, click the View menu, point to Visual Aids, and then click Invisible Elements.*

4. Open the Properties panel.

5. Click the red form outline to select the form.

6. Type a name to identify the form for reference purposes with a scripting language.

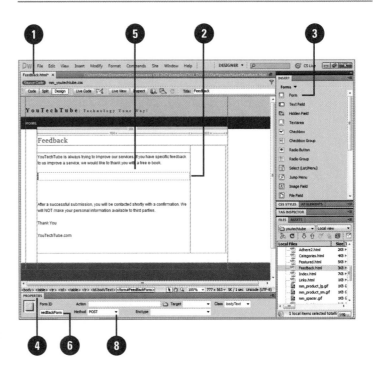

7 Enter the path to the page or script that processes the form data, or click the **Browse For File** button to select a file (if you don't have this information, you can add it later).

8 Click the **Method** list arrow, and then select one of the following options:

- ◆ **Default.** Uses the browser's default setting to send the form data to the server. Typically the default is the GET method.

- ◆ **GET.** Appends the value to the URL requesting the page.

- ◆ **POST.** Embeds the form data in the HTTP request.

9 Insert the form objects you want and specify the information in the Input Tag Accessibility Attributes dialog box. When you create form objects, follow these guidelines:

- ◆ **Unique Names.** Use a unique name that identifies the object for scripting purposes. Avoid using spaces or special characters.

- ◆ **Layout.** Use line and paragraph breaks, formatted text, and tables to design the form layout.

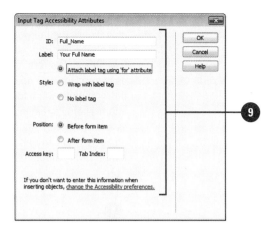

Form with text element

See Also

See "Inserting Form Objects" on page 304 for information on inserting form objects.

For Your Information

Starting a Form from a Sample

Instead of creating a form from scratch, you can start a form from a sample, and then make the changes you want to suit your own needs. Click the File menu, click New, click the Page From Sample category, click Starter Page (Basic), click the sample page you want, such as Survey, Multiple Choice or Register (Basic), and then click Create.

Inserting Form Objects

After you create a form, you can starting inserting form objects. Form objects are the individual elements—such as text field, text area, button, check box, radio button, or menu—that make up the form and visitors fill out. The form objects allow you to create a form that makes it easy for visitors to use, yet still provide you with the important information you need. Each form object is designed to gather a specific type of information. For example, if you have a list of categories and you can select more than one category, you should use the check box form object. If you can only select one category, you should use the radio button form object instead.

Insert Form Objects

1. Open a page that contains a form, or create a new document and insert a form.

2. Click to place the insertion point to where you want to insert a form object.

3. Click the **Forms** tab on the Insert panel, or click the **Insert** menu, point to **Form**, and then select from the following commonly used form objects:

   ◆ **Text Field.** Select to create a text field that consists of one line or multiple lines. In addition, text fields are used to create a password field that hides the text the user enters.

   ◆ **Text Area.** Select to create a large text area that is commonly used by a visitor to enter large amounts of data; for example, a comment field.

   ◆ **Button.** Select to create a button object. Buttons are used to submit form data to the server or to reset the form. Standard form buttons are typically labeled Submit, Reset, or Send. You can also assign other processing tasks that you've defined in a script.

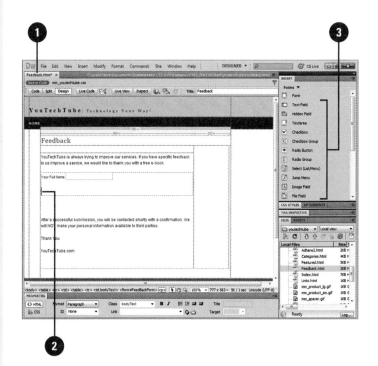

- **Checkbox.** Select to let users select more than one option from a set of options.

- **Radio Button.** Select to let users select only one choice from a set of options. Radio buttons are typically used in groups.

- **List/Menu.** Select to let users select one or more items from a list.

④ In the Input Tag Accessibility Attributes dialog box, specify the following options:

- **ID.** Enter a unique ID for the form object.

- **Label.** Enter a label for the form object.

- **Style.** Select a style for the form object.

- **Position.** Select a position for the label in relation to the form object.

- **Access Key.** Enter a keyboard equivalent (single letter) in the Access Key text box. For example, if you entered the letter N into the field, pressing Alt+N (Win) or Control+N (Mac) in the browser automatically selects that field.

- **Tab Index.** Enter a numerical value for the tab order of the form object in the Tab Index text box. For example, if you entered the number 3 into the field, pressing the tab key three times would cause the field to be selected.

⑤ Click **OK**.

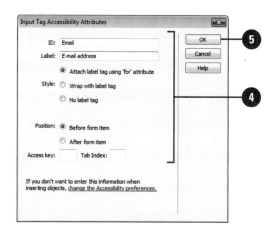

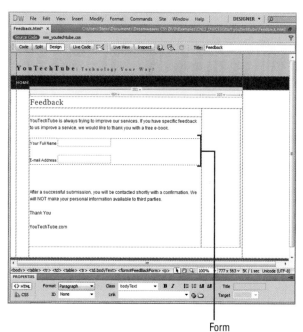

Form

Modifying Text Fields and Text Areas

A text field consists of one line or multiple lines used to enter small distinct amounts of data or information, such as your name or address. You can also use a text field to create a password field that hides the text the user enters. A text area is a large text field commonly used to enter large amounts of data or information, such as comments. After you create a text field or text area, you can use the Properties panel to set or change options for the form objects.

Work with Text Field and Text Area Properties

1. Select a text input field or text area within a form document.

2. Open the Properties panel.

3. Select from the following text field or text area options:

   ◆ **Char Width.** Enter the maximum number of characters that can be displayed in the field.

   ◆ **Max Chars.** Enter the maximum number of characters that can be entered in the field for single-line text fields.

   ◆ **Num Lines.** Enter the height of the field for multiple-line text fields.

   ◆ **Wrap.** Determines how the user's input will be displayed when the user enters more information than can be displayed within the defined text area.

      ◆ **Off.** Prevents text from wrapping to the next line.

      ◆ **Virtual.** Sets word wrap in the text area.

      ◆ **Physical.** Sets word wrap in the text area, as well as to the data when it is submitted for processing.

3 Text field

- **Type.** Designates the field as a single-line, multiple-line, or password field.

  - **Single-line.** Selecting to cause the Char Width and Max Chars settings to map to a single line with defined boundaries.

  - **Password.** Select to create a password field (information typed into the field appears as asterisks or dots).

  - **Multi-line.** Select to create a multi-line field.

NOTE *The default for text area fields is multi-line.*

- **Init Value.** Enter an initial value that displays when the field first loads.

- **Class.** Click to apply CSS rules to the object directly or through a CSS Style sheet.

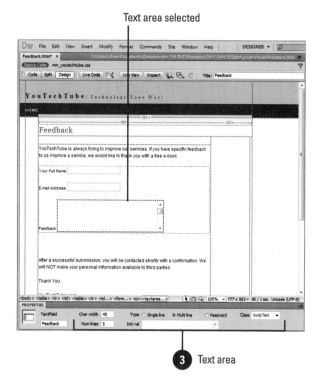

Text area selected

3 Text area

Modifying Radio Buttons and Check Boxes

Radio buttons and check boxes allow you to create options for users to select. A radio button allows a user to select only one choice from a set of options, while a check box allows a user to select more than one option from a set of options. Radio buttons are typically used in groups. Both form objects are very often used when you want to create a survey. After you create a radio button or check box, you can use the Properties panel to set or change options for the form objects.

Work with Radio Button and Checkbox Properties

1 Select a radio button or checkbox within a form document.

2 Open the Properties panel.

3 Select from the following radio button options:

- **Radio Button/Checkbox.** Enter a name for the Radio Button or Checkbox object.

NOTE *If the name of a group of radio buttons is the same, then the user will only be able to select one button (i.e. male or female). The name cannot contain spaces or special characters.*

NOTE *Unlike radio buttons, every checkbox must have a unique name.*

- **Checked Value.** Enter in a value to be sent to the server when the button is selected. For example, male or female.

- **Initial State.** Select whether to have the button selected or not when the form first loads.

- **Class.** Click to apply CSS rules to the object directly or through a CSS Style Sheet.

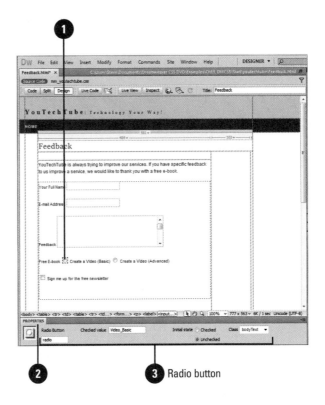

Radio button

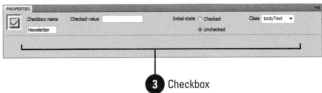

Checkbox

Modifying Lists and Menus

Lists and menus perform similar tasks; each allows you to select an item from a list of related items. However, there are some differences. A list allows you to scroll through the items as well as select multiple items, while a menu doesn't. When you select an item from a list or menu, you can execute an action using a script or behavior. After you create a list or menu, you can use the Properties panel to set or change options for the form objects.

Work with List/Menu Properties

1. Select a list/menu field within a form document.

2. Open the Properties panel.

3. Select from the following list/menu options:

   ◆ **List/Menu.** Enter a unique name for the menu.

   ◆ **Menu.** Select to have the menu drop down when clicked.

   ◆ **List.** Select to display a scrollable list of items when clicked.

   ◆ **Height.** Enter a value to determine the number of items displayed in the menu (List type only).

   ◆ **Selections.** Select to allow the user to select multiple items from the list (List type only).

   ◆ **List Values.** Click to add items to the menu.

   ◆ **Class.** Click to apply CSS rules to the object directly or through a CSS Style Sheet.

   ◆ **Initially Selected.** Select from the available items to make the item initially selected when the browser loads the form.

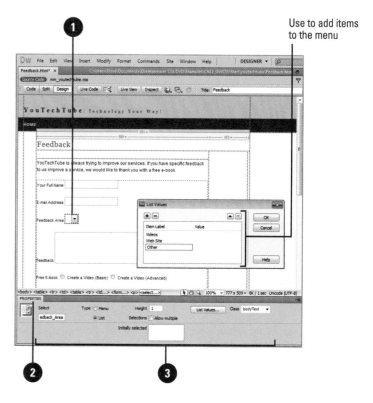

Use to add items to the menu

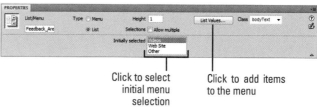

Click to select initial menu selection

Click to add items to the menu

Modifying Buttons

Buttons are used to execute an action. Form buttons are generally used to submit form data to the server or to reset the form. Standard form buttons are typically labeled Submit, Reset, or Send. In addition to the standard form buttons, you can assign other processing tasks that you've defined in a script or behavior to create a custom button. After you create a button, you can use the Properties panel to set or change options for the form objects.

Work with Button Properties

1 Select a button field within a form document.

2 Open the Properties panel.

3 Select from the following button options:

◆ **Label.** Use to add a label next to a text field, check box, or radio button option. Click next to the object, and then type the label.

◆ **Value.** Enter the name of the button (appears directly on the button).

◆ **Action.** Determines what happens when the button is clicked.

◆ **Submit Form.** Select to submit the form data for processing when the button is clicked.

◆ **Reset Form.** Select to clear the contents of the form when the button is clicked.

◆ **None.** Select if you want to add a JavaScript behavior for the button.

◆ **Class.** Click to apply CSS rules to the object directly or through a CSS Style Sheet.

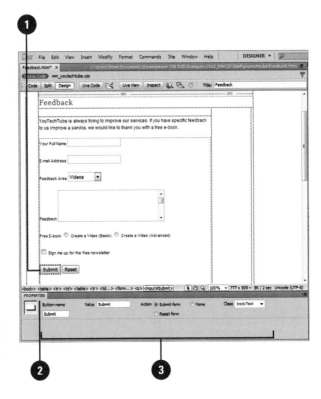

Inserting an Image Button

Instead of using one of the built-in buttons provided by Dreamweaver, you can insert an image and use it as a button. This allows you to create a custom look for your form, yet still provide the functionality you want. After you insert an Image button, you can use the Properties panel to set or change options for the form object.

Insert an Image Button

1 Create a new HTML document, or open an existing page.

2 Click to place the insertion point where you want to insert an image button.

3 Insert the image using one of the following options:

   ◆ Click the **Forms** tab on the Insert panel, and then click the **Image Field** button.

   ◆ Click the **Insert** menu, point to **Form**, and then click **Image Field**.

4 Locate and select the image you want to use as a button.

5 Click **OK**.

6 In the Properties panel, select from the following options:

   ◆ **Image Field.** Enter a unique name for the image.

   ◆ **Src.** Enter the path and name for the image or click the **Browse For File** button to select the image file.

   ◆ **Alt.** Enter a description of the image.

   ◆ **Align.** Click to select an alignment option.

   ◆ **Edit Image.** Click to edit the image in your default editor.

   ◆ **Class.** Click to apply CSS rules to the object directly or through a CSS Style Sheet.

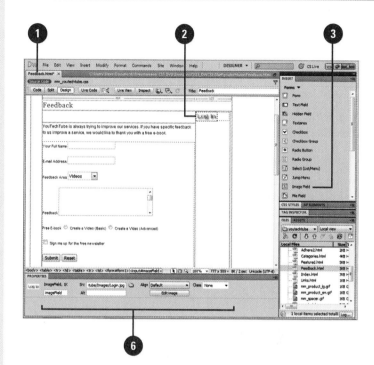

Making Form Objects Dynamic

Instead of setting static form options in Dreamweaver, you can set form options dynamically (on the fly) from your Web server, known as a dynamic form object. For example, you can dynamically set a form menu or list menu with entries from a database, display content in text fields when viewed in a browser, or preset a radio button or check box when viewed in a browser.

When a page with a dynamic form object is displayed from a Web server, the initial state is determined by the server. Making form objects dynamic makes updating and maintaining a Web site much easier. Instead of manually changing a menu item, you can simply change an entry in a database table where the information is stored.

In order to use dynamic form objects, you need to have a data source set up, such as a MySQL database, and available on your Web server. The set up and connection of a data source is outside the scope of this book, so you should see your ISP or Web administrator for more details.

Make Form Objects Dynamic

1 Select the form object you want to make dynamic within a form document.

2 Open the Properties panel.

3 Click the **Dynamic** button or click the **Lighting Bolt** icon.

4 Select the options you want to make the form object dynamic; the options vary depending on the form object.

◆ Select an existing data source, or click the **Plus** (+) button to define a new data source.

5 Click **OK**.

Using Tables to Control Forms

When you create a table, it's a simple matter to add form elements on a line-by-line basis. However, in many cases this simplistic method may not suit your particular form layout. In that case, it's tables to the rescue. A smart form designer can use a table within the form (just like in standard design), to control the look and positioning of all the form elements. Once the table is inserted into the form, it's a simple matter to use the individual table cells to insert the various elements (for more information on the creation of a table, turn to Chapter 8). The only requirement for the table is that it must be placed within the red dotted lines defining the form.

Control the Form with Tables

1. Create a new document or open an existing page.

2. Click to place the insertion point to where you want to insert a form.

3. Insert the form using one of the following options:

   ◆ Click the **Forms** tab on the Insert panel, and then click the **Form** button.

   ◆ Click the **Insert** menu, point to **Form**, and then click **Form**.

   An empty form appears with a dotted red outline.

4. Select the form.

5. Click the **Insert** menu, click **Table**, select the table options that you want, and then click **OK**.

6. Click into an individual cell.

7. Click the **Forms** tab on the Insert panel, or click the **Insert** menu, point to **Form**, and then select from the available form objects.

   The table cells control the placement and design of the form.

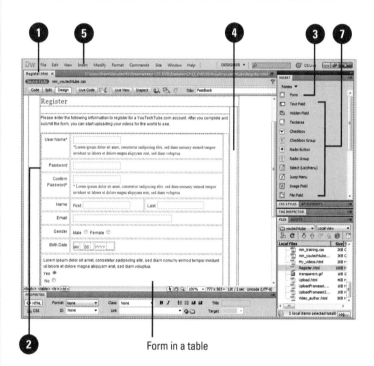

Form in a table

Validating Forms

The Validate Form action checks the contents of specified text fields to ensure that the user has entered the correct type of data. You can attach this action to individual text fields using an onBlur event to validate the fields as the user is filling out the form, or attach it to the form with the onClick event to evaluate several text fields at once when the user clicks the Submit button. Attaching this action to a form prevents the form from being submitted to the server if any of the specified text fields contains invalid data. In addition, Dreamweaver can add JavaScript code that checks the contents of specified text fields to ensure that the user has entered the correct type of data.

Validate HTML Form Data

1. Open a form document, or create a new form document.

   IMPORTANT *The form document must contain at least one text field and a Submit button. In addition, all text fields must have unique names.*

2. Select the **Submit** button inside the form that you want to validate.

3. Click the **Window** menu, and then click **Behaviors** to display the Behaviors panel.

4. Click the **Add Behavior** button (the Plus (+) sign), and then click **Validate Form**.

5. Select the form input fields one at a time, and then validate the form using the following options:

   ◆ **Required.** Select to make the form object required.

   ◆ **Anything.** Accepts any input entered by the user.

   ◆ **Number.** Restricts input to numeric.

   ◆ **Email address.** Looks for an e-mail address with the @ sign.

   ◆ **Number from.** Enables you to enter a minimum and maximum range for numeric values.

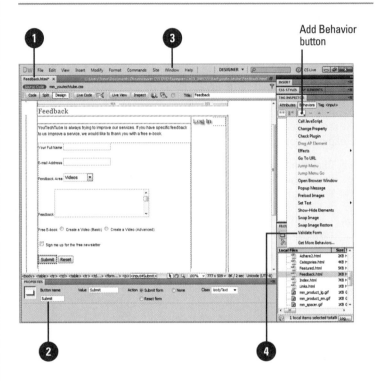

Add Behavior button

6 Click **OK** to add the validation information (in script) to the HTML form document.

7 Click the **Action** button in the Behaviors panel, and then select one of the following options:

   ◆ **OnClick.** Select if you are validating multiple fields when the user submits the form.

   ◆ **OnBlur.** Select if you are validating individual fields.

8 Click the **File** menu, point to **Preview In Browser**, and then check the current validation actions.

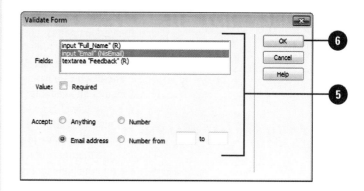

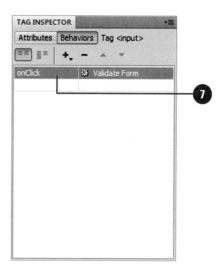

Creating and Editing a Jump Menu

Most Web sites employ buttons to helps the visitor navigate through the various pages; however, it's possible to create a jump menu, using a simple form element. A jump menu utilizes a form object to create a list of menu options. When the visitor clicks on the list, a drop-down menu displays a listing of all the available page options. Displaying a listing of all available page options within a single drop-down menu is a creative use of form objects that makes navigation through a complex site much easier for your visitors. After you create a jump menu, you can make changes to it as needed. You can add, delete, rename or change the order of items in the menu. In addition, you can modify the file an item links to. If you want to change the location in which a linked file opens, or to add or change a menu selection prompt, you need to apply the Jump Menu behavior from the Behaviors panel.

Create a Jump Menu

1. Create a new Web page or Open the Web page where you want to insert a jump menu.

2. Click to place the insertion point to where you want to insert a jump menu.

   NOTE *Dreamweaver inserts a form at the insertion point (if you haven't already created one).*

3. Click the **Forms** tab on the Insert panel, or click the **Insert** menu, point to **Forms**, and then click **Jump Menu**.

4. Create the jump menu using the following options:

   ◆ Menu Items. Click the **Plus** (+) sign to add more "unnamed" menu items to the list. Click the **Minus** (-) sign to remove "unnamed" items from the list. Use the up and down arrows buttons to move selected items within the list.

   ◆ Text. Select an "unnamed" menu item in the Menu Items box, and then enter a name in the text field. Continue selecting "unnamed" items until all have been properly named.

Jump menu

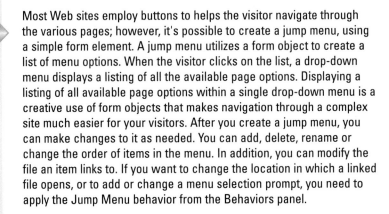
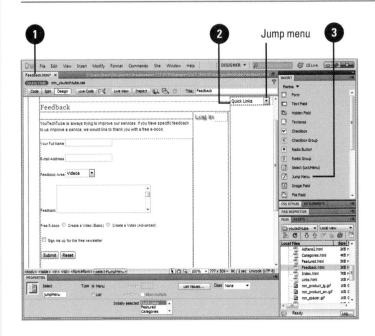

- ◆ **When Selected Go To URL.**
  Select a menu item in the Menu
  Items box, and then enter the
  path and filename of the page
  you want opened for the
  selected item or click **Browse**
  to select the file.

- ◆ **Open URLs In.** If you're not
  working within a frameset, you
  have only one option: Main
  Window.

- ◆ **Menu ID.** Enter a unique name
  for the menu in the input field
  (optional).

- ◆ **Insert Go Button After Menu.**
  Select to add a button that
  activates the jump menu.

- ◆ **Select First Item After URL
  Change.** Select to reset the
  menu selection to the top item
  after each jump.

5 Click **OK**.

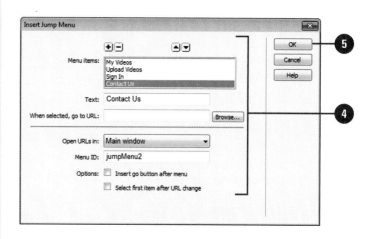

Edit a Jump Menu

1 Open the Web page where you
want to edit a jump menu.

2 Open the Properties panel.

3 Select a jump menu object.

4 Click the **List Values** button.

5 Make the changes you want.

- ◆ Click the **Plus** (+) sign to add
  more "unnamed" menu items to
  the list. Click the **Minus** (-) sign
  to remove "unnamed: items
  from the list. Use the up and
  down arrows buttons to move
  selected items within the list.

6 Click **OK**.

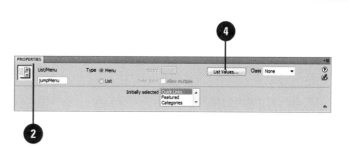

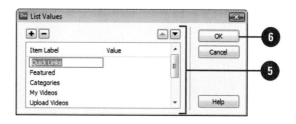

Viewing Example Code for Forms

The <form></form> Tags

The first step in the creation of a form is to place the HTML <form></form> tags on your page. The form tags, when inserted into the document will be delineated by a red line, which will be invisible when the page loads into a standard browser. The red line is a visible design element that lets you know you're working on a form. All items defining the form must be placed within those lines.

```
<html>
<head>
<meta http-equiv="Content-Type"
content="text/html; charset=ISO-8859-1" />
<title>Untitled Document</title>
</head>
<body>
<form id="form1" name="form1" method="post"
action="">
</form>
</body>
</html>
```

```
<body>
<form id="form1" name="form1" method="post"
action="">
  <label>Name
  <input type="text" name="textfield" />
  </label>
<label>Address
    <input type="text" name="textfield2" />
    </label>
<label>City
    <input type="text" name="textfield3" />
    </label>
<label>State
    <input type="text" name="textfield4" />
    </label>
<label>Zip
    <input type="text" name="textfield5" />
    </label>
</form>
</body>
```

Form Elements

Forms can be populated with any number of elements. For example, you could create a simple bio form that asks for information such as name, address, phone number, sex, age, social security number, etc. Because of all this information, it's a good idea to sketch out the general look and feel of the form on a piece of paper, and then use that as a visual guide to the creation of the form in Dreamweaver. When you create an interactive field, Dreamweaver inserts the code necessary to display the field in the browser. The following is an example of the HTML code necessary to display a text input field for a person's name, address, city, state, and zip code.

Form Validation

Once the various form elements are ironed out, you can look at the possibility of validating some of the fields. For example, it might be difficult to create a validation for a name field; however, you at least check to see that the field is not blank. In addition, you could check to see if all zip code fields contain five numbers and not alphabetic characters. Options that require specific answers, such as sex (male/female) could be placed as a pop-up with the correct choices, and other options could be designed using check boxes or radio buttons. In most cases, using check boxes allows the user to choose more than one option (check all that apply), and radio button typically allow for a single choice from a group (choose only one).

When you choose form validation, Dreamweaver creates a script that instructs the browser how to handle the input. The following is an example of a form validation script that validates an email address input field:

```
function MM_validateForm() { //v4.0
  var
i,p,q,nm,test,num,min,max,errors=",args=MM_valida
teForm.arguments;
  for (i=0; i<(args.length-2); i+=3) { test=args[i+2];
val=MM_findObj(args[i]);
    if (val) { nm=val.name; if ((val=val.value)!="") {
      if (test.indexOf('isEmail')!=-1) {
p=val.indexOf('@');
        if (p<1 || p==(val.length-1)) errors+='- '+nm+'
must contain an e-mail address.\n';
      } else if (test!='R') { num = parseFloat(val);
        if (isNaN(val)) errors+='- '+nm+' must contain
a number.\n';
        if (test.indexOf('inRange') != -1) {
p=test.indexOf(':');
          min=test.substring(8,p); max=test.sub-
string(p+1);
          if (num<min || max<num) errors+='- '+nm+'
must contain a number between '+min+' and
'+max+'.\n';
      } } } else if (test.charAt(0) == 'R') errors += '-
'+nm+' is required.\n'; }
    } if (errors) alert('The following error(s)
occurred:\n'+errors);
  document.MM_returnValue = (errors == ");
```

Viewing the HTML Behind the Page

Introduction

In the world of the Internet, the graphics, text, animation, and all the "stuff" that the visitor sees displayed in their browser is the front end of a Web page, and the power behind the page is the HTML code. The HTML code sits quietly behind the scenes, letting the front end get all the credit; however, without the code, the Internet would fall apart. It's the cosmic glue that holds the whole thing together.

Designers, like myself, remember when there were no graphical design interfaces (like Dreamweaver), and all Web pages were designed code line, by tedious code line. I remember working by candlelight into the wee hours of the morning, until I thought my head was going to burst... okay, so maybe I didn't use candles, but it was a lot of painstaking work. Although Dreamweaver changed all of that with its intuitive graphical design interface, the code is still there. However, we're not the ones doing the coding, Dreamweaver is... and isn't that nice?

What You'll Do

Understand HTML

Use the Reference Panel

Use Code View

Use Live Code View

Set Code View Options

Enter HTML Code

Use Code Hints

Work with HTML Head Tags

Insert HTML Comments

Use the Coding Toolbar

Use Quick Tag Editor

Use the Tag Inspector and Chooser

Open Related Files

Navigate to Related Code

Set Site Specific Code Hints

Set Code Hint Preferences

Set Code Format Preferences

Set Code Rewriting Preferences

Set Code Color Preferences

Understanding HTML

HTML stands for the HyperText Markup Language. HTML code is the major language of the Internet's World Wide Web. Web sites and Web pages are written in HTML code. With HTML code and the World Wide Web, you have the ability to bring together text, pictures, sounds, and links... all in one place! HTML code files are plain text files, so they can be composed and edited on any type of computer... Windows, Mac, UNIX, whatever.

HTML documents look a lot like word processing documents. You can have text that's bold and italicized, larger and smaller, or it can look typewritten. The HTML code might look something like this:

You can have <b>bold</b> and <i>italicized</i>, <font size=+2>Larger</font> and <font size=-2>Smaller</font>, or it could look <tt>typewritten</tt>.

Most HTML code is enclosed within braces < >, and when you place the code between the braces it's said to be a tag. An HTML **tag** is code inserted in a document that specifies how the document, or a portion of the document, should be formatted. For example, the <b> tag is saying to start bold text, and the </b> tag is saying to stop bold text. The tag with the slash (/) is known as the closing tag. Many opening tags require a following closing tag, but not all do. Tags make up the entire structure of an HTML document.

HTML files are just normal text files; they usually have the extension of .htm, .html, or .shtml. HTML documents have two parts, the head and the body. The body is the larger part of the document, as the body of a letter you would write to a friend. The head of the document contains the document's title and similar information, and the body contains most everything else.

Common Tags

Symbol	Defines
<html>	Start of the HTML document
<head>	The document heading
<body>	The body of the document
<title>	The document title
<div>	A section in a document
<span>	A section in a document
<h1>	Text heading
<p>	A paragraph
<style>	Format of text
<img>	An image placeholder
<a>	A hyperlink
<iframe>	An inline frame
<!-- comment -->	A comment

Here's an example of a basic HTML document:

    <html>

    <head><title>Title goes here</title></head><body>Body goes here</body>

    </html>

You may find it easier to read if you add extra blank lines such as follows...

    <html>
    <head>
    <title>Title goes here</title>
    </head>
    <body>
    Body goes here
    </body>
    </html>

Extra spaces and line breaks (blank lines) are ignored when the HTML is interpreted (displayed) by a Web browser, such as Microsoft Explorer or Apple Safari... so add them if you wish.

When working with HTML code, it's all about the tags. The HTML tags instruct the text how to look and how it's formatted. In addition, tags control graphics, animation, in short... everything. For example the following uses the <b> or bold tag:

The cow jumped <b>OVER</b> the moon.

When displayed within a browser it would look like this:

The cow jumped **OVER** the moon.

The start tag <b> instructs the text following the tag to use boldface; the end tag </b> instructs the text to stop boldface and return to normal.

HTML page in Code view

HTML page in Design mode

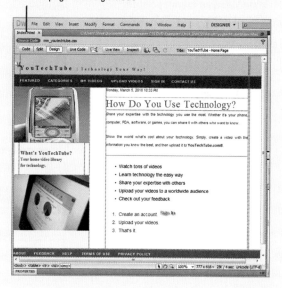

Using the Reference Panel

It doesn't matter whether you're an experienced Web designer, or a newcomer to the field. Sooner or later you're going to need a bit of help, in the form of reference material. I'll admit that I'm a big reader... I love to read. I have a library full of books on creativity and design. Unfortunately, I can't carry all those books with me when I'm on a lecture tour. That's why one of my favorite features in Dreamweaver is the Reference panel. The Reference panel gives you instant (on screen) access to 10 O'Reilly reference manuals, 2 Adobe manuals, and a UseableNet Accessibility Reference. Now that's a lot of reading material, and instant information at your fingertips. For example, you're coding a page, and you need a bit more information on the HTML body tag... it's there, or you need a bit of help with the new syntax of XHTML... it's there. As a matter of fact, when you first open the Reference panel, the information displayed is based on the selected element on the active Web page.

Access the Reference Panel

1. Open Dreamweaver (do not open a document).

2. Click the **Window** menu, point to **Results**, and then click **Reference**.

3. Select information based on the following options:

   - Click the **Select Book** list arrow to select from the list of available reference manuals.

   - Click the **Select Tag** list arrow to select from a list of available HTML tags.

   - Click the **Select Attribute** icon to choose from a list of available attributes for the selected tag.

   The reader window displays the information based on your selections.

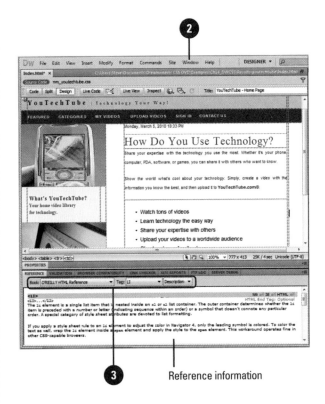

Reference information

Access Specific Information

1. Open the Web page you want to access specific information.

2. Perform one of the following:

   ◆ **Code View.** Select a specific HTML tag, CSS style rule, or other HTML text.

   ◆ **Split View.** Select an item in the Code pane or select an object or text in the Design pane.

   ◆ **Design View.** Select an object, graphic, or portion of text.

3. Select the element for which you want specific information.

4. Press Shift+F1 (Shortcut for accessing the Reference panel).

   The panel opens and displays information about the selected page element.

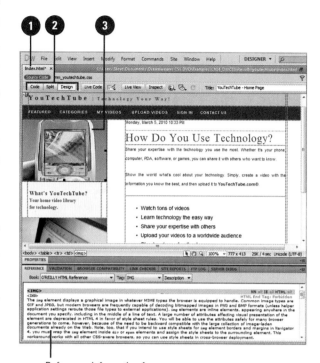

Reference information for the selected element

Did You Know?

You can search for tags, attributes, or text in code. Click the Edit menu, click Find And Replace, specify the Find in document, select Source Code in the Search list arrow, enter the text you want to find, enter the replace text (optional), specify any options, and then click the Find or Replace buttons you want.

You can save and reuse searches. Click the Edit menu, click Find And Replace, set the search criteria you want, click the Save Query button (the disk icon), navigate to the folder where you want to save the search, and then click Save. To reuse a search, click the Load Query button (the folder icon), navigate to the folder with the saved search query file, select it, click Open, and then use the Find or Replace buttons you want.

Using Code View

Dreamweaver utilizes three document code views: Code and Design, Code, and Split Code. The Code and Design view gives you a look at the code and the visual design, the Code view gives you a straight look at the HTML code of your Web page, and the Split Code view gives you a multi-pane look at the HTML code. When you work in any of the code views, you're going back to the basics of Web design... the actual code that makes it all happen. Some designers never look at the code, and some designers claim that you can't be good at creating Web pages without knowing the code. To be honest, I'm in the second camp. I believe that to really understand the design of a Web page, you need to know how the code makes a page function.

Access the Code View

1. Open the Web page you want to view code.

2. Access the Code view using one of the following methods:

   - **Code and Design View.** Click the **View** menu, and then click **Code and Design**, or click the **Split View** button on the document window.

   - **Code View.** Click the **View** menu, and then click **Code**, or click the **Code View** button on the document window.

   - **Split Code View.** Click the **View** menu, and then click **Split Code**.

   The document view changes to display the current page code.

3. To change the placement of content in a split screen, click the **View** menu, and then click **Split Vertically** (horizontal when unchecked), or **Design View on Left** or **Design View on Top**.

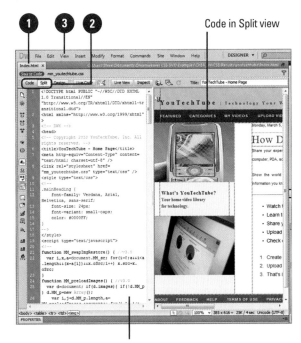

Code in Split view

Split views appear vertically by default.

Did You Know?

You can adjust the size of the panes in Split view. Drag the splitter bar located between the two panes.

View Code in a Separate Window Using Code Inspector

① Open the Web page you want to view code.

② Click the **Window** menu, and then click **Code Inspector**.

③ Use the toolbar to select from the following options:

◆ **File Management.** Get, put, check in or check out a file.

◆ **Preview/Debug In Browser.** Preview or debug the file in a browser or Device Central.

◆ **Refresh Design View.** Refreshes Design view to reflect code changes in Code view.

◆ **Reference.** Opens the Reference panel.

◆ **Code Navigation.** Allows you to move quickly in the code.

◆ **View Options.** Allows you to change the way code appears in Code view.

④ When you're done, click the **Close** button.

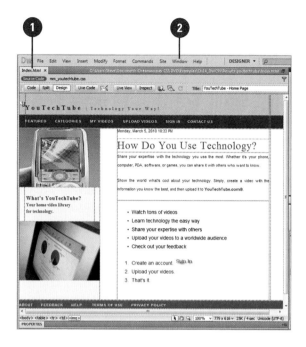

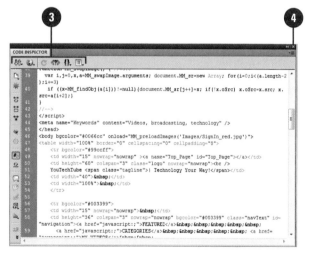

Did You Know?

You can use the coder-oriented work-space. The workspace displays the panel groups docked on the left side of the main window, and the Document window appears in Code view. The Properties panel is collapsed. Click the Window menu, point to Workspace Layout, and then click Coder.

Using Code Live View

As you work in Live view, you can also view live code. Similar to Live view, Live Code view is a non-editable view. Live code view appears displaying the code that the browser uses to execute the page. The non-editable code is highlighted in yellow. If you want to edit the code, all you need to do is return to Live view, and then switch to Code view, which is editable. After making your code changes, you can return to Live view and then refresh it to see your changes.

Access Live Code View

① Open the Web page you want to view.

② Switch to Design view or Code and Design view.

③ Click the **Live View** button.

④ To go to Live Code view, click the **Live Code** button.

Live code view appears displaying the code that the browser uses to execute the page. The non-editable code is highlighted in yellow.

⑤ To return back to Live view, click the **Live Code** button again.

⑥ To return back to Design view, click the **Live View** button again.

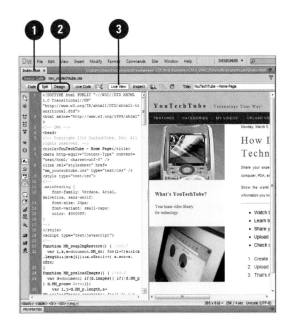

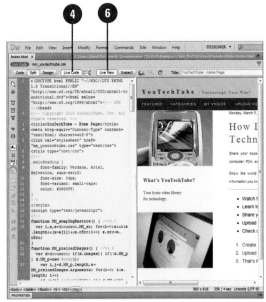

Did You Know?

You can print code. Open the Web page you want to print in Code view, click the File menu, click Print Code, specify the options you want, and then click OK (Win) or Print (Mac).

See Also

See "Previewing Pages in Live View" on page 32-33 for more information on viewing pages in Live View and Live Code View.

Setting Code View Options

You can select Code view options to change the way code appears in Code view. When you select the Code View Options command on the View menu or use individual buttons on the Code toolbar, you can set options to set word wrapping, display line numbers, hide characters, highlight invalid code, color code, indent code automatically, and display syntax error alerts in the Info bar.

Use Code View Options

1. Open the Web page you want to view code.

2. Switch to the Code view.

3. Click the **View** menu, point to **Code View Options**, and then select from the following options:

   - **Word Wrap.** Forces the HTML code to wrap, based on the width of the Code view window.

   - **Line Numbers.** Displays line numbers to the left of the HTML code.

   - **Hidden Characters.** Displays hidden code elements, such as tabs and character returns.

   - **Highlight Invalid Code.** Highlights any code that Dreamweaver considers incorrect.

   - **Syntax Coloring.** Colorizes the HTML code, to visibly separate it from the text.

   - **Auto Indent.** Automatically indents the HTML code to aid in readability.

   - **Syntax Error Alerts in Info Bar.** Displays syntax code error alerts in the Info bar.

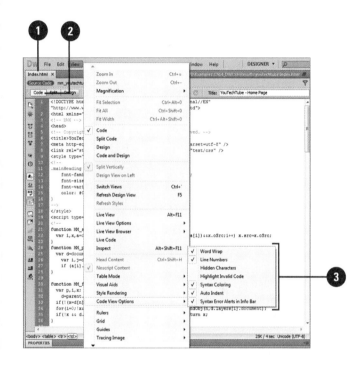

Entering HTML Code

You can enter HTML code in Code view like you are typing text into a word processor. However, when you type HTML code, it uses a specific structure and layout. As you type, the Code Hints popup menu appears to help you enter correct HTML code tag names, attributes, and values as you type code in Code view or the Quick Tag Editor. For example, when a tag requires the selection of a color, Dreamweaver displays a color palette. When a font is required, a font list is automatically displayed, and when a file is required a browse button magically appears allowing you to select and insert the file. If a page does contain invalid code, it appears in Design view and optionally highlights in Code view. When you select the invalid code, the Properties panel displays information as to why the code is invalid and steps to fix it.

Enter HTML in Code View

1 Open the Web page you want to view code.

2 Switch to the Code view.

3 Click to the right of a tag and press Enter to create a space between the opening and closing body tag.

4 Enter the HTML code you want on the new line.

◆ **Code Hints**. When you type the left brace "<" the Code Hints popup menu appears, listing all possible HTML codes. Begin entering in the code name, and Code Hints will display the correct code. Double-click it or select it and press Enter (Win) or Return (Mac) to add the tag.

TIMESAVER *Press Control+Spacebar to display a Code Hints popup menu or press Esc to close the Code Hints menu.*

5 To indent the selected code, press Tab; to outdent the selected code, press Shift+Tab.

6 To add a closing tag, type a left brace and forward slash "</", and Dreamweaver will automatically insert the correct closing tag.

7 To remove a tag, right-click in the tag, and then click **Remove Tag**.

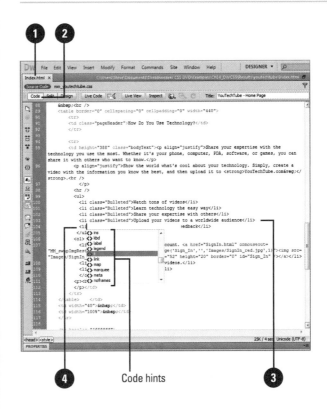

Code hints

Using Code Hints

Code hints makes it easy to insert and edit code accurately in a variety of languages. Dreamweaver supports code hinting for the following languages and technologies: HTML, CSS, DOM, JavaScript, Ajax, Spry, Adobe ColdFusion, JSP, PHP (**New!** for functions, variables, and classes and tooltip help), MySQL, ASP JavaScript, ASP VBScript, ASP.NET C#, and ASP.NET VB. As you start to type code for a particular code type, the Code Hints popup menu appears to help you enter it correctly. When you type a right angle bracket (<), code hint displays HTML tag names. When you type a period (dot operator) after an object, code hint displays JavaScript code possibilities. Dreamweaver also provides code hinting for your own or third-party custom JavaScript classes that are not built in to the language. If Dreamweaver detects problems with your code, code hints doesn't always work properly. Use the Syntax Error Information Bar to help you fix the code problems.

Use Code Hints

1. Open the Web page you want to view code.

2. Place the insertion point where you want to add code.

3. Start to type the code you want or press Control+Spacebar to manually display the code hints popup menu.

4. Scroll through the list by using the scroll bar or pressing the Up Arrow and Down Arrow keys.

5. To insert a code hint, double-click an item, or select it and then press Enter (Win) or Return (Mac).

   ◆ Press Backspace (Win) or Delete (Mac) to dismiss the list of code hints.

6. To edit code, delete the code, and then start typing what you want to use for code hints.

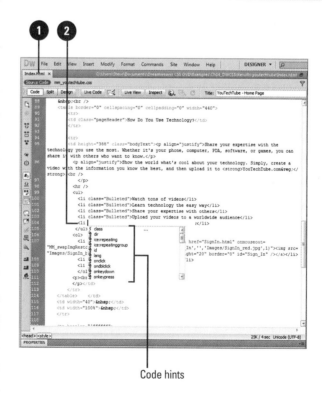

Code hints

See Also

See "Setting Code Hint Preferences" on page 344 for more information on setting options for code hints.

Working with HTML Head Tags

Each page contains information about the document in the head section. You can set the properties of head elements to control how your pages are identified on the Web by search browsers. You can insert the following head tags: meta, keywords, description, refresh, base, or link. A **meta** tag records information about the current page, such as encoding, author, copyright, or keywords. The **keywords** and **description** tags record information many search engines, such as Google or Yahoo, look for to create an index for your page for use in their search results databases. For the best results, specify a few descriptive keywords and a short description for a page. The **refresh** tag specifies the amount of time before the page is refreshed in a browser. The **base** tag sets the base URL that all document-relative paths in the page use. The **link** tag defines a relationship between the current page and another file. After you insert a head tag, you can always make changes and adjustments by using the head content, selecting the head element, and making changes in the Properties panel.

View and Insert Head Tags

1. Open the Web page you want to view and change head properties.

2. To insert head tags, click the **Insert** menu, point to **HTML**, point to **Head Tags**, and then select the tag you want: Meta, Keywords, Description, Refresh, Base, or Link.

3. Enter the information or specify the options you want, and then click **OK**.

4. Click the **View** menu, and then click **Head Content**.

5. To edit an element, click one of the icons in the head section to select it, and then change the properties you want in the Properties panel.

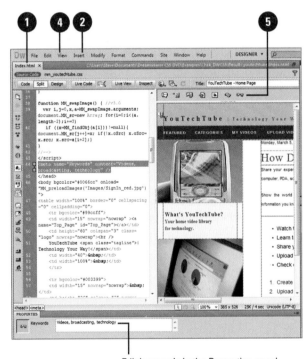

Edit keywords in the Properties panel

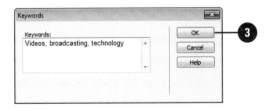

Did You Know?

You can check for balanced tags and braces. In Code view, click to place the insertion point where you want to check, click the Edit menu, and then click Select Parent Tag or Balance Braces. You can select the commands again to check the next level out.

Inserting HTML Comments

If you're writing large sections of code or working with other people to develop a site, it's important to insert comments into your HTML code. An HTML comment is descriptive text that explains the purpose and process for the page's code. The comment text only appears in Code view; the information is for internal development purposes only. You can insert comments in Code view or Design view. After you insert a comment, you can edit it directly in Code view, or select the comment marker and make changes in the Properties panel.

Insert HTML Comments

1. Open the Web page you want to insert comments.

2. Click to place the insertion point where you want to insert a comment (in Code or Design view).

3. Click the **Insert** menu, and then click **Comment**.

4. Type the comment you want.

5. Click **OK** (in Design view).

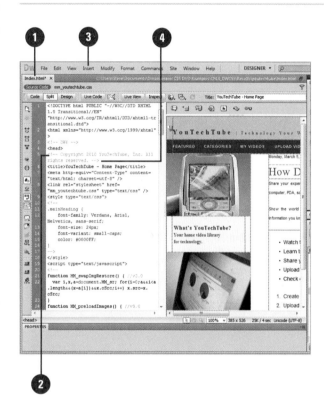

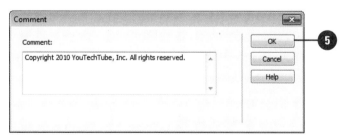

Did You Know?

You can change the code using the Selection submenu. Select the code you want in Code view, right-click (Win) or control-click (Mac) it, point to Selection, and then click the selection command you want.

You can copy and paste code. Copy the code from Code view or from another program, click to place the insertion point in Code view where you want to paste the code, click the Edit menu, and then click Paste.

See Also

See "Working with Invisible Elements" on page 88 for information on displaying comment markers in Design view.

Using the Coding Toolbar

When you switch to Code or Split view, the Coding toolbar appears along the left side of the Code view pane. The toolbar provides easy access to the most common coding related commands. If the Code view pane is not large enough, an expander arrow appears, which you click to access additional buttons. Some of the tools allow you to collapse and expand the content between a set of opening and closing tags, select tags, insert and remove comments, format code, and highlight invalid code.

Use the Coding Toolbar

1. Open the Web page you want to view code.

2. Switch to Code or Split view.

3. Click to place the insertion point in the code or select a block of code.

4. Click the button you want on the Coding toolbar:

   ◆ **Open Documents.** Displays a list of open documents. Click the one you want to open it.

   ◆ **Show Code Navigator.** Displays the Code Navigator in the code.

   ◆ **Collapse Full Tag.** Collapses the content between a set of opening and closing tags. You need to place the insertion point in the opening or closing tag.

   ◆ **Collapse Selection.** Collapses the selected code.

   ◆ **Expand All.** Restores all collapsed code.

   ◆ **Select Parent Tag.** Selects the code tag immediately outside of the line with the insertion point.

   ◆ **Balance Braces.** Selects the code tag and surrounding parentheses, braces, or square brackets of the line with the insertion point.

   ◆ **Line Numbers.** Shows or hides the numbers at the beginning of each line of code.

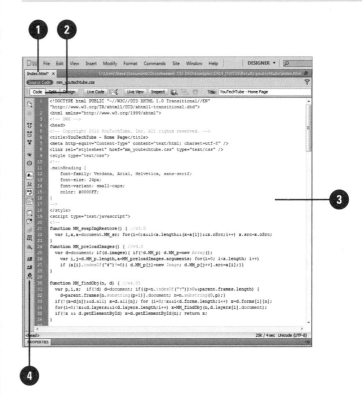

- **Highlight Invalid Code.** Highlights invalid code in yellow.

- **Syntax Error Alerts in Info Bar.** Displays syntax code error alerts in the Info bar.

- **Apply Comment.** Inserts comment tags around the selected code, or opens new comment tags.

- **Remove Comment.** Deletes comment tags from the selected code.

- **Wrap Tag.** Wraps selected code with the selected tag from the Quick Tag Editor.

- **Recent Snippets.** Inserts a recently used code snippet from the Snippets panel.

- **Move or Convert CSS.** Moves CSS to another location or converts inline CSS to CSS rules.

- **Indent Code.** Shifts the selection to the right.

- **Outdent Code.** Shifts the selection to the left.

- **Format Source Code.** Displays options to apply source code formatting to selected code, or to the entire page if no code is selected. You can also access Code Format Settings from the Preferences dialog box or the Tag Library Editor.

TIMESAVER *You can perform many of these same commands on the Insert panel.*

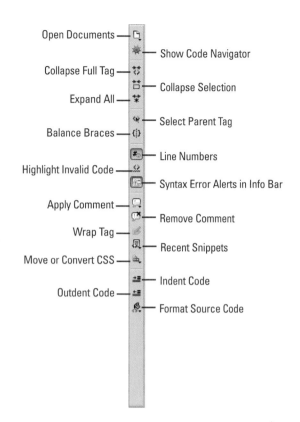

See Also

See "Moving CSS Rules" on page 226 for information on moving CSS rules to a style sheet.

For Your Information

Identifying Syntax Errors

If you open a page with syntax errors, Dreamweaver displays a semi-transparent red color to mark the code view gutter on all the lines that have syntax errors. In addition, Dreamweaver displays an alert message in the Info bar to inform you the first error line number and warn you that code hinting might not work property. It's important to know that even though all errors are shown, often only the first error is the real error location. The rest of the errors are an indirect consequence of the first error.

Using Quick Tag Editor

Creating Web documents in the Design view is a beautiful and elegant way to design Web pages; however, sometimes you just need to get under the hood and make changes directly to the code. Dreamweaver gives you a way to make alterations to the code using the Quick Tag Editor. When activated, the Quick Tag Editor displays as a small pop-up window and allows you to edit a tag, add a tag, or enclose the current selection within a tag. In addition, you can use a list of tags and attributes to help jog your HTML memory, and save you some typing. Dreamweaver's Quick Tag Editor can be used in three ways: Insert HTML (used for adding new tags and code at the current cursor position), Wrap Tag (wrap one tag around one or more other tags and content) and Edit HTML (displays the entire selected tag with all the attributes). It is a great time-saver for making those small tweaks to the code of any Web document. While most designers will perform most of the creative process using the Design view, it's nice to know that you have a powerful tool like the Quick Tag Editor when you need to get back to coding basics.

Open the Quick Tag Editor

1. Open the Web page you want to view code.

2. Open the Quick Tag Editor using any of the following methods:

   ◆ Click the **Modify** menu, and then click **Quick Tag Editor**.

   ◆ Use the keyboard shortcut Ctrl+T (Win) or ⌘+T (Mac).

   ◆ Click the **Quick Tag Editor** icon in the Properties panel.

Did You Know?

Dreamweaver helps you with the syntax of the code. If you fail to add the quotation marks around a parameter's value, the Quick Tag Editor will do it for you. If you want to add more than one tag, you can use the right arrow key to move beyond the first set of braces in the Quick Tag Editor. Then, simply enter in a left brace and add the additional tag.

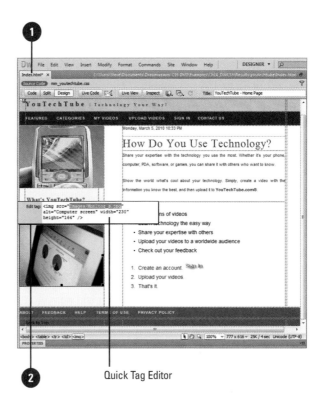

Quick Tag Editor

Use Quick Tag Editor in Wrap Tag or Insert HTML Mode

1. Open the Web page you want to view code.

2. Select a portion of text within the document (for Wrap Tag mode) or click in the text area (do not select any text) to place an insertion point (for Insert HTML mode).

3. Open the Quick Tag Editor.

4. Use the HTML tags in the pop-up hint list to insert a tag, or manually enter a customized XML tag.

5. Press Enter (Win) or Return (Mac) to wrap the selected text with the tag.

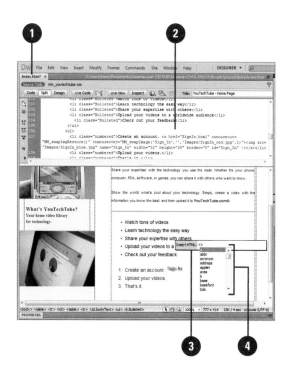

Use Quick Tag Editor in Edit Tag Mode

1. Open the Web page you want to view code.

2. Select a complete tag in Code view (e.g., img), or select an object, such as an image, in Design view.

3. Open the Quick Tag Editor.

   The tag with all its attributes will be displayed within the Quick Tag Editor window.

4. Manually enter any changes to the tag and attributes.

5. Press Enter (Win) or Return (Mac) to add the tag to the document.

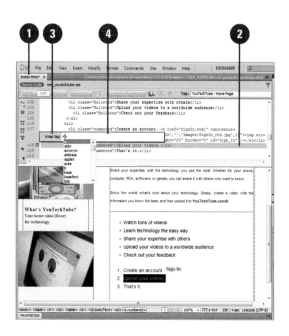

Using the Tag Inspector

Dreamweaver's Tag Inspector gives you control over your code by displaying a collapsible outline of the tags used on the current page. This feature allow you to quickly determine if tags are correctly nested, and to view and change tag attributes. For example, you may want to change the attributes of the <body> tag, or change the overall color and size of the default font; both these and many more options are available using the Tag Inspector. When selected, the Tag Inspector displays a collapsible structure of all the attributes within the selected Web element. This view gives you an overall view of the code and how it's laid out. When you select a tag, all the attributes for that tag are displayed for you to view and edit.

Access the Tag Inspector

1. Open the Web page you want to view in the Tag Inspector.

2. Make a selection using one of the following methods:

   ◆ **Code View.** Select a specific HTML tag or section of text.

   ◆ **Split View.** Select a HTML tag in the Code pane or select an object in the Design pane.

   ◆ **Design View.** Select an object in the window, or create a selection of text.

3. Click the **Window** menu, and then click **Tag Inspector** to display the Tag Inspector.

4. Select from the following views:

   ◆ **Category View.** Displays a list of general categories within collapsible headings. Click the plus (+) or minus (-) sign icon to display all available attributes.

   ◆ **List View.** Displays a list of all available attributes for the selected Web element.

5. Select the attribute that you want to add or modify, and enter the correct value in the input field.

6. Press the Enter key to record your changes.

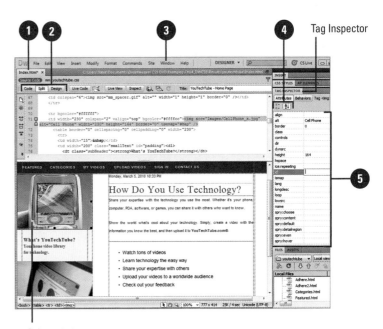

Tag Inspector

Selected element

Using the Tag Chooser

The Tag Chooser allows you to insert any tag from the Dreamweaver tag libraries in your page. A tag library is a collection of tags for a certain type that contains tag information, code hints, target browser checks, and other features. You can insert tags from the following types: HTML, CFML, ASP.NET, JSP, JRun custom library, ASP, PHP, and WML. If you are looking for a specific tag in a specific category, the Tag Chooser can help you insert it into your code with the right syntax.

Insert Tags Using the Tag Chooser

1. Open the Web page you want to insert a tag using the Tag Chooser.

2. Click to place the insertion point in the code where you want to insert a tag.

3. Right-click (Win) or control-click (Mac) near the insertion point, and then click **Insert Tag**.

4. Select a category of tags from the tag library, or expand the category and select a subcategory.

5. Select a tag from the right pane.

6. To view syntax and usage information for the selected tag, click **Tag Info**.

7. To insert the selected tag into your code, click **Insert**.

8. If a tag requires more information, enter the required information in the tag editor, and then click **OK**.

9. Click **Close**.

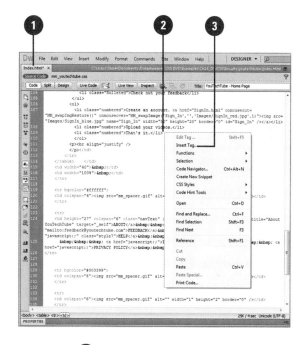

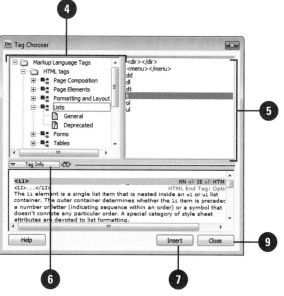

Did You Know?

You can add or remove tags, attributes, and libraries from the Tag Library.
Click the Edit menu, click Tag Libraries, click the Plus (+) or Minus (-) buttons to select commands to add or remove tags, attributes, and libraries.

Opening Related Files

If you have a related file attached to a document, you can use the Related Files toolbar to quickly open it while keeping the main page available. When the Enabled Related Files option and an Discover Dynamically-Related Files option is selected in General Preferences, Dreamweaver displays the names of all static and dynamically (**New!**) related files related to a main document in a Related Files toolbar. The related files include external CSS rules, server-side includes (multi-level), PHP files, external JavaScript files, parent templates files, library files, and iframe source files. Status files appear first starting from the left, followed by external files (such as .css and .js), and concluding with dynamic path server included files (such as .php, .inc, and .mod-ule). When the Related Files toolbar contains too many files to fit on the toolbar, scroll arrows appear on the right and left to access files. To help you reduce the number of files on the toolbar, you can filter files by type to hide the ones you don't want to display. In addition, when you click a link to a code source file in the Code Navigator, the file appears in the related files area (if enabled).

Set Related Files Preferences

1. Click the **Dreamweaver** (Mac) or **Edit** (Win) menu, and then click **Preferences**.

2. Click the **General** category.

3. Select the **Enable Related Files** check box.

4. Click **OK** to the alert. The change takes effect after restarting Dreamweaver.

5. Click the **Discover Dynamically-Related Files** list arrow (**New!**), and then select an option:

   ◆ **Automatically.** Displays static and dynamically-related files on the Related Files toolbar.

   ◆ **Manually.** Displays static related files and displays the Info bar for dynamic-related ones. Click the **Discover** link on the Info bar to display it on the Related Files toolbar.

   ◆ **Disabled.** Turns off the discovery of dynamically-related files. Static related files are still displayed.

6. Click **OK**.

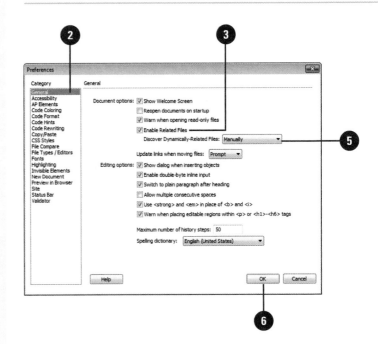

Use the Related Files Toolbar

◆ **Open a Related File.** Click a file named button on the Related Files toolbar.

◆ **Open a Related File as a Separate File.** Right-click (Win) or Control-click (Mac) a file named button on the Related Files toolbar, and then click **Open as Separate File**.

◆ **Return to the Main Document Source Code.** Click the **Source Code** button on the Related Files toolbar.

◆ **Filter Files on the Toolbar.** Click the **Filter Related Files** button (**New!**) on the Related Files toolbar, and then select the file types you want to filter (checked to show or unchecked to hide) or click **Show All File Types** to show all files.

The list of file types on the menu is built based on the file types connected to the current open document. You cannot filter out all the file types. When you close a document, the filter settings are not saved.

Related Files toolbar with buttons to access files

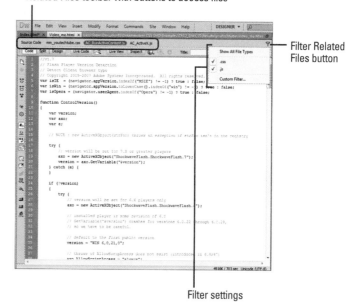

Filter Related Files button

Filter settings

Navigating to Related Code

Code Navigator displays a list of linked code sources related to a part of a page. The related codes sources include internal and external CSS rules, server-side includes, external JavaScript files, parent templates files, library files, and iframe source files. When you click a linked code source, the file appears in the related files area (if enabled) or opens as a separate file in the Document window. If the code source is an internal CSS rule, the rule appears in Split view. You can open Code Navigator from Design, Code, and Split views and the Code Inspector.

Open the Code Navigator

1. Open the Web page you want to view.

2. Alt-click (Win) or command-option-click (Mac) anywhere on the page.

   ◆ You can also click the **Code Navigator indicator** icon to open the Code Navigator. The Code Navigator indicator icon appears near the insertion point when the mouse remains idle for 2 seconds.

   The Code Navigator displays links to the code related to the section of the page you clicked. The code sources are grouped by file and listed alphabetically.

3. Click a link to display it in the related files area or open it as a separate file in the Document window.

4. To close the Code Navigator, click outside of it.

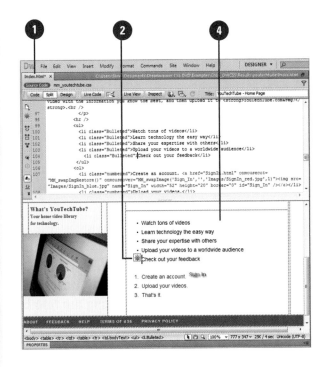

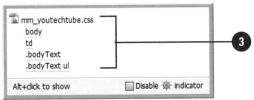

Did You Know?

You can enable or disable the Code Navigator indicator. Alt-click (Win) or command-option-click (Mac) on a page, select or clear the Disable Indicator check box, and then click outside to close the Code Navigator.

Setting Site Specific Code Hints

When you're working with PHP files in Dreamweaver, you can discover code hints for functions, variables, and classes (**New!**). The built-in hint support also includes tooltips with documentation from php.net, which you can enable in Code Hints preferences. Added dynamic PHP code hinting support allows you to customize CMS (Content Management System) frameworks, like Drupal, Wordpress, and Joomla. If a PHP code hint is not available by default in Dreamweaver, you can create or edit a configuration file in your local site with the site-specific code hints extension (**New!**) that allows PHP code hinting to inspect the specified files and folders for functions, objects, and global variables you want as code hints. The configuration file, named *dw_php_codehinting.config*, is saved to your site's root.

Set Site Specific Code Hints

1. Open a PHP page, and make sure a server site is set up.

2. Click the **Structure** list arrow, and then select a built-in option (**Drupal**, **Joomla**, or **Wordpress**), or click **<New from blank>** to create your own.

3. Click the **Browse for Folder** icon to select a sub-root folder for the configuration file and the base for searches within the site.

4. To add or remove a file or folder to your site scan, click the **Plus** button, specify a file or folder, and then click **Add**, or select a file or folder, and then click the **Minus** button.

5. Use any of the following:

   ◆ **Scan This Folder.** Includes the selected folder in the site scan.

   ◆ **Recursive.** Includes subfolders when a folder is selected.

   ◆ **Extensions.** Specifies the file extensions to check.

6. To manage structures, use the **Import**, **Save**, **Rename**, or **Delete** buttons.

7. Click **OK**.

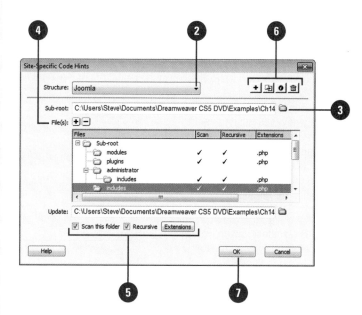

Setting Code Hint Preferences

You can use the Code Hint section of the Preferences dialog box to set options for the Code Hints popup menu. Code Hints does more than help you type in a simple HTML code tag. It helps you insert tag names, attributes, and values as you type code in Code view or the Quick Tag Editor. For example, when a tag requires the selection of a color, Dreamweaver displays a color palette. When a font is required, a font list is displayed, and when a file is required, a browse button magically appears allowing you to select and insert the file. If you want additional tooltip help, you can enable it for php code hints (**New!**).

Set Code Hint Preferences

1. Click the **Dreamweaver** (Mac) or **Edit** (Win) menu, and then click **Preferences**.

2. Click the **Code Hints** category.

3. Select from the following check boxes:

   ◆ **Close Tags.** Select an option to specify how you want to insert closing tags. The default inserts tags automatically after you type the characters </. You can also insert it after a final bracket >, or not at all.

   ◆ **Options.** Select the **Enable Code Hints** check box to use code hints, and then drag the slider to set the code hints popup menu delay you want. Select the **Enable Description Tooltips** check box (**New!**) to use tooltip help for PHP files.

   ◆ **Menus.** Select the check boxes for the types of code hints you want to display, and clear the others you don't want.

   IMPORTANT *Even if you disable code hints, you can display a popup hint in Code view by pressing Control+Spacebar.*

4. To add or remove tags and attributes, click the **Tag Library Editor** link.

5. Click **OK**.

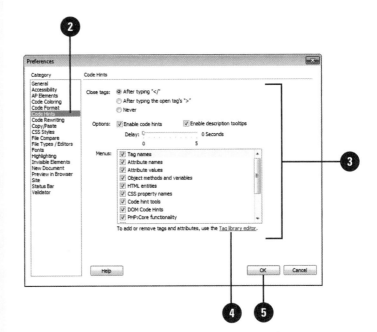

Setting Code Format Preferences

You can use the Code Format section of the Preferences dialog box to change the way your code looks in Code view. The options you set in the Code Format section, except the Override Case Of option, are automatically applied only to new documents or additions to documents you create in the future. If you want to reformat an existing document, you can use the Apply Source Formatting on the Commands menu.

Set Code Format Preferences

1. Click the **Dreamweaver** (Mac) or **Edit** (Win) menu, and then click **Preferences**.

2. Click the **Code Format** category.

3. Select from the following options:

   ◆ **Indent.** Select to have Dreamweaver indent generated code, and then specify how many spaces or tabs to indent.

   ◆ **Tab Size.** Specify how many spaces for a tab character.

   ◆ **Line Break Type.** Select the type of remote hosting server (Windows, Macintosh, or UNIX).

   ◆ **Default Tag Case and Default Attribute Case.** Select <lowercase> or <uppercase>.

   ◆ **Override Case Of: Tags and Attributes.** Select whether to override your case settings.

   ◆ **TD Tag: Do Not Include A Break Inside The TD Tag.** Select to prevent problems with white space and line breaks on older browsers.

   ◆ **Advanced Formatting.** Click to set formatting options for CSS code and individual tags and attributes in the Tag Library Editor.

4. Click **OK**.

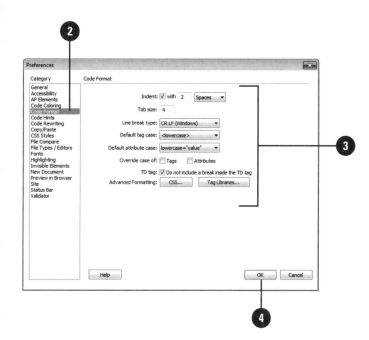

Setting Code Rewriting Preferences

You can use the Code Rewriting section of the Preferences dialog box to specify how and if Dreamweaver changes your code. Some of the rewriting options allow you to fix invalid nesting and unclosed tags; prevent duplicate names for form objects; ensure attributes values and URLs contain legal characters; and add the right JavaScript tags upon opening active content files. These options have no effect when you edit your code in Code view. If you disable the rewriting options, invalid HTML code that would have been rewritten is displayed in the Document window.

Set Code Rewriting Preferences

1. Click the **Dreamweaver** (Mac) or **Edit** (Win) menu, and then click **Preferences**.

2. Click the **Code Rewriting** category.

3. Select from the following options:

   ◆ **Fix Invalidly Nested and Unclosed Tags.** Select to rewrite overlapping or transposed tags and inserts closing quotation marks and to insert closing brackets as needed.

   ◆ **Rename Form Items When Pasting.** Select to prevent duplicate names for form objects.

   ◆ **Remove Extra Closing Tags.** Select to delete closing tags that don't have an associated opening tag.

   ◆ **Warn When Fixing Or Removing Tags.** Select to display a summary of invalid HTML code Dreamweaver wants to fix.

   ◆ **Never Rewrite Code: In Files With Extensions.** Select to prevent code rewriting in files with specific file extensions, and then specify the files extensions you want separated by a space.

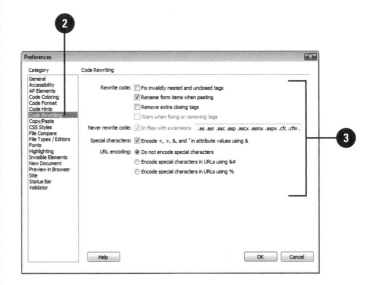

- **Encode <, >, &, And " In Attribute Values Using &.** Select to make sure attribute values you enter outside Code view contain legal characters.

- **Do Not Encode Special Characters.** Select to prevent Dreamweaver from changing URLs to use only legal characters.

- **Encode Special Characters In URLs Using &#.** Select to make sure URLs you enter outside Code view contain legal characters (use the &# encoding method).

- **Encode Special Characters In URLs Using %.** Select to make sure URLs you enter outside Code view contain legal characters (use the % encoding method).

4 Click **OK**.

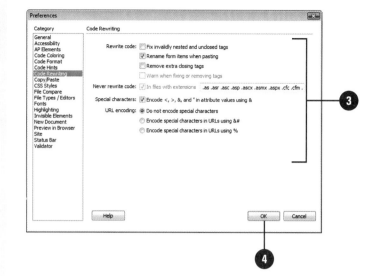

Setting Code Color Preferences

You can use the Code Coloring section of the Preferences dialog box to specify colors for general categories of tags and code elements, such as HTML Image or style tags, Library items, or CSS properties. For a selected tag or code element, you can specify the text color, background color, and any formatting (Bold, Italic, or Underline) you want to make it easier to work with your code. In Code view and Live Code view (**New!**), you can specify different colors for backgrounds and code to make it easier to read.

Set Code Color Preferences

1. Click the **Dreamweaver** (Mac) or **Edit** (Win) menu, and then click **Preferences**.

2. Click the **Code Coloring** category.

3. Click any of the color boxes, and then select a color.

   ◆ **Default Background.** Default Code view background color.

   ◆ **Hidden Characters.** Hidden character code color. (**New!**)

   ◆ **Live Code Background.** Live Code view background color. (**New!**)

   ◆ **Live Code Changes.** Live Code view code change color. (**New!**)

   ◆ **Read Only Background.** Read only background color. (**New!**)

4. Click the document type in which you want to set code colors.

5. Click **Edit Coloring Scheme**.

6. Select the style for the document type you want to change.

7. Specify the text color, background color, and any formatting (Bold, Italic, or Underline) you want.

   The sample code in the Preview pane displays the new styles and colors.

8. Click **OK**.

9. Click **OK**.

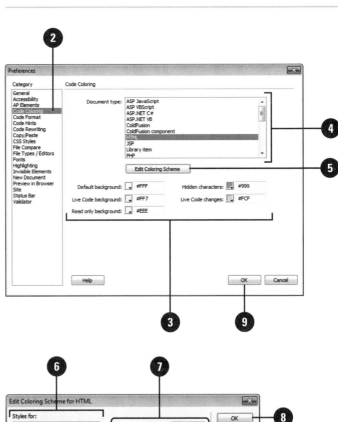

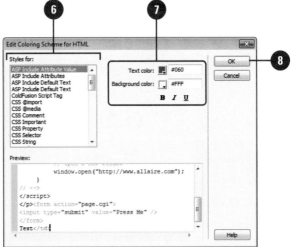

Working with Behaviors

Introduction

Everybody loves the versatility that JavaScript can bring to a Web page, yet not that many people love programming in JavaScript, to make it happen. Dreamweaver makes your life easier by allowing you to insert Behaviors, most of which directly translate into JavaScript. Using behaviors, you can do things like insert pop-up windows, create disjointed rollovers, check to see if users have a certain plug-in or what browser they're running.

The best thing about behaviors and commands is that they are extendable. Many third party companies and individuals write commands and behaviors for Dreamweaver. You can download these extensions from the Web, most often for free!

A **behavior** is a combination of an event with an action triggered by that event. In the Behaviors panel, you add a behavior to a page by specifying an action and then specifying the event that triggers that action. Adobe Dreamweaver behaviors insert JavaScript code in documents to allow users to interact with a Web page, change the page, or to produce certain tasks. Behaviors are attached to a specific element on your page, whether it's a text link, an image, and even certain HTML specific tags.

An action consists of pre-written JavaScript code that performs a specific task, such as opening a browser window, showing or hiding an AP element, playing a sound, or stopping a Flash movie. The actions provided with Dreamweaver are written by engineers to provide maximum cross-browser compatibility.

In this chapter you'll learn how to apply behaviors to Web elements, how to edit and modify behaviors; even how to create and maintain a library of all your important behaviors.

What You'll Do

Introduce Behaviors

Apply Behaviors to Page Elements

Apply Behaviors to Entire Page

Edit Behaviors

Work with Behaviors

Add Behavior Effects

Go to Another Web Page

Open Another Browser Window

Display Text Messages

Preload and Swap Images

Change Element Properties

Drag an AP Element

Show and Hide Elements

Execute a JavaScript

Introducing Behaviors

Dreamweaver helps non-programmer types (you know who you are) use built-in JavaScript functions that are useful to any Web project. The code generated is well optimized so you do not have to worry about performance. A Dreamweaver behavior consists of two parts: An **action** that instructs the browser what to do, and an **event** that triggers the specific actions.

Dreamweaver comes supplied with dozens of behavior actions, the most useful being:

- **Check Plug-in.** The Check Plug-in action sends visitors to different pages depending on whether they have the specified plug-in installed.

- **Go To URL.** The Go To URL action opens a new page in the current window or in the specified frame.

- **Open Browser Window.** The Open Browser Window action opens a URL in a new window.

- **Popup Message.** The Popup Message action displays a JavaScript alert with the message you specify.

- **Preload Images.** The Preload Images action loads images that do not appear on the page right away (i.e., rollover images) into the browser cache.

- **Show Pop-Up Menu.** The Show Pop-Up Menu behavior creates a pop-up menu within a page.

- **Show/Hide Elements.** The Show/Hide Elements action causes specified layers to be shown or hidden.

- **Swap Image.** The Swap Image action creates button rollovers and other image effects (including swapping more than one image at a time).

- **Swap Image Restore.** The Swap Image Restore action restores the last set of swapped images to their previous source files (automatically added whenever you attach the Swap Image action).

- **Validate Form.** The Validate Form action checks the contents of selected text fields to ensure that the user has entered the correct type of data.

NOTE *Behavior code is client-side JavaScript code; that is, it runs in browsers, not on servers.*

Behaviors are attached to a specific element on your page, whether it's a text link, an image, and even certain HTML specific tags. After you attach a behavior to a page element, whenever the event you've specified occurs for that element, the browser calls the action (the JavaScript code) that you've associated with that event. (The events that you can use to trigger a given action vary from browser to browser.) For example, if you attach the Popup Message action to a link and specify that it will be triggered by the onMouseOver event, then whenever someone points to that link with the mouse pointer in the browser, your message pops up in a dialog box. A single event can trigger several different actions, and you can specify the order in which those actions occur.

In order to make a behavior work, an action is linked to an event. Events are, effectively, messages generated by browsers indicating that a visitor to your page has done something. For example, when a visitor moves the pointer over a link, the browser generates an onMouseOver event for that link; the browser then checks to see whether there's some JavaScript code that the browser is to call when the event is generated. Different events are defined for different page elements; for example, in most browsers onMouseOver and onClick are events associated with links, where onLoad is an event associated with images and with the body section of the document. Notice the specific way that JavaScript code is written. It's not only important to get the spelling of a code piece correct; in addition, case is important. For example onBlur is correct... onblur is not. The good news is that Dreamweaver inserts the correct code into the document through the use of the Behaviors panel.

The possible Events associated with an Action are:

- **onBlur.** Activates when a blur event occurs. A field gains focus when the user clicks inside the text box, and the focus is lost (onblur) when the user clicks outside the box, anywhere on the page.

- **onClick.** Activates when the user clicks the left mouse button on the object.

- **onDblClick.** Activates when the user double-clicks the object.

- **onError.** Activates when an error occurs during object loading.

- **onFocus.** Activates when the object receives focus. A field gains focus when the user clicks inside the object.

- **onKeyDown.** Activates when the user presses a key.

- **onKeyPress.** Activates when the user presses an alphanumeric key.

- **onKeyUp.** Activates when the user releases an alphanumeric key.

- **onLoad.** Activates after the browser loads the object.

- **onMouseDown.** Activates when the user clicks the object with either the mouse or a form button.

- **onMouseMove.** Activates when the user moves the mouse over the object.

- **onMouseOut.** Activates when the user moves the mouse pointer outside the boundaries of the object.

- **onMouseOver.** Activates when the user moves the mouse pointer into the object.

- **onMouseUp.** Activates when the user releases a mouse button while the mouse is over the object.

- **OnUnload.** Activates immediately before the object is unloaded.

The target browser you select determines which events are supported for a given element.

The power of Behaviors lies in the fact that they use JavaScript code to create dynamic and interactive Web pages. Although JavaScript is not new to Web page design, it's quickly becoming more and more popular as the days roll by, and the World Wide Web Consortium (*www.w3c.org*) is working overtime to make all the code pieces work the same on all browsers. However, no matter how good the code is, there will always be times when the code warrior (you) decides that the code needs to be edited or completely eliminated. Thankfully, with Dreamweaver, this is no problem whatsoever.

Applying Behaviors to Page Elements

Dreamweaver allows you to attach behaviors to links, images, form elements, or any of several other HTML elements. The Behaviors panel allows you to attach, modify, and manage behaviors embedded in a page. In the Behaviors panel, you can use options to show all events for a specific category, or only the ones currently attached to the page. The target browser you select determines which events are supported for a given element. Dreamweaver works well with current browsers. However older ones may be more limited. Internet Explorer 4.0, for example, has a much wider array of events for each element than Netscape Navigator 4.0 or any 3.0 browsers. If you need additional functionality, you can attach more than one event to a specific action; for example, when you user clicks on a specific image, the image changes, and a prerecorded sound plays. When you use multiple actions, they occur in the order in which they're listed in the Actions column of the Behaviors panel.

Apply One or More Behaviors to a Page Element

1. Open the Web page you want to apply a behavior to an element.

2. Click the **Window** menu, and then click **Behaviors** to display the Behaviors panel.

3. Select an element (image or link) on the page in Design view.

4. Click the **Add Behavior** button (plus sign), and then select a behavior action from the Actions menu.

    NOTE *Actions dimmed in the menu can't be chosen for that particular Web element.*

    IMPORTANT *The Deprecated submenu provides features for those who used them in Dreamweaver 8 or earlier. Dreamweaver CS3 or later provides new ways to perform the same tasks.*

5. Enter the parameters and options you want for the selected action; the parameters and options vary depending on the selected action.

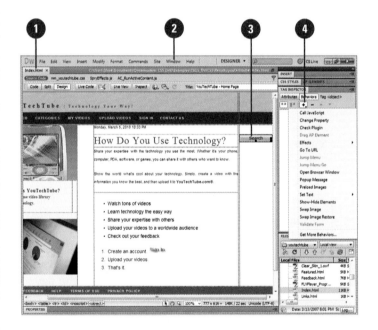

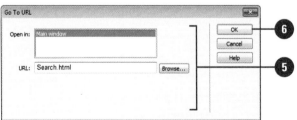

6 Click **OK**.

The action is embedded into the HTML code and appears in the Behaviors panel. The default event is onClick.

7 Click the default Event (onClick), and then click the **Event** list arrow to select the event you want to associate with this action (in this example, onMouseOver).

8 If you want to apply more than one behavior, repeat steps 4-7.

9 Click the **File** menu, point to **Preview In Browser**, and then select a browser to test your Web page.

10 In your browser, perform the event to trigger the action.

Did You Know?

You can show events for a specific browser. Open the Behaviors panel, click the Add Behavior button, point to Show Events For, and then select the browser that you want to show events.

You can show all events or only the ones currently attached to the page. Open the Behaviors panel, click the Show All Events button to show all available events, or click the Show Set Events button to show only the events currently attached behaviors.

See Also

See "Checking for CSS Browser Compatibility" on page 234 for information on using browser compatibility.

For Your Information

Testing Browser Compatibility

Unlike CGI scripts, the client interprets Behavior JavaScript code. The good news is that there are currently many early browsers that support JavaScript. Each browser supports different JavaScript features. Some bugs are platform-specific, while others are browser-specific. To ensure that your site will function correctly, Dreamweaver gives you the ability to check the site, and list any problems that might occur with earlier browsers. The two most important ways are to check the code live in various browsers, or let Dreamweaver check the page for browser incompatibility issues. To check the code live, click the File menu, point to Preview In Browser, and then select a browser. Dreamweaver opens the active page in the selected browser, and you can check the page for errors live. To check browser compatibility, click the File menu, point to Check Page, and then select Browser Compatibility. Dreamweaver checks the current page, and gives you a list of any possible errors by browser type and version.

Applying Behaviors to Entire Page

In addition to attaching behaviors to links, images, form elements, or any of several other HTML elements, you can also attach behaviors to an entire document (using the <body> tag). The process to apply a behavior to an entire page is similar to the one you use to attach a behavior to an individual page element. The difference is what you select. For a page element, you select the element; for an entire page, you select the <body> tag, which applies the behavior to the document. For example, you can use the Check Plug-in behavior to check for the existence of media players, such as Adobe Flash, Apple QuickTime, and Microsoft Windows Media Player, and then redirect a visitor.

Apply a Behavior to a Web Page

① Open the Web page you want to apply a behavior to an entire page.

② Click the **Window** menu, and then click **Behaviors** to display the Behaviors panel.

③ Click the <body> tag in the tag selector at the bottom left of the Document window.

④ Click the **Add Behavior** button (plus sign), and then select a behavior action from the Actions menu.

⑤ Enter the parameters and options you want for the selected action; the parameters and options vary depending on the selected action.

⑥ Click **OK**.

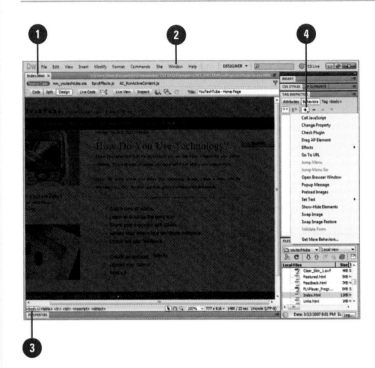

Did You Know?

You can download and install third-party behaviors. If you don't find the behavior functionality you need, you can download and install behaviors created by third-party developers. Open the Behaviors panel, click the Plus (+) button, and then click Get More Behaviors from the Actions menu. In your browser, search for the behavior you want on the Exchange site, and then download and install it according to the site instructions.

Apply the Check Plugin Behavior to a Web Page

1. Open the Web page you want to apply a behavior to an entire page.

2. Click the **Window** menu, and then click **Behaviors** to display the Behaviors panel.

3. Click the <body> tag in the tag selector at the bottom left of the Document window.

4. Click the **Add Behavior** button (plus sign), and then click **Check Plugin**.

5. Select the following options from the Check Plugin dialog box.

   ◆ **Select.** Click the **Select** option, and then select a plugin from the menu (in this example, Flash).

   ◆ **Enter.** Click the **Enter** option, and then enter or browse for the name of the required plugin (use if your plugin is not displayed in the Select menu).

   ◆ **If Found Go To URL.** Enter or browse for the name of the URL to go to, if the required plugin is found on the visitor's computer.

   ◆ **Otherwise Go To URL.** Enter or browse for the name of the URL to go to, if the plugin is not found on the visitor's computer.

   ◆ **Always Go To First URL If Detection Is Not Possible.** Select if the visitor's computer does not allow for plugin checking, and the browser loads the first URL.

6. Click **OK**.

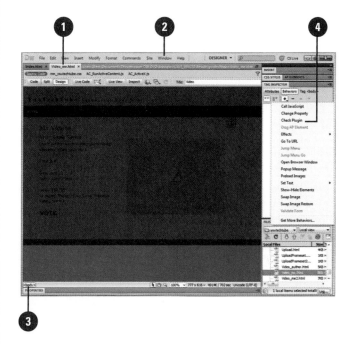

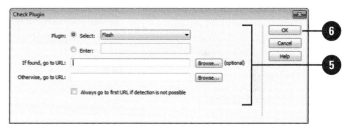

Editing Behaviors

After you create a behavior, you can quickly and easily change the parameters for the action or the event that triggers the action. When you complete your changes to a behavior, all occurrences of the behavior on the page are updated. If other pages use the same behavior, you need to update the behavior on each page.

Edit the Parameters for a Behavior

1. Open the Web page with the behavior you want to change.

2. Click the **Window** menu, and then click **Behaviors** to display the Behaviors panel.

3. Select an element on the Web page that contains an attached behavior, or if the behavior is attached to the document, click the <body> tag in the tag selector at the bottom left of the Document window.

   The behaviors attached to the element appear in the Behaviors panel.

4. Select the specific event for the action that you want to edit.

5. Click the **Behaviors Options** button, and then click **Edit Behavior**.

   TIMESAVER *Double-click the event to open the dialog box; you can also select it, and then press Enter (Win) or Return (Mac).*

6. In a behaviors dialog box, make the changes you want; the dialog box options differ depending on the behavior.

7. Click **OK**.

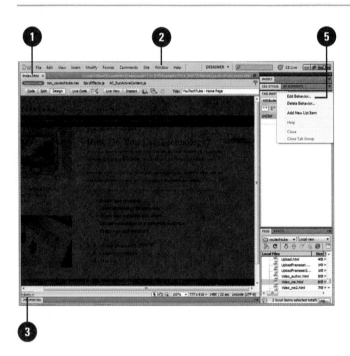

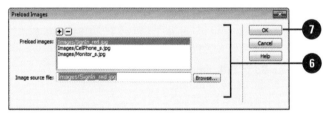

Change the Event for a Behavior

1. Open the Web page with the behavior you want to change.

2. Click the **Window** menu, and then click **Behaviors** to display the Behaviors panel.

3. Select an element on the Web page that contains an attached behavior, or if the behavior is attached to the document, click the <body> tag in the tag selector at the bottom left of the Document window.

   The behaviors attached to the element appear in the Behaviors panel.

4. Click the specific event that you want to edit.

5. Click the **Event** list arrow, and then select the event you want to trigger the action from the available options.

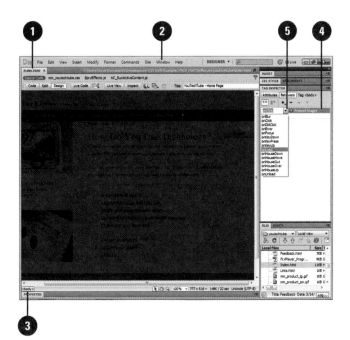

Working with Behaviors

Behaviors you have attached to a selected page element appear in the Behaviors panel in the behaviors list by event in alphabetical order. If you have multiple actions for a specific event, the behaviors are executed by the browser in the order in which they appear in the behavior list. You can use the Behaviors panel to change the order. If you no longer need a behavior, you can remove it from the list.

Change Multiple Behavior Order

① Open the Web page with the behavior you want to change.

② Click the **Window** menu, and then click **Behaviors** to display the Behaviors panel.

③ Select an element on the page that contains multiple behaviors.

The behaviors attached to the element appear in the Behaviors panel.

④ Select the behavior action you want to change.

⑤ Click the **Up** or **Down** buttons to move the action to a different stacking order.

> **TIMESAVER** *Press the Up and Down arrow keys to move the selected action.*

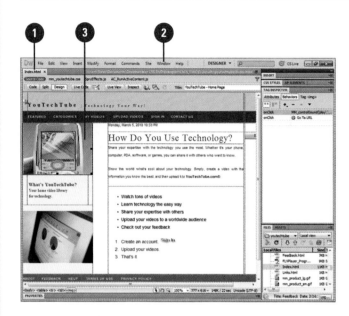

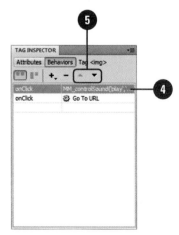

Remove a Behavior

① Open the Web page with the behavior you want to remove.

② Click the **Window** menu, and then click **Behaviors** to display the Behaviors panel.

③ Select an element on the Web page that contains an attached behavior, or if the behavior is attached to the document, click the <body> tag in the tag selector at the bottom left of the Document window.

The behaviors attached to the element appear in the Behaviors panel.

④ Select the behavior action you want to delete.

⑤ Click the **Remove Event** button (minus sign).

The behavior is removed from the document.

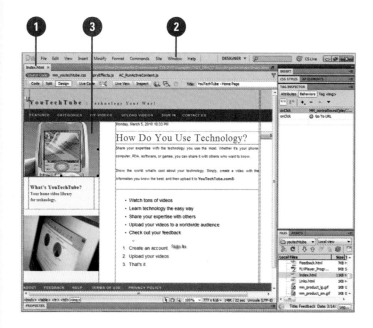

Adding Behavior Effects

Dreamweaver Effects give you one more way to create dynamic Web pages. For example, you can use Behavior Effects to make a Web element shrink to half size, or to slowly fade away, there's even an event that lets you make objects shake. While these options are fun to use, remember that Web design is not about what you can do to a site to make it dynamic. You have to ask yourself this question: Are the special effects that I'm using helping me to keep my visitor's attention, and are they in line with the message that I'm trying to send? If the answer to those questions is "yes," then by all means, use effects; however, if the answer is "no," then stay away from using the effects.

Adding Effects

1. Open the Web page you want to apply a behavior effect to an element.

2. Click the **Window** menu, and then click **Behaviors** to display the Behaviors panel.

3. Select an element on the page to which you want to attach an effect.

4. Click the **Add Behavior** button (plus sign), point to **Effects**, and then select an effect from the following options:

   ◆ **Appear/Fade.** Use this effect when you want the element to slowly appear or fade from the Web page.

   ◆ **Blind.** Use this effect when you want the element to slowly rise or lower on the page (like opening or closing a blind).

   ◆ **Grow/Shrink.** Use this effect when you want the element to increase or decrease in size.

   ◆ **Highlight.** Use this effect when you want the element (typically text) to change color.

   ◆ **Shake.** Use this effect when you want the element to shake side to side.

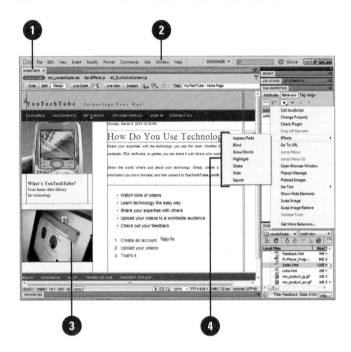

- **Slide.** Use this effect when you want the element to slide. Works by selecting the container tag of the content tag that you want to slide.

- **Squish.** Use this effect when you want the element to slowly reduce in size until gone (the anchor point for the squish effect is the upper-left corner of the Web object).

5 Specify the options you want in the dialog box for the specific effect; the options vary depending on the effect.

IMPORTANT *Not all the behavior effects work for all the elements in Dreamweaver; an error message may appear.*

6 Click **OK** to attach the effect to the Page, Document, or Tag.

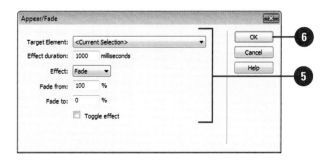

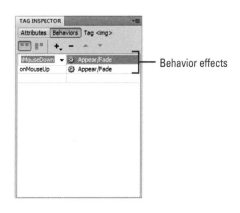

Behavior effects

Going to Another Web Page

The Go To URL behavior gives you the ability to link an element on a Web page to an URL address. For example, you can create a Web page, and then use the Go To URL behavior to direct visitors to other sites and pages, or you can create a set of interactive buttons for use on a standard HTML driven Web site. Whichever option you choose, the ability to direct a visitor to other Web sites is essential to creating Internet-oriented documents.

Use the Go To URL Behavior

① Open the Web page you want to apply a behavior.

② Click the **Window** menu, and then click **Behaviors** to display the Behaviors panel.

③ Click the element you want to add the Go To URL behavior.

④ Click the **Add Behavior** button (plus sign), and then click **Go To URL**.

A dialog box appears, allowing you to set the details of the action.

⑤ Type the URL or click **Browse**, select the URL from the Select File dialog box, and then click **OK**.

⑥ Click **OK**.

⑦ To change the trigger, click the event, click the **Event** list arrow, and then select the event you want.

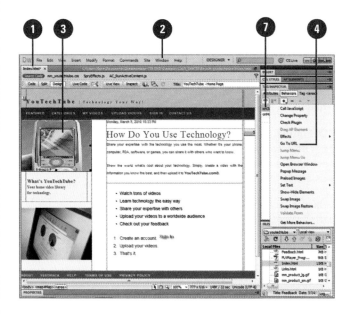

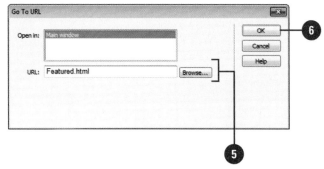

Opening Another Browser Window

The Open Browser behavior allows you to set a hyperlink to open in a new browser window. When you use the Open Browser behavior, you need to specify the URL you want to open in the new browser window and any window attributes, such as width, height, navigation and location toolbar, status bar, menu bar, scrollbar as needed and resize handles. If you want to use this behavior with text, you can also use the Change Property and Change Property Restore behaviors to change the pointer to a hand when visitors hover over your text link.

Open Another Browser Window

1. Open the Web page you want to apply a behavior.

2. Click the **Window** menu, and then click **Behaviors** to display the Behaviors panel.

3. Click the element you want to add the Open Browser Window behavior; typically link text or graphic.

4. Click the **Add Behavior** button (plus sign), and then click **Open Browser Window**.

   A dialog box appears, allowing you to set the details of the action.

5. Type the URL or click **Browse**, select the URL from the Select File dialog box, and then click **OK**.

6. Enter a window size (width and height in pixels).

7. Select the check boxes with the window attributes you want to use.

8. Enter a window name. The window name is used in the behavior script, so it cannot have any spaces or special characters.

9. Click **OK**.

10. To change the trigger, click the event, click the **Event** list arrow, and then select the event you want.

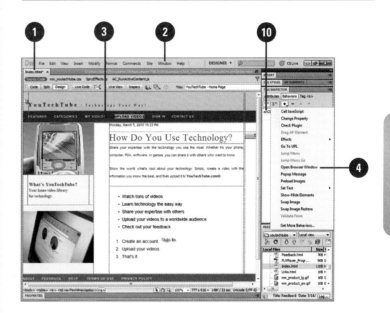

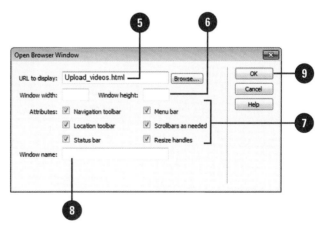

Displaying Text Messages

Dreamweaver provides several behaviors to display user text messages, including Popup Message and Set Text. The Set Text behavior consists of four individual behaviors: Set Text of Container, Set Text of Frame, Set Text of Status Bar, and Set Text of Text Field. These behaviors allow you to display text in an alert dialog box, a container, specific frame, text field, or the Status bar.

Create a Popup Message Window

1 Open the Web page you want to apply a behavior.

2 Click the **Window** menu, and then click **Behaviors** to display the Behaviors panel.

3 Click the element you want to add the Popup Message behavior.

4 Click the **Add Behavior** button (plus sign), and then click **Popup Message**.

A dialog box appears, allowing you to set the details of the action.

5 Type the message you want.

6 Click **OK**.

7 To change the trigger, click the event, click the **Event** list arrow, and then select the event you want.

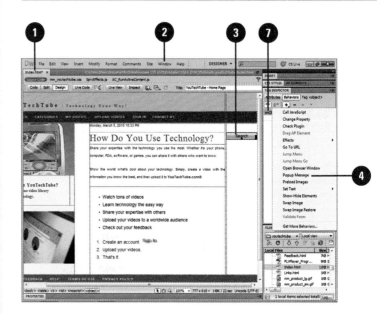

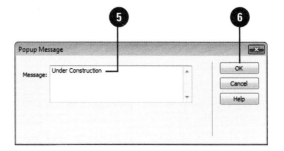

Create a Status Bar Message

1 Open the Web page you want to apply a behavior.

2 Click the **Window** menu, and then click **Behaviors** to display the Behaviors panel.

3 Click the element you want to add a behavior.

4 Click the **Add Behavior** button (plus sign), point to **Set Text**, and then click **Set Text Of Status Bar**.

A dialog box appears, allowing you to set the details of the action.

5 Type the message you want.

6 Click **OK**.

7 To change the trigger, click the event, click the **Event** list arrow, and then select the event you want.

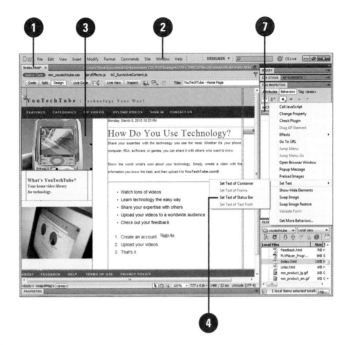

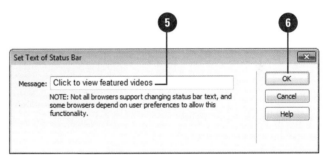

Preloading and Swapping Images

The Preload Images behavior allows you to preload images when a Web page initially loads. This is useful when you want to swap images on mouse rollover buttons. The Preload Images behavior loads the rollover image when the page initially loads, so visitors will not experience a delay while the image loads the first time a visitor points to the button. The Swap Images behavior allows you to swap one image for another when an event occurs. The most common use of this behavior is to create rollover buttons. Along with the Swap Image behavior, you can also use the Swap Image Restore behavior, which restores the images that were swapped by the Swap Image behavior.

Preload Images

1. Open the Web page you want to apply a behavior.

2. Click the **Window** menu, and then click **Behaviors** to display the Behaviors panel.

3. Click the element or <body> tag in the tag selector for the entire page you want to add the Preload Images behavior.

4. Click the **Add Behavior** button (plus sign), and then click **Preload Images**.

   A dialog box appears, allowing you to set the details of the action.

5. Click **Browse**, locate and select the image you want to preload, and then click **OK**.

6. Click the **Add Items** button (plus sign).

7. To add more images, repeat steps 5 and 6.

8. Click **OK**.

9. To change the trigger, click the event, click the **Event** list arrow, and then select the event you want.

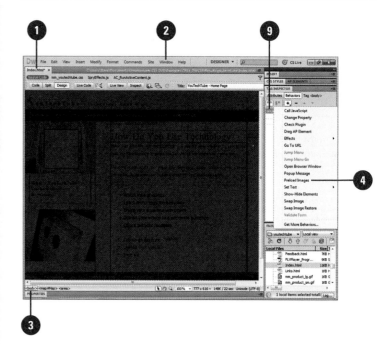

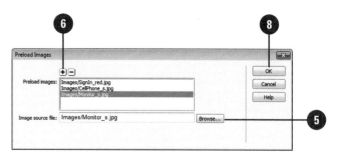

Swap Images

1. Open the Web page you want to apply a behavior.

2. Click the **Window** menu, and then click **Behaviors** to display the Behaviors panel.

3. Click the image you want to swap.

4. Click the **Add Behavior** button (plus sign), and then click **Swap Image**.

   The selected image appears highlighted in the Swap Image dialog box.

5. Click **Browse**, locate and select the image you want to swap it with, and then click **OK**.

6. To insert a Preload Images behavior, select the **Preload Images** check box.

7. To insert a Swap Image Restore behavior, select the **Restore Images onMouseOut** check box.

8. To remove a swap, select an image in the list, and then delete the file and path in the Set Source To box.

9. Click **OK**.

10. To change the trigger, click the event, click the **Event** list arrow, and then select the event you want.

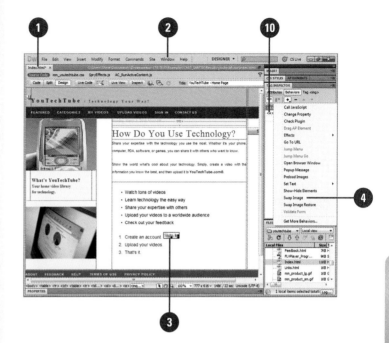

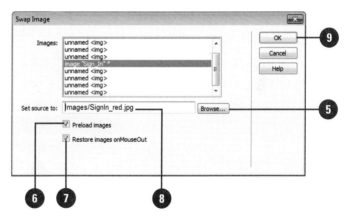

Changing Element Properties

The Change Property behavior allows you to change properties, such as font styles, borders or visibility, for an element on a Web page. The Change Property behavior is useful for adding interactivity to a Web page. For example, you can have the Change Property behavior display a text description or link address when a user points to a picture on a page. Along with the Change Property behavior, you can also use the Change Property Restore behavior, which restores the most recent property changes made by the Change Property behavior. When you use the Change Property Restore behavior, Dreamweaver displays a message dialog box acknowledging the use of the behavior. You can double-click the behavior to display a list of properties being restored.

Use the Change Property Behavior

1. Open the Web page you want to apply a behavior.

2. Click the **Window** menu, and then click **Behaviors** to display the Behaviors panel.

3. Click the element you want to add the Change Property behavior (in this example, select the cell phone image).

4. Click the **Add Behavior** button (plus sign), and then click **Change Property**.

   A dialog box appears, allowing you to set the details of the action.

5. Click the **Type Of Element** list arrow, and then select the type you want to change (in this example, select DIV).

6. Click the **Element ID** list arrow, and then select an ID (in this example, select div "apTextSign").

   The AP element to the right of the cell phone image contains text, which you'll change the font size to a larger size.

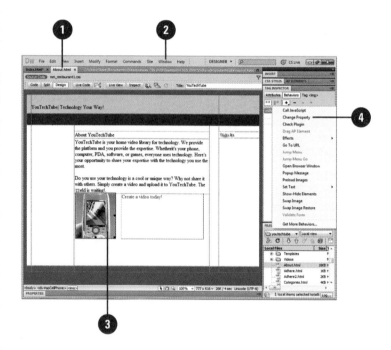

7 Click the **Select** option and select the property you want to change (in this example, select fontSize), or click the **Enter** option and enter the property you want to change.

8 Enter the new value you want (in this example, enter 24).

9 Click **OK**.

10 To change the trigger, click the event, click the **Event** list arrow, and then select the event you want.

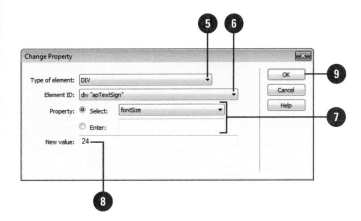

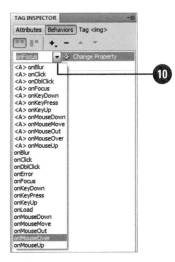

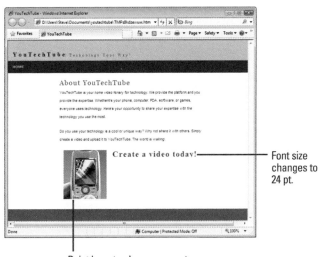

Font size changes to 24 pt.

Point here to change property

Dragging an AP Element

The Drag AP Element behavior allows you let visitors on a Web page to drag an AP (Absolute Positioned) element. This behavior is useful for creating interactive training, games, and interface controls, such as a slider. The behavior allows you to specify how you want the AP element to move. You can constrain the movement in a specific direction, to a specific location or target, or to snap to another element. In order to use the Drag AP Element behavior, you need to call the behavior before the visitor can drag the element. To achieve this, you need to attach the Drag AP Element behavior to the body object with the onLoad event.

Use the Drag AP Element Behavior

1. Open the Web page you want to apply a behavior.

2. Click the **Window** menu, and then click **Behaviors** to display the Behaviors panel.

3. Create the AP Element you want to add the Drag AP Element behavior.

4. Click <body> in the tag selector in the Document window.

5. Click the **Add Behavior** button (plus sign), and then click **Drag AP Element**.

   A dialog box appears displaying the Basic tab.

6. Click the **Movement** list arrow, and then click **Constrained** or **Unconstrained**.

7. If you selected the Constrained option, enter values for Up, Down, Left, and Right (in pixels).

   The values are relative to the starting position of the AP element. To constrain movement, use the following methods:

   ◆ Rectangle. Enter positive values in all four boxes.

   ◆ Vertical. Enter positive values for Up and Down and 0 for Left and Right.

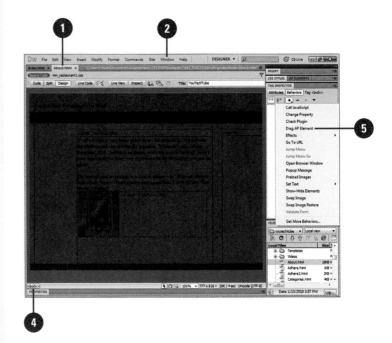

◆ **Horizontal.** Enter positive values for Left and Right and 0 for Up and Down.

⑧ Enter values for the Drop Target in the available Up, Down, Left, and Right boxes (in pixels), or click **Get Current Position** to automatically insert the current position of the AP element.

The drop target is the spot where you want the visitor to drag the AP element. Values are relative to the top left corner of the browser window.

⑨ Enter a Snap If Within value (in pixels) to specify how close the visitor needs to be to the drop target before the AP element snaps to the target.

⑩ To define the drag handle, track movement, and trigger an action, click the **Advanced** tab.

◆ **Drag Handle.** Click the list arrow, and then select **Entire Element** or **Area Within Element**. For an area, enter values for the area you want within the element.

◆ **While Dragging.** Select the **Bring Element To Front, then** check box, select a position, and then enter the script code or function you want executed during the drag.

◆ **When Dropped.** Enter the script code or function you want executed when dropped, and then select the **Only If Snapped** check box to execute the code only if snapped.

⑪ Click **OK**.

⑫ To change the trigger, click the event, click the **Event** list arrow, and then select the event you want.

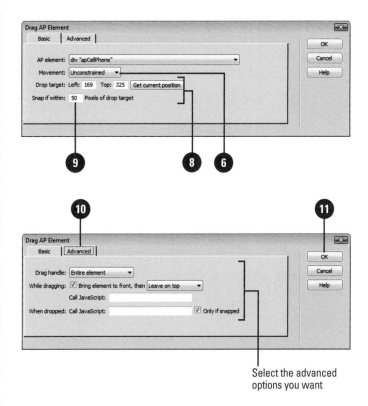

Select the advanced options you want

Showing and Hiding Elements

The Show-Hide Elements behavior allows you to show, hide, or restore the visibility of elements on a page. This behavior is useful for displaying information or providing interaction when a visitor points to an element. For example, when a visitor points to a picture or a text box, you can display information about the item to provide added value and some interactivity. When the visitor moves the pointer away, you can restore the element back to its original state.

Show or Hide Page Elements

1. Open the Web page you want to apply a behavior.

2. Click the **Window** menu, and then click **Behaviors** to display the Behaviors panel.

3. Click the element you want to add a behavior.

4. Click the **Add Behavior** button (plus sign), and then click **Show-Hide Elements**.

   A dialog box appears, allowing you to set the details of the action.

5. Click the element you want to show, hide, or restore.

6. Click **Show**, **Hide**, or **Default**, which restores the default visibility of the element.

7. Repeat steps 5 and 6 for each element you want.

8. Click **OK**.

9. To change the trigger, click the event, click the **Event** list arrow, and then select the event you want.

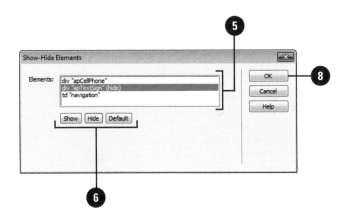

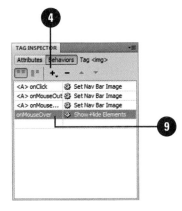

Executing a JavaScript

The Call JavaScript behavior runs a line of script when an event occurs. The behavior only runs one line of script, which means you can execute a single line of code or a procedure that calls a section of code. To use the Call JavaScript behavior, you need JavaScript experience and coding knowledge, which is outside the scope of this book.

Use the Call JavaScript Behavior

1 Open the Web page you want to apply a behavior.

2 Click the **Window** menu, and then click **Behaviors** to display the Behaviors panel.

3 Click the element you want to add a behavior.

4 Click the **Add Behavior** button (plus sign), and then click **Call JavaScript**.

A dialog box appears, allowing you to set the details of the action.

5 Type the line of script you want to run.

6 Click **OK**.

7 To change the trigger, click the event, click the **Event** list arrow, and then select the event you want.

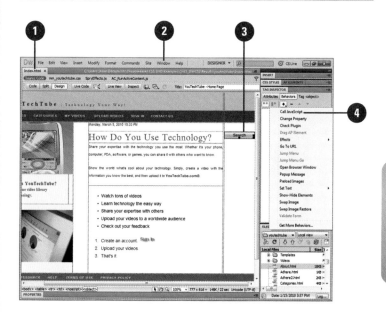

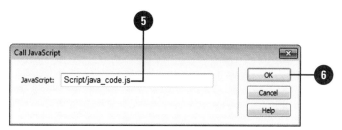

Using Spry Widgets and Effects

Introduction

The Spry framework is a JavaScript library that allows you to use built-in HTML, CSS, and JavaScript code to create widgets, add special effects, and integrate HTML or XML data in your Web pages.

A spry widget is a page element, such as a menu bar, tabbed or collapsible panels, or form validation, that provides added functionality without all the scripting. A widget consists of three different parts: structure, behavior, and styling. A widget structure is HTML code that defines the structure of the widget. A widget behavior is JavaScript that specifies what happens to a widget when an event occurs. Widget styling is CSS code that determines the look of the widget.

You can insert a built-in spry widget, Dreamweaver takes care of all three aspects of the widget. It provides the HTML, CSS, and JavaScript as well as the style of the widget, which you can modify to suit your own needs. For example, you can edit menu items, modify panels, and change the appearance of the page. The CSS and JavaScript files related to the widget are named with the same name as the spry widget, and stored in a SpryAssets folder in your site.

Dreamweaver also includes built-in spry effects that allow you to apply visual effects, such as highlighting information or creating transitions, to elements on a page. You can apply one or more effects, such as a fade, highlight, blind up and down, slide up and down, grow and shrink, shake, and squish, to create a dynamic user experience.

In this chapter you'll learn how to insert and work with spry widgets, and add spry effects to elements on your Web pages with minimal or no knowledge of JavaScript. If you have a strong knowledge of JavaScript you can create your own spry widgets or effects.

Inserting Spry Widgets

Dreamweaver provides a wide variety of spry widgets you can insert in your Web pages. Some of the widgets include page region definition, tables, menu bars, form validation, and panels to store data in a compact space. When you insert a spry widget, Dreamweaver creates a SpryAssets folder (on first use) in your local root site to store the widget, data, and any spry effects. The CSS and JavaScript files related with the widget are named with the same name as the spry widget and also stored in a SpryAssets folder. If you want (which is not recommended), you can change the default folder location where Dreamweaver saves and stores your spry assets.

Insert a Spry Widget

1. Open the Web page you want to insert a spry widget.

2. Click to place the insertion point where you want to insert the spry widget.

3. Click the **Spry** tab on the Insert panel, or click the **Insert** menu, and then point to **Spry**.

4. Click the spry widget you want to insert:

   ◆ **Spry Data Set.** Access HTML or XML data for regions, tables, or lists.

   ◆ **Spry Region.** Creates an area to wrap around objects, such as tables and repeat lists.

   ◆ **Spry Repeat.** Creates a duplicate region.

   ◆ **Spry Repeat List.** Creates an ordered, unordered, definition list, or drop-down list.

   ◆ **Spry Validation.** Create form validation for a text field or area, check box, password, confirm, or radio group.

   ◆ **Spry Menu Bar.** Creates a set of navigational menu buttons.

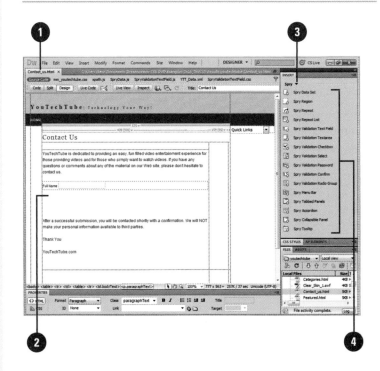

For Your Information

Downloading Spry Files Before You Begin

Before you add Spry widgets, you need to download and link the latest required Spry Framework files from the Adobe Labs Web site (http://labs.adobe.com/technologies/spry/). Unzip the Spry Framework files into the SpryAssets folder on your local root site. You can put all the files (includes **great samples**) to the SpryAssets to make sure you have everything. If space is tight, make sure you copy the includes and widgets folders, and the SpryData.js, SpryEffect.js, and xpath.js files. When you transfer files to your Web server for delivery on the Web, you need to transfer the files in the SpryAssets folder too.

- ◆ **Spry Tabbed Panels.** Creates a set of panels to store data in a compact space.

- ◆ **Spry Accordion.** Creates a set of collapsible panels to store large amounts of data in a compact space.

- ◆ **Spry Collapsible Panel.** Creates a set of collapsible panels to store data in a compact space.

- ◆ **Spry Tooltip.** Creates a tooltip for page elements.

5 If prompted, specify widget or input tag accessibility attribute options; the widget options vary depending on the widget.

6 Click **OK**. If prompted, click **Yes** or **No** to add a form tag.

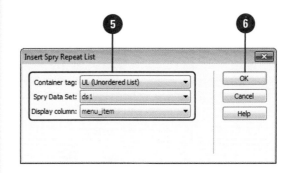

Change the Default Spry Assets Folder

1 Click the **Sites** menu, and then click **Manage Sites**.

2 Select the site you want to change, and then click **Edit**.

3 Click the **Advanced Settings** category.

4 Click the **Spry** category.

5 Enter a path and folder name to the location where you want to store spry assets, or click the **Browse For Folder** icon to select a folder location.

6 Click **Save**, and then click **OK** to cache files, if necessary.

7 Click **Done** to close the Manage Sites dialog box.

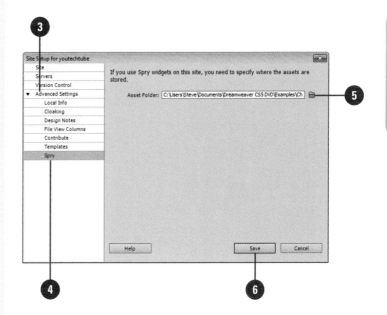

Selecting and Editing Spry Widgets

After you insert a spry widget, you can select and edit the widget to customize it for your specific needs. You can edit the parameters and options for a spry widget or modify the style, or appearance, of a spry widget using CSS. Before you can edit a spry widget, you need to select it first by pointing to the widget until you see the widget's blue tabbed outline and then clicking the widget's tab in the upper left corner.

Select and Edit a Spry Widget

1. Open the Web page with the spry widget you want to edit.

2. Point to the widget until you see the blue tabbed outline, and then click the widget tab to select it.

3. Click the **Window** menu, and then click **Properties** to display the Properties panel.

4. Specify the options you want in the Properties panel for the selected widget; the options vary depending on the widget you select.

5. Make changes to the content of the widget in the Design window.

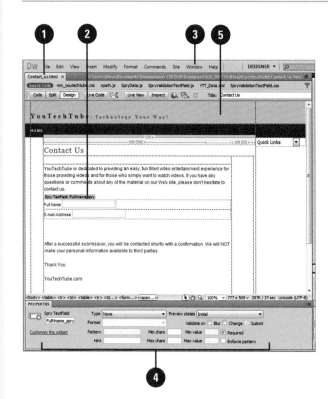

Did You Know?

You can edit the style of a spry widget in the related CSS file. You can open the CSS file located in the SpryAssets folder, make the changes you want, and then save it, or open the CSS panel and change the CSS styles for the spry widget.

Change the Appearance of a Spry Widget

1. Open the Web page with the spry widget you want to edit.

2. Click in the part of the spry widget you want to change.

3. Click the **Window** menu, and then click **Properties** to display the Properties panel.

4. Specify the options you want in the Properties panel for the selected widget.

   ◆ **Widget.** Specify the settings you want for the selected widget. For example, for a selected text field, you can specify name, character width, maximum characters, type, class, or initial value.

   ◆ **CSS.** Click **CSS** to change cascading style sheet options in the CSS Styles panel. Click the **Target Rule** list arrow to change the current style.

   ◆ **HTML.** Click **HTML** and then use the normal formatting options, such as: Format, Font, Size, Bold, Italic, and alignment and spacing buttons.

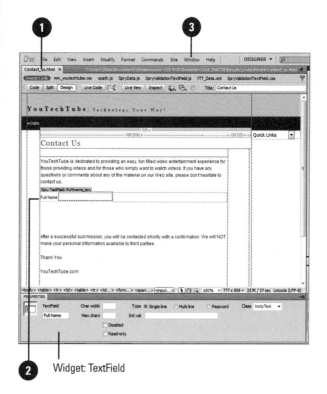

Widget: TextField

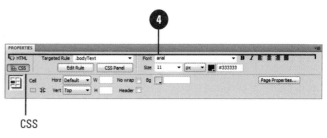

CSS

HTML

Working with Spry Panel Widgets

A spry panel widget allows you to store content in a compact space using tabs. Dreamweaver provides three different types of spry panels: accordion, collapsible, and tabbed. Each spry panel type provides a tab-like interface that displays content when a visitor clicks a tab. The differences between the spry panel types lies in the display and style of the tabs. If you have a large amount of content, the accordion panel is your best bet. Try each one to see which one works best with the content you want to display.

Insert and Work with Spry Panel Widgets

1. Open the Web page you want to insert a spry widget, and then click to place the insertion point where you want it.

2. Click the **Spry** tab on the Insert panel, or click the **Insert** menu, point to **Spry**, and then select the spry panel element you want:

   ◆ **Spry Tabbed Panels.** Creates a set of panels to store data in a compact space.

   ◆ **Spry Accordion.** Creates a set of collapsible panels to store large amounts of data in a compact space.

   ◆ **Spry Collapsible Panel.** Creates a set of collapsible panels to store data in a compact space.

3. Select the panel widget.

4. Point to a tab, click the eye icon (if available) to edit the panel contents, or select the panel contents and edit it.

5. Click the **Window** menu, and then click **Properties** to display the Properties panel.

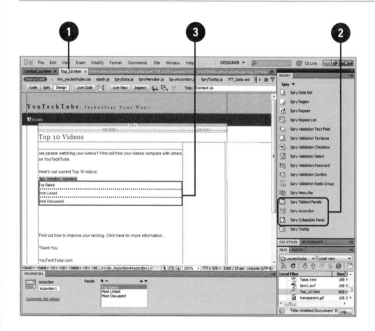

6 Specify the options you want in the Properties panel for the selected widget; the options vary depending on the widget. Some of the options include:

◆ **Panel Order.** Click the **Up** or **Down Arrow** buttons.

◆ **Default Panel.** Click the **Default Panel** list arrow, and then select the panel you want.

◆ **Delete Panel.** Select the panel, and then click the **Minus** button.

◆ **Animate Panel.** Select the panel, and then select or clear the **Enable Animation** check box.

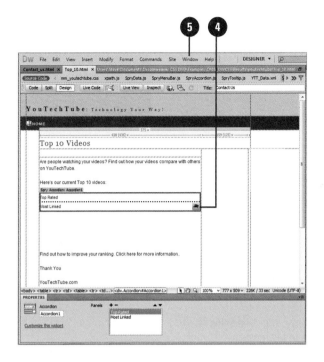

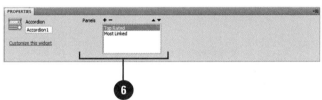

Working with Spry Validation Widgets

A spry validation widget allows you to determine whether information or data in a form is valid or invalid. Dreamweaver provides several types of spry validation elements: text field, text area, select (from a drop-down menu), and check box. When you insert a spry validation element, the Input Tag Accessibility Attributes dialog box opens, requesting information and options to make the form object accessible to the visually impaired. After you insert a spry validation element, you can use the Properties panel to specify the validation options you want; each element provides different validation options.

Insert and Work with Spry Validation Widgets

1. Open the Web page you want to insert a spry widget, and then click to place the insertion point where you want it.

2. Click the **Spry** tab on the Insert panel, or click the **Insert** menu, point to **Spry**, and then select the spry validation element you want:

   ◆ **Spry Validation Text Field.** Creates a text box that displays valid or invalid states when a visitor enters text or doesn't enter text as a required field.

   ◆ **Spry Validation Textarea.** Creates a text area that displays valid or invalid states when a visitor enters text or doesn't enter text as a required field.

   ◆ **Spry Validation Checkbox.** Creates a check box that displays valid or invalid states when a visitor selects or doesn't select a check box.

   ◆ **Spry Validation Select.** Creates a drop-down menu with a list of options divided into sections that displays valid or invalid states when a visitor selects an element in the list.

   ◆ **Spry Validation Password.** Creates a password text field that enforces password rules.

◆ **Spry Validation Confirm.**
Creates a text or password field
that displays valid or invalid
states.

◆ **Spry Validation Radio Group.**
Creates a group of radio buttons
with validation
support.

③ Specify the Input Tag Accessibility
Attributes dialog box options you
want.

④ Click **OK**.

⑤ Select the panel widget.

⑥ Click the **Window** menu, and then
click **Properties** to display the
Properties panel.

⑦ Specify the options you want in the
Properties panel for the selected
widget; the options vary depending
on the widget. Some of the general
options include:

◆ Initial State. Indicates the state
when the page loads in the
browser or when the form is
reset.

◆ Focus State. Indicates the state
with the insertion point.

◆ Valid State. Indicates the state
when the visitor entered
information correctly.

◆ Required State. Indicates the
state when the visitor fails to
enter information.

◆ Minimum or Maximum Number
of Characters State. Indicates
the state when the visitor has
not entered enough characters
or entered too many characters.

◆ Minimum or Maximum Value
State. Indicates the state when
the visitor has entered a value
that is less or greater than the
allowed value.

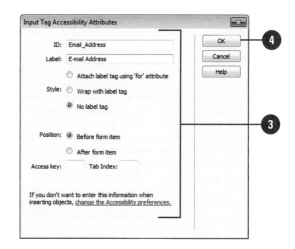

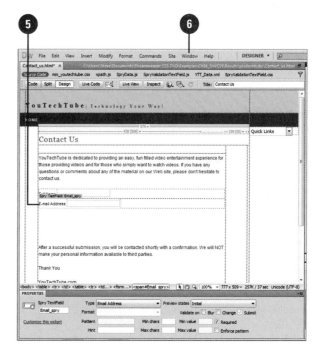

Working with Spry Menu Bar Widgets

A spry menu bar widget allows you to create a set of navigational menus that come with submenus. A menu bar makes it easy for visitors to navigate to different parts of your site in the same way they choose commands in a program, such as Dreamweaver. You can insert two types of menu bars: horizontal or vertical. You can link a menu item to a specific place or execute a script. In addition, you can add tool tips to provide a short description of menu items for visitors.

Insert and Work with Spry Menu Bar Widgets

1. Open the Web page you want to insert a spry widget, and then click to place the insertion point where you want it.

2. Click the **Spry** tab on the Insert panel, or click the **Insert** menu, point to **Spry**, and then click **Spry Menu Bar**.

   IMPORTANT *If your page contains Flash content, the DHTML layers used to create the menu bar may cause problems.*

3. Click the **Horizontal** or **Vertical** option.

4. Click **OK**.

5. Select the panel widget.

6. Click the **Window** menu, and then click **Properties** to display the Properties panel.

7. Specify the options you want in the Properties panel for the selected widget:

   ◆ Add Main Menu. Click the **Plus** (+) button above the first column, and then rename the menu in the Text box.

   ◆ Add Submenu. Select a main menu item, click the **Plus** (+) button above the second column, and then rename the menu in the Text box.

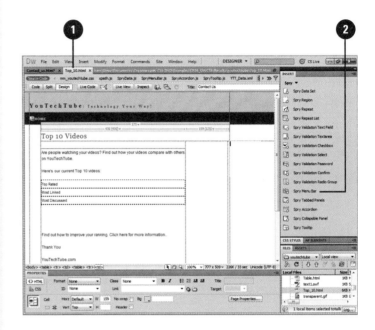

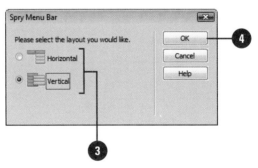

◆ **Delete Menu.** Select the main menu or submenu item you want to delete, and then click the **Minus** (-) button.

◆ **Change Menu Order.** Select the menu item you want to reorder, and then click the **Up** or **Down** buttons.

◆ **Link Menu.** Select the menu item you want to apply a link, and then type the link in the Link box or click the **Browse** button to select a file.

◆ **Add Tool Tip.** Select the menu item you want to create a tool tip, and then type the text for the tool tip in the Title text box.

◆ **Target.** Enter one of the following options:

 ◆ **_blank.** Opens the linked page in a new window.

 ◆ **_parent.** Loads the linked document in the immediate frameset of the active document.

 ◆ **_self.** Loads the linked document in the same browser window (default).

 ◆ **_top.** Loads the linked document in the topmost window of a frameset.

◆ **Styles.** Click the **Turn Styles Off** button to disable the styling of a menu bar, which is helpful to see the HTML structure of the widget. Click the **Turn Styles On** button to enable it again.

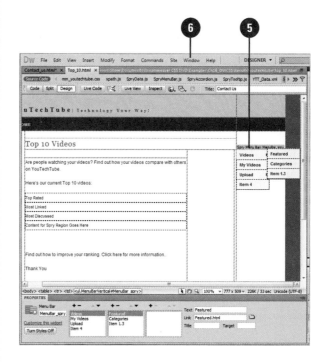

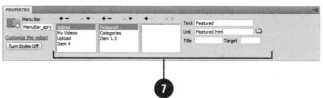

Creating a Spry Tooltip

With the spry tooltip widget, you can add screen information for elements on a web page. When you hover over an element, a tooltip with information about the element, a title or short description, appears for a short period of time or until you stop hovering over the element. A spry tooltip consists of a container, page element, and JavaScript. When you insert a spry tooltip, a container appears with a blue tab on top and a placeholder sentence inside. You can add formatting for a tooltip by using standard CSS styles. When you display the tooltip, by default, it appears 20 pixels down and to the right of the cursor.

Create a Spry Tooltip

1. Open the Web page you want to insert a spry tooltip.

2. Select the full tag element you want to add a tooltip.

3. Click the **Spry** tab on the Insert panel, or click the **Insert** menu, point to **Spry**, and then click **Spry Tooltip**.

   A container with a placeholder sentence for the tooltip appears. The container displays a blue tab with the Spry Tooltip name.

4. Select the placeholder text, and then enter the tooltip text that you want.

5. Select the spry tooltip widget, and then select from the following options in the Properties panel:

   ◆ **Name.** Specifies a name for the tooltip container.

   ◆ **Trigger.** Identifies the elements that triggers the tooltip.

   ◆ **Follow Mouse.** Causes the tooltip to follow the mouse.

   ◆ **Hide on Mouse Out.** Keeps the tooltip open as long as the mouse is hovering over the tooltip (even if the mouse leaves the trigger). Helpful for selecting links in a tooltip.

- ◆ **Horizontal or Vertical Offset.** Specifies the tooltips horizontal or vertical position in relation to the mouse. The offset value is in pixels.

- ◆ **Show Delay.** Specify the delay in milliseconds before the tooltip appears after the tooltip has been triggered.

- ◆ **Hide Delay.** Specify the delay in milliseconds before the tooltip disappears after the tooltip has been triggered.

- ◆ **Effect.** Specify the type of effect you want when the tooltip appears. The **Blind** option acts like a window blind to display and hide the tooltip. The **Fade** option fades the tooltip in and out.

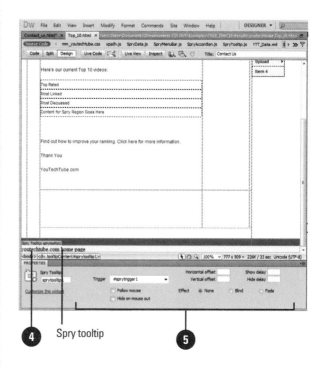

Spry tooltip

Edit a Spry Tooltip

1. Open the Web page with the spry tooltip.

2. Hover over or place the insertion point in the tooltip content on the page.

3. Click the tooltip's blue tab to select it.

4. Modify the text in the tooltip or change the tooltip options in the Properties panel.

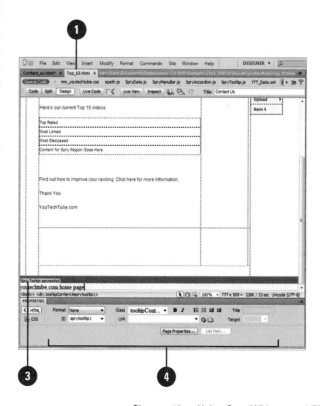

Displaying Spry Data Sets

A spry data set allows you to provide interactive data to visitors on your site. The data on the page changes based on the visitors' selections. For example, you can select an option in one part of a page, and then display other content somewhere else on a page without requiring a full-page refresh. To use data sets to create a dynamic page, you need to take a few steps. First, you identify one or more data sets (HTML or XML source files) that contain the data you want to use. Next, you insert one or more spry data objects to display the data on a page. When a visitor opens the page in a browser, the data set loads like a normal table containing columns and rows.

Display the Spry HTML Data Set

1. Open the Web page you want to use.

2. Click the **Spry** tab on the Insert panel, or click the **Insert** menu, point to **Spry**, and then click **Spry Data Set**.

3. Click the **Select Data Type** list arrow, and then click **HTML**.

4. Enter a name for the spry data set or use the default one, ds1.

5. Click the **Detect** list arrow, and then select the type of HTML elements in your data source that you want to detect.

6. Click **Browse**, navigate to and select the HTML data file, and then click **OK**.

   ◆ To use a sample feed on your test server, click the **Design Time Feed** link.

7. In the Data Selection window, click one of the yellow arrows with the element for your data container. You can also select an ID from the Data Containers list arrow.

8. If you want to specify CSS data selectors, select the **Advanced data selection** check box, and then enter a data selector, such as .product, to filter the data.

9. Click **Next** to continue.

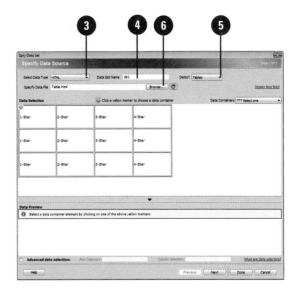

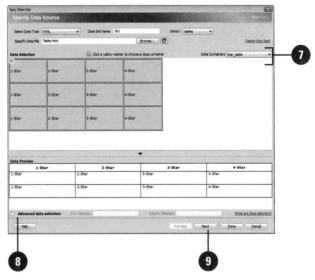

10 Select the column you want to use in the Data Preview window.

11 If you want to validate the data to a specific type, click the **Type** list arrow, and then select a data type.

12 If you want to sort the data as it loads, click the **Sort Column** list arrow, select a sort option, click the **Direction** list arrow, select the direction you want, and then select or clear the sort check boxes.

13 Select the **Filter Out Duplicate Rows** check box to eliminate any duplicate columns.

14 Select the **Disable Data Caching** check box to load data directly from the server, otherwise it caches it on your local computer.

15 Select the **Auto Refresh Data** check box, and then enter an interval value in milliseconds to refresh the data from the server.

16 Click **Next** to continue.

17 Select a display option for the data, and then click **Set Up** to specify how you want to layout the data.

◆ **Insert Table.** Creates a dynamic Spry Table.

◆ **Insert Master/Detail Layout.** Creates a master region on the left that updates information in the detailed region on the right.

◆ **Insert Stacked Containers.** Creates a stacked repeating container structure for data.

◆ **Insert Stacked Containers with Spotlight Area.** Creates a stacked repeating container structure (2 columns) with a spotlight area (for a picture).

◆ **Do Not Insert HTML.** Creates a data set without inserting a data layout.

18 Click **Done**.

Continue Next Page

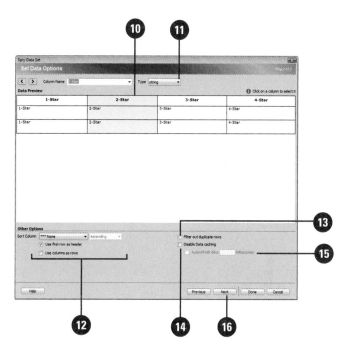

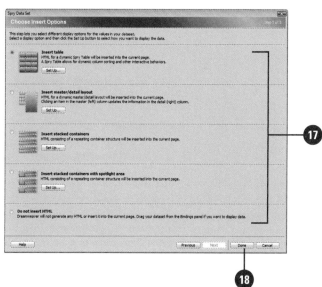

Continued from Previous Page

Display the Spry XML Data Set

① Open the Web page you want to use.

② Click the **Spry** tab on the Insert panel, or click the **Insert** menu, point to **Spry**, and then click **Spry XML Data Set**.

   TIMESAVER *If you don't have an XML data set, you can get a sample at www.adobe.com/go/ learn_dw_spryframework.*

③ Click the **Select Data Type** list arrow, and then click **HTML**.

④ Enter a name for the spry data set or use the default one, ds1.

⑤ Click **Browse**, navigate to and select the XML data file, and then click **OK**.

   ◆ To use a sample feed on your test server, click the **Design Time Feed** link.

⑥ Click **Get Schema** to populate the Row Elements panel.

⑦ Select the element that contains the data you want to display. The element typically is a repeating node with one or more subfields.

   The XPath text box shows the data found in the data set. A preview of the data set appears in the Data Preview window.

⑧ Click **Next** to continue.

⑨ Select the column you want to use in the Data Preview window.

⑩ If you want to validate the data to be a specific type, click the **Type** list arrow, and then select a data type.

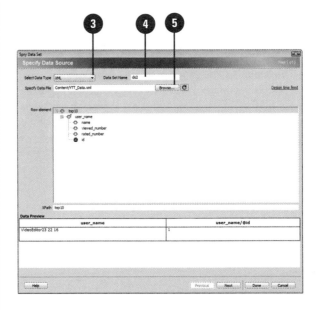

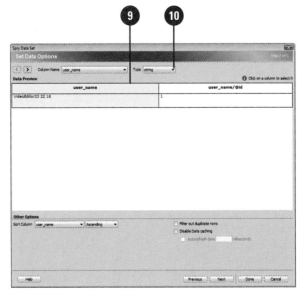

11 If you want to sort the data as it loads, click the **Sort Column** list arrow, select a sort option, click the **Direction** list arrow, and then select the direction you want.

12 Select the **Filter Out Duplicate Rows** check box to eliminate any duplicate columns.

13 Select the **Disable Data Caching** check box to load data directly from the server, otherwise it caches it on your local computer.

14 Select the **Auto Refresh Data** check box, and then enter an interval value in milliseconds to refresh the XML data from the server.

15 Click **Next** to continue.

16 Select a display option for the data, and then click **Set Up** to specify how you want to layout the data.

17 Click **Done**.

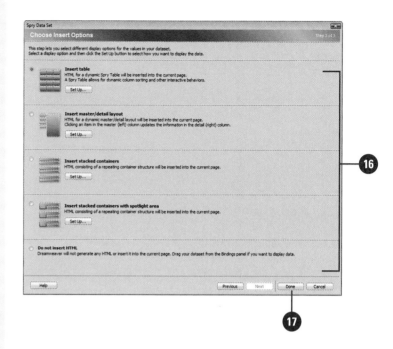

View the Spry XML Data Set

1 Open the Web page with the spry XML data set you want to view.

2 Click the **Window** menu, and then click **Bindings** to display the Bindings panel.

The spry XML data set appears, displaying the structure of the data.

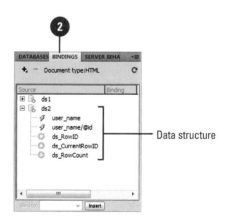

Data structure

Creating a Spry Region

After you identify the data sets (HTML or XML source files) you want to use, you can insert one or more spry data objects to display the data on a page. A spry data object is enclosed in a spry region on a page, so you need to insert one first or let Dreamweaver do it for you. You can create a region or a repeated region. There are two types of regions: a region and a detail region. A spry region is a page section that wraps around data objects. A spry detail region updates data based on changes made in a master table object (also known as a spry table) somewhere else on a page. A repeat region is a data structure you can format to display your data. A repeat region is useful for elements you want to repeat within a page layout, such as a gallery of images.

Create a Spry Region

1. Open the Web page you want to insert a spry region, and then click to place the insertion point where you want it.

2. Click the **Spry** tab on the Insert panel, or click the **Insert** menu, point to **Spry**, and then click **Spry Region**.

3. Select the **DIV** or **SPAN** option.

4. Click the **Region** or **Detail Region** option to specify the type of region you want to insert.

5. Click the **Spry Data Set** list arrow, and then select the data set you want to use.

6. Click the **Wrap Selection** option to insert a new region around an object, or the **Replace Selection** option to replace an existing region for an object.

7. Click **OK**.

   Dreamweaver inserts a region placeholder on your page.

   You can replace the placeholder with spry data objects, such as a table or repeat list, or with dynamic data from the Bindings panel.

Spry region

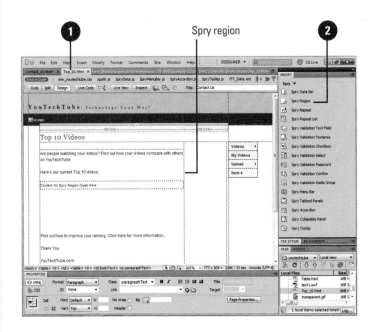

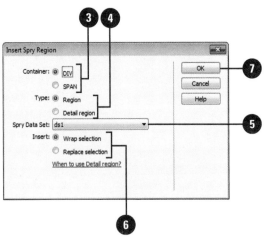

Create a Spry Repeat Region

1. Open the Web page you want to insert a spry region, and then click to place the insertion point where you want it.

2. Click the **Spry** tab on the Insert panel, or click the **Insert** menu, point to **Spry**, and then click **Spry Repeat**.

3. Select the **DIV** or **SPAN** option.

4. Click the **Repeat** or **Repeat Children** option to specify the type of region you want to insert.

   Use the Repeat Children option when data validation is done for each line in a list at the child level.

5. Click the **Spry Data Set** list arrow, and then select the data set you want to use.

6. Click the **Wrap Selection** option to insert a new region around an object, or the **Replace Selection** option to replace an existing region for an object.

7. Click **OK**.

   Dreamweaver inserts a region placeholder on your page.

   You can replace the placeholder with spry data objects, such as a table or repeat list, or with dynamic data from the Bindings panel.

Spry repeat region

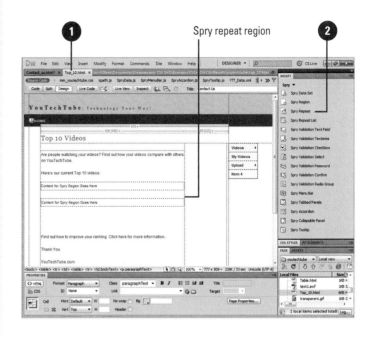

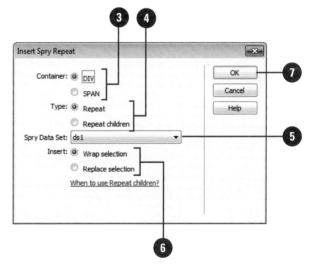

Creating a Spry Repeat List

A spry data object, such as a repeat list, displays data from a spry data set. A spry data object is enclosed in a spry region on a page, so you need to insert one first. If you don't, Dreamweaver inserts one for you. The repeat list data object allows you to display your data as an ordered list, an unordered (bulleted) list, a definition list, or a drop-down list.

Create a Spry Repeat List

1. Open the Web page you want to insert a spry region, and then click to place the insertion point where you want it.

2. Click the **Spry** tab on the Insert panel, or click the **Insert** menu, point to **Spry**, and then click **Spry Repeat List**.

3. Click the **Container Tag** list arrow, and then select the tag you want to use: UL (Unordered List), OL (Ordered List), DL (Definition List), or SELECT (Drop-down List).

   ◆ If you choose the SELECT (Drop-down List) option, you also need to select a display column and value column (the value sent to the background server).

4. Click the **Spry Data Set** list arrow, and then select the data set you want to use.

5. Click the **Display Column** list arrow, and then select the column you want to display.

6. Click **OK**.

   Dreamweaver inserts a repeated region in your page.

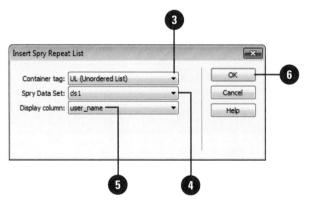

Customizing a Spry Widget

Each spry widget is associated with a CSS and JavaScript file. The CSS file contains all the styling for the widget and the JavaScript file provides all the functionality for the widget. (For example, the files associated with the Validation Radio Group widget are called SpryValidationRadio.css and SpryValidationRadio.js). When you insert a widget in a saved page, Dreamweaver creates a SpryAssets folder in your site and saves the associated files in it. If you want to customize the styling for a spry widget, all you need to do is open the CSS file in the SpryAssets folder, make the changes you want, and then save it.

Change the Style of a Spry Widget

1. Click the **File** menu, click **Open**, navigate to the SpryAssets folder in your site, select the CSS file for the widget that you want to change, and then click **Open**.

   The CSS file becomes available in the SpryAssets folder after you use it on a web page.

2. Locate the CSS rule for the part of the widget that you want to change.

   The available CSS rules vary depending on the spry widget.

3. Make the changes you want.

   ◆ You can also make changes to a CSS file in the CSS Styles panel.

4. Click the **File** menu, and then click **Save** to save your changes.

5. Click the **File** menu, and then click **Close**.

See Also

See Chapter 9, "Working with CSS Rules" on page 224 for more information on changing CSS styles.

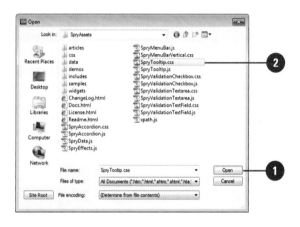

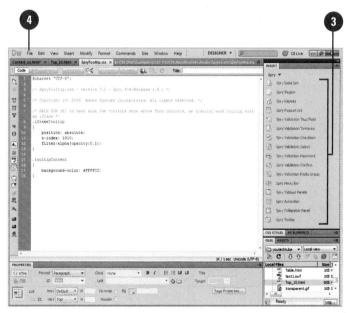

Adding and Removing Spry Effects

Dreamweaver goes a step further with spry widgets that allows you to add special effects to page elements. A spry effect is useful for high-lighting information or creating an animated transition. You can use the Behaviors panel to add a variety of spry effects including fades, high-lights, blinds, slides, shakes, and squishes. You can combine more than one effect to an element to create a unique display. If you no longer want to use an effect, you can quickly remove it.

Apply a Spry Effect

1. Open the Web page with the element you want to apply a spry effect.

2. Select the element on the page you want to change.

3. Click the **Window** menu, and then click **Behaviors** to display the Behaviors panel.

4. Click the **Add Behavior** button (plus sign), point to **Effects**, and then select the effect you want:

   ◆ **Appear/Fade.** Makes the element appear or fade away.

   ◆ **Highlight.** Changes the element background color.

   ◆ **Blind.** Displays the element with a window blind effect.

   ◆ **Slide.** Moves the element up or down.

   ◆ **Grow/Shrink.** Makes the element increase or decrease in size.

   ◆ **Shake.** Makes the element shake from left to right.

   ◆ **Squish.** Makes the element disappear in the upper left corner.

5. Specify the options you want for the selected spry effect; the options for the effect vary depending on the one you select.

6. Click **OK**.

Add Behavior button

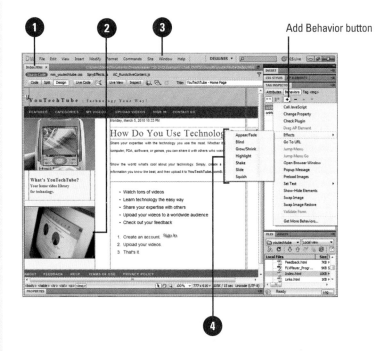

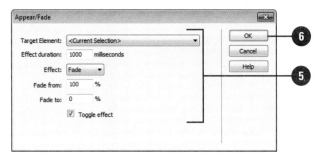

Remove a Spry Effect

1. Open the Web page with the effect you want to remove.

2. Select the element on the page with the spry effect.

3. Click the **Window** menu, and then click **Behaviors** to display the Behaviors panel.

4. Select the effect you want to remove in the Behaviors panel.

5. Click the **Remove Event** button in the subpanel title bar.

   ◆ You can also right-click (Win) or control-click (Mac) the behavior, and then click **Delete Behavior**.

Did You Know?

Applying a spry effect adds code to your Web page file. When you apply a spry effect, Dreamweaver adds code to the document that initiates and identifies the SpryEffects.js file, which provides the executable code to perform the effect. Do not remove or modify this code in Code view.

You can add multiple effects to an element. Select the element you to which want to apply multiple effects, open the Behaviors panel, click the Add Behavior button (plus sign), point to Effects, select the effect you want on the submenu, select the element's ID from the target element list, or select <Current Selection>, specify the other options you want, and then click OK.

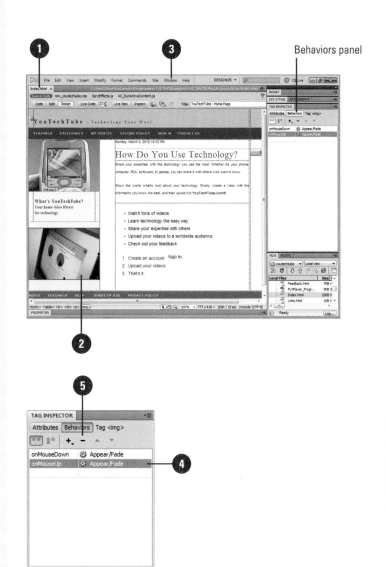

Behaviors panel

Checking Out Spry Samples

Before you add Spry widgets, you need to download and link the latest required Spry Framework files from the Adobe Labs Web site (http://labs.adobe.com/technologies/spry/). When you unzip the Spry Framework files, you also get some samples and demo files that show you by example how to use a spry widget.

In addition to spry widgets, there are also other widgets available that work with Dreamweaver. You can browse for widgets on the Adobe Exchange web site, which you can quickly access from Dreamweaver. Click the Browse for Web Widgets from the Extend Dreamweaver menu on the Applications bar.

Using Code Snippets and Libraries

17

Introduction

The Snippets panel is a collection of Scripts (called Snippets) that you can drop into your Web pages. Essentially, a snippet is a pre-built selection of code. The Snippets panel in turn acts like a code library, with sections or folders for different snippets. There are ten major folders, and some folders have subfolders to organize content.

Each folder has a small triangle, located to the right of the folder name. Clicking this icon expands or contracts the folders contents, revealing either more folders or snippets of code. For example, expanding the JavaScript folder reveals 16 more sub-folders, jam-packed with cool features to add to your Web site. There are thousands of JavaScript codes that can be executed within a Web browser, so Dreamweaver categorized JavaScript into sub-folders to help you better understand where to find the code you need. You will find a group of scripts for managing and controlling Browser functions, cookies, readable functions and a whole host of additional tools. All said and told, the JavaScript folder alone has over 80 individual snippets.

Most well designed Web sites have areas that are repeated from page to page. These would include header areas, navigation bars, information boxes, footers, etc. Occasionally, changes need to be made in these areas. There are wonderfully easy-to-use components in Dreamweaver to make those changes appear on multiple pages when the change is made at one location. Dreamweaver has two such components, Libraries and Templates. Library items are sections of a Web page that can be used over and over again. Dreamweaver Templates are really large Library items.

In this chapter, you'll learn how to work with and add snippets to your Web pages, as well as modify and edit them. In addition, you'll learn how Library items can streamline your workflow in the creation of a complex Web site.

What You'll Do

Introduce Snippets

Insert a Snippet

Edit Existing Snippets

Create Snippets

Introduce Assets and Libraries

Use the Assets Panel

Insert an Asset

Work with Site Assets

Work with Color and URL Assets

Work with Favorite Assets

Create and Insert Library Items

Edit Library Items

Work with Library Items

Create an External JavaScript Library

Insert and Edit an External JavaScript

Use Server-Side Includes

Introducing Snippets

If you build a complex Web site, it's almost a certainty that you will use design elements over and over again. However each time you need them you either have to recall a particular command, or more likely copy and paste the code containing the content you want to reuse. Knowing that is not the most efficient way to work, Dreamweaver created a solution that most people don't know about called Code Snippets.

Similar in philosophy to Microsoft's macros or Adobe's actions, snippets are a incredible way to automate some of your repetitive tasks and make your job easier. They are composed of bits of code and/or content that you can save, edit, use, and reuse as often as you want on any Web site you happen to be working on.

Dreamweaver snippets allow you to save and reuse chunks of code over and over. This saves time and effort in maintaining a large Web site. Plus Dreamweaver has a lot of pre-written snippets to use. Use snippets to store things like headers and footers, logos, and scripts.

Snippets offer a simple and convenient method of creating fragments of reusable code. Snippets can be a single line or a considerable sized chunk of code such as HTML, XHTML, CSS, CFML, PHP, JavaScript and other types of code. Since they are reusable, snippets save you hours of time because you don't have to recreate the same code over and over. You have the ability to create snippets in Dreamweaver, or in another application, and bring them into the Snippets panel, use the pre-designed snippets supplied by Dreamweaver, or use snippets created by other designers.

Snippet Example

The following is an example of snippet code, written in JavaScript that checks for the current location of the mouse.

```
/*
Example:
function test()
{
  if (document.layers) getMouseLoc;    //NS
  else if (document.all) getMouseLoc(); //IE
  alert(mouseLocation.x+","+mouseLocation.y);
}
in the BODY: <a href="#"
    onMouseOver="test()">test</a> */
function Point(x,y) {  this.x = x; this.y = y; }
mouseLocation = new Point(-500,-500);
function getMouseLoc(e)
{
  if(!document.all)  //NS
  {
    mouseLocation.x = e.pageX;
    mouseLocation.y = e.pageY;
  }
  else           //IE
  {
    mouseLocation.x = event.x +
        document.body.scrollLeft;
    mouseLocation.y = event.y +
        document.body.scrollTop;
  }
  return true;
}
//NS init:
if(document.layers){
    document.captureEvents(Event.MOUSEMOVE);
    document.onMouseMove = getMouseLoc; }
```

Information on the current location of the mouse can be used to trigger a variety of actions. For example, when the user hovers over an image, a dialog box could appear to describe the image.

Block and Wrap

Dreamweaver employs two types of snippets: a wrap snippet and a block snippet. Wrap snippets will insert code above and below any selected content on the page. Block snippets, by contrast, simply drop in the snippet content after the insertion point on the page.

To use a block snippet, place an insertion point inside an open document, select the snippet from the Snippets panel, and then click the Insert button at the bottom of the panel. You can also drag and drop the snippet from the panel into an open document, as you would an image or any other media file.

To use a wrap snippet, select the content in Design view that the snippet will wrap around, select the snippet in the Snippets panel, and then click the Insert button at the bottom of the panel.

Summary

Snippets are a great way to reduce the time spent reproducing repetitive tasks. They're easy to use and apply to the documents. However, they do require some experience in writing code in languages such as: HTML, XHTML, CSS, CFML, PHP and JavaScript.

While it's not the purpose of the chapter to teach you how to write snippet code, there are a lot of Web sites out there that offer free (and for cash) snippets, which you can download and use in the construction of your Web sites. Some of these sites include:

http://www.assonetriver.com/snippets/

http://www.luckychair.com/downloads.html

http://www.programmersheaven.com/search/ LinkDetail.asp?Typ=1&ID=13270

As a matter of fact, simply do a Web search using the words "free" and "snippets" and sort through the hundreds of hits. One word of caution: not all snippets are created equal, and may contain code that is not compatible with every browser, so checking and testing is the rule of the day, when it comes to downloading snippets. In addition, some sites might use the downloading of a snippet to also download a virus onto your computer, so know the sites that you're using to downloading the snippets.

Inserting a Snippet

As mentioned in the previous section, you can apply (add) a snippet to a Dreamweaver document in one of two ways: block or wrap. The blocking method requires that you click to create an insertion point in the document and then add the snippet; the wrapping method requires that you select (in Design mode) the selection of the page that you want to wrap the code around. Both methods have their advantages; for example, you could use the block method to insert a snippet into the HTML code that would pre-load rollover images, or you could use the wrap method to select a section of text, or an image, that turns the selection into a link, but is masked from appearing in the status window of the browser. Although Dreamweaver contains many pre-designed snippets, they may require a bit of editing before use.

Add a Block Snippet

1. Open the document you want to insert the block snippet.

2. Click the **Window** menu, and then click **Snippets** to display the Snippets panel.

   TIMESAVER *Press Shift+F9 to display the Snippets panel.*

3. Click in the page where you want to insert the snippet.

4. Click the **Plus** (+) icon next to the folder in the Snippets panel with the snippet you want to insert (in this example, click the (+) next to the Footers folder).

5. Select the snippet you want to insert.

6. Click the **Insert** button in the Snippets panel.

   TIMESAVER *You can also drag a snippet from the Snippets panel directly into the document at the insertion point of the cursor, or double-click the snippet in the Snippets panel.*

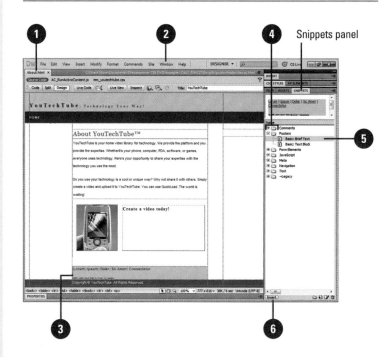

Snippets panel

Add a Wrap Snippet

1. Open the document you want to insert the Wrap snippet.

2. Click the **Window** menu, and then click **Snippets** to display the Snippets panel.

3. Select the text in Design view that you want to apply this snippet.

4. Click the **Plus** (+) or **Minus** (-) icon next to the folder to display the snippet you want to insert from the Snippets panel (in this example, click the (+) next to the Text folder).

5. Select the snippet you want to insert (in this example, click Service Mark).

6. Click the **Insert** button in the Snippets panel to wrap the snippet around the selected text.

   NOTE *The snippet will have to be edited to include the proper URL.*

Did You Know?

You can insert a recent snippet. Click the Insert menu, point to Recent Snippet, and then select the recently used snippet you want.

You can add or edit a keyboard shortcut for a snippet. Open the Snippets folder, right-click (Win) or control-click (Mac) in the Snippets panel, click Edit Keyboard Shortcuts, click the Commands list arrow, select Snippets (if necessary), select the snippet you want to change, enter a keyboard shortcut in the Press key box, and then click OK.

Service Mark

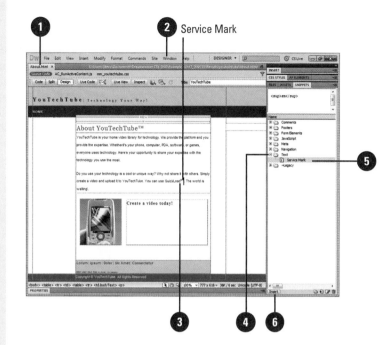

Editing Existing Snippets

In Dreamweaver, you can use one of the many pre-designed snippets, one you developed yourself or others you downloaded from the Web. If any of these snippets is not exactly what you need, you can edit the snippet code directly in Dreamweaver. In addition to editing snippet code, you can also change snippet options, including name, description, snippet type (either block or wrap), and preview type (either in Design or Code view). The blocking method requires that you click to create an insertion point in the document and then add the snippet; the wrapping method requires that you select (in Design view) the selection of the page that you want to wrap the code around.

Edit a Snippet

1. Click the **Window** menu, and then click **Snippets** to display the Snippets panel.

2. Click the **Plus** (+) or **Minus** (-) icon next to the folder to display the snippet you want to insert from the Snippets panel (in this example, click the (+) next to the Footers folder).

3. Select the snippet that you need to edit (in this example, click Title and Hanging List).

4. Click the **Edit Snippet** button in the Snippets panel.

   NOTE *If you don't want to change the original snippet, simply make a copy of the snippet you want to change, and perform the edit to the copy.*

5. Edit the snippet using the following options:

   ◆ **Name.** Change the name for the snippet, if desired.

   ◆ **Description.** Change the description of this snippet, if desired.

   NOTE *Name and Description appear in the Snippets panel.*

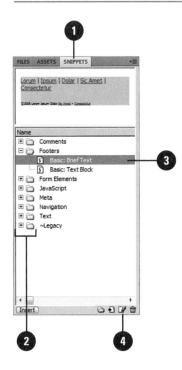

- ◆ **Snippet Type.** Select the **Wrap Selection** option for the wrap type or the **Insert Block** option for the block type.

- ◆ **Insert Code.** Modify the code to fit the particular situation (in this example, the copyright date, and links were updated to reflect the current project).

- ◆ **Preview Type.** Select the **Design** or **Code** option to specify how you want to preview the snippet in the Document window.

6 Click **OK**.

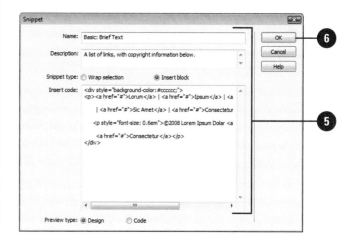

Did You Know?

You can delete a code snippet or snippet folder. Open the Snippets folder, click the snippet folder or code snippet you want to remove, click the Remove button, and then click Yes. When you delete a folder, all the snippets in the folder are also deleted.

You can share a snippet. Snippets are located in the Program Files (Win) or Applications (Mac) folder in the following subfolders: Adobe/Adobe Dreamweaver CS5/Configuration /Snippets/*snippet type name*. You can copy and paste a snippet file into the same location to share it with others.

Creating Snippets

Although Dreamweaver supplies you with dozens of useful sections of snippet code, there will always be the time when you need something that isn't supplied. One method is to jump out onto the Web, go to your friendly search engine, and look for something that might fit the bill. Not only are there a lot of sites out there that have free code for you to use, it's very possible that you might be able to modify an existing piece of code to suit your purposes. And let's not forget Adobe; they've given us the exchange that is just jam packed with high-end code snippets for just about any occasion; many of them free. Just point your browser to: *http://www.adobe.com/cfusion/exchange/* While this section is not designed to make you a snippet programmer, there are probably a lot of you code warriors out there (myself included), who have the ability to write our own snippets. And here's a bit of advice... if you design what you think is a really cool snippet, you can post it on the Adobe Exchange and share it with others.

Create a New Snippet Folder

1. Click the **Window** menu, and then click **Snippets** to display the Snippets panel.

2. Select the folder where you want to create a new snippet folder.

3. Click the **New Snippet Folder** button.

    The new folder appears selected with the name, untitled.

4. Type a name for the folder, and then press Enter (Win) or Return (Mac).

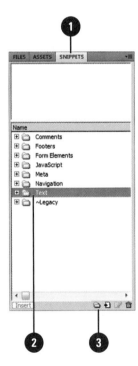

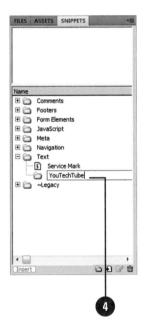

Did You Know?

You can rename a snippet folder or a code snippet. Open the Snippets folder, click the snippet folder or code snippet you want to rename, click the item again, edit the name, and then press Enter (Win) or Return (Mac).

Create a Snippet

1. Click the **Window** menu, and then click **Snippets** to display the Snippets panel.

2. Select the folder that you want to add your new snippet.

3. Click the **New Snippet** button.

4. Use the following options to create the snippet:

   ◆ **Name.** Enter a name for the snippet.

   ◆ **Description.** Enter a description of the snippet.

   ◆ **Snippet Type.** Select the **Wrap Selection** option for the wrap type or the **Insert Block** option for the block type (in this example, Insert Block).

   ◆ **Insert Code.** Enter or paste the code for the snippet. For the Wrap Selection option, enter or paste the code in the Insert Before or Insert After box (in this example, JavaScript code was added to create a date last modified area to the page; the file is called Snippet.xml in the Scripts folder).

   TIMESAVER *You can copy code from another text program (even Microsoft Word), and paste it using Ctrl+V (Win) or ⌘+V (Mac) into the Snippet dialog box.*

   ◆ **Preview Type.** Select the **Design** or **Code** option to specify how you want to preview the snippet in the Document window.

5. Click **OK**.

   Dreamweaver saves the code and adds it to the Snippets panel.

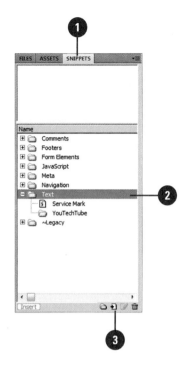

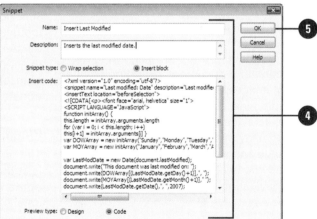

Introducing Assets and Libraries

Introducing Assets

Assets are individual elements, such as images, movies, colors, scripts, and URL links, you add to your Web site. You create assets when you insert elements from other programs, such as Adobe Photoshop or Adobe Flash. The assets are stored in the Assets panel, where you can insert and manage them for use in other parts of your Web site.

Introducing Libraries

Dreamweaver provides two special types of assets: libraries and templates. A library is a Dreamweaver file that contains individual assets or copies of assets, while a template is a Dreamweaver file that contains editable regions. The assets in a library are called **library items**.

Library items are sections of a Web page that can be used over and over again. You can create a library item from any element in the body section of a document, including navigation bars, images, text, tables, forms, Java applets, plug-ins, and ActiveX controls. For example, a navigation system that you want to use on many of the pages in your site is best created and saved as a library item. That way when you need it, all you have to do is add the navigation to the page by dragging it out of the Assets panel.

This gives you a tremendous savings in terms of time creating all those replicating items in Web design. And another benefit is the consistency factor. You know that if the original Library item works, they all work, because they are based on the original item.

Library items also give you a grand advantage when it comes to changes. Again, let's say that you've created a catalog Web site with hundreds of pages that contain images, and descriptions of your products. However, they're not the only things on those pages; you've got a header, footer, navigation, background image or color. There's a lot of stuff going on... and then something happens. You make a modification to the site that requires you to add another button to the Navigation bar... OOPS.

No problem. You created the navigation system for those pages as a library item, and then you inserted that item into a template (more about Templates in a later chapter). So all you have to do is open the original library item, make your changes, and instruct Dreamweaver to update the site. Sounds too good to be true, doesn't it?

Dreamweaver stores library items in a Library folder within the local root for each site. However, for linked items, such as images, the library stores only a reference to the item. When you insert a library item in a page, Dreamweaver creates a link to it instead of inserting it, so the item is able to be updated later.

Planning is the Key

The time to begin the creation of library items is at the very beginning stages of site development. As you are working out the natty details, look at sketches of your pages, and decide what items are worth creating library items and/or templates, and what are not. It's a bit late in the process (after the site is designed) to think back and wish that you had converted this item or that into a library item or template. Think up-front... begin with the end in mind.

Using the Assets Panel

While the Files panel gives you access to your Web site and allows you to add, delete, and link files, quickly and efficiently, it doesn't help you in the actual placement of assets into the documents. That job is left to the Assets panel. The Assets panel holds all of the individual elements that make up your Web pages; they're the puzzle pieces that when properly assembled create awesome Web sites. The Assets panel includes a variety of elements that you store in a site, such as images, movie files, colors, and library elements.

Use the Assets Panel

① Click the **Window** menu, and then click **Assets** to display the Assets panel.

② Click the **Site** option to show all of the assets in your site, or click the **Favorites** option to show only the assets you set as a favorite.

③ Click any of the following category buttons to display the assets you want:

- ◆ **Images.** Displays images in the GIF, JPEG, or PNG formats.

- ◆ **Colors.** Displays the colors that are used in pages and style sheets in your site.

- ◆ **URL.** Displays any external links in your current site documents.

- ◆ **Flash.** Displays files in any version of the Flash format.

- ◆ **Shockwave.** Displays files in any version of the Shockwave format.

- ◆ **Movies.** Displays files in QuickTime or MPEG format.

- ◆ **Scripts.** Displays JavaScript or VBScript files.

- ◆ **Templates.** Displays a list of all the templates in the site.

- ◆ **Library.** Displays a list of all library items (elements used in multiple pages).

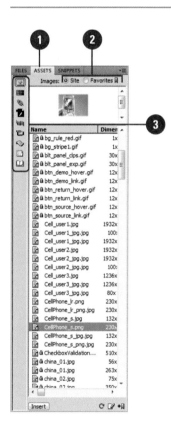

Inserting an Asset

Once an asset is part of a Web site, you can insert it in another page using several different methods. You can drag the asset from the Assets panel directly into Design or Code view or click to place the insertion point where you want the asset and use the Insert button at the bottom of the Assets panel.

Insert an Asset

1. Open the Web page you want to insert an existing asset.

2. Click in the document to add an insertion point.

3. Click the **Window** menu, and then click **Assets** to display the Assets panel.

4. Click the **Site** option to show all of the assets in your site, or click the **Favorites** option to show only the assets you set as favorites.

5. Select the category that contains the asset you want to insert.

   IMPORTANT *You cannot select the Templates category. Templates are applied to an entire document.*

6. Insert the asset using one of the following methods:

   ◆ Click the **Insert** button in the Assets panel. The asset appears at the insertion point.

   ◆ Click and drag the asset from the Assets panel directly into the active document. The asset appears where you release your mouse.

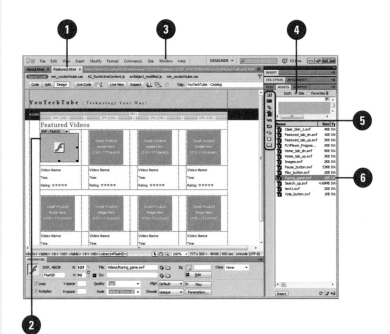

Did You Know?

You can view an asset in the preview area. Open the Assets panel, select the category that contains the asset you want to view, and then select the asset.

Working with Site Assets

The Assets panel does much more than let you look at assets of your site. As a matter of fact, it's a powerful tool to help you manage and edit all the elements that make up a Web site. You can use the Assets panel to edit an image, or even create a new image. Once an asset is edited, it will impact all Web pages that use that particular asset. For example, you use the Assets panel to reopen an image that's used on several Web pages, perform a bit of touchup, and then save the file. In response, all the pages that used that particular asset will update to reflect the changes. Now that's power.

Modify an Asset

1. Select the **Window** menu, and then click **Assets** to display the Assets panel.

2. Select the category that contains the asset you want to edit.

3. Double-click the asset you want to edit, or select the asset, and then click the **Edit** button.

   Dreamweaver launches the program required to edit the image (default application is Fireworks).

4. Make changes to the image, save the file, and then close the edit program.

   The image is resaved with the changes, and all Web pages that utilize the image automatically reflect the changes when loaded.

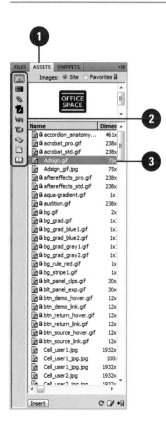

Did You Know?

You can select multiple items in the Assets panel. Open the Assets panel, select an asset, and then use Shift-click to select a consecutive series of assets, or use Ctrl-click (Win) or ⌘-click (Mac) to include or exclude individual assets in the selection.

Working with Color and URL Assets

If you regularly use the same color or URL in a Web site, you can add it to the Assets panel in the Favorites list, so it's available whenever you need it. After you add a color or URL, you can apply it to selected text or images in Design view. For example, you can select text on a page and apply a color asset to change text color or select text or an image on a page and apply a URL link to it.

Add a New Color Asset

1. Open the Web page you want to insert an existing asset.

2. Click the **Window** menu, and then click **Assets** to display the Assets panel.

3. Click the **Favorites** option.

4. Click the **Color** category.

5. Click the **New Color** button.

6. Select the color from the color list.

Add a New URL Asset

1. Open the Web page you want to insert an existing asset.

2. Click the **Window** menu, and then click **Assets** to display the Assets panel.

3. Click the **Favorites** option.

4. Click the **URLs** category.

5. Click the **New URLs** button.

6. Enter the URL and nickname (optional) you want.

   A nickname helps you identify a URL; it doesn't affect the link.

7. Click **OK**.

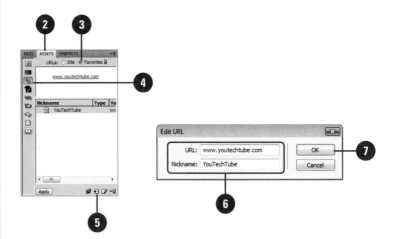

Apply a Color to Text

1 Open the Web page you want to apply a color to text.

2 Select the text you want to apply a color.

If you click to place the insertion point, the color applies to the text appearing after the insertion point.

3 Click the **Window** menu, and then click **Assets** to display the Assets panel.

4 Click the **Color** category.

5 Select the color you want to apply.

6 Click the **Apply** button.

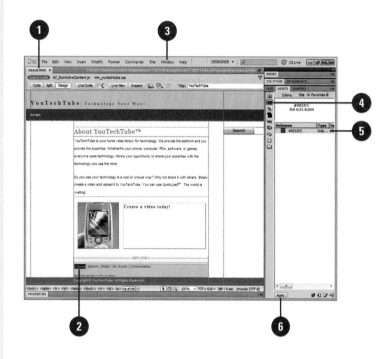

Apply a URL to an Image or Text

1 Open the Web page you want to apply a URL to an image or text.

2 Select the image or text you want to apply a URL.

3 Click the **Window** menu, and then click **Assets** to display the Assets panel.

4 Click the **URLs** category.

5 Select the URL you want to apply.

6 Click the **Apply** button.

TIMESAVER *Drag the URL from the Assets panel to the selected image or text in Design view.*

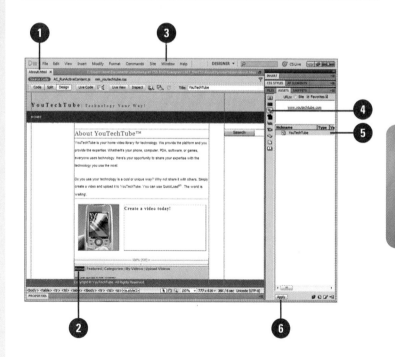

Working with Favorite Assets

When the list of assets for a Web site becomes long, it's difficult to find the assets you want to use. For the assets you frequently use, you can add them to a Favorites list to make them easier to find, and even group related ones together. If the names of the assets in your Favorites list are difficult to identify, you can give them nicknames to make them easier to locate and use. When you give a nickname to an asset, it doesn't affect the real filename of the asset.

Add or Delete a Favorite Asset

1 Select the **Window** menu, and then click **Assets** to display the Assets panel.

2 Select the category that contains the asset that you want to modify.

3 Select one or more assets you want to add from the Site list or remove from the Favorites list.

4 Use any of the following methods:

◆ **Add.** Click the **Add To Favorites** button in the Assets panel.

◆ **Delete.** Click the **Remove From Favorites** button in the Assets panel.

Did You Know?

You can sort assets. Open the Assets panel, select the category that contains the assets you want to sort, and then click the column heading you want to sort by.

You can resize the Assets panel. Open the Assets panel, and then drag the splitter bar between the preview area and the list of assets to resize the panel.

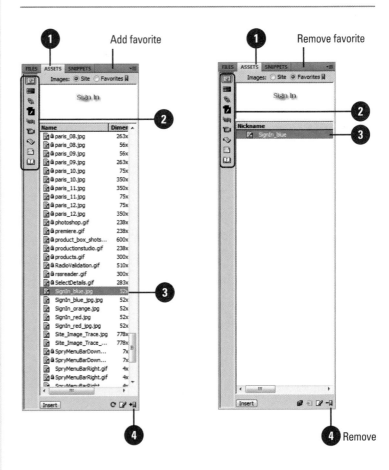

Add favorite

Remove favorite

Remove

Group Assets in a Favorites Folder

1 Click the **Window** menu, and then click **Assets** to display the Assets panel.

2 Select the category that you want to create a group.

3 Click the **Favorites** option.

4 Click the **New Favorites Folder** button.

5 Type a name for the folder, and then press Enter (Win) or Return (Mac).

6 Drag assets into the folder.

Did You Know?

You can copy assets from the Assets panel to another site. Open the Assets panel, select the category that contains the assets you want to copy, right-click (Win) or control-click (Mac) one or more assets (or a Favorites folder) in either the Site list or Favorites list, click Copy To Site, and then select the target site name from the submenu list of all the defined sites.

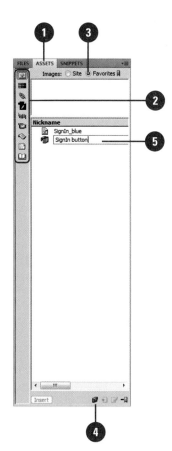

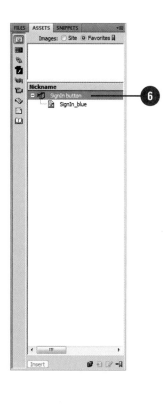

For Your Information

Creating a Nickname for a Favorite Asset

In order to help make assets easier to identify, you can give items placed into the favorites list a nickname, which doesn't impact the real file name. Nicknames can help you identify items that have boring file names like: DCSN0002.JPG, and change it to Sunrise_in_Paris.JPG (assuming, of course, that it actually is a sunrise in Paris). Right-click (Win) or control-click (Mac) the assets name or icon, click Edit Nickname, type a nickname, and then press Enter (Win) or Return (Mac).

Creating and Inserting Library Items

Library items are elements in a Web page you store in a library that you can reuse to quickly create other pages. It can't be overstated just how valuable library items are; not only to increased speed in construction, but perfect consistency between pages. Creating and using library items is fairly straightforward; you create and select an element, such as a navigation bar, and then use the New Library Item button in the Library category to create a library item. After you create a library item, you can use it on any page with a simple click and a drag.

Create a Library Item

1. Open a page that contains information you want to convert to a library item.

2. Click the **Window** menu, and then click **Assets** to display the Assets panel.

3. Click the **Library** category.

4. Select the item or items that you want converted into a library item.

5. Click the **New Library Item** button.

   Dreamweaver adds the item to the Assets panel as an untitled library item.

6. Enter a name for the library item, and then press Enter (Win) or Return (Mac).

   NOTE *Dreamweaver creates all Library Items with the .lbl extension.*

   NOTE *If this is the first library item created, Dreamweaver creates a new subfolder called Library, and place it in the working site folder. All library items are placed within this folder.*

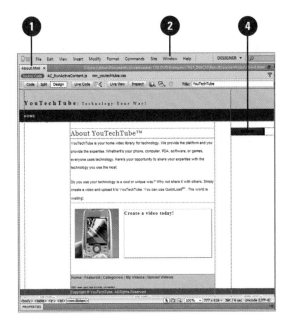

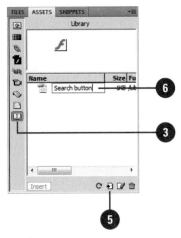

Use a Library Item

① Open the Web page you want to insert a library item.

② Click the **Window** menu, and then click **Assets** to display the Assets panel.

③ Click the **Library** category.

④ Use one of the following methods to add a library item to a page:

◆ Drag and drop the item from the Library in the Assets panel directly into the page.

◆ Click to place the insertion point in the active document, select the library item you want to insert, and then click the **Insert** button in the Assets panel.

Did You Know?

You can disconnect a library item from a library. If you to edit a library item on a specific page and not everywhere else it's used, you need to disconnect the library item from the library. Open the Assets panel, select the Library category, right-click the library item you want to disconnect, and then click Detach From Original.

Drag or insert item here

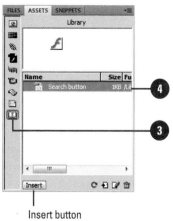

Insert button

Editing Library Items

Creating and using library items, such as a navigation bar, is fairly straightforward. The creation, saving, and subsequent use of library items is discussed in the previous section. After you create an object, you can use it on any Web page with a simple click and a drag. The fun part (and it's easy) is when you need to make a modification to a library item. When you think about it, that's the real power of library items. When you make changes to a library item, Dreamweaver changes the item everywhere it was used.

Edit a Library Item

1 Click the **Window** menu, and then click **Assets** to display the Assets panel.

2 Click the **Library** category.

3 Open the library item using one of the following methods:

◆ Select the item, and then click the **Edit** button in the Assets panel.

◆ Double-click on the library item.

◆ In the Properties panel, click the **Open** button.

Dreamweaver opens the document in a new window.

4 Make changes to the item using standard editing techniques.

5 Click the **File** menu, and then click **Save**.

Dreamweaver opens the Update Library Items dialog box.

6 Choose from the following options:

◆ **Update Library Items In These Files.** Displays a list of all files associated with this library item.

◆ **Update.** Click the **Update** button to perform an update on all displayed files.

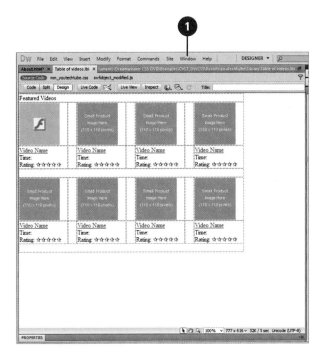

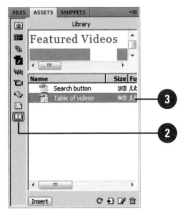

◆ **Don't Update.** Click the **Don't Update** button to cancel the update.

Dreamweaver opens the Update Pages dialog box.

⑦ Choose from the following options:

◆ **Look In.** Click the **Look In** option to update all files within a specific site, or click the **Entire Site** option to update all files within the working site.

◆ **Update.** Select to update **Library Items**, **Templates** (associated with the Library Item), or both.

◆ **Show Log.** Select to show a log of the update when finished.

⑧ Click **Start** to begin the update process, if necessary, and then click **Close**.

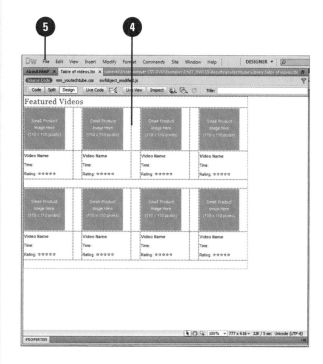

Did You Know?

You can display the filename and location of the source file for a library item. Select the item on one of your pages, open the Properties panel, and then view the filename and location in the Src box.

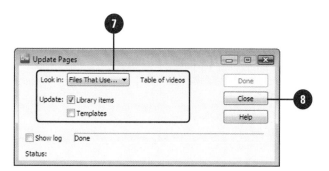

Working with Library Items

If you choose not to update a library item when you edit it, you can still update it later using the Update Current Page or Update Pages commands. The Update Current Page allows you to update the active document in the Document window, while the Update Pages command allows you to update the entire Web site. In addition to updating library items, you can also rename individual items or delete the ones you no longer use.

Update Library Items on a Page or an Entire Site

1. Open the Web page with library items you want to update.

2. Update the library items using either of the following methods:

   ◆ **Update Current Page.** Click the **Modify** menu, point to **Library**, and then click **Update Current Page**.

   ◆ **Update Entire Site.** Click the **Modify** menu, point to **Library**, click **Update Pages**, specify what to update in the **Look In** list arrow, select the **Library Items** check box, and then click **Start**.

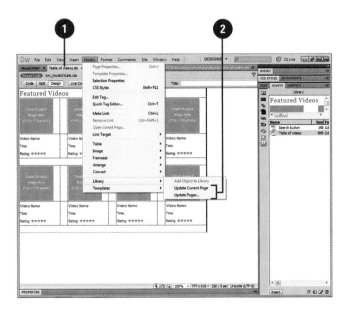

Did You Know?

You can customize the highlight color of library items. Click the Dreamweaver (Mac) or Edit (Win) menu, click Preferences, select the Highlighting category, select the Library Items check box, select a highlighting color, select the Show check box, and then click OK.

You can show or hide highlighting. Click the View menu, point to Visual Aids, and then click Invisible Elements.

Rename or Delete a Library Item

1. Open the Web page with library items you want to rename or delete.

2. Click the **Window** menu, and then click **Assets** to display the Assets panel.

3. Click the **Library** category.

4. Select the library item you want to rename or delete.

5. Use any of the following methods:

   ◆ **Rename a Library Item.** Right-click the library item, click **Rename**, type a new name, and then press Enter (Win) or Return (Mac).

   ◆ **Delete a Library Item.** Right-click the library item, click **Delete**, or click the **Delete** button, and then click **Yes** to confirm the deletion.

Did You Know?

You can recreate a missing or deleted library item. Select the item on one of your pages, open the Properties panel, and then click the Recreate button.

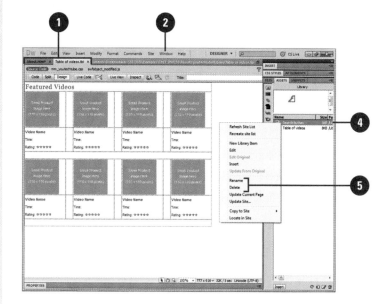

Creating an External JavaScript Library

As you develop a site, you use some Dreamweaver behaviors and JavaScript code constantly. The basic rollover image, for example, is so useful for navigation bars, you may end up putting it on every page of your site. Unfortunately, each time you add a behavior to a page, Dreamweaver adds lines of JavaScript code as well, and more code means slower downloads. You usually end up using the same behaviors repeatedly, so it makes sense to collect these functions and save them in an external JavaScript file. External JavaScripts help you speed up the download of your Web pages. When the scripts are downloaded, they are cached on the visitor's computer. Once your scripts are cached, each subsequent page that is downloaded only requires the browser to download the HTML... and not the scripts, which saves time. You can create a JavaScript file (.js) in Dreamweaver or an external editor, and then copy the JavaScript code that Dreamweaver produces or enter your own code in the JavaScript file (.js) and save it in your site folder (typically in a folder called Scripts) for easy access from the Assets panel.

Create a JavaScript File in Dreamweaver

1. Click the **File** menu, and then click **New**.

   The New Document dialog box opens.

2. Click the **Blank Page** category.

3. Click the **JavaScript** page type.

4. Click **Create**.

5. Enter your JavaScript code, or copy and paste Dreamweaver generated JavaScript code (located in Code view) in the JavaScript file.

6. Click the **File** menu, and then click **Save**.

7. Navigate to the folder location in your local root site folder where you want to store the script file, typically called Scripts folder.

8. Enter a name for the script file.

9. Click **Save**.

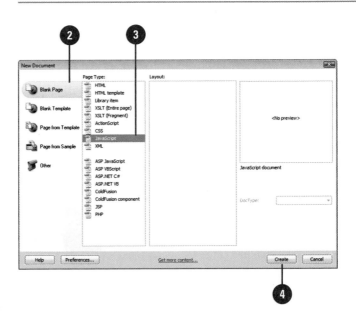

Create an External JavaScript Library Item by Dragging

1 Open the local root site folder for your Web site from the desktop.

2 Drag the user-created JavaScript file from the desktop into the internal folder named, Scripts.

3 Open Dreamweaver.

4 Click the **Site** menu, point to **Manage Sites**, select the site that you dragged the JavaScript code, and then click **Done**.

5 Click the **Window** menu, and then click **Assets** to display the Assets panel.

6 Click the **Scripts** category.

7 Click the **Refresh** button.

The new JavaScript code appears in the Assets panel.

Did You Know?

You can create an external JavaScript library item by dragging a JavaScript file directly to a page. Open a page in Dreamweaver, drag the user-created JavaScript file (.js) from the desktop directly to the page in Dreamweaver, and then click Yes to save the code in the active site folder (recommended). Open the Assets panel, click the Scripts category, and then click the Refresh button to display the JavaScript file.

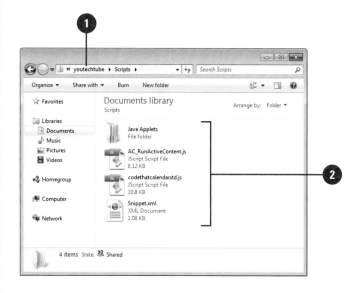

Assets panel

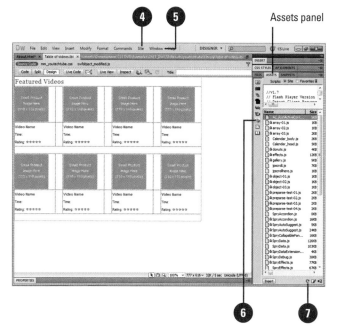

Inserting and Editing an External JavaScript

After you create an external JavaScript file in Dreamweaver or another external editor and store it in a folder, typically called Scripts, in your local root site folder, you can insert the JavaScript into any page in your site and reduce page download times. If you need to make a change to an external JavaScript file, you can do it directly from Dreamweaver using the Assets panel. When you make a change to a JavaScript file, the new code is automatically used when the script is called.

Insert an External JavaScript

1. Open the Web page you want to insert an external script.

2. Click in the document where you want to insert the JavaScript code.

   NOTE *If the script is to be attached to the entire Web page, click the <body> tag in the tag selector at the bottom left of the Document window.*

3. Click the **Window** menu, and then click **Assets** to display the Assets panel.

4. Click the **Scripts** category.

5. Select the script you want attached to the page.

   TROUBLE? *If the script is not available in the list, click the Refresh button.*

6. Click the **Insert** button.

   Dreamweaver inserts the script into the page.

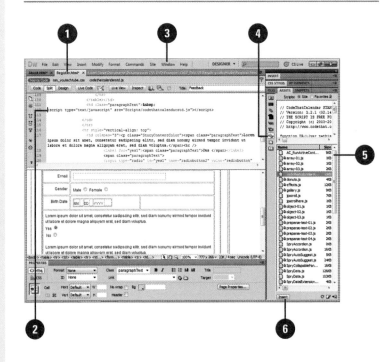

Did You Know?

You can get free javascripts on the Web. Check out the free scripts at *www.java-script.net*. You can also perform a search for free javascripts from additional Web sites.

Edit External Scripts

1. Click the **Window** menu, and then click **Assets** to display the Assets panel.

2. Click the **Scripts** category.

3. Select the script you want to edit.

4. Click the **Assets Options** button, and then click **Edit**.

   The script appears within a window, the same size as the current document window.

5. Make the necessary changes to the script.

6. Click the **File** menu, and then click **Save**.

7. Click the **Close** button to close the JavaScript document.

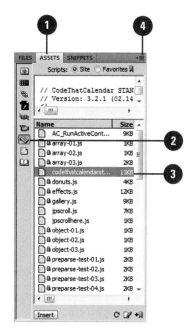

Using Server-Side Includes

A server-side include is a file that the Web server uses in your pages when a browser opens the page. In Dreamweaver, you can insert server-side includes in your pages, edit the includes, or preview pages containing includes.

When you insert a server-side include in a Web page, Dreamweaver places a reference to an external file; the actual contents of the server-side include are not placed in the file. However, Dreamweaver displays the contents of the server-side include in Design view to make it easier to create and layout your pages. In addition, you can preview your pages in your browser to display them as if they were on your Web server. When you display a page with a server-side include in your browser, the server creates a new page inserting the contents of the file and displays the result. This can make updating files more flexible, however it does take a little longer to display the page.

There are two types of server-side includes: Virtual and File. The type you need depends on the Web server you use. Some servers can only use certain types of files for server-side includes, so check the documentation of your server software to determine which is the best type for you. Or, you can just try each type to see which one works for you.

Insert a Server-Side Include

1. Open the Web page where you want to place the server-side include.

2. Click the **Insert** menu, and then click **Server-Side Include**.

3. Locate and select the server-side include file you want to insert.

4. Click **OK**.

Modify a Server-Side Include

1. Open the Web page with the server-side include you want to modify.

2. Select the server-side include.

3. Open the Properties panel.

4. Use the options in the Properties panel to modify server-side settings or change/update the server-side include file.

   ◆ If your server is an Apache Web server, click Virtual. This works well for Apache Web server where File doesn't always.

   ◆ If your server is a Microsoft Internet Information Server (IIS), click File. This works well for IIS where Virtual only works in certain circumstances.

Creating Templates

Introduction

A template is a common structure of a Web site design. Usually Web sites follow a standard structure, such as a header, a navigation bar and a footer that are common to all your pages. Now, imagine that your site has 50 pages. If you need to make one small change, for example adding a new link, you would need to go to each of those pages and change it manually. But using a template you only need to change it in the template and all the pages will be updated automatically.

Think of Dreamweaver templates as really large library items. Instead of occupying a small part of a page, templates control all areas of a page that are to be kept consistent throughout the majority of a Web site. Once created, areas within the template are then made editable so new content can be inserted from page to page.

If nothing else, templates are a fantastic timesaving tool. They allow you to create pages that share the same design but contain different content, and if you modify a template document, you immediately update the design of all pages that were created from that template.

In this chapter, you'll learn how templates can streamline your workflow.

What You'll Do

Introduce Templates

Create a Template

Open a Template

Define Editable Regions

Define Editable Attributes

Create Repeating Regions

Create Optional Regions

Create InContext Editing Editable Regions

Create InContext Editing Repeating Regions

Create Nested Templates

Create a Web Page from a Nested Template

Create a Web Page from a Custom Template

Update a Template

Attach or Detach a Template

Import XML into a Template

Export Template Data as XML

Introducing Templates

Think of templates as really big library items. For example, an entire Web page can be saved as a template. You could have the navigation built into the page; along with editable areas for text or graphics. Let's face it; large and complex Web sites have many pages that have a similar look and feel. Think of a catalog Web site where you would click to view items in the catalog. Let's say that the site has hundreds of items, and the only difference between the pages is the description of the item and an image. Instead of creating hundreds of pages from scratch, you need only create one template and have editable areas for the description and image.

Templates can be comprised of virtually any Web design components. They can include graphics, images, CSS, Flash, just about anything that you would place on a normal Web page. Since a template will contain areas that are editable, and areas that are locked, most templates are designed using a series of tables, or AP elements. As the designer of the template, you decide what areas of the template are editable and what areas are locked out. Of course, this means little to your visitors; locked and editable areas only define to the Web designer what areas can be changed and what areas remain the same.

For example, you create a Web page that emulates a newsletter. The navigation, footers, and the e-newspaper flag remain the same; however, there are areas of the page that you want to update with the latest news. When you design the template, the navigation, footers, and flag are locked, and the areas for the news are editable.

Templates don't control what visitors do with the page; they control how other designers edit the page. When the template is used, the designer assigned to change the data can only access and change the areas you mark as editable. This prevents the accidental (or purposeful) changing of the page, except where you as the Template designer decide.

Editable Regions

If you're a regular template user (and you should be), you'll find a lot of flexibility as you create editable areas for a template page. There are four types of editable areas on a template page: editable region, repeating region, optional region, and editable tag attributes. **Editable regions** are unlocked areas that you can add content in a template page. **Repeating regions** are unlocked areas where you can add or delete copies of the repeating regions in a template page. There are two types of repeating regions: region and table. With a table region, for example, you can increase or decrease the rows in a table while keeping the table structure intact. **Optional regions** are unlocked areas that allow you to show or hide content in a template page. In addition to using editable regions, you can also use **editable tag attributes** to modify specific attributes related to an element. You can make some attributes editable while leaving other attributes locked.

The Internet is full of sites containing pre-designed templates. Some are quite elaborate. You can find templates for entire sites, such as shopping carts, and sites complete with Paypal pages. Listed here are a few of the sites that carry templates:

http://allwebcodesign.com/

http://www.dreamweaver-templates.org/

http://www.adobe.com/products/dreamweaver /download/templates/

Creating a Template

Templates allow you to create pages that share the same design but different content, and if you modify a template document, you immediately update the design of all pages that were created from that template. One of the best ways to create a template is to actually design a Web page, place everything where you want it to be (navigation, text areas, image areas, footers, possibly a library item, etc.), and then convert (save) the page as a template. Templates contain editable and locked areas, so they are typically enclosed within a table structure or AP elements. When you create a template, Dreamweaver saves the file by default to the Templates folder for your site and manages any links, so updates are properly maintained.

Create a Template

1. Create a document (including editable regions) that you want to use as a template.

2. Click the **File** menu, and then click **Save As Template**.

3. Save the template using the following options:

   ◆ **Site.** Choose the site to save the template (default: working site).

   ◆ **Existing Templates.** Choose to save as an existing template.

   ◆ **Description.** Enter a meaningful description of the template.

   ◆ **Save As.** Enter a file name for the template.

4. Click **Save**.

5. Click **Yes** as necessary to update the site with any needed files.

   Dreamweaver saves the template file with the .dwt extension in the default Templates folder within the local root site folder.

   NOTE *If you attempt to close a template file without an editable region, Dreamweaver warns you.*

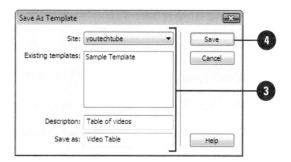

For Your Information

Checking Template Syntax

When you insert a region in a template, Dreamweaver uses HTML comment tags, known as template tags, to specify the region in the code to make sure it remains valid HTML. For example, <!--TemplateBeginEditable name ="..." -->. There are a few important rule to be aware of: (1) white space can be any length; (2) attributes can be in any order; (3) comment and attribute names are case sensitive; and (4) all attributes need to be in quotation marks, either single or double quotes. When you save a template, Dreamweaver checks the template syntax. However, you can also check it whenever you want. Open the template you want to check, click the Modify menu, point to Templates, and then click Check Template Syntax. If there are problems, an error message appears, describing the problems.

Opening a Template

After you create and save a template, you can open it using several different methods in Dreamweaver. You can use the Assets panel or the Open dialog box. When you save a template file, the default location is typically in the Templates folder of the local root site folder. When you use the Assets panel to open a template, the default location automatically appears displaying the current templates. When you use the Open dialog box, you need to navigate to the Templates folder. If you have recently saved or opened a template, you can also open it again quickly using the Open Recent submenu on the File menu. When you open a template file, the title bar in the Document window contains the word <<Template>> followed by the name of the template along with the .dwt file extension for templates.

Open a Template File Using the Assets Panel

1. Click the **Window** menu, and then click **Assets** to display the Assets panel.

2. Click the **Templates** category.

3. Open the template using one of the following options:

   ◆ Select the template in the Names window, and then click the **Edit** button in the Assets panel.

   ◆ Double click on the name of the template in the Assets panel.

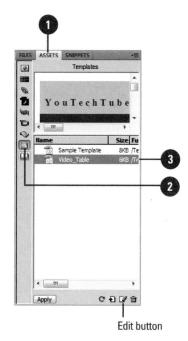

Edit button

Did You Know?

You can create a blank template from the Assets panel. Open the Assets panel, click the Templates category, click the New Template button, type a name, and then press Enter (Win) or Return (Mac).

See Also

See "Creating a Web Page from a Blank Template" on page 22 for information on using a blank template.

Open a Template File Using the Open Dialog Box

1. Click the **File** menu, and then click **Open**.

   TIMESAVER *Press Ctrl+O (Win) or ⌘+O (Mac).*

2. Click the **Files Of Type** list arrow (Win) or **Popup** (Mac), and then click **Template Files (*.dwt)**.

3. Locate and select the template file you want to open.

   The default location is typically in the Templates folder of the local root site folder.

4. Click **Open**.

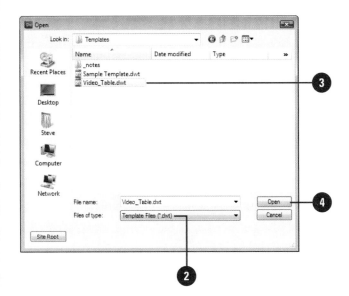

Did You Know?

You can open the template file attached to the current page file. Open the Web page based on the template you want to open, click the Modify menu, point to Templates, and then click Open Attached Template.

You can rename a template. Open the Assets panel, click the Templates category, click the name of the template, click the name again, enter a new name, and then press Enter (Win) or Return (Mac).

You can delete a template. Open the Assets panel, click the Templates category, click the template you want to delete, and then click the Delete button in the Assets panel.

Defining Editable Regions

When you first create a template, the entire page is locked and uneditable to the designer. Without editable areas, you would not be able to make any changes to the page. To correct this problem, you need to create editable areas in the template. Editable areas are for the designers who want to use templates to create Web pages. Web pages based on a template enable Dreamweaver users to edit parts of a Web page within the editable regions without the risk of accidentally changing the locked regions. Editable regions in Design view appear with a rectangular outline and a small tab in the upper-left corner with the name of the region. You can click the tab to select the editable region.

Define Editable Regions

1. Open the template you want to add editable regions.

2. Select the content (including tables, table cells, or AP elements) in the template you want to make editable, or click to place the insertion point.

    NOTE *If the area is going to contain text, make sure you apply any formatting options, using HTML or CSS to the area before making it an editable area.*

3. Click the **Insert** menu, point to **Template Objects**, and then click **Editable Region**.

    The New Editable Region dialog box opens.

4. Enter a unique name for the new region.

5. Click **OK**.

    The editable region appears with the name in the tab.

Did You Know?

You can remove or relock an editable region. Select the area you want to change, click the Modify menu, point to Templates, and then click Remove Template Markup.

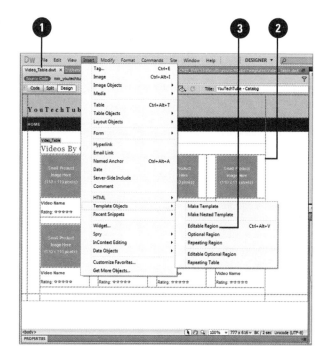

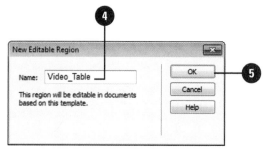

Defining Editable Attributes

In addition to making regions of a page editable, you can also make specific HTML tag attributes editable (for example, the background color of the page). This combination not only gives you control over a general area such as a table, individual cell, or an AP element; you now have control over specific elements. You can use this option to allow contributors to the Web page the ability to duplicate the region. For example, when creating a table that holds customer comments, the contributor needs the ability to add more rows to the table. In addition, you can also create template variables, such as boolean, text, number, color or URL, for use in template expressions.

Define Editable Attributes

1. Open the template you want to define editable attributes.

2. Select the tag or object that you want to make editable.

3. Click the **Modify** menu, point to **Templates**, and then click **Make Attribute Editable**.

4. Select from the following options in the Editable Tag Attributes dialog box:

   ◆ **Attribute.** Select the attribute, or click the Add button and enter the attribute manually.

   ◆ **Make Attribute Editable.** Select to make this attribute editable.

   ◆ **Label.** Enter a unique name for the editable attribute.

   ◆ **Type.** Select a type from the available options: Text, URL, Color, True/False, or Number.

   ◆ **Default.** Enter the initial default value for the attribute.

5. Click **OK**.

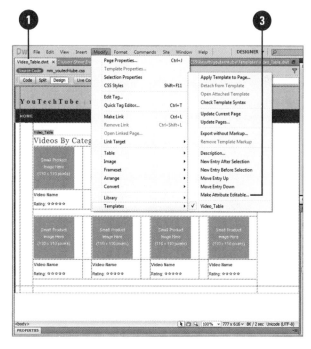

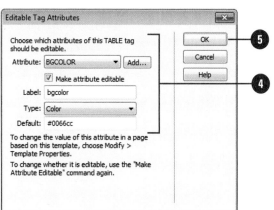

Did You Know?

You can modify the properties of an editable attribute. Click the Modify menu, click Template Properties, select the attribute or variable you want, make any changes, and then click OK.

Creating Repeating Regions

Repeating regions are unlocked areas that allow you to add or delete copies of the repeating regions in a template page. There are two types of repeating regions: region and table. With a repeating region, you can specify the layout you want by duplicating repeating page elements, such as a gallery of photographs. With a repeating table region, you can increase or decrease the rows in a table while keeping the table structure intact. You can define table attributes and set which table cells are editable.

Create a Repeating Region

1. Open the template you want to add a repeating region.

2. Select the content in the template you want to change, or click to place the insertion point where you want it.

3. Click the **Insert** menu, point to **Template Objects**, and then click **Repeating Region**.

   The New Editable Region dialog box opens.

4. Enter a unique name for the new region.

5. Click **OK**.

   The repeating region appears with the name in the tab.

   NOTE *If the area is to contain text, make sure you apply any formatting options, using HTML or CSS to the area before making it an editable area.*

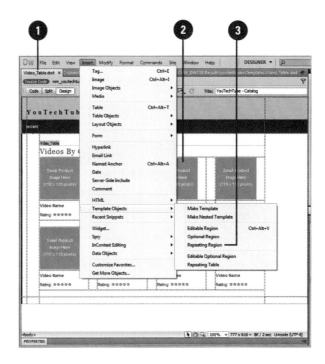

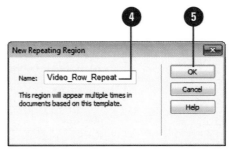

Did You Know?

You can add, delete and change the order of a repeating region entry. Open the template-based page, place the insertion point, and then click the Plus (+), Minus (-), Down Arrow, or Up Arrow buttons to change the entries. You can also use the Repeating Entries submenu on the Edit menu to cut, copy, and paste entries.

Create a Repeating Table

① Open the template you want to add editable regions.

② Click to place the insertion point where you want to insert the table.

③ Click the **Insert** menu, point to **Template Objects**, and then click **Repeating Table**.

④ Select from the following options in the Insert Repeating Table dialog box:

◆ **Rows.** Enter the number of rows for the table.

◆ **Columns.** Enter the number of columns for the table.

◆ **Cell Padding.** Specify the number of pixels between a cell's contents and the cell border.

◆ **Cell Spacing.** Specify the number of pixels between the table cells.

◆ **Width.** Enter the width (in pixels) or as a percentage of the browser window's width.

◆ **Border.** Enter the width (in pixels) for the table border.

◆ **Repeat Rows Of The Table.** Specify the table rows you want in the repeating region.

◆ **Starting Row.** Enter the row number for the first row.

◆ **Ending Row.** Enter the row number for the last row.

◆ **Region Name.** Enter a unique name for the table region.

⑤ Click **OK**.

The repeating table region appears with the name in the table.

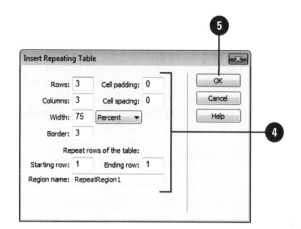

Creating Optional Regions

Content within an optional region may or may not be displayed, depending on certain conditions set by the template designer. Optional regions are just that: optional. Optional regions define content or editable regions that you can turn on or off (be visible or not). Optional regions, therefore, enable designers to show and hide specially marked regions. The template tab of an optional region is preceded by the word *If*. There are two types of optional regions: non-editable and editable. A **non-editable optional region** allows you to show or hide the region without the ability to edit the content, while an **editable optional region** allows you to edit the content.

Create a Non-Editable Optional Region

1. Open the template you want to add an optional region.

2. Select the item, or an AP element within the template that you want converted into an optional region.

3. Click the **Insert** menu, point to **Template Objects**, and then click **Optional Region**.

4. Click the **Basic** tab.

5. Enter a unique name for the region.

6. Select the **Show By Default** check box to toggle between showing or hiding this optional region (default: show).

7. To set values for the optional region, click the **Advanced** tab.

   ◆ Click the **Use Parameter** option, and then select a parameter from the popup, or click the **Enter Expression** option, and then write a template expression.

8. Click **OK**.

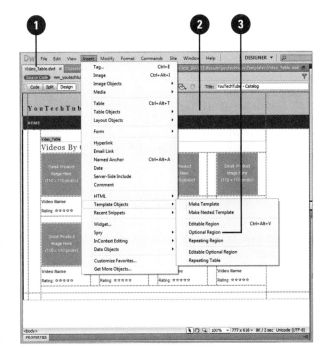

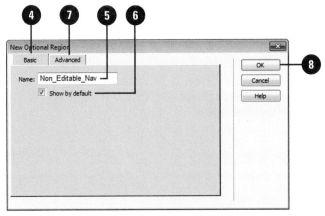

Create an Editable Optional Region

1. Open the template you want to add an optional region.

2. Click to place the insertion point where you want to insert an editable optional region.

3. Click the **Insert** menu, point to **Template Objects**, and then click **Optional Region**.

4. Click the **Basic** tab.

5. Enter a unique name for the region.

6. Select the **Show By default** check box to toggle between showing or hiding this optional region.

7. To set values for the optional region, click the **Advanced** tab.

   ◆ Click the **Use Parameter** option, and then select a parameter from the popup, or click the **Enter Expression** option, and then write a template expression.

8. Click **OK**.

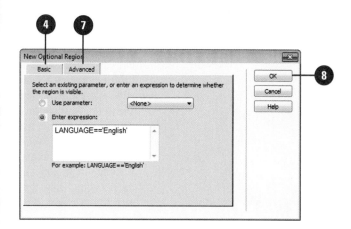

Did You Know?

You can change the settings for an optional region. Select the optional region, open the Properties panel, and then click the Edit button.

You can modify optional regions template parameters. Open the template-based page, click the Modify menu, click Template Properties, select the property you want to change, edit the value of the property, select or clear the Show check box, select or clear the Allow Nested Templates To Control This check box, and then click OK.

Design By Example

Creating an Optional Region

A simple use of an optional region is to allow content to either be visible or not in a page based on a template. For example, you maintain a Web site for a garden center called the Green Thumb (now that's original). The site sells three types of items: Flowers, Vegetables, and Garden Equipment. The pages are essentially the same. There will be two editable areas: one describing the product, and another for an image displaying the product. The remainder of the areas (navigation, footers, background, etc.), are all locked... except for one thing. You want a generic image on each of the pages so that the customer can identify the pages for the three products (it could even be a background image contained in an AP element). To solve this problem, you create an optional region, load all three changeable images into the area, and then let the designer of the page decide which image to use.

Creating InContext Editing Editable Regions

Adobe InContext Editing (ICE) is an online service that allows users to make simple edits to your web pages without any previous knowledge of HTML code or web editing. Before a user can edit a page, you need to specify what areas on the page that you want to enable users to edit directly in a browser. You can specify areas of a page for users to edit by creating an ICE editable region. An ICE editable region is a pair of HTML tags that includes the ice:editable attribute in the opening tab. These tags transform a non-editable region of a page into an editable one. To edit a page, a user opens the page in a browser, logs in to the InContext Editing service, and then edits the content in the ICE editable region. If you are creating an ICE editable region to a template, the new ICE editable region must be placed within an editable region. For details about using the Adobe ICE online editing service, see the Adobe web site at *www.adobe.com*.

Create an InContext Editing Editable Region

1. Open the Web page that you want to transform into an ICE repeating region.

2. Do any of the following to select the region that you want to make editable:

   - Select a div, th, or td tag.

   - Place the insertion point or select content.

   - Select one editable region in a template.

3. Click the **Insert** menu, point to **InContext Editing**, and then click **Create Editable Region**.

4. Based on your selection in Step 2, take the appropriate action:

   - If you selected a div, th, or td tag, you're done.

   - If you placed the insertion point or selected content, select an option to create a new editable region, and then click **OK**.

   - If you selected one editable region in a template, click **OK**.

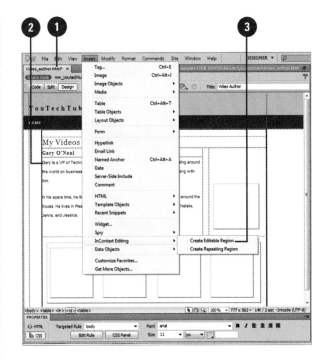

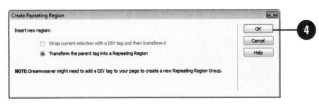

5. Click the blue tab of the editable region to select it.

6. Specify the editing options that you want to make available to users in the Properties panel.

   The options you select in the Properties panel will be available to users when they edit the page in a browser.

7. Click the **File** menu, and then click **Save**.

8. If prompted, click **OK** for Dreamweaver to add supporting files to your site for ICE. These files need to be uploaded to your server for ICE to work properly.

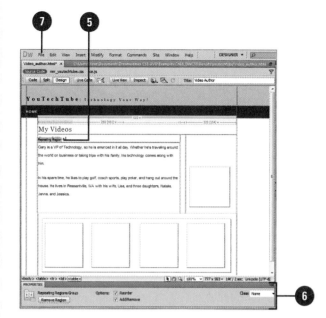

Click to display options

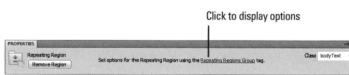

Delete Editable Region

1. Open the Web page with the ICE editable region.

2. Select the editable region that you want to delete.

3. Click the **Remove Region** button in the region's Properties panel.

4. Click **OK** to confirm the removal.

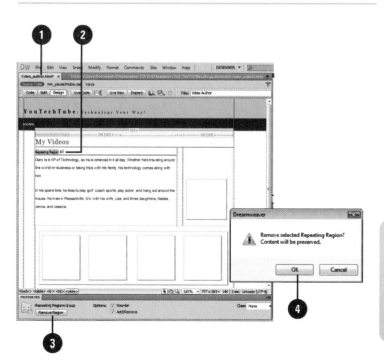

Creating InContext Editing Repeating Regions

In addition to creating an editable region, you can also create a repeating region for use with Adobe InContext Editing (ICE), an online service that allows users to make simple edits to your web pages without any previous knowledge of HTML code or web editing. An ICE repeating region creates an area on the page that a user can repeat and add content. When you create an ICE repeating region, Dreamweaver adds a pair of HTML tags that includes the ice:repeating attribute in the opening tab. To edit a page, a user opens the page in a browser, logs in to the InContext Editing service, and then edits the content in the ICE repeating region. If you are creating an ICE repeating region to a template, the new ICE editable region must be placed within an editable region. For details about using the Adobe ICE online editing service, see the Adobe web site at *www.adobe.com*.

Create an InContext Editing Repeating Region

① Open the Web page that you want to transform into an ICE editable region.

② Do any of the following to select the region that you want to make editable:

◆ Select any of the following tags: a, abbr, acronym, address, b, bif, blockquote, center, cite, code, dd, dfn, dir, dive, dl, dt, em, font, h1, h2, h3, h4, h5, h6, hr, i, img, ins, kbd, label, li, menu, ol, p, pre, q, s, samp, small, span, strike, strong, sub, sup, table, tbody, tr, tt, u, ul, and var.

◆ Place the insertion point or select content.

◆ Select one editable region in a template.

③ Click the **Insert** menu, point to **InContext Editing**, and then click **Create Repeating Region**.

④ Based on your selection in Step 2, take the appropriate action:

◆ If you selected a tag, you're done.

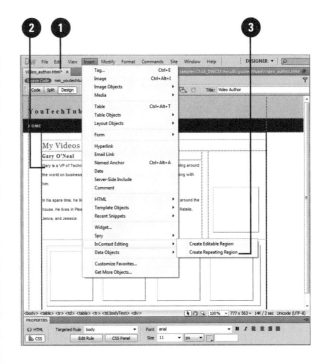

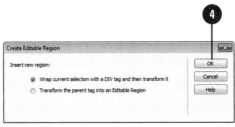

- ◆ If you placed the insertion point or selected content, select an option to create a new editable region, and then click **OK**.

- ◆ If you selected one editable region in a template, click **OK**.

5. Click the blue tab of the editable region to select it.

6. Specify the editing options that you want to make available to users in the Properties panel.

The options you select in the Properties panel will be available to users when they edit the page in a browser.

7. Click the **File** menu, and then click **Save**.

8. If prompted, click **OK** for Dreamweaver to add supporting files to your site for ICE. These files need to be uploaded to your server for ICE to work properly.

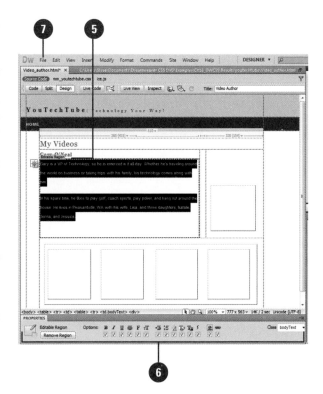

Creating Nested Templates

Nested templates are essentially templates within templates. Nested templates allow for different levels of control on pages created from these templates. For example, you create a Web site that has a similar overall appearance (navigation, logo, color scheme, etc.), yet also has sections that have a different appearance. For the separate sections of the site, you can make nested templates that will have common elements and layout features for that section. The differences represent a different type of page in the site. First, you create the navigation templates; each with their own differences, and save them. Next, you create the main body of the page (which will also be a template), and "nest" the navigation template into the main template. The nested template is now defined as the "child" template. Now, any time you need to make changes to the navigation, you simply edit the child template, just like any other template, and the changes will be applied specifically to the pages that contain the child. Nested templates do not increase the size of the Web page, nor do they create any additional complexity. All they do is give you control over your site.

Create a Nested Template

1. Create a normal template, the same as any other template.

   This template will act as the parent template. There must be at least one editable region in the template (this is the area you will insert your nested template).

2. Click the **File** menu, and then click **Save As Template**.

3. Save the template using the following options:

   - **Site.** Choose the site to save the template (default: working site).

   - **Description.** Enter a meaningful description of the template.

   - **Save As.** Enter a file name for the template.

4. Click **Save**.

5. Click **Yes** as necessary to update the site with any needed files.

6. Click the **File** menu, click **Close**, and then click **OK** as necessary to the alert message.

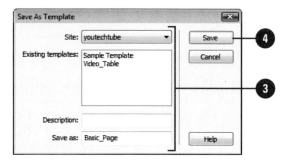

Now, you want to create a new page based on the template.

7 Click the **File** menu, and then click **New**.

8 Select from the following options in the New Document dialog box:

◆ Click the **Page From Template** category.

◆ Select the site where the template is located.

◆ Select the template you just saved in step 4.

◆ Click **Create** to open the new document.

9 Click to select the area of the document that will contain the nested template.

10 Click the **Window** menu, and then click **Assets** to display the Assets panel.

11 Click the **Templates** category.

12 Select your previously created nested template (in this example, a template that contains the navigation).

13 Click the **Apply** button in the Assets panel.

Dreamweaver adds the nested template to this new document.

14 Click the **File** menu, click **Save As Template**, and then follow the instructions in steps 3 through 5 to save this template.

See Also

See "Setting Highlighting Color Preferences" on page 66 for information on setting highlight colors for editable regions, nested editable regions, and locked regions.

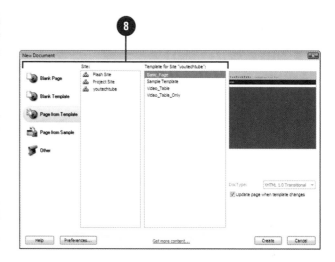

For Your Information

Dealing with Inconsistent Region Names

The Inconsistent Region Names dialog box appears automatically when Dreamweaver finds regions that do not match in a template and the document to which the template is being applied. You can map the content in the document to any region in the template or discard the content.

Creating a Web Page from a Nested Template

In addition to standard templates, you can create nested templates. A nested template is a template whose design is based on another template. By creating nested templates, you can control content in pages that share the same layout but also have slight design variations. When you open and change a nested template, it modifies that section of all the files that use the nested template without changing any other areas of the template or the pages to which they are attached. This takes Web page customization and reusability to the next level.

Create a Nested Template

1. Click the **File** menu, and then click **New**.

   The New Document dialog box opens.

2. Click the **Page From Template** category.

3. Select the site that contains the template you want.

4. Select the template you want to use.

5. Click **Create**.

   Dreamweaver opens a new Web page based on the selected template.

6. Add something to the new template, such as a pre-existing navigational system, an image, or possibly some changeable text.

7. Click the **Insert** menu, point to **Template Objects**, and then click **Make Nested Template**.

8. Enter a Description in the input field (optional), and then enter a name for the nested template into the Save As input field.

9. Click the **Save** button.

   Dreamweaver now saves the nested template.

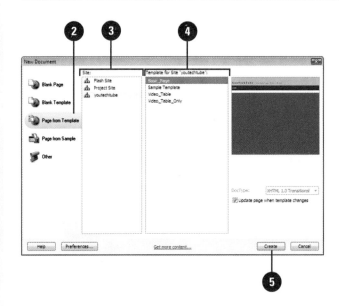

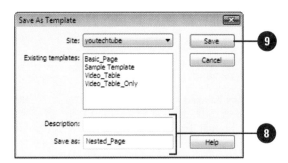

Creating a Web Page from a Custom Template

After you create your own custom template, you can use it to create Web pages. A document created from a template is known as an instance of that template. When you create a page based on a template, it contains all the attributes of the template; however, it won't be a template, it will be a Web page. When you open a page based on a template, the editable regions in Design view appear with a rectangular outline and a small tab in the upper-left corner with the name of the region. You can click the tab to select the editable region. In addition, the entire page is surrounded by a different colored outline with the template name on the tab that reminds you the page is based on a template and you can only change editable areas.

Create a Web Page from a Custom Template

1. Click the **File** menu, and then click **New**.

   The New Document dialog box opens.

2. Click the **Page From Template** category.

3. Select the site that contains the template you want.

4. Select the template you want to use.

5. Select the **Update Page When Template Changes** check box to instruct Dreamweaver to update all pages when the template changes (default).

6. Click **Create**.

   Dreamweaver generates a new document based on the selected template.

7. Edit and add content to all editable areas of the page.

8. Click the **File** menu, click **Save**, select a location, specify a name, and then click **Save** to save your new page.

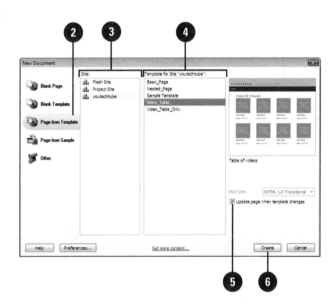

Updating a Template

If all you did with templates was to create new pages based on their design, that would be very powerful. However, there's more to a template than simply streamlining the creation of a simple Web page. The power of a template is that when you change one template, you have the option of changing all the associated pages. Now, that's what I'm talking about. When you edit and save a template, Dreamweaver asks you whether you want to automatically update the page files based on that template. If you decide not to automatically update the page files, you can manually change an individual page, all the pages that use a template, or the entire site using the Update commands.

Update a Template and All the Pages Based on the Template

① Open the template you want to update.

② Make changes to the template, using standard editing techniques.

③ Click the **File** menu, and then click **Save**.

The Update Templates Files dialog box opens, displaying all the page files based on the templates.

④ Click **Update** to continue the update process, or click **Don't Update** to cancel the process.

⑤ If you clicked Update, the Update Pages dialog box opens.

  ◆ **Look In.** Select **Entire Site** to update all the documents that use this template, or select **Files That Use** to update pages using a particular template.

  ◆ **Templates and Library Items.** Select to update templates, library items, or both.

  ◆ **Show Log.** Select to show a log upon completion.

⑥ Click **Start** to update the files, if necessary, and then click **Close**.

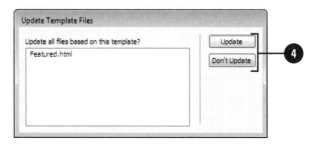

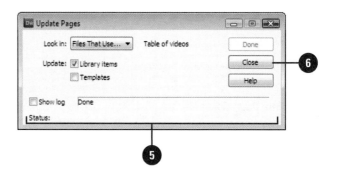

Update Pages Based on a Template Manually

1. Open the template-based Web page you want to update.

2. Click the **Modify** menu, point to **Templates**, and then click **Update Pages**.

   The Update Pages dialog box opens.

3. Click the **Look In** list arrow, and then click **Files That Use** or **Entire Site**.

4. Select the **Templates** and **Library Items** check boxes to update templates and library items in the template-based files.

5. Select the **Show Log** check box to show a log upon completion.

6. Click **Start** to update the files, and then click **Close**.

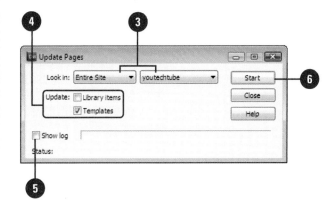

Did You Know?

You can manually apply template changes to a page based on the template. Open the Web page based on the template, click the Modify menu, point to Templates, and then click Update Current Page.

You can find an editable region and select it. Click the Modify menu, point to Templates, and then select the name of the region you want to find and select. Editable regions inside a repeated region do not appear in the menu.

Design By Example

Saving Time by Using Templates

Let's say that you've just created this huge Web site for your university (I volunteered to oversee the one for my university, and it wasn't pretty). Now, the project is completed, you unveil to the students and staff, and what happens: Well in my case one of the deans decided they didn't like the look of their section of the site, and another one decided that the graphics for her section were wrong. Understand everyone signed off on the design; however, things will happen. So, now all eyes are on me... I have to get this site up and running in a week, if we're to meet our deadlines for school enrollment. I looked about the room, asked each department head to give me their changes (in writing) by 5:00PM. The next day, when the faculty came in and checked the site all the changes were implemented (some people still weren't happy). How did I manage to change literally hundreds of Web pages in a single night (it actually took 3.5 hours)? How did I manage this great feat? Templates, my friend, templates.

Attaching or Detaching a Template

If you didn't create a new page based on a template, you can still attach (apply) the template to the file later. When you apply a template to a page file, Dreamweaver tries to match the existing content to a region in the template. You can apply a template to a page using menu commands from the Document window or from the Assets panel. If you no longer want a page to be based on a template, you can detach the page from the template. The page doesn't lose any content, however, changes made to the template will not be applied to the page after it is detached.

Attach and Detach a Template to a Page

1. Open the Web page you want to apply the template to.

2. Click the **Modify** menu, point to **Templates**, and then click **Apply Template To Page**.

   ◆ To detach a page from the template, click the **Modify** menu, point to **Templates**, and then click **Detach From Template**.

3. Select the template you want to apply.

4. Click **Select**.

   ◆ You can also open the Assets panel, click the **Templates** category, select a template, and then click the **Apply** button.

   If the Inconsistent Region Names dialog box opens, content on the page cannot be automatically assigned to a template region.

5. Select a destination for the content. Select a region in the new template or select **Nowhere** to remove the content.

6. To move all unresolved content to the selected region, click **Use For All**.

7. Click **OK**.

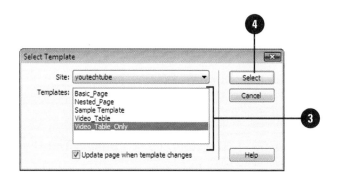

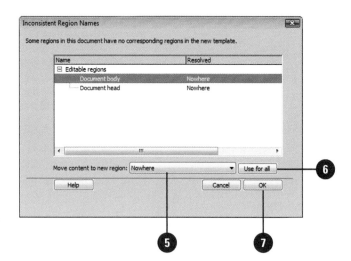

Importing XML into a Template

Dreamweaver provides an Import command for XML you can use to create a new document based on the template specified in an XML file. The command fills in the contents of each editable region in the new document using data from the XML file. If Dreamweaver has problems importing the data, the XML file might not have the right structure. To correct the problem, use the Export command for XML to view the file structure and then make the adjustments to the XML file you want to import.

Import XML into a Template

1. Click the **File** menu, point to **Import**, and then click **XML Into Template**.

2. Navigate to the drive and folder location where you want to import the XML file.

3. Select the XML file you want to import.

4. Click **Open**.

   Dreamweaver creates a new Web page based on the template specified in the XML file. The XML data in the file is placed in the editable region in the new Web page.

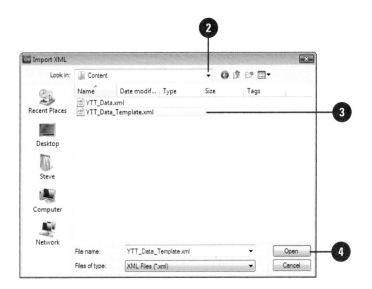

Exporting Template Data as XML

If you have data in a template that you want to use in another program, you can export the data as XML. The XML Export command creates an XML file with the data contained in your template's editable regions and parameters. The exported XML file includes the name of the template and editable regions for round trip purposes. You can also use the XML Export command if you are having problems importing XML data into Dreamweaver. You can export data as an XML file in order to view the file structure and then make adjustments to the XML file you want to import.

Export Template Data as XML

1. Open the template-based Web page with the data you want to export as XML.

2. Click the **File** menu, point to **Export**, and then click **Template Data As XML**.

3. Select the Notation option you want.

    ◆ **Use Standard Dreamweaver XML Tags**. Use this option if the template contains repeating regions or template parameters.

    ◆ **Use Editable Region Names As XML Tags**. Use this option if the template doesn't contain repeating regions or template parameters.

4. Click **OK**.

5. Navigate to the drive and folder location where you want to export the data as an XML file.

6. Type a name for the file, or use the suggested name.

7. Click **Save**.

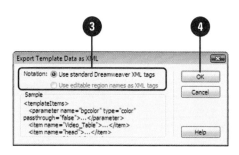

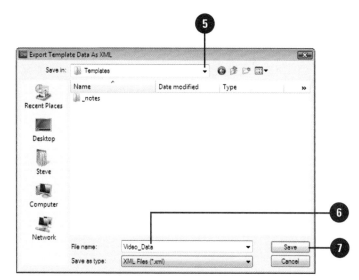

Testing a Web Site

Introduction

Testing is an integral part of the design of a Web site. In fact, the term used to describe a good Web site is bullet proof. Without the ability to test a site, you would never know what works, and what needs help. Dreamweaver gives you a host of tools to help make sure that your visitors have a pleasant experience. Some of the things Web testing can and should look for are:

- ◆ **Validation.** Is your HTML and CSS code compatible with your visitors? Do your Web pages have any broken links? If problems arise on your site, visitors will go elsewhere, which isn't the goal.

- ◆ **Browser Independence.** Do your Web pages load and function on the various browsers used by your visitors? Your site may be viewed in a large variety of situations: different browsers, different operating systems, or different features enabled or disabled.

- ◆ **Accessibility.** Do your Web pages conform to the standards set by the government on accessibility standards? Your site may be viewed by those with physical limitations, such as the visually impaired.

- ◆ **Speed.** Is it easy and fast to access your Web pages? Remember, visitors do not like to wait. The 8-second rule is a good guideline to remember.

All of these items are important because they make your site more compatible to your visitors. It gives them a better experience, and it helps to keep them at your site.

What You'll Do

Find Broken Links

Fix Broken Links

Validate Web Pages

Check for HTML Browser Compatibility

Check for Balanced Code

Clean Up HTML

Clean Up Word HTML

Add Accessibility

Run Reports to Test a Site

View and Save Reports

Gather Download Statistics

Finding Broken Links

One of the most absolute, worst, horrible (enough adjectives for you) things is to create a Web site with links that don't work. You know what I'm talking about; you click on a link and a page pops up saying the link can't be found... I HATE it when that happens. A broken link to another site, although not acceptable, is sometimes understandable. For example, you have a link to a photography site that you like, the site goes down, and the owner never bothered to tell you. A few weeks later, you discover the problem and fix it; however, you know a lot of your visitors clicked that link. The worst types of broken links are those to pages within your own document... to pages that you created. The good news is that Dreamweaver provides you with the tools to make sure that all of your links (external and internal) function correctly using the Link Checker in the Results panel. You can check links in the current document, for the entire site, or for selected files.

Find Links

1. Open the Web page you want to find links (if you plan to check just one page).

2. Click the **Window** menu, point to **Results**, and then click **Link Checker**.

    ◆ You can also click the **Site** menu, and then click **Check Links Sitewide**.

3. Select from the following Link Checker options:

    ◆ Check Links. Click the **Check Links** button, and then select the command you want:

        ◆ **Check Links In Current Document.**

        ◆ **Check Links For Entire Current Local Site.**

        ◆ **Check Links For Selected Files In Site.**

    ◆ Stop. Click the **Stop** button to stop the current link check.

    ◆ Save Report. Click the **Save Report** button to save the report.

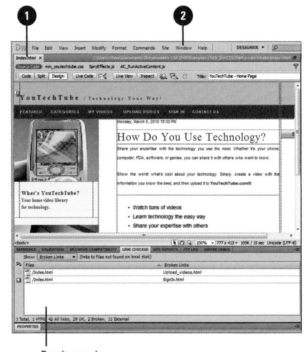

Results panel

④ Click the **Show** list arrow, and then choose from the following options:

◆ **Broken Links.** Select to display a listing of all files that contain broken links (default).

◆ **External Links.** Select to display a listing of all external links.

◆ **Orphaned Links.** Select to display all the files with no incoming links (available when choosing Check Links For Entire Local Site).

③   Link Checker tab

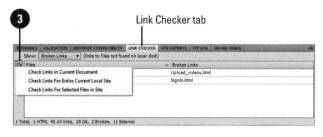

④ Shows broken links

Shows external links

Shows orphaned links

4a

Fixing Broken Links

After you find the broken links in your site using the Link Checker in the Results panel, you can use Dreamweaver tools to fix them. It's pretty simple. All you need to do is relink it. In the Link Checker, a broken link appears with a folder icon, which you can use to open a dialog box and select a reference to an active link. In the dialog box, you can enter a URL, select related parameters, and select whether the link is relative to the Document or Site Root. If a link changes over the entire site, you can use the Change Link Sitewide command to quickly redirect it to another place. If you want to delete a link, you can use this command.

Fix Links

1. Open the Web page you want to fix (if you plan to check just one page).

2. Click the **Window** menu, point to **Results**, and then click **Link Checker**.

3. If needed, click the **Check Links** button, and then select a Check Links command.

4. Select a broken link from the Link Checker panel.

5. Click the folder icon, associated with the broken link (located to the right of the broken link).

   The Select File dialog box appears.

6. Choose to select file names from the **Site Root**, **Server**, or **Data Sources** (default: Site Root).

7. Select the correct link from the Select File dialog box, or enter the correct link directly into the URL input box.

8. Select whether the link is relative to the **Document** or **Site Root** (default: Document).

9. To add any additional parameters to the link, click **Parameters**.

10. Click **OK** to update the link, and then click **Yes**, if prompted to fix remaining broken references to this file.

Fixing a broken link

Link Checker panel

Quick Link Change Sitewide

1 Click the **Site** menu, and then click **Change Link Sitewide**.

2 Enter a path or click the folder icon to browse and select the target file from which to unlink.

3 Enter a path or click the folder icon to browse and select the new file to link to.

4 Click **OK**.

Did You Know?

You can check links sitewide. Click the Site menu, and then click Check Links Sitewide to generate a quick report of all the links associated with the working site.

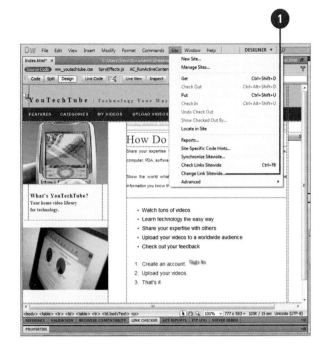

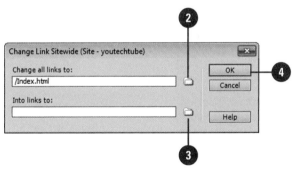

Validating Web Pages

The Validator in Dreamweaver allows you to quickly locate tag or syntax errors in your code. You can specify the tag-based languages against what the Validator should check, the specific problems that the Validator should check, and the types of errors that the Validator should report. Validating Web pages differs from checking for browser support in that the Validator checks for specific problems such as support for a specific version of HTML, or ColdFusion. Understanding the specific problems associated with a Web page help you to further refine the document to generate compliant code.

Set Validator Preferences

1 Click the **Dreamweaver** (Mac) or **Edit** (Win) menu, and then click **Preferences**.

2 Click the **Validator** category.

> **TIMESAVER** *Click the Validation button on the Validation tab in the Results panel, and then click Settings.*

3 Select the items that you want to validate by checking the box, located to the left of the item.

4 Click **Options**.

5 Select from the following validator options:

- ◆ **Display.** Select what options you want to display (**Errors, Warnings, Custom Messages,** or **Nesting Errors**).

- ◆ **Check For.** Select the options to check for **Quotes In Text** or **Entities In Text**.

6 Click **OK**.

7 Click **OK**.

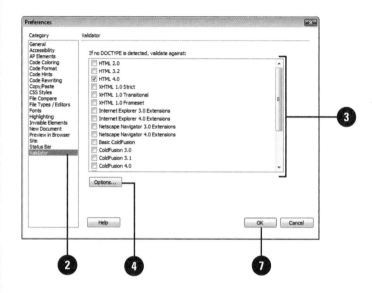

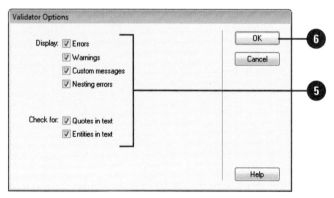

Validate a Web Page

1 Click the **Window** menu, point to **Results**, and then click **Validation**.

2 Select from the following Validator options:

◆ **Validate.** Click the **Validate** button, and then select the validate command you want: Validate Current Document, Validate Entire Current Local Site, and Validate Selected Files In Site, Settings.

◆ **Stop.** Click the **Stop** button to stop the current validation check.

◆ **More Info.** Select an item from the validator list of errors, and then click the **More Info** button to receive more information on the selected error.

◆ **Save Report.** Click the **Save Report** button to save the document as an XML file.

◆ **Browse Report.** Click the **Browse Report** button to view an ordered listing of the current errors in your default browser.

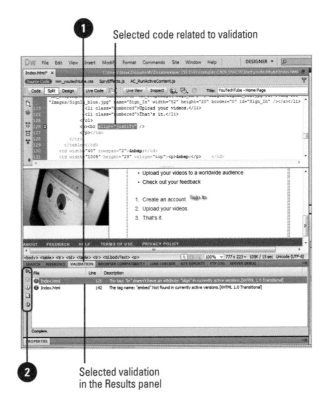

Selected code related to validation

Selected validation in the Results panel

Did You Know?

You can do further validation of your Web site online. The World Wide Web Consortium gives you the ability to check your HTML and CSS according to the latest standards. Visit *http://validator.w3.org/* to validate your HTML, or use *http://jigsaw.w3.org/css-validator/* to check your CSS.

Checking for HTML Browser Compatibility

The Browser Compatibility Check (BCC) analyzes the HTML and CSS on the open page and determines whether it has problems in certain browsers. When you run the BCC, it scans the open page and reports any potential HTML problems in the Results panel. Each potential problem is given a confidence rating, a circle. The amount of the circle filled in—quarter, half, three-quarter, or full—determines the occurrence probability level of the problem. Browser problems fall into three categories: serious (visible problem), warning (not supported), and informational (no visible effect). You can also check browser compatibility in Code view. When you refresh a page, Dreamweaver checks the code and inserts a wavy red underline under the name of every item creating an error in one of your predefined target browsers.

Check for HTML Browser Compatibility

1. Click the **File** menu, point to **Check Page**, and then click **Browser Compatibility**.

   The Results panel appears with the Browser Compatibility tab, indicating any potential problems.

2. Double-click an issue to select it.

   Information about the potential problem appears to the right in the Results panel.

3. To display the issue in the code, click the **Check Page** button on the Document window, and then click **Next Issue** or **Previous Issue**.

4. To exclude an issue from future checking, right-click the issue in the Results panel, and then click **Ignore Issue**.

   ◆ To edit the Ignore Issues list, click the green arrow in the Results panel, click **Edit Ignored Issues List**, delete the issue from the Exceptions.xml file, and then save and close the file.

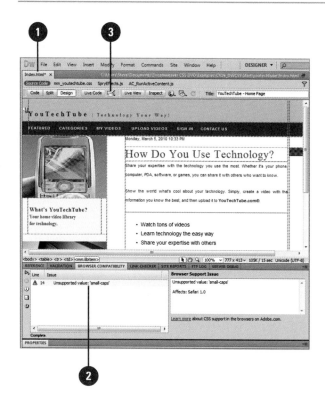

Check for HTML Browser Compatibility Using Code View

1 Open the document you want to check.

2 Switch to Code view.

3 After making a change in Code view, click the **Refresh** button in the Properties panel, or press F5.

A wavy red underline appears under the name of every item that's an error in one of your pre-defined target browsers.

NOTE *If Dreamweaver finds no unsupported markup, then nothing is underlined, and the Target Browser Check menu icon in the Document toolbar changes to indicate that there are no errors.*

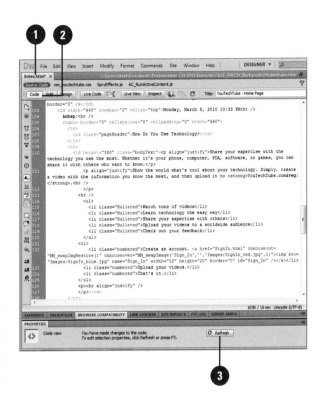

Did You Know?

You can check to see exactly what browser is not supported. Simply position the pointer to point to the red-underlined text, and a tool tip appears, indicating which browsers don't support that item.

You can select browsers to check. Click the Check Page button on the Document window, click Settings, select the browser and versions you want, and then click OK.

See Also

See "Checking for CSS Browser Compatibility" on page 234 for information on viewing and saving a BCC report.

Checking for Balanced Code

HTML is a very structured language and needs to follow specific rules to be error free. HTML code includes tags, parentheses (( )), braces ({ }), and square brackets ([ ]) that need to be balanced, meaning every opening tag, parentheses, brace, or bracket has a corresponding closing one. If HTML is not balanced, the code will not work properly and cause errors. You can use commands in Dreamweaver to make sure the tags, parentheses (( )), braces ({ }), and square brackets ([ ]) in a page are correctly balanced.

Check for Balanced Tags

① Open the Web page in Code view you want to check.

② Click to place the insertion point in the nested code you want to check.

③ Click the **Edit** menu, and then click **Select Parent Tag**.

The enclosing matching tags (including the contents) are selected in Code view.

④ Click the **Edit** menu, and then click **Select Parent Tag** again to continue checking tags.

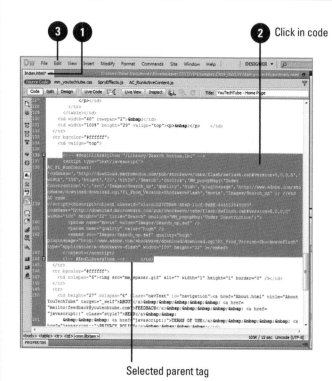

Click in code

Selected parent tag

Check for Balanced Parentheses, Braces, or Brackets

1 Open the Web page in Code view you want to check.

2 Click to place the insertion point in the code you want to check.

3 Click the **Edit** menu, and then click **Balanced Braces**.

The code between the enclosing parentheses, braces, or square brackets are selected in Code view.

4 Click the **Edit** menu, and then click **Balanced Braces** again to continue checking parentheses, braces, and square brackets.

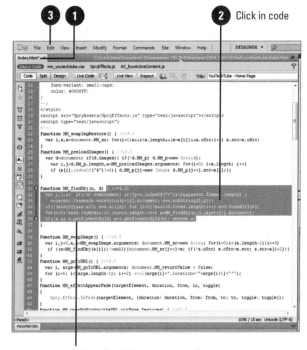

Click in code

Selected code between parentheses, braces, or square brackets

Cleaning Up HTML

Not all HTML documents are created equal. Some HTML documents contain problems with the overall coding; empty tags, individual font tags, improperly implemented tables… the list goes on and on. The good news is that Dreamweaver can automatically remove empty tags, combine nested font tags, and otherwise improve messy or unreadable HTML or XHTML code, and more. The question to ask is where did this sloppy code come from? Did Dreamweaver generate code that subsequently must be cleaned up? The answer to that question is no. However, not all the code associated with a particular Web page is generated by Dreamweaver. For example, you might switch from Design view to Code view, and enter your own code, or (and this is more likely), you might want to insert an HTML page into your Dreamweaver site that was written by another designer, or generated by another application. If that's the case, Dreamweaver can help you straighten out the code with a click of a button. It's really that simple.

Clean Up HTML or XHTML

1. Open the Web page you want to clean up.

2. Click the **Commands** menu, and then click **Clean Up HTML** or **Clean Up XHTML**.

3. Select the Remove check boxes you want from the following options:

   ◆ **Empty Container Tags.** Removes tags that have no content.

   ◆ **Redundant Nested Tags.** Removes all redundant instances of a tag.

   ◆ **Non-Dreamweaver HTML Comments.** Removes all comments not inserted by Dreamweaver.

   ◆ **Dreamweaver Special Markup.** Removes comments related to Dreamweaver code for automatically updating templates and library-based documents.

   ◆ **Specific Tags.** Removes custom tags specified in the Adjacent text box.

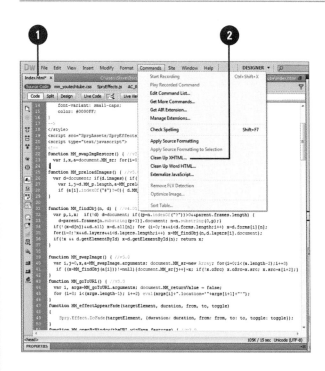

4 Select the Options check boxes you want from the following options:

◆ **Combine Nested <font> Tags When Possible.** Combines two or more font tags when they control the same range of text.

◆ **Show Log On Completion.** Displays an alert with details about the changes made to the document when the cleanup is complete. A pop-up window will appear listing what actions were performed in cleaning up the document.

5 Click **OK** to clean up the active document.

6 Review the clean up summary results, and then click **OK**.

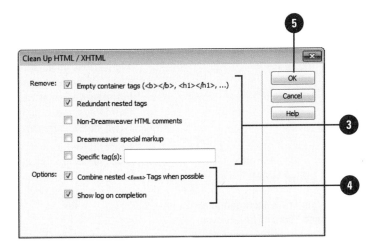

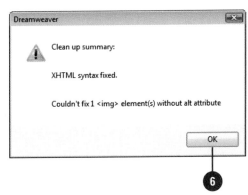

Cleaning Up Word HTML

If you have a Microsoft Word document saved as an HTML file, you can open it in Dreamweaver, and then use the Clean Up Word HTML command to convert the file into HTML compliant Web pages. The Clean Up Word HTML command removes unnecessary HTML code generated by Word. Before you convert a Word HTML file to a compliant Web page in Dreamweaver, it's a good idea to create a backup of the original Word (.doc and .htm) files, because you may not be able to reopen the HTML document in Word once you've applied the Clean Up Word HTML command.

Clean Up Word HTML

1. Open the HTML file created in Microsoft Word 97 or later you want to use in Dreamweaver.

2. Click the **Commands** menu, and then click **Clean Up Word HTML**.

3. Click the **Clean Up HTML From** list arrow, and then select the Word version you want to use.

4. Select from the following Basic options:

   ◆ **Remove All Word Specific Markup.** Removes Word-specific HTML code. You can select the options you want on the Details tab.

   ◆ **Clean Up CSS.** Removes Word-specific CSS.

   ◆ **Clean Up <font> Tags.** Removes HTML tags, converting the default body text to size 2 HTML text.

   ◆ **Fix Invalidly Nested Tags.** Removes the font markup tags generated by Word.

   ◆ **Apply Source Formatting.** Uses source formatting in the HTML Format Preferences dialog box.

◆ **Show Log On Completion.**
Displays an alert with details
about the changes made to the
document when the cleanup is
complete. A pop-up window
will appear listing what actions
were performed in cleaning up
the document.

5 Click the **Detailed** tab.

6 Select from the following
Advanced options:

◆ **Remove Word Specific
Markup.** Select to enable the
options.

  ◆ XML from <html> tag

  ◆ Word meta and link tags
  from <head>

  ◆ Word XML markup

  ◆ Conditional tags and their
  contents

  ◆ Remove empty paragraphs
  and margins from styles

◆ **Clean Up CSS.** Select to enable
the options.

  ◆ Remove inline CSS styles
  when possible

  ◆ Remove any style property
  that starts with "mso"

  ◆ Remove any non-CSS style
  declaration

  ◆ Remove all CSS styles from
  table rows and cells

7 Click **OK** to perform the
conversion.

8 Review the clean up summary
results, and then click **OK**.

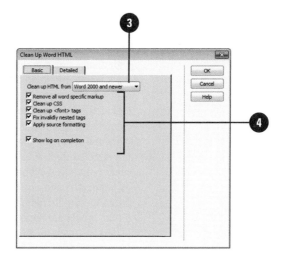

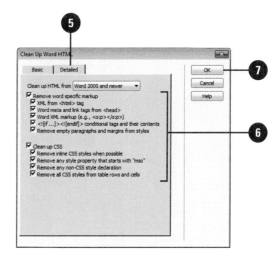

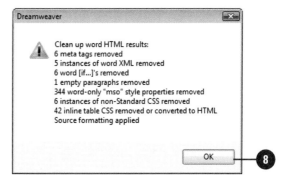

Adding Accessibility

When you create accessible pages, you need to associate information, such as labels and descriptions, with your page objects to make your content accessible to all users. Web accessibility means that people with disabilities can use the Web. In addition, older people with changing abilities due to aging have better access to the Web. Web accessibility encompasses all disabilities that affect access to the Web, including visual, auditory, physical, speech, cognitive, and neurological disabilities. Dreamweaver understands the importance of Web accessibility and gives you the means to make your pages more accessible to the handicapped. As a matter of fact, Dreamweaver offers screen reader support, keyboard navigation, and operating system accessibility support. A screen reader speaks the text that appears on the computer screen. In addition, it reads non-textual information, such as button labels or image descriptions in the application. Dreamweaver supports JAWS for Windows from Freedom Scientific, and Window-Eyes screen readers from GW Micro. When designing pages to be compliant with screen readers, understand that the screen reader starts reading in the upper-left corner of the Document window. In addition, since the policy on accessibility standards changes every year, Dreamweaver gives you the ability to check your pages against the current standards. Whenever you create a new Form object, Frame, Media or Images item, a dialog box appears with accessibility options.

Set Accessibility Preferences

1. Click the **Dreamweaver** (Mac) or **Edit** (Win) menu, and then click **Preferences**.

2. Click the **Accessibility** category.

3. Select the items you want to display accessibility options for:

   ♦ **Form Objects**

   ♦ **Frames**

   ♦ **Media**

   ♦ **Images**

4. Click **OK**.

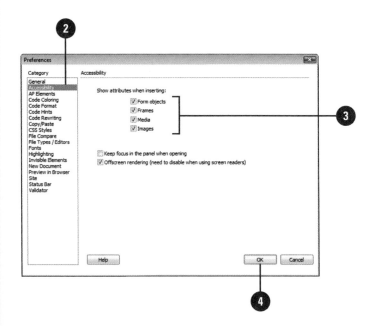

Add Accessibility

1. Open the Web page with the accessibility you want to add.

2. Add a specific item to the Web page (in this example, an image was added).

3. Select from the following options in the Image Tag Accessibility Attributes dialog box:

   ◆ **Alternate Text.** Reader programs use the text to describe the item to the visually impaired. For example, if it were a Home button, you might add the text, Home Page. In addition, the text pops up in a small window, when the visitor's mouse hovers over it.

   ◆ **Long Description.** Displays a file that contains a longer textual description of the object. For example, you might have an image of a sunset, and you want to give visually impaired readers a more in depth description. Enter the URL to the file, or click the folder icon to browse for it.

4. Click **OK**.

3 For an image

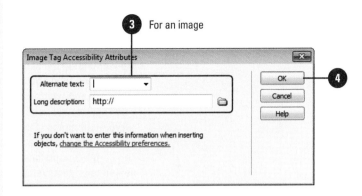

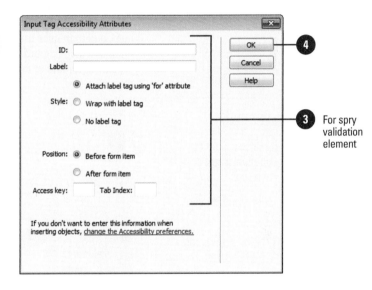

3 For spry validation element

Running Reports to Test a Site

Dreamweaver has a lot of site reports for you to select from; for example, you can run site reports on workflow or HTML attributes, including accessibility, for the current document, selected files, or the entire site. In addition, workflow reports can improve cooperation among designers working on the same Web site. Workflow reports display checked out files and who checked them out, which files have Design Notes attached, and what, if any, files have been modified. To generate workflow reports, you need active Design notes and access to the remote server holding the information. In addition, HTML reports enable you to compile and generate reports for HTML attributes. For example, you can check for combinable nested font tags, missing Alt text, redundant nested tags, removable empty tags, and untitled documents. Many of the site report items have options to help you further refine what you're looking for. For example, the Recently Modified item has options to allow you to define what recently modified means. Simply select the item, and then click the Report Settings button located at the bottom of the Reports dialog box. Site reports can and should be conducted on a regular basis during the construction of any Web site, be it complex or simple.

Run Reports to Test a Site

1. Open the Web page you want to get a report (if you plan to get a report on just one page).

2. Click the **Site** menu, and then click **Reports**.

3. Click the **Report On** list arrow, and then select from the following options:

   ◆ **Current Document.**

   ◆ **Entire Current Local Site.**

   ◆ **Selected Files In Site.**

   ◆ **Folder.** Select the folder you want a report.

4. Select from the following site Workflow (requires remote server access) options:

   ◆ **Checked Out By.** Lists what designer checked out what files and when.

   ◆ **Design Notes.** Lists all design notes for the selected report.

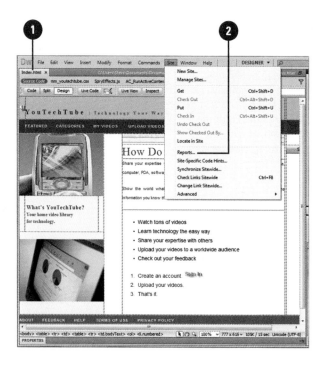

- ◆ **Recently Modified.** Lists all files modified since the last check.

⑤ Select from the following site HTML Reports options:

- ◆ **Combinable Nested Font Tags.** Lists any nested font tags that can be combined to create tighter code.

- ◆ **Missing Alt Text.** Lists any missing alternate <alt> text.

- ◆ **Redundant Nested Tags.** Lists any redundant nested tags.

- ◆ **Removable Empty Tags.** Lists any empty tags.

- ◆ **Untitled Documents.** Lists any documents named Untitled.

⑥ To set specific options for a report, select the report, click **Report Settings**, specify the options you want (options vary depending on the report), and then click **OK**.

⑦ Click the **Run** button to generate the report.

> **IMPORTANT** *After you run an HTML report, use the Clean Up HTML command on the Site menu to correct any HTML errors the reports listed.*

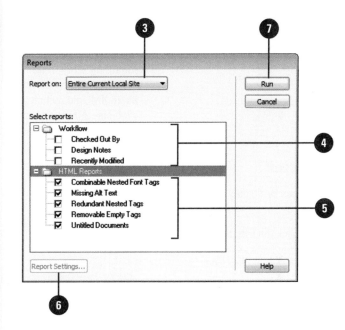

Report results

Did You Know?

You can access more reports on the Dreamweaver Exchange Web site. If you need additional reports, click the Help menu, and then click Dreamweaver Exchange to search for the ones you want.

Viewing and Saving Reports

After you run a report, the results appear on the Site Reports tab in the Results panel. The Site Reports tab displays information in columns relating to the reports you selected. If you don't see enough information regarding a report item, you can display additional reference material in the Results panel. In the Site Reports tab, you can also save a report as an XML file, which you can import into a database, spreadsheet, or Web site. After you import the XML data into another file, you can print or use the report information like any other XML data.

View a Site Report

1. Create a report or display an existing one.

   ◆ **Create.** Click the **Site** menu, click **Reports,** select report options, and then click **Run**.

   ◆ **Existing.** Click the **Window** menu, point to **Results**, and then click **Site Reports**.

   The Results panel appears, displaying the Site Reports tab with report details.

2. The Site Reports tab in the Results panel displays the following:

   ◆ **Item Icon.** An icon appears to the left of the item indicating the type of error or problem associated with the file.

   ◆ **File.** Contains the name of the file.

   ◆ **Line.** Displays the line number of the code associated with the file.

   ◆ **Description.** Displays a description of the error.

3. To find out more information about a report item, select the report item, and then click **More Info**.

   The information appears on the Reference tab in the Results panel.

4. To open the document associated with the problem or error, double click the report item.

Site report results

Save a Site Report

1. Create a report or display an existing one.

   ◆ **Create.** Click the **Site** menu, click **Reports,** select report options, and then click **Run.**

   ◆ **Existing.** Click **Window,** point to **Results,** and then click the **Site Reports** tab.

   The Results panel appears, displaying the Site Reports tab with report details.

2. Click the **Save Report** button in the Results panel.

3. Select a location where you want to save the site report.

4. Click **Save.**

See Also

See "Running Reports to Test a Site" on page 468 for information on creating a site report.

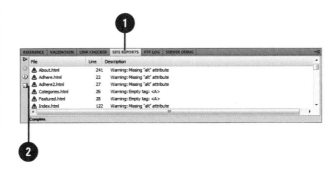

Gathering Download Statistics

There's an expression, and I'm sure that you've heard it before. It goes something like this: Build it and they will come. That might be true of baseball fields; however, I'm not so sure it's true of Web sites. Building it is one thing… building it in an efficient way so that visitors will stay for the experience is quite another. Dreamweaver gives you the ability to gauge how well your pages download, based on a user-defined value. For example, the rule on the Internet today is called the 8-second rule. That simply means that visitors, on average, will only wait 8 seconds for your initial (home) page to load, before they get bored and go somewhere else… that's not a whole lot of time. In response, Dreamweaver lets you view download statistics, based on the average bandwidth of your average viewer.

Change Download Statistics Preferences

1 Click the **Dreamweaver** (Mac) or **Edit** (Win) menu, and then click **Preferences**.

2 Click the **Status Bar** category.

3 Click the **Connection Speed** list arrow, and then select from the pre-defined bandwidth options, or enter in a user-defined bandwidth.

4 Click **OK**.

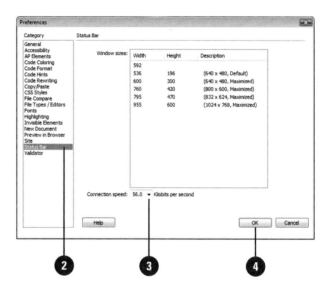

Did You Know?

You can quickly view Download statistics. View the file size and subsequent download time in the Download Statistics section of the Document window (located in the lower-right corner of the document window).

You can determine the speed of your file transfer rate to the Internet. Bandwidth is the amount of data that can be transferred over the network in a fixed amount of time. On the Net, it is usually expressed in bits per second (bps) or in higher units like Mbps (millions of bits per second). A 28.8 modem can deliver 28,800 bps, a T1 line is about 1.5 Mbps.

Managing a Web Site

Introduction

In Chapter 2, you learned how to defined a site using Basic site settings. With the basic settings in place, you can use the Advanced site settings to fine-tune and customize the site to meet your specific needs. In this chapter, you learn how to modify advanced site setup settings to better manage and control your site.

The Site Setup dialog box allows you to define how you want your local site, remote site, and testing server to work, and set related options for updating and managing different types of files on your site.

The local site contains all the Web page files for the site as well as all images, cascading style sheet (CSS) files, templates, and other dependent files. In order to publish your site on the Web, you need to define the remote site on a Web server, and then upload the files from the local site to the remote site. If you created dynamic pages in Dreamweaver, you need to define a testing server to try them out. Dreamweaver needs a testing server to generate and display dynamic pages during development.

In addition to the main site settings for the local, remote and testing sites, you can also set related options in the following areas: cloaking, design notes, file view columns display, Adobe Contribute compatibility, templates, and spry assets.

Setting Advanced Site Definitions

Dreamweaver provides a choice of two methods to define a site: the Basic and Advanced site settings (**New!**). In Chapter 2, you defined a site using the Basic settings. In addition to the basic site settings, you can set up remote and testing servers, set up version control, and specify other advanced settings. The Advanced settings—Local Info, Cloaking, Design Notes, File View Columns, Contribute, Templates, and Spry categories—allow you to fine-tune and customize the site to meet your specific needs. The Site Setup dialog box (**New!**) doesn't force you to complete the site setup unless it's required. As you work on your site and a task needs information from the Site Setup dialog box, Dreamweaver opens it and highlights the required setting.

Set Advanced Site Definitions

1. Click the **Site** menu, point to **Manage Sites**, click **New,** and then click **Site**, or select a site, and then click **Edit**.

2. Select a category, and then specify the site options you want:

   ◆ **Servers.** Specifies the Web site server location to upload the site files to the Web server and creates a place to act like a public server to test the applications and connections to the database. (**New!**)

   ◆ **Version Control.** Adds the version control system provided by Subversion to manage file and folder changes.

3. Click the **Advanced Settings** category.

4. Select a category, and then specify the site options you want:

   ◆ **Local Info.** Specifies the site files location and enables site management options.

   ◆ **Cloaking.** Cloaking allows you to specify file types or specific files that you do not want uploaded to the server.

   ◆ **Design Notes.** Adds notes to files in the working site. Notes are stored in a separate file.

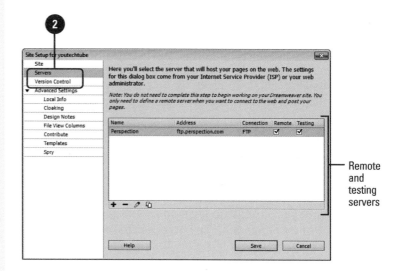

Remote and testing servers

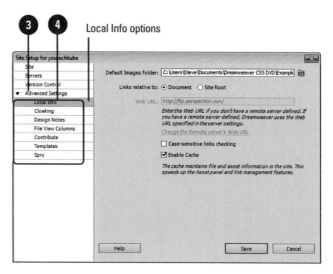

Local Info options

◆ **File View Columns.** Customizes the appearance of the expanded Files panel.

◆ **Contribute.** Adobe Contribute allows you to maintain and update content on existing Web sites, requiring no training or knowledge of HTML.

   ◆ **Compatibility.** Select to enable the Contribute feature (requires the installation of the Contribute program).

◆ **Templates.** This option controls how templates are used within a site.

   ◆ **Template Updating.** Select to prevent the rewriting of a document's relative path (recommended).

◆ **Spry.** Spry is a JavaScript library for Web designers that provides functionality that allows designers to build pages that provide a richer experience for their users.

   ◆ **Spry Assets Folder.** Enter the path to the Spry folder, or click the folder icon to browse and select the Spry folder.

⑤ Click **Save**, and then click **OK** to cache files, if necessary.

⑥ Click **Done** to close the Manage Sites dialog box.

See Also

See "Creating a Web Site" on page 18 for information on using the Basic tab in the Site Setup dialog box.

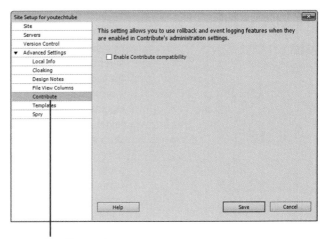
Contribute options

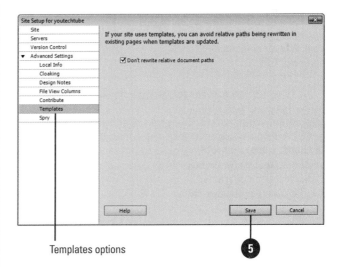
Templates options

Defining Local Info for a Site

In order for Dreamweaver to keep track of links between Web pages and dependent files, it is necessary to define a folder on the hard disk, or mapped drive, as the local root folder and to save all the files for the site in that folder. The local root folder contains the Web page files for the site as well as all images, cascading style sheet (CSS) files, templates, and other dependent files. After the site is defined, Dreamweaver creates and saves pages for the site inside the local root folder. Then the contents of that local root folder are uploaded to the Web server. The local root folder and the folder on the server should have exactly the same folder structure. Dreamweaver automatically replicates the folder structure of the local root folder on the server when it uploads your files, and that make future maintenance of the site efficient and easy. When you define the site, the local folder should be easy to access.

Define the Local Info for a Site

1. Click the **Site** menu, point to **Manage Sites**, click **New,** and then click **Site**, or select a site, and then click **Edit**.

2. Click the **Site** category.

3. Specify the following information for the Local Info category:

   ◆ **Site Name.** Enter a name for your site in the Site Name box; avoid any special characters, but it may contain capitals and spaces.

   ◆ **Local Site Folder.** Enter the path to the Local root folder, or click the folder icon to browse and select the folder that you want to contain the site files.

   IMPORTANT *Avoid using the Dreamweaver program folder as the location for the local root folder.*

4. Click the **Advanced Settings** category.

5. Click the **Local Info** category.

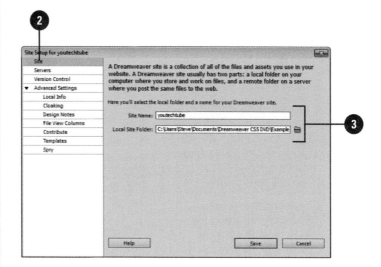

6 Select the options you want:

♦ **Default Images Folder.** Enter the path to the Default Images folder, or click the folder icon to browse and select the folder you want to contain the site image files. Select a folder in the local root folder.

♦ **Links Relative To.** Select to set your links relative to the documents or the site's root folder.

♦ **Web URL.** Click the **Change the Remove server's Web URL** link, enter an HTTP Web URL address for your site, and then click **Save**.

NOTE *The HTTP Address field is useful if you are using absolute paths to refer to local files within your site, and for the link checker to determine if your links refer to your own site.*

♦ **Case-sensitive Links Checking.** Select to check your links to make sure the case of the links matches the case of the filenames. This option is useful on UNIX systems where file names are case-sensitive.

NOTE *This option is only for checking in Dreamweaver, and does not impact how the links are used on the server.*

♦ **Enable Cache.** Select to maintain file and asset information in a separate cache file (recommended), which speeds up most Dreamweaver operations.

7 Click **Save**, and then click **OK** to cache files, if necessary.

8 Click **Done** to close the Manage Sites dialog box.

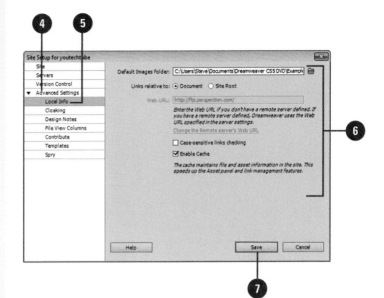

Defining Remote Info for a Site

In order to publish your site, you will first have to define the remote site, and then upload the files to a remote folder on that site. A remote folder is where you store your files for testing and publication. Dreamweaver defines this folder as the remote site. You can define the remote server at any time during the development process. However, before you can define the remote site, you must have access to a remote Web server, such as your ISP's server, and you will need information such as: path, password, and login ID. You'll also need to find out the best access method, either FTP (File Transfer Protocol), SFTP (Secure File Transfer Protocol), Local/Network, WebDAV (Web-based Distributed Authoring and Versioning), or RDS (Remote Data Services). Once you have this information, you simply add it to the setup for the working site.

Define the Remote Info for a Site

1. Click the **Site** menu, point to **Manage Sites**, click **New**, and then click **Site**, or select a site, and then click **Edit**.

2. Click the **Servers** category.

3. Click the **Add New Server** button, or select an existing server, and then click the **Edit Existing Server** button.

4. Click the **Basic** tab.

5. Enter or revise a server name.

6. Click the **Connect Using** list arrow, select a remote server, and then specify the following information for the remote server:

   - **FTP** or **SFTP.** Select if you connect to your remote server using File Transfer Protocol (FTP) or Secure FTP, which is useful for fast file transfer and working remotely.

     - **FTP Address.** Enter the FTP address or IP address that calls the server, and then specify a port number as needed.

     - **Username.** Enter your login name to access the server.

Use to add, delete, edit, and duplicate servers.

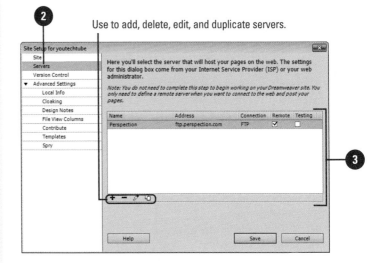

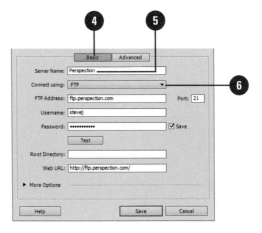

◆ **Password.** Enter your password to access the server. Select the **Save** check box to save it.

NOTE *Click the Test button to test the connection between the local and remote server.*

◆ **Root Directory.** Enter the host directory name. The Host Directory specifies the exact folder on the server where the files will go (optional).

◆ **Web URL.** Enter the Web address URL to the server.

◆ For FTP Only, click **More Options** arrow to expand the dialog box.

◆ **Use Passive FTP.** Select if the server security requires the files to be transferred in passive mode.

◆ **Use IPv6 Transfer Mode.** Select if you are using an IPv6 (Internet Protocol version 6) enabled FTP server.

◆ **Use Proxy, as defined in Preferences.** Select if your computer is behind a Firewall. Click the **Preferences** link to set options in Site Preferences.

◆ **Use FTP Performance Optimization.** Deselect if Dreamweaver cannot connect to your server.

◆ **Use Alternative FTP Move Method.** Select if you get errors either when rollbacks are enabled or when moving files.

Continue Next Page

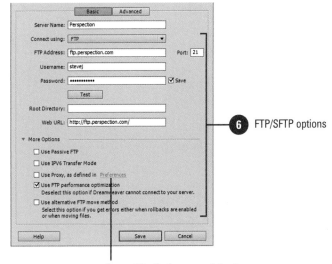

6 FTP/SFTP options

Opens Site Preferences dialog box

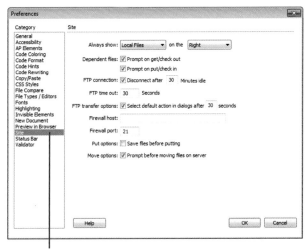

Site preferences

Continued from Previous Page

◆ **Local/Network.** Select if the server lives on a local area network.

    ◆ **Server Folder.** Enter the path to the Local/Network folder, or click the folder icon to browse and select the folder on the server that you want to contain the site files.

    ◆ **Web URL.** Enter the Web address URL to the server.

◆ **WebDAV.** WebDAV (Web-based Distributed Authoring and Versioning) allows you to manage pages to and from a WebDAV server.

    ◆ **URL.** Enter the address for the WebDAV server.

    ◆ **Username.** Enter your login name to access the server.

    ◆ **Password.** Enter your password to access the server. Select the **Save** check box to save it.

NOTE *Click the Test button to test the connection between the local and remote server.*

    ◆ **Web URL.** Enter the Web address URL to the server.

◆ **RDS.** RDS (Remote Data Services) allows you to work with live Web pages on the server.

    ◆ **Settings.** Click Settings, enter in the Host Name, Port, Full Host Directory, User Name, Password for the RDS site, and then click OK.

Local/Network options

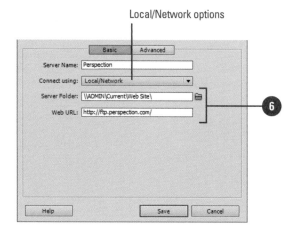

WebDAV options

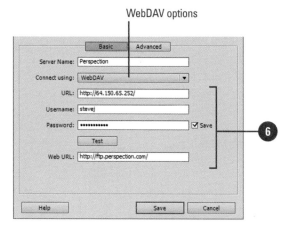

RDS options

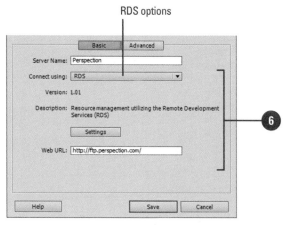

(7) Click the **Advanced** tab.

(8) Specify the following information for the remote server:

- ◆ **Maintain Synchronization Information.** Select to automatically synchronize your local and remote files.

- ◆ **Automatically Upload Files To Server On Save.** Select to automatically upload files to the Web server each time the page is saved (not recommended).

- ◆ **Enable File Check Out.** Select to use the Check In/Out system to manage file development by a team.

  - ◆ **Check Out Files When Opening.** Enter the address for the WebDAV server.

  - ◆ **Check-out Name.** Enter your login name to access the server.

  - ◆ **Email Address.** Enter your password to access the server.

(9) Click **Save** to save the server settings.

(10) To enable or disable a remote server, select or deselect the server check box under Remote.

(11) Click **Save**, and then click **OK** to cache files, if necessary.

(12) Click **Done** to close the Manage Sites dialog box.

Configure RDS server settings

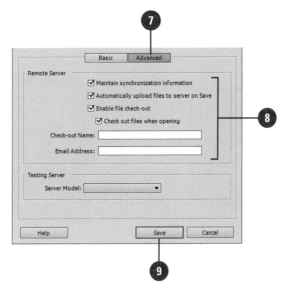

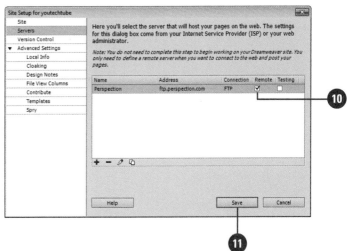

Defining the Testing Server

If you created dynamic pages in Dreamweaver, you need to define a testing server to try them out. Dreamweaver needs a testing server to generate and display dynamic pages during development. You can define a testing server on your local computer, a network development server, or a remote production server. For example, you can create a place to act like a public server to test the applications and connections to the database. Before you can define a testing server, you need to define a local site folder and remote site server.

Define the Testing Server

1. Click the **Site** menu, point to **Manage Sites**, click **New**, and then click **Site**, or select a site, and then click **Edit**.

2. Click the **Servers** category.

3. Click the **Add New Server** button, or select an existing server, and then click the **Edit Existing Server** button.

4. Click the **Basic** tab.

5. Click the **Connect Using** list arrow, and then select an access method: FTP, SFTP, Local/Network, or WebDAV.

6. Specify the options you want for the selected Connect type; options vary depending on the type.

7. Click the **Advanced** tab.

8. Click the **Server Model** list arrow, and then select a server: ASP JavaScript, ASP VBScript, ASP.NET C#, ASP.NET VB, ColdFusion, JSP, or PHP MySQL.

9. Click **Save** to save the server settings.

10. To enable or disable a testing server, select or deselect the server check box under Testing.

11. Click **Save**, and then click **OK** to cache files, if necessary.

12. Click **Done** to close the Manage Sites dialog box.

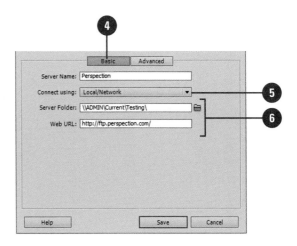

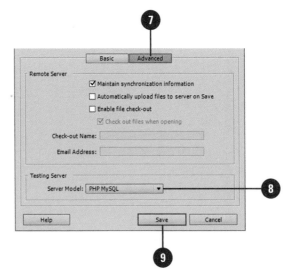

Defining Version Control

When you work in a team environment where many contributors make changes to site files, you'll want to use a version control system to keep track of them. Subversion is a version control system that works along with Dreamweaver to help you maintain version histories of your site files. Subversion maintains a repository of the file and folder structure of your site on the Subversion server, which is the normal installation (available at *http://subversion.tiggris.org*), however, you can set it up on your own computer. The files and folders are not actually stored on the server. Subversion maintains a database of changes, which allows you to view a file history and compare it with previous versions. Before you can use Subversion, you need to define server settings in the Site Setup dialog box.

Define Version Control

1. Click the **Site** menu, point to **Manage Sites**, click **New,** and then click **Site**, or select a site, and then click **Edit**.

2. Click the **Version Control** category.

3. Click the **Access** list arrow, and then click **Subversion**.

4. Click the **Protocol** list arrow, and then select a server protocol used by the Subversion server: **HTTP**, **HTTPS**, **SVN**, or **SVN+SSH**.

5. Enter the URL address to the Subversion server.

6. Enter the folder location for your web site files. This can be the root or a subfolder.

7. Enter a port number as needed.

8. Enter a username and password.

9. Click **Test** to make sure your connection to the server is valid.

10. Click **Save**, and then click **OK** to cache files, if necessary.

11. Click **Done** to close the Manage Sites dialog box.

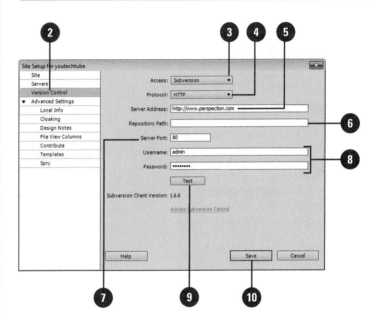

Defining Site Cloaking

Site cloaking allows you to exclude folders and files from certain operations, such as using Put, Get, Check In, and Check Out commands, generating reports, finding newer local and newer remote files, checking and changing sitewide links, synchronizing, using the Assets panel, and updating templates and libraries. You can cloak individual folders and specific file types; however, you cannot cloak a specific individual file. Before you can use site cloaking, you need to enable it and specify the file types you want to cloak.

Define Site Cloaking

1. Click the **Site** menu, point to **Manage Sites**, click **New**, and then click **Site**, or select a site, and then click **Edit**.

2. Click the **Advanced Settings** category.

3. Click the **Cloaking** category.

4. Select the **Enable Cloaking** check box to turn on cloaking.

5. Select the **Cloak Files Ending With** check box to turn on cloaking for specific file types, and then add the file extensions to the list of cloaked items. Separate multiple file types with one space (do not use a comma or semicolon). You can also enter or delete file suffixes you want to cloak or uncloak.

6. Click **Save**, and then click **OK** to cache files, if necessary.

7. Click **Done** to close the Manage Sites dialog box.

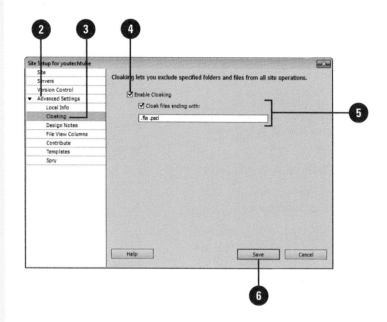

Setting File View Columns Options

When you view a Web site in the expanded Files panel, information about the files appears in columns in a similar fashion as files in Windows Explorer (Win) or the Finder (Mac). You can use the File View Columns options to customize the appearance of the expanded Files panel. For example, you can hide, add, delete, rename, and reorder columns. In addition, you can share columns with connected users, and associate columns with a Design Note.

Set File View Columns Options

1. Click the **Site** menu, point to **Manage Sites**, click **New,** and then click **Site**, or select a site, and then click **Edit**.

2. Click the **Advanced Settings** category.

3. Click the **File View Columns** category.

4. Specify any of the following File View Columns options:

   ◆ **Enable Column Sharing.** Select to modify anything but the order of preexisting columns.

   ◆ **Add, Delete, or Edit Column.** Select a column, click a button, specify the info below, and then click **Save**.

     ◆ **Column Name.** Enter a name for the selected column.

     ◆ **Associate With Design Note.** Select a design note setting.

     ◆ **Align.** Click and choose how column data are aligned.

     ◆ **Show.** Select to show the specific column.

     ◆ **Share With All Users Of This Site.** Select to share with all users of the site.

   ◆ **Move Up or Down.** Use the arrows to change the order.

5. Click **Save**, and then click **OK** to cache files, if necessary.

6. Click **Done** to close the Manage Sites dialog box.

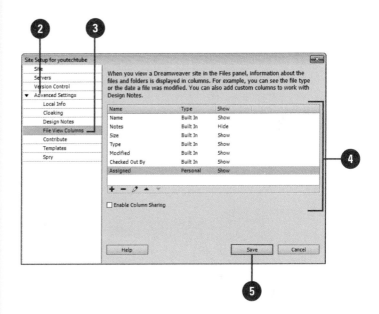

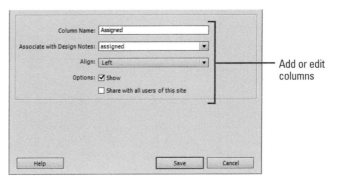

Add or edit columns

Using Design Notes

Design Notes are notes that you create for the files in the working site. Although Design Notes are connected with the file they describe, they are stored separately in a file. Design Notes help you to keep track of file data related with your individual site documents. For example, if you copy a document from one site to another, you can add Design Notes for that document, with the comment that the original document is in the other site folder. In another way, Design Notes can keep track of sensitive information that you can't put inside a document for security reasons. When importing graphics into Dreamweaver, the Design Notes file is automatically copied into your site along with the graphic. Design Notes also can keep track of integration with Fireworks and Flash and allow communication on subjects ranging from the status of the page to marketing tactics. Before you can attach Design Notes to files, you need to enable it.

Enable Design Notes

1. Click the **Site** menu, point to **Manage Sites**, click **New**, and then click **Site**, or select a site, and then click **Edit**.

2. Click the **Advanced Settings** category.

3. Click the **Design Notes** category.

4. Select the **Maintain Design Notes** check box to enable Design Notes.

5. Select the **Enable Upload Design Notes For Sharing** check box to share your notes with others working on the site.

6. Click **Save**, and then click **OK** to cache files, if necessary.

7. Click **Done** to close the Manage Sites dialog box.

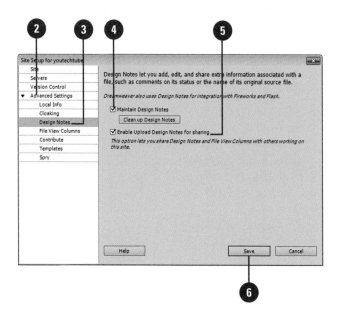

Did You Know?

You can erase all Design Notes not associated with a file. In the Site Setup dialog box, click the Design Notes category, click the Clean Up button to permanently erase all Design Notes not directly associated with a file, and then click OK.

Link Design Notes with Files

1. Click the **Window** menu, and then click **Files** to display the Files panel.

2. Right-click (Win) or Control-click (Mac) the file you want to add notes, and then click **Design Notes**.

    The Design Notes dialog box opens.

3. Click the **Basic Info** tab, and then add notes using the following options:

    ◆ **Status.** Click the list arrow, and then select the current status from the available options.

    ◆ **Notes.** Enter in notes on this file.

    ◆ **Insert Date.** Click the button to add the current date to the notes.

    ◆ **Show When File Is Opened.** Select to display these notes whenever the file is first opened.

4. Click the **All Info** tab, and then view and modify notes using the following options:

    ◆ **Add/Subtract.** Click the Plus (+) or Minus (-) buttons to add or remove specific notes.

    ◆ **Info.** Displays a list of all Design Notes for the selected file.

    ◆ **Name.** Displays the name of the note, or allows you to type in a name, if this is a new note.

    ◆ **Value.** Displays the content of the note, or allows you to enter content, if this is a new note.

5. Click **OK**.

Selected file for notes

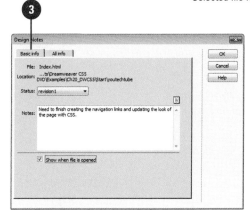

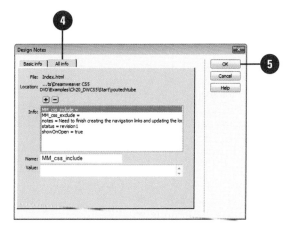

Viewing Design Notes

After you create notes for files in your working site, you can display the files that contain notes in the expanded Files panel. A Design Notes icon appears in the Notes column. The Design Notes icons only appear in the expanded Files panel when the Notes option is set to show in the File View Columns category of the Site Setup dialog box. In the Files panel, you can double-click the Design Notes icon to open the Design Notes dialog box, where you can view the Design Notes for the selected file on the Basic Info tab.

View Design Notes

1 Click the **Window** menu, and then click **Files** to display the Files panel.

2 Use one of the following methods:

◆ Right-click (Win) or Control-click (Mac) the file with notes you want to view, and then click **Design Notes**.

◆ Double-click the file with notes you want to open in the Files panel; the Show When File Is Opened check box needs to be selected in the Design Notes dialog box.

◆ Double-click the yellow Design Notes icon in the Notes column of the Files panel.

IMPORTANT *To show the yellow Design Notes, click the Site menu, click Manage Sites, select your working site, click Edit, click the File View Columns category, select Notes in the list panel, and then select the Show check box on the Advanced tab.*

The Design Notes dialog box opens, displaying the Basic Info tab with any notes for the page. You can click the All Info tab to display HTML note information about the page.

3 Click **OK**.

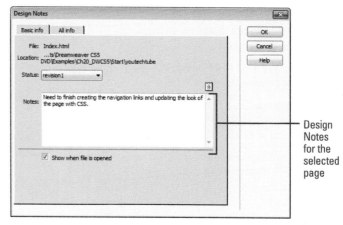

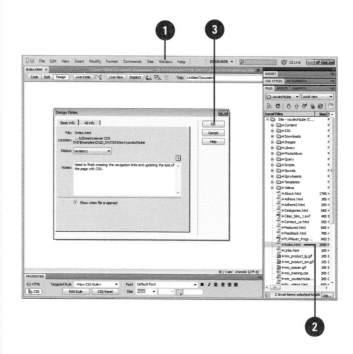

Design Notes for the selected page

Moving Your Site to the Internet

Introduction

You've worked a long time; created graphics, wrote text, built tables and layers. Now, the big moment has come... it's moving day for your Web site. However, this is not like any moving day you've ever experienced. No packing of bags, or calling the movers, because Dreamweaver has taken care of all the little details.

Dreamweaver includes a number of features for managing files and transferring files to and from a remote site (also called the remote folder). When you transfer files between local and remote sites, Dreamweaver maintains copies of the file and folder structures between the local and remote sites. If you're transferring files to the remote site, Dreamweaver will automatically create necessary folders when they do not exist. It's even possible to synchronize the files between your local and remote sites; Dreamweaver copies files in both directions as necessary and removes unwanted files when appropriate.

Dreamweaver contains features to make collaborative work on a Web site easier. You can check files in and out of a remote server so that other members of a Web team can see who is working on a file. You can also use Subversion, a version control system that works along with Dreamweaver, to help you maintain version histories of your site files.

In addition, Dreamweaver allows you to use the Business Catalyst extension to connect you directly to a hosted online business site, where you can add, edit, delete, upload pages and templates in Dreamweaver, and use pre-build code modules, such as search, forums, blogs, password protected areas, web forms, and online stores, without programming from the Business Catalyst panel.

What You'll Do

Set Site File Preferences

Manage Site Files with the Files Panel

Transfer Files

Compare Local and Remote Files

Check Site Files In and Out

Manage Site Files Versions with Subversion

Work with Business Catalyst Site Files

Synchronize Site Files

Cloak and Uncloak Files

Setting Site File Preferences

Before you start transferring files from your local site to a remote site, you should specify site preferences to control the way files transfer over the Web. You can set FTP (File Transfer Protocol) connection options and firewall settings. If you're not sure how to set these options, check with your ISP (Internet Service Provider). In addition to file transfer settings, you can also set preferences for the viewing of your files in the Files panel. You can indicate which site, either local or remote, you want to always display in the Files panel, whether to prompt for confirmation when you get/check out or put/check in files, and whether to automatically save files before being put onto the remote site.

Set Site Preferences

1. Click the **Dreamweaver** (Mac) or **Edit** (Win) menu, and then click **Preferences**.

2. Click the **Site** category.

3. Select from the following options:

    ◆ **Always Show.** Indicates which site (local or remote) is always shown, and in which Files panel pane (left or right) the local and remote files appear.

    ◆ **Dependent Files.** Displays a prompt for transferring dependent files (such as images, external style sheets, etc.) that the browser loads when it loads the HTML file. The Prompt On Get/Check Out and Prompt On Put/Check In are selected by default.

    ◆ **FTP Connection.** Enter whether the connection to the remote site is terminated after the specified number of minutes has passed with no activity.

    ◆ **FTP Time Out.** Enter the number of seconds in which Dreamweaver attempts to make a connection with the remote server.

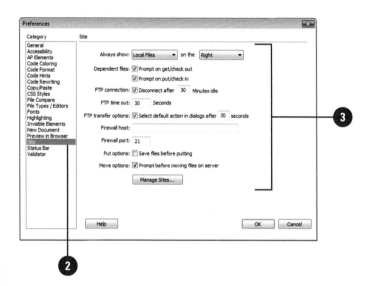

- ◆ **FTP Transfer Options.** Select whether Dreamweaver chooses the default option, after a specified number of seconds, when a dialog box appears during a file transfer and there is no user response.

- ◆ **Firewall Host.** If your site is behind a firewall, enter the address of the proxy server through which you connect to outside servers.

- ◆ **Firewall Port.** Enter the port in your firewall through which you pass to connect to the remote server. Leave Firewall host, and Firewall port blank, if you are not behind a firewall.

- ◆ **Put Options.** Select to automatically save files before being put onto the remote site.

- ◆ **Move Options.** Select to prompt you before moving files on the server.

- ◆ **Manage Sites.** Click to open the Manage Sites dialog box.

④ Click **OK**.

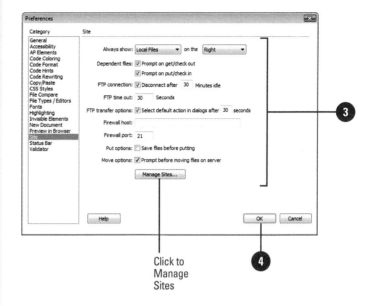

Click to
Manage
Sites

Manage Sites dialog box

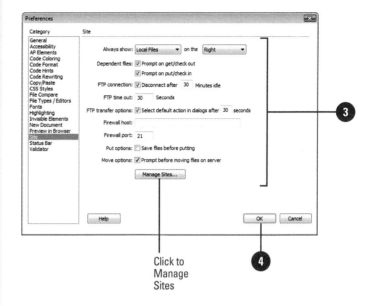

Managing Site Files with the Files Panel

Once a site is created, it's important to work with and organize all of the files associated with the active working site. You can organize and manage your site files and folders whether they are part of a Dreamweaver site on a server you've connected to, or on your local drive or desktop. The Files panel gives you access to all of the files associated with the working site and allows you to work on files and locate files within the local and remote site.

Work with the Files Panel

1. Click the **Window** menu, and then click **Files** to display the Files panel.

2. To expand the Files panel into a split window, click the **Expand** button.

3. Use any of the following options in the Files panel:

   ◆ Click the **Show** list arrow to display a listing of all active Dreamweaver sites.

   ◆ Click the **Connect/Disconnect** button to create or exit a connection between the local and remote sites.

   NOTE *If you have not set up the remote site hosting information, Dreamweaver prompts you to do so before continuing.*

   ◆ Click the **Refresh** button to refresh the contents of the Files panel.

   TIMESAVER *Press F5 to refresh the Files panel.*

   ◆ Click the **View Site FTP Log** button to display the FTP Log tab in the Results panel.

   ◆ Click the **Site Files** button to display a listing of files on the site.

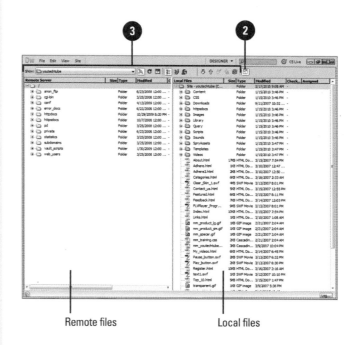

Remote files   Local files

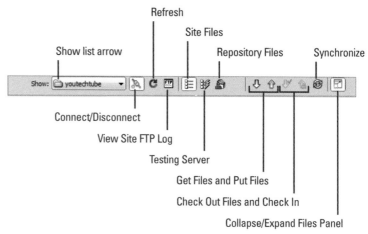

Show list arrow   Refresh   Site Files   Repository Files   Synchronize

Connect/Disconnect

View Site FTP Log

Testing Server

Get Files and Put Files

Check Out Files and Check In

Collapse/Expand Files Panel

- ◆ Click the **Testing Server** button to display a listing of all files located on the testing server.

- ◆ Click the **Repository Files** button to display the repository of the file and folder structure of your site on the Subversion server. Subversion is a version control system that helps you maintain version histories of your site files.

- ◆ Click the **Get Files** and **Put Files** buttons to receive from or send files to the remote server, respectively.

- ◆ Click the **Check Out Files** or **Check In** buttons to check files in or out.

NOTE *This option requires you to enable the file check in and out option in the Site Setup dialog box.*

- ◆ Click the **Synchronize** button to match up the files on the remote and local servers.

- ◆ Click the **Collapse/Expand** button to toggle between a split panel view (local and remote), and single view.

Click to collapse Files panel

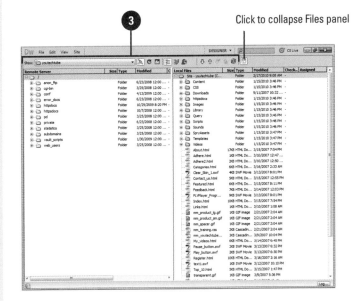

Transferring Files

Once a remote site has been established, the next step is to begin the transfer of files from the local (working) folder, to the remote site. Since you've already defined the remote server, it's a simple question of deciding what files and folders you want to move. Dreamweaver lets you move files (Put) to the remote site, and it allows you to move files from the remote server, back to the local site (Get). The amount of time it takes to transfer your files is directly related to your bandwidth. If you're moving a large site, it might be a good idea to perform the move at night. That way the site will be moved and ready the next day.

Transfer Files to the Remote Site

1. Click the **Site** menu, click **Manage Sites**, select the site you want to use, and then click **Done**.

2. Click the **Window** menu, and then click **Files** to display the Files panel.

3. Click the **Expand** button to show local and remote sites.

4. Click the **Connect To Remote Host** button to gain access to the remote site.

5. Select files (in the right window) using one of the following options:

   ◆ **Site.** Click the site folder to move the entire site to the remote folder.

   ◆ **Files.** Ctrl-click (Win) or ⌘ -click (Mac) to select the non-contiguous files for moving to the remote folder.

6. Click the **Put** button.

7. If prompted, click **Yes** to save a file or click **No** to use the existing one.

8. If prompted, click **Yes** to upload dependent files along with the selected files, or click **No** to not upload dependent files.

   Dreamweaver moves the entire site, or selected file/folders to the remote site.

9. To stop a file transfer, click **Cancel**.

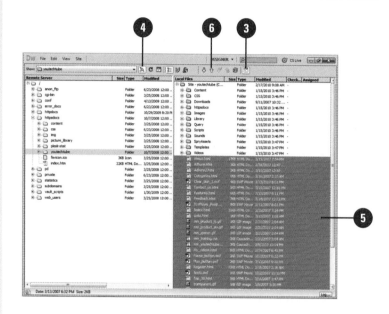

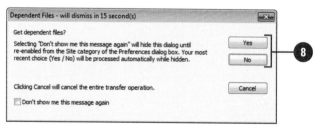

Transfer Files from the Remote Site

1 Click the **Site** menu, click **Manage Sites**, select the site you want to use, and then click **Done**.

2 Click the **Window** menu, and then click **Files** to display the Files panel.

3 Click the **Expand** button to show local and remote sites.

4 Click the **Connect To Remote Host** button to gain access to the remote site.

5 Select files from the remote site (left window) using one of the following options:

- ◆ Site. Click the site folder to move the entire site to the local folder.

- ◆ Files. Ctrl-click (Win) or ⌘ - click (Mac) to select the non-contiguous files for moving to the local folder.

6 Click the **Get** button.

7 If prompted, click **Yes** to download dependent files along with the selected files, or click **No** to not download dependent files.

Dreamweaver moves the entire site, or selected file/folders to the local site.

8 To stop a file transfer, click **Cancel**.

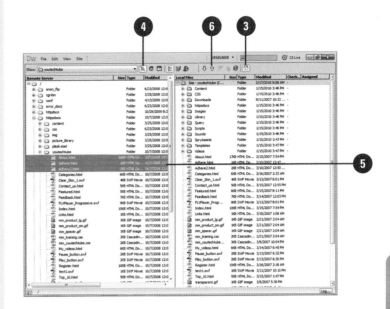

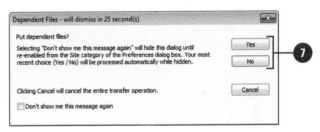

Did You Know?

You can display the FTP log. Open the Files panel, click the Options button in the upper-right corner, point to View, and then click Site FTP Log.

For Your Information

Managing File Transfers

You can cancel a file transfer or view the status of a file transfer by using the Background File Activity dialog box, which you can open by clicking the Log button at the bottom of the Files panel. In the Background File Activity dialog box, close the dialog box to cancel a transfer, click the Details expander to view more details, click Hide to minimize the dialog box, or click Save Log to save a log of the last file transfer.

Comparing Local and Remote Files

If you have a third-party file comparison tool, also known as a diff tool, installed on your computer, you can use it with Dreamweaver to compare versions of the same file located on your local and remote sites. If you're not sure whether two files are the same, a file comparison tool can save you a lot of time. You can compare local and remote site versions of the same file as well as different versions of the same file on the local or remote site. Before you can use a comparison tool, you need to select it in Dreamweaver preferences. File comparison programs are designed to compare text files, not binary files, such as images. You can compare the text files you can edit in Dreamweaver, including HTML, CSS, XML, ASP.NET, ColdFusion, and PHP.

Set Compare File Preferences

1. Click the **Dreamweaver** (Mac) or **Edit** (Win) menu, and then click **Preferences**.

2. Click the **File Compare** category.

3. Select from the following File Compare options:

   ◆ In Windows, click **Browse** to select the comparison program you have installed on your computer.

   ◆ On the Macintosh, click **Browse** to select the comparison tool or script (typically located in the user/bin folder) that starts the file comparison program from the command line. Some of the tools include FileMerge, BBEdit, and TextWrangler.

4. Click **OK**.

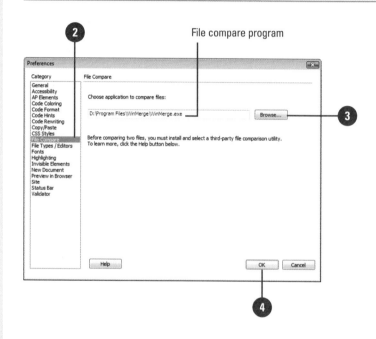

File compare program

Did You Know?

You can find a third-party file comparison tool on the Web. In your browser, perform a search for *file comparison* or *diff* tools. Dreamweaver works with most tools, including FileMerge (Mac) or WinMerge (Win). Many of them are free to download.

Compare Files

◆ **Two Local Files.** In the Files panel, select the two files on your local site, right-click the selected files, and then click **Compare Local Files**.

◆ **Two Remote Files.** In the Files panel, select the two files on your remote site, right-click the selected files, and then click **Compare Remote Files**.

◆ **Local File With Remote File.** In the Files panel, right-click a file on your local site, and then click **Compare With Remote Server**.

◆ **Remote File With Local File.** In the Files panel, right-click a file on your remote site, and then click **Compare With Local**.

◆ **Open File With Remote File.** Open the file in the Document window, click the **File** menu, and then click **Compare With Remote Server**.

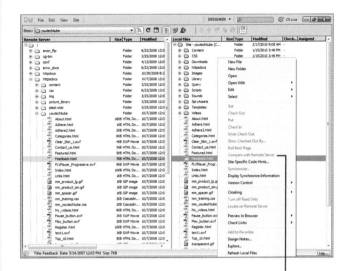

Click to compare files on local site with remote site

Did You Know?

You can compare files when synchronizing. When you synchronize files from your local site to the remote site, you can also compare files. Right-click anywhere in the Files panel, click Synchronize, complete the options you want in the Synchronize dialog box, click Preview, select each file you want to compare, and then click the Compare button.

You can check for newer files without synchronizing. In the Files panel, click the Options button in the Files panel, point to Edit, and then click Newer Local or Newer Remote.

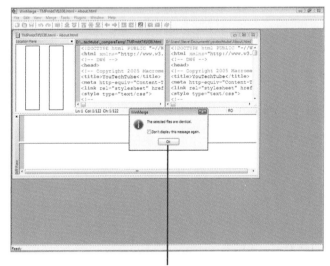

File compare complete; the files are the same.

Checking Site Files In and Out

It's important to understand that if you've enabled File Check In and Check Out, you can put files from the local site to the remote site without changing the file's checked out status. Checking out a file prevents other designers from working on the same file at the same time. When a file is checked out, Dreamweaver displays the name of the person who checked out the file in the Files panel, along with a red check mark (if a team member checked out the file) or green check mark (if you checked out the file) next to the file's icon. When you or another designer has finished with the file, checking in makes the file available for other team members to check out and edit.

Use Check Out

1. Click the **Window** menu, and then click **Files** to display the Files panel.

2. Click the **Expand** button to show local and remote sites.

3. Click the **Connect To Remote Host** button to gain access to the remote site.

4. Select the file or files that you want to checkout in the remote site window on the left.

    NOTE *A red check mark indicates that another team member has the file checked out and a lock symbol indicates that the file is read-only (Win) or locked (Mac).*

5. Click the **Check Out** button in the Files panel toolbar.

6. If prompted, click **Yes** to download dependent files along with the selected files, or click **No** not to download dependent files.

    NOTE *A green check mark appears beside the local file's icon indicating that you have checked it out.*

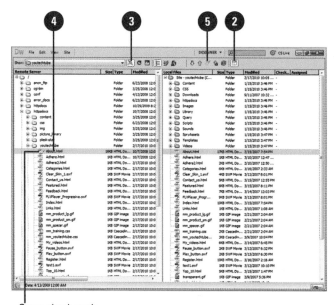

Green check mark

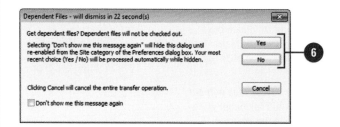

Use Check In

1. Click the **Window** menu, and then click **Files** to display the Files panel.

2. Click the **Expand** button to show local and remote sites.

3. Click the **Connect To Remote Host** button to gain access to the remote site.

4. Select the file or files that you want to check in.

5. Click the **Check In** button in the Files panel toolbar.

6. If prompted, click **Yes** to upload dependent files along with the selected files, or click **No** not to upload dependent files.

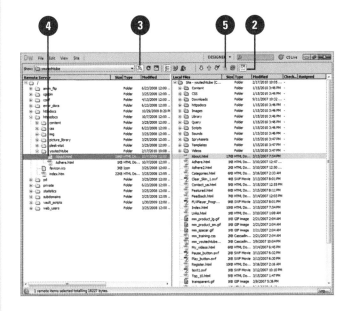

Enable Check In and Check Out

1. Click the **Site** menu, point to **Manage Sites**, select a site, and then click **Edit**.

2. Click the **Servers** category.

3. Select the server, and then click the **Edit Existing Server** button.

4. Click the **Advanced** tab.

5. Select the **Enable File Check-Out** check box.

6. To automatically check out files when you double-click to open them, select the **Check Out Files When Opening** check box.

7. Enter a check out name and an e-mail address.

8. Click **Save**.

9. Click **Save**, and then click **OK** to cache files, if necessary.

10. Click **Done** to close the Manage Sites dialog box.

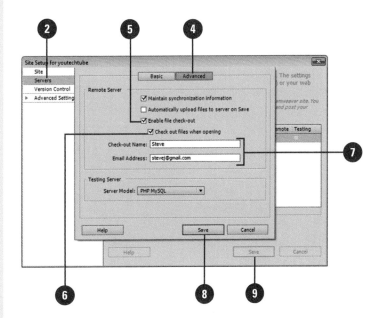

Managing Site Files Versions with Subversion

Subversion is a version control system that works along with Dreamweaver to help you maintain version histories of your site files. Subversion maintains a repository of the file and folder structure of your site on the Subversion server, which is the normal installation (software available at *http://subversion.tiggris.org*), however, you can set it up on your own computer. The files and folders are not actually stored on the server; Subversion maintains a database of changes. Before you can use Subversion, you need to define server settings in the Site Setup dialog box. You can access Subversion in Dreamweaver from the Files panel. When you change a file, a plus sign (+) appears next to the file name. If you want to keep your changes, click the Check In button, where you can view your changes and commit to them. When you commit to your changes, they are sent to the Subversion server and unmarked in the Files panel. In addition, you can move, copy, and delete files, as well as revert to file changes not yet committed (**New!**).

View and Commit to File Changes

1. Click the **Window** menu, and then click **Files** to display the Files panel.

2. Click the **Expand** button to show local and remote sites.

3. Make changes to files on your site.

    A plus sign (+) appears next to the file name that you have modified.

4. Select the file or files that you want to commit to your changes.

5. Click the **Check In** button in the Files panel toolbar.

6. To change an action, select a file, and then click one of the change buttons.

7. When you're ready to commit your changes, click **Commit**.

See Also

See "Defining Version Control" on page 483 for more information on setting Subversion in Dreamweaver.

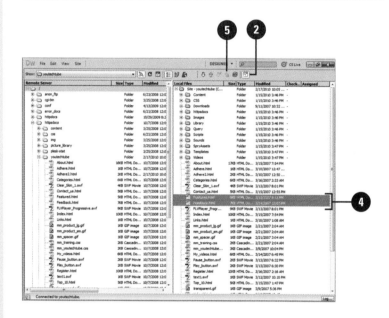

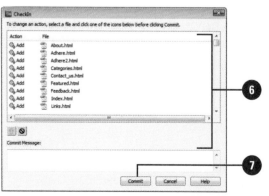

Manage Files with Subversion

1 Click the **Window** menu, and then click **Files** to display the Files panel.

2 Click the **Expand** button to show local and remote sites.

3 Select one or more files that you want to manage and view changes.

4 To move or copy the selection, drag or Ctrl+drag it to a new location.

5 To delete the selection, press Delete, and then click **Delete From Version Control** or **Delete Locally**.

6 To perform other operations, right-click the selection, point to **Version Control**, and then select any of the following commands:

◆ **Get Latest Versions.** Access the latest versions of files from the Subversion server.

◆ **Update Status.** Refreshes the current status of files.

◆ **Mark as Resolved.** If there are conflicts with the server version, it marks your local copy as current. The command is grayed out if there are no conflicts.

◆ **Show Revisions.** Displays a history of changes for a file or set of files where you can compare different versions.

◆ **Lock and Unlock.** Locks and unlocks files from changes by other contributors.

◆ **Go Offline.** Disconnects you from the server.

◆ **Clean Up.** Cleans up the server.

◆ **Commit.** Commits to file changes.

◆ **Revert.** Reverts to file changes not yet committed.

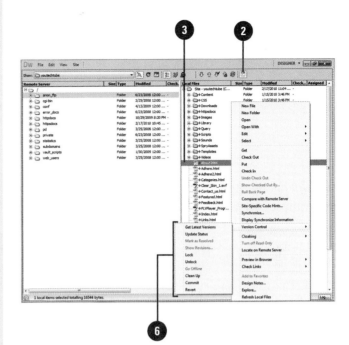

Working with Business Catalyst Site Files

Adobe Business Catalyst is a hosted Web site solution that allows you to build dynamic, data-driven Web sites with some advanced features, such as search, forums, blogs, password protected areas, web forms, and online stores (**New!**). Dreamweaver uses the Business Catalyst extension to connect you directly to your online business site, where you can add, edit, delete, upload pages and templates in Dreamweaver, and use pre-build code modules without programming from the Business Catalyst panel. You can get the extension by using the Business Catalyst panel and install it by using the Adobe Extension Manager.

Download and Install the Business Catalyst Extension

1. Click the **Window** menu, and then click **Business Catalyst** to display the Business Catalyst panel.

2. Click the **Get the Extension** button to access the Business Catalyst Web site.

3. Follow the online instructions to access and download the Business Catalyst extension, and then close your browser.

4. Click the **Help** menu, and then click **Manage Extensions**.

5. Click the **Install** button, navigate to and select the Business Catalyst extension, click **Open**, and then complete the install.

6. To enable the extension, select the **Enable** check box.

7. Click the **Close** button.

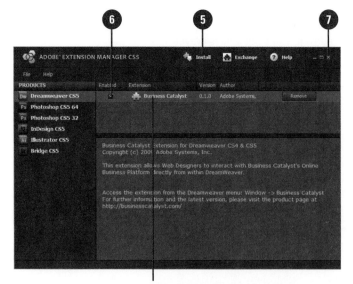

Adobe Business Catalyst extension

Get Started with a Business Catalyst Site

1. Click the **Window** menu, and then click **Business Catalyst** to display the Business Catalyst panel.

    ◆ If you have not created a Business Catalyst site, visit *www.businesscatalyst.com*, click **Free Sign Up**, and then follow the online instructions.

    ◆ The first time you work with Dreamweaver, you need to define the local root folder in the Site Setup dialog box.

2. Enter your username (e-mail address) and password, and then click **Login**.

3. Click the **Site** list arrow, and then select your site.

    ◆ To define a site, click the **Quick Site Setup** icon in the Business Catalyst panel, and then follow the wizard instructions. Select the **Download Site Locally** check box, and then click **Done**. This sets up your testing server.

4. Use the toolbar in the Files panel to work with files on the remote and local sites. To open a local file, double-click it.

    ◆ Click the **Window** menu, and then click **Files** to display the Files panel, and then click the **Expand** button to show local and remote sites.

5. To add a module to an open Web page, open the Web page you want, click to place the insertion point, select the module in the Business Catalyst panel, double-click the wizard icon, follow the step-by-step instructions, and then click **Insert**.

Setting up an online business catalyst site

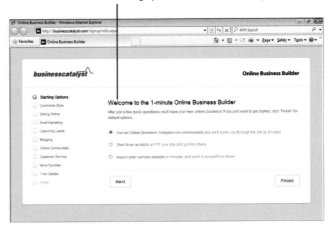

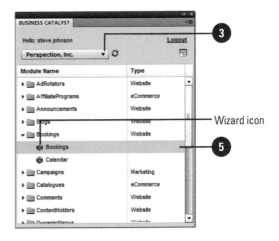

Wizard icon

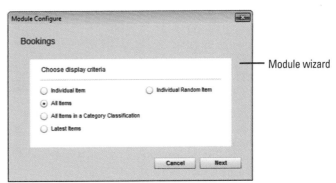

Module wizard

Synchronizing Site Files

In Web development, sometimes it can get confusing managing versions of files. Where is the most recent file? This question is one that you'll probably ask yourself more than once throughout the development of a site. Dreamweaver solves this problem with an option called File Synchronization. This feature compares files between the local and remote site and will determine which is the latest version. If the latest version lives on the local site, it will upload that file accordingly. File Synchronization can also delete files on either the local or remote site, if the file doesn't appear in both versions of the site. You can apply the synchronize command to selected files, or apply it site-wide.

Synchronize Files

1. Click the **Window** menu, and then click **Files** to display the Files panel.

2. Click the **Expand** button to show local and remote sites.

3. Select the file or files that you want to synchronize (local or remote).

4. Click the **Synchronize** button.

   TIMESAVER *Click the Site menu, and then click Synchronize Sitewide.*

5. Select from the following synchronize options:

   ◆ **Synchronize**. Select between synchronizing the entire site, or only selected files.

   ◆ **Direction**. Select Put Newer Files To Remote (default), Get New Files From The Remote, or Get And Put Newer Files (wherever they exist).

   ◆ **Delete Remote Files Not On Local Drive**. Select to allow Dreamweaver to delete any files found on the remote server, but not on the local drive.

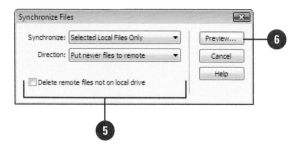

6 Click **Preview** to view the proposed changes.

7 Select a file or files, and make modifications using the following options:

- ◆ Mark selected files to get the remote version.

- ◆ Mark selected files to put the local version.

- ◆ Mark selected files for deletion.

- ◆ Ignore selected files during this synchronization.

- ◆ Mark selected files as already synchronized.

- ◆ Compare the local and remote versions of the selected files.

  NOTE *If no synchronization is required, Dreamweaver prompts you with a dialog box, asking if you want to see a list of the files, and then change them manually.*

8 Click **OK**.

Once the synchronization is complete you can save a log of the actions performed by pressing the Save Log button.

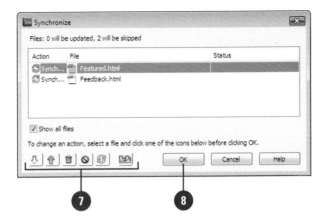

Did You Know?

You can display detailed information for a synchronized file. In the Files panel, right-click (Win) or control-click (Mac) the file you want information, and then click Display Synchronize Information. This command is available only when the Maintain Synchron-ation Information check box is selected in the Remote Info category of the Site Setup dialog box.

Cloaking and Uncloaking Files

Cloaking files hides the selected files from many of the file transfer commands, such as: Get, Put, Check In, and Check Out; however, it doesn't protect files when using Synchronize. For example, you have a folder on you local site that contains original uncompressed source documents, such as Photoshop and Flash. There would be no need for these files to be uploaded to the remote server, so you cloak them. Any file format you cloak remains in your local folder and will not be uploaded unless you manually override the cloak setting. In addition, cloaked files do not appear in the Assets panel. Cloaked files can be controlled by extension, such as all FLA files, or they can be controlled individually, regardless of their extension. You can cloak specific folders, even multiple ones; however, you cannot cloak all folders or an entire site.

Cloak and Uncloak Files

1. Click the **Window** menu, and then click **Files** to display the Files panel.

2. Click the **Expand** button to show local and remote sites.

3. Select the files or folder within the site files, right-click (Win) or control-click (Mac) the selection, point to **Cloaking**, and then click **Cloak** or **Uncloak**.

   A red line through the folder icon appears or disappears, indicating the folder is cloaked or uncloaked.

Did You Know?

You can uncloak all files at the same time. In the Files panel, select any file or folder in the local site, right-click (Win) or control-click (Mac) the selection, point to Cloaking, and then click Uncloak All.

See Also

See "Defining Site Cloaking" on page 484 for information on enabling cloaking and specifying the file types you want to cloak.

Automating Dreamweaver

Introduction

You can't change time; it plods forward at sixty minutes an hour, twenty-four hours a day. Unfortunately, when you're involved in creating a complex Web site, and up against a deadline, there never seems to be enough time in the day.

Adobe understands the need for efficiency in their applications, and Dreamweaver is no exception. Built into the structure of the program are ways to help you get the job done, and get it done quickly. However, it's not just about finishing a project fast, it's also about doing it right. Again, Dreamweaver creates a perfect balance between efficiency and quality.

For example, you're working along, and suddenly decide that 6 steps ago, you deleted something that should not have been deleted. No problem, just use the History panel to go back in time and correct the error. That's great, but the History panel is much more than multiple undos. It actually allows you to automate repetitive tasks by creating commands out of selected history steps.

Here's another one: You're almost finished with your site; it's 75 pages, all nicely checked out and ready to go. Then you discover a misspelling that occurs on all the pages. No problem, you simply access Find and Replace and correct the error. But Find and Replace is more that just a simple text corrector; you can search for specific source code, text within tags, even search for a specific tag. In addition, if it's something that you search for often, you can save the search as a query and use it over and over again.

What You'll Do

Use the History Panel

Undo and Redo History Steps

Replay History Steps

Copy History Steps Between Documents

Save History Steps as Commands

Use and Manage History Commands

Record Commands for Temporary Use

Set History Panel Preferences

Use Advanced Find and Replace for Text

Use Advanced Find and Replace for Tags

Create and Use a Search Query

Using the History Panel

The History panel helps you automate and streamline the way you work in Dreamweaver. As you work in Dreamweaver, the History panel tracks all your steps behind the scenes for the entire document or only for individual or all objects. With the History panel, you can undo or redo steps to correct mistakes, replay selected steps for new tasks to streamline repetitive work, or record steps for replay from the Commands menu to automate your work.

The History panel doesn't replace the Undo, Redo, and Repeat commands on the Edit menu, it simply tracks every step you perform. When you undo or redo one or more commands, the History panel displays the results; the Undo/Redo slider moves according to the commands you select.

You can open the History panel using the Window menu like any of the other panels in Dreamweaver. Each step you take in the active document during a work session (since you created or opened the document) appears on a separate line in the History panel. Steps you take in one Dreamweaver document don't appear in other documents' History panel lists. The first step you perform in a session appears at the top of the list and the last step appears at the bottom. If a red X appears in the icon for a step, it indicates Dreamweaver cannot save or replay the step. Unlike other panels in Dreamweaver, the History panel includes a slider on the left side you can use to undo/redo steps; the Undo/Redo slider initially points to the last step you performed. As the History panel records each step taken to the active document, it consumes memory and hard disk space. If you no longer need the steps in the History panel and want to free up some memory, you can clear the entire list with the Clear History command on the Options menu. When you close a document, Dreamweaver clears the History panel. The bottom of the History panel includes buttons to replay selected steps, copy selected steps to the Clipboard, and create a command from selected steps.

History panel

History steps

Options menu

Clear History command

Undoing and Redoing History Steps

As you change the current open document, you begin to see the History panel record each action you make. For example, type in a line of text and a typing layer displays in the History panel. Now, select the text and change it to italic: the History panel displays the change. Each action in the document creates a new action layer in the panel. Now, continue on for a few steps, and then you realize that you didn't want to italicize the text. As long as that history step is still in the History panel, you can go in and undo it. If the step you need to change is the last one, then all you need to do is press ⌘+Z (Mac), or Ctrl+Z (Win). If you change your mind you can always press ⌘+Y (Mac), or Ctrl+Y (Win) to redo the last undo... sound confusing? Not really; however, if it is, then the History panel eliminates the confusion by giving you a visual list of all your history steps.

Undo or Redo Multiple History Steps

① Open the Web page you want to use.

② Open the History panel.

③ Perform several actions within the document to create a running history.

◆ To redo steps, undo one or more actions.

④ In the History panel, perform a multiple undo or redo using one of the following methods:

◆ Drag the slider up (undo) or down (redo) on the History panel to the desired step in the History panel.

◆ Click the slider bar next to the step you want to undo or revert to and the slider will scroll automatically to that step.

NOTE *Any actions performed after the undo overwrite the undone actions and create a new history for the document from that point forward. A redo can be performed only so long as you haven't performed a multiple undo, and then created new steps.*

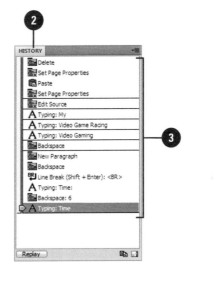

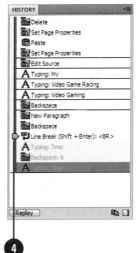

Replaying History Steps

You can replay steps from the History panel to the same object or to a different object in the document. You can replay steps only in the order in which you performed them; you can't rearrange the order of the steps in the History panel. If a red X appears in the icon for a step, it indicates Dreamweaver cannot save or replay the step.

Replay History Steps to the Same Object or Another Object

1. Open the Web page containing the steps you want to replay.

2. Open the History panel.

3. Select the steps you want:

   ◆ **One Step.** Click a step.

   ◆ **Adjacent Steps.** Drag from one step to another or click the first step, hold down the Shift key, and then click the last step.

   ◆ **Nonadjacent Steps.** Hold down the ⌘ (Mac) or Ctrl (Win) key, and then click steps.

4. Select the same object used in the History steps or another object.

5. Click **Replay** in the History panel.

   The steps are replayed in order, and a new step called Replay Steps appears in the History panel.

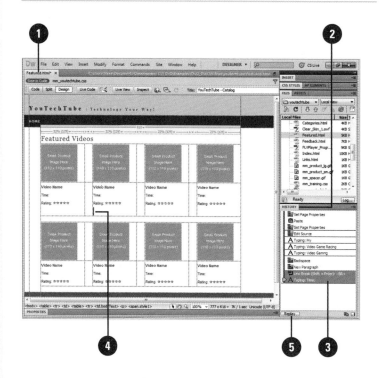

Copying History Steps Between Documents

Each document only tracks its own set of steps in the History panel. When you close a document, Dreamweaver clears the History panel. If you want to use a set of steps in another document, you need to copy them from one History panel and paste them to another document. You can use the Copy Steps button on the History panel or the same command on the Options menu to complete the task. When you paste steps into another document, Dreamweaver replays the steps and the History panel shows the steps as only one step called Paste Steps (Mac) or Paste (Win).

Copy Steps Between Documents

1. Open the Web page containing the steps you want to copy.

2. Open the History panel.

3. Perform several actions within the document to create a running history.

4. Select the steps (called a History action) that you want to copy.

5. Click the **Copy Steps** button in the History panel.

6. Click in the document to place the insertion point where you want to paste the steps or select an object to apply the steps.

7. Click the **Edit** menu, and then click **Paste**.

   Dreamweaver executes the saved History steps at the insertion point of the cursor.

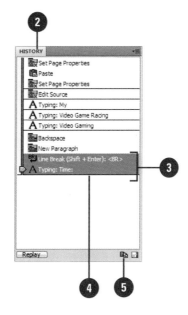

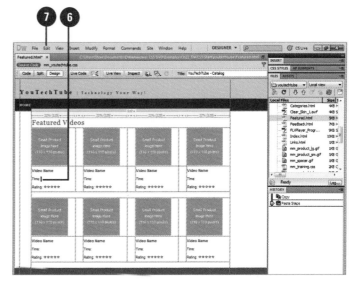

Saving History Steps as Commands

The History panel records the steps you take in the order in which you perform them in Dreamweaver. If you perform the same set of steps several times while you work on a document, you can save the steps in the History panel as a command on the Commands menu, which you can reuse again and again. This is where the real power is located. Dreamweaver stores the commands you save for future use in any document. While History records most actions performed while working on a page, there are some things that it can't record, such as dragging an object from one place on the page to another. If a black line separating the steps or a red X appears in the icon for a step, it indicates Dreamweaver cannot save or replay the step.

Save History Steps as a Command

1. Open the Web page you want to use.

2. Open the History panel.

3. Perform several steps within the page (in this example, a copyright notice is created using a specific font and formatting).

   IMPORTANT *When selecting the text to change its formatting do not click and drag; instead use the left arrow key while holding down the shift key.*

   Dreamweaver records all of the steps within a box in the History panel.

   NOTE *If you see a black line separating the steps, or a red X, that indicates the steps cannot be saved or replayed as a single command.*

4. When finished creating the copyright symbol, select all of the steps that you want saved as a command, by clicking and dragging on the steps in the History panel.

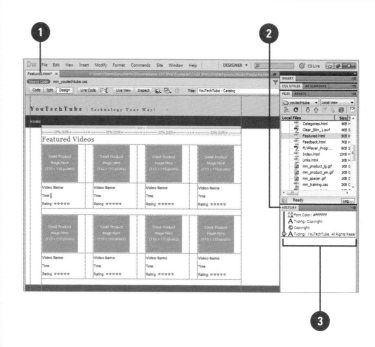

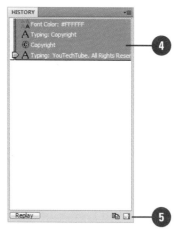

5 Click the **Save Steps** button in the History panel.

6 Enter a descriptive name for the command.

7 Click **OK**.

8 To reuse the command, click the **Commands** menu, and then click the command name.

The bottom of the Commands menu displays a list of your saved history commands.

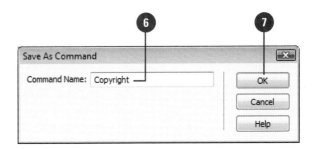

Using and Managing History Commands

The History panel is one of those tools in Dreamweaver that many users don't take full advantage of. Most designers use it as a tool for multiple undos. While that's a fine way to use it (I love multiple undos), there's more to the History panel than that. The History panel's job is to record all the actions you make in an open document, based on a user-defined number of steps, and lets you take multiple steps backwards with the use of the panel's slider. Its real power, however, is the ability to record, play, save, and reuse user-defined commands. User-defined commands are great timesaving tools when you build complex Web sites and know that you'll do certain things over and over again. For example, you might want to insert a copyright statement at the bottom of each page. We're not talking about a library item, just some simple italicized text. That's just perfect for a command. After you save steps as a command, you can run, rename, or delete commands.

Run a History Command

1. Open the Web page you want to run (apply) a Command.

2. Click in the document where you want to run the Command.

3. Click the **Commands** menu, and then select the command from the list at the bottom of the menu (in this example, Copyright).

Dreamweaver applies the command at the insertion point of the cursor.

Manage History Commands

1. Click the **Commands** menu, and then click **Edit Command List**.

2. Select from the following options in the Edit Command List dialog box:

   ◆ **Rename.** Select a command from the list, and enter a new name, if desired.

   ◆ **Remove.** Select a command from the list, and then click the **Delete** button.

3. Click **Close** to save your changes.

Did You Know?

You can get more commands. Click the Commands menu, and then click Get More Commands. Your browser opens the Adobe Exchange, where you can pick up hundreds of specific commands (many for free).

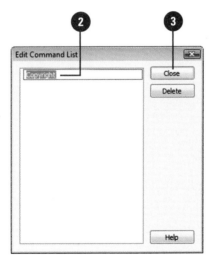

Recording Commands for Temporary Use

If you need to quickly create a command for temporary use, such as your current working session, you can use the Start Recording and Stop Recording commands on the Commands menu. The actions you take during the recording process are stored internally by Dreamweaver and cannot be edited. Dreamweaver stores only one recorded command at a time. This means when you record a new command, the old command is erased. However, if you like a recorded command, you can save it for future use.

Record and Play a Command for Temporary Use

1. Open the Web page you want to use for recording purposes.

2. Click the **Commands** menu, and then click **Start Recording**.

   TIMESAVER *Ctrl+Shift+X (Win) or ⌘+Shift+X (Mac) to start recording.*

3. Perform the steps you want to record (the cursor changes to indicate you're recording).

4. When you're done, click the **Commands** menu, and then click **Stop Recording**.

   TIMESAVER *Ctrl+Shift+X (Win) or ⌘+Shift+X (Mac) to stop recording.*

5. To play back the recorded command, click the **Commands** menu, and then click **Play Recorded Command**.

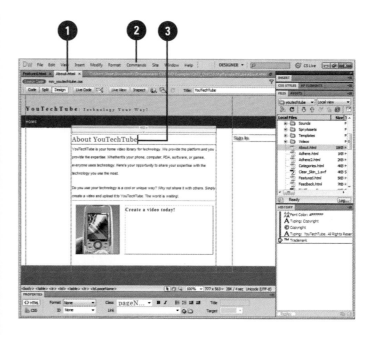

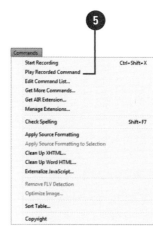

Setting History Panel Preferences

By default, the History panel is set for a maximum of 50 undos. Your first job is to determine whether 50 undo steps is enough (or too many), and modify the History panel by using the General category in the Preferences dialog box. You can set the number of history steps to any number between 2 and 9999. As the History panel records each step taken in the active document, it consumes memory and hard disk space. The larger the number of history steps you specify, the more memory and hard disk space Dreamweaver consumes on your computer.

Define History Steps

1. Click the **Dreamweaver** (Mac) or **Edit** (Win) menu, and then click **Preferences**.

2. Click the **General** category.

3. Enter a numeric (2-9999) value into the Maximum Number Of History Steps box.

4. Click **OK**.

Using Advanced Find and Replace for Text

Dreamweaver's Find and Replace is a powerful tool for searching for and changing HTML text, tags and their attributes within the document you are working on. Conducting a simple find/replace on text allows you to search for a specific phrase, words or characters, and replace them. The advanced text option allows you to search for and replace text strings inside or outside of a target tag with the specific criteria you want; this acts as a filter for the search.

Conduct an Advanced Text Find and Replace

1. Open Dreamweaver (it is not necessary to open a document).

2. Click the **Edit** menu, and then click **Find And Replace**.

3. Select the following options from the Find and Replace dialog box:

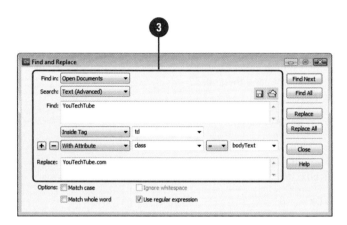

- ◆ **Find In.** Click the list arrow to look for the find text by the desired area for the search.

- ◆ **Search.** Click the list arrow, and then click **Text (Advanced)**.

- ◆ **Find.** Enter the text to search.

- ◆ **Replace.** Enter the text to replace.

- ◆ **Tag.** Click the list arrow, click **Inside Tag** or **Not Inside**, and then select a target tag to look for text in (to the right).

- ◆ **Criteria.** Click the **Plus** (+) button or the **Minus** (-) button to add or remove search criteria.

  When you add a criteria, click to select what to look for in the tag (**With Attribute, Without Attribute,** or **Containing,** or **Not Containing**), and then specify the criteria you want.

  For example, with Attribute chosen, the attribute is color, and the equal sign was used to indicate we're looking for a specific color (990000).

4. Select from the following Find and Replace options:

- **Match Case.** Select to make the Find text case sensitive.

- **Match Whole Word.** Select to match whole words.

- **Ignore Whitespace.** Select to treat all whitespace as a single space for the purpose of matching.

- **Use Regular Expression.** Select to use string expressions to help locate information.

5. Click **Find Next**, **Find All**, **Replace**, **Replace All** to perform the find and replace.

6. Click **Close** to end the Find and Replace routine.

Did You Know?

You can repeat the last search.
Dreamweaver remembers your last search. So, if you close the Find and Replace dialog box to do additional editing, you can resume the prior search. Click the Edit menu, and then click Find Again.

See Also

See "Finding and Replacing Text or Code" on page 120 for information on using the Find and Replace command.

Find all results

Using Advanced Find and Replace for Tags

When you need to find a specific tag within the document you are working on, you can use the advanced features in the Find and Replace dialog box. The advanced options allow you to search for and replace specific tags inside or outside of a target tag with the specific criteria you want, including tag attributes. In other words, you can set conditions that act as a filter for the search. Searching the source code takes you into the code and stops at each occurrence of the search.

Conduct a Specific Tag Find and Replace

1. Open Dreamweaver (it is not necessary to open a document).

2. Click the **Edit** menu, and then click **Find And Replace**.

3. Select the following options from the Find and Replace dialog box:

   ◆ **Find In.** Click to look for the find text by the desired area for the search.

   ◆ **Search.** Click the list arrow, and then click **Specific Tag**.

   ◆ **Tag.** Click the list arrow, and then select the tag to look for from the list (to the right).

   ◆ **Tag Criteria.** Click to select what to look for in the tag (**With Attribute, Without Attribute,** or **Containing,** or **Not Containing**), and then specify the criteria you want.

   For example, with Attribute chosen, the attribute is color, and the equal sign was used to indicate we're looking for a specific color (990000).

   ◆ **Criteria.** Click the **Plus** (+) button or the **Minus** (-) button to add or remove search criteria.

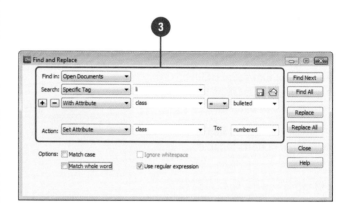

- **Action.** Click to select from the available actions to perform, when a match is made.

4. Select from the following Find and Replace options:

- **Match Case.** Select to make the Find text case sensitive.

- **Match Whole Word.** Select to match whole words.

- **Ignore Whitespace.** Select to treat all whitespace as a single space for the purpose of matching.

- **Use Regular Expression.** Select to use string expressions to help locate information.

5. Click **Find Next**, **Find All**, **Replace**, **Replace All** to perform the find and replace.

Dreamweaver looks for the specific tag and makes the change you specify.

6. Click **Close** to end the Find and Replace routine.

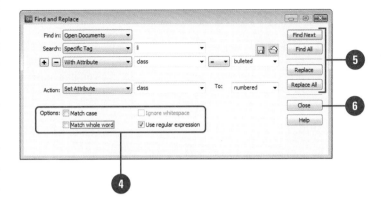

Find all results

See Also

See "Finding and Replacing Text or Code" on page 120 for information on using the Find and Replace command.

Creating and Using a Search Query

If you create a complex search and want to use it again, you can save it as a query, and use it over and over again. When you save a query in the Find and Replace dialog box, Dreamweaver saves the file with the extension DWR. After you save a query, you need to load (open) it before you can use it. In addition to the DWR extension, some queries from older versions of Dreamweaver may use the extension DWG.

Create a Query

1. Click the **Edit** menu, and then click **Find And Replace**.

2. Create a Find and Replace search using any of the methods described in the previous sections.

3. Click the **Save Query** button.

4. Select a location for the query (default: working site folder).

5. Enter a descriptive name for the query.

6. Click **Save** to record and save the query.

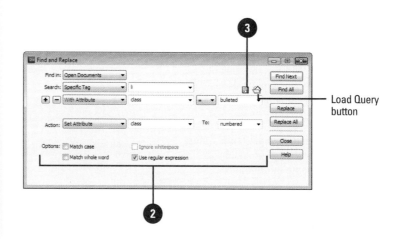

Load Query button

Use a Query

1. Click the **Edit** menu, and then click **Find And Replace**.

2. Click the **Load Query** button.

3. Select the folder that contains the query, and then select the query file you want to use.

4. Click the **Open** button to load the query into the Find and Replace dialog box.

5. Perform the Find and Replace.

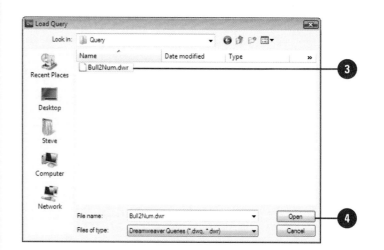

New! Features

Adobe Dreamweaver CS5

Adobe Dreamweaver CS5 means superior results faster, with new features and enhancements that help you build Web sites and Internet applications. It provides a combination of visual layout tools, application development features, and code editing support, enabling developers and designers at every skill level to create visually appealing, standards-based sites and applications quickly and easily.

Only New Features

If you're already familiar with Dreamweaver CS4, you can access and download all the tasks in this book with Adobe Dreamweaver CS5 New Features to help make your transition to the new version simple and smooth. The Dreamweaver CS5 New Features as well as other Dreamweaver CS4 to Dreamweaver CS5 transition helpers are available on the Web at *www.perspection.com.*

What's New

If you're searching for what's new in Dreamweaver CS5, just look for the icon: **New!**. The new icon appears in the table of contents and throughout this book so you can quickly and easily identify a new or improved feature in Dreamweaver CS5. The following is a brief description of each new feature and its location in this book.

Dreamweaver CS5

- **Simplified Site Setup (p. 18-19, 69, 474-475)** The Site Setup dialog box is redesigned and doesn't force you to complete the site setup unless it's required. As you work on your site and a task needs information from the Site Setup dialog box, Dreamweaver opens it and highlights the required setting.
- **Enable ICE for New File (p. 20-21)** In the New Document dialog box, you can add an editable region for a blank HTML page.
- **Save All Related Files (p. 26-27)** Use the Save All Related Files command on the File menu to save all web site related files at one time.
- **Lock Icon (p. 28)** When you open a read-only document, a lock icon appears in the Document tab to the left of the name.
- **Vertical Split View (p. 30)** Split views display the screen in half vertically by default.

◆ **Live View Changes (p. 32-33, 182-183, 348)** In Live view, you can set options to follow links in pages, type URLs using the Browser Navigation bar, and edit browsed pages from your site in a new tab. When code states change, Live Code highlights the code in different colors for easy viewing. You can specify different colors for backgrounds and code to make it easier to read.

◆ **Navigation Bar (p. 32-33, 44)** The Browser Navigation bar allows you to navigate to pages in Live view using similar options to those in a Web browser.

◆ **Adobe Community Help (p. 36-37)** In the Adobe Community Help window, you can search product help from Local Help, Community Help, or Adobe.com by using keywords or phrases or browsing through a list of categories.

◆ **Adobe Updater (p. 38-39)** The Adobe Updater Preferences dialog box allows you to set update options for Dreamweaver and other installed Adobe products, including one to have Adobe notify you of updates in the menu bar.

◆ **CS Live (p. 43, 296-298)** Adobe CS Live is an online service that allows you to set up or manage an Adobe account, and access Adobe related Web sites using the CS Live menu on the Application bar.

◆ **Application Bar (p. 44)** You can show and hide the Application bar using the Application Bar command on the Window menu.

◆ **Dynamically-Related Files (p. 60, 217, 340-341)** The Related Files toolbar displays static and dynamically-related files for a Web page. To help you reduce the number of files on the toolbar, you can filter files by type to hide the ones you don't want to display.

◆ **Spell Checking Dictionaries (p. 125)** Adobe uses the LILO (Linguistic Library Optimized) speller engine, which supports 37 different dictionaries.

◆ **CSS Enable/Disable (p. 219, 228)** Instead of deleting a CSS rule that you might want to use later, you can disable one or more rule properties. When you disable a CSS rule property, Dreamweaver wraps the CSS code as a comment.

◆ **CSS Inspect (p. 229)** CSS Inspect works together with Live View to quickly identify HTML elements and their associated CSS styles to give you immediate feedback. With CSS Inspect enabled, you can move the mouse over elements on your page to see the CSS box model attributes for any block level element.

◆ **PHP Code Hinting (p. 331)** PHP for functions, variables, and classes have been added to code hinting along with tooltip help.

◆ **Info Bar (p. 341)** The Info bar is a yellow bar that appears when certain types of errors occurs. The Info bar shows information error messages for dynamically-related files, Live View, standard related files, code hinting, etc.

◆ **Site-specific Code Hints (p. 343)** If a PHP code hint is not available by default, you can create or edit a configuration file in your local site with the site-specific code hints extension that allows PHP code hinting to inspect the specified files and folders for functions, objects, and global variables you want as code hints.

◆ **Subversion Enhancements (p. 500-501)** Dreamweaver uses Subversion 1.6 or later for file version management. In this version, you can move, copy, and delete files, as well as revert to file changes not yet committed.

◆ **Business Catalyst (p. 502-503)** Dreamweaver uses the Business Catalyst extension to connect you directly to your online business site, where you can use templates, and pre-build code modules without programming from the Business Catalyst panel.

Adobe Certified Expert

About the Adobe Certified Expert (ACE) Program

The Adobe Certified Expert (ACE) program is for graphic designers, Web designers, systems integrators, value-added resellers, developers, and business professionals seeking official recognition of their expertise on Adobe products.

What Is an ACE?

An Adobe Certified Expert is an individual who has passed an Adobe Product Proficiency Exam for a specific Adobe software product. Adobe Certified Experts are eligible to promote themselves to clients or employers as highly skilled, expert-level users of Adobe software. ACE certification is a recognized worldwide standard for excellence in Adobe software knowledge. There are three levels of ACE certification: Single product certification, Specialist certification, and Master certification. To become an ACE, you must pass one or more product-specific proficiency exam and sign the ACE program agreement. When you become an ACE, you enjoy these special benefits:

- ◆ Professional recognition
- ◆ An ACE program certificate
- ◆ Use of the Adobe Certified Expert program logo

What Does This Logo Mean?

It means this book will prepare you fully for the Adobe Certified Expert exam for Adobe Dreamweaver CS5. The certification exam has a set of objectives, which are organized into broader skill sets. The Adobe Certified Expert objectives and the specific pages throughout this book that cover the objectives are available on the Web at *www.perspection.com*.

 DW 3.1

Choosing a Certification Level

There are three levels of certification to become an Adobe Certified Expert.

◆ **Single product certification.** Recognizes your proficiency in a single Adobe product. To qualify as an ACE, you must pass one product-specific exam.

◆ **Specialist certification.** Recognizes your proficiency in multiple Adobe products with a specific medium: print, Web, or video. To become certified as a Specialist, you must pass the exams on the required products. To review the requirements, go online to *http://www.adobe.com/support/certification/ace_certify.html*.

◆ **Master certification.** Recognizes your skills in terms of how they align with the Adobe product suites. To become certified as a Master, you must pass the exam for each of the products in the suite.

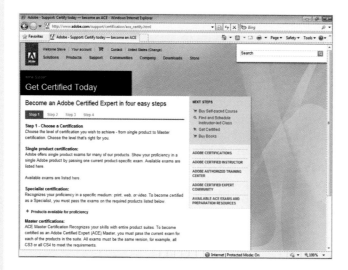

Preparing for an Adobe Certified Expert Exam

Every Adobe Certified Expert Exam is developed from a list of objectives, which are based on studies of how an Adobe program is actually used in the workplace. The list of objectives determine the scope of each exam, so they provide you with the information you need to prepare for ACE certification. Follow these steps to complete the ACE Exam requirement:

1. Review and perform each task identified with a Adobe Certified Expert objective to confirm that you can meet the requirements for the exam.

2. Identify the topic areas and objectives you need to study, and then prepare for the exam.

3 Review the Adobe Certified Expert Program Agreement. To review it, go online to *http://www.adobe.com/support/certification/ace_certify.html*.

You will be required to accept the ACE agreement when you take the Adobe Certified Exam at an authorized testing center.

4 Register for the Adobe Certified Expert Exam.

ACE testing is offered at more than a thousand authorized Pearson VUE and Thomson Prometric testing centers in many countries. To find the testing center nearest you, go online to *www.pearsonvue.com/adobe* (for Pearson VUE) or *www.2test.com* (for Prometric). The ACE exam fee is US$150 worldwide. When contacting an authorized training center, provide them with the Adobe Product Proficiency exam name and number you want to take, which is available online in the Exam Bulletin at *http://www.adobe.com/support/certification/ace_certify.html*.

5 Take the ACE exam.

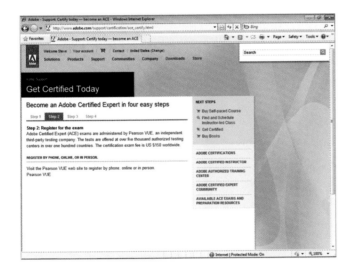

Getting Recertified

For those with an ACE certification for a specific Adobe product, recertification is required of each ACE within 90 days of a designated ACE Exam release date. There are no restrictions on the number of times you may take the exam within a given period.

To get recertified, call Pearson VUE or Thomson Prometric. You will need to verify your previous certification for that product. If you are getting recertified, check with the authorized testing center for discounts.

Taking an Adobe Certified Expert Exam

The Adobe Certified Expert exams are computer-delivered, closed-book tests consisting of 60 to 90 multiple-choice questions. Each exam is approximately one to two hours long. A 15-minute tutorial will precede the test to familiarize you with the function of the Windows-based driver. The exams are currently available worldwide in English only. They are administered by Pearson VUE and Thomson Prometric, independent third-party testing companies.

Exam Results

At the end of the exam, a score report appears indicating whether you passed or failed the exam. Diagnostic information is included in your exam report. When you pass the exam, your score is electronically reported to Adobe. You will then be sent an ACE Welcome Kit and access to the ACE program logo in four to six weeks. You are also placed on the Adobe certification mailing list to receive special Adobe announcements and information about promotions and events that take place throughout the year.

When you pass the exam, you can get program information, check and update your profile, or download ACE program logos for your promotional materials online at:

http://www.adobe.com/support/certification/community.html

Getting More Information

To learn more about the Adobe Certified Expert program, read a list of frequently asked questions, and locate the nearest testing center, go online to:

http://www.adobe.com/support/certification/ace.html

To learn more about other Adobe certification programs, go online to:

http://www.adobe.com/support/certification

Index

WYSIWYG view, 30

X

XHTML (Extensible Hypertext Markup
Language)
cleaning up, 462-463
definitions, selecting, 62
XML (Extensible Markup Language), 29
file format, 79
spry XML data set, displaying, 390
templates, importing and exporting XML
data into, 449-450
XSL format, 29

Y

Yahoo submission options, 8

Z

z-index to AP element, applying, 249
zooming
on images, 151
Zoom tool, 52
changing view with, 54